P9-DWP-832

DATE DUE

DE 23 '94			
DE 8 '95			
NO 3 '97			
MR 19 '98			
FE 27 '99			
MY 25 '99			
JE 6 '00			
AUG 05 2004			
DE 17 '04			
DE 17 '05			
JE 5 '06			
NO 12 '08			

Management Mistakes
& Successes

Management Mistakes
& Successes

Fourth Edition

Robert F. Hartley
Cleveland State University

JOHN WILEY & SONS, INC.

New York • Chichester • Brisbane • Toronto • Singapore

Acquisitions Editor   Timothy Kent
Marketing Manager   Debra Riegert
Senior Production Editor   Marjorie Shustak
Manufacturing Manager   Inez Pettis
Illustration Coordinator   Gene Aiello

This book was set in Palatino by V&M Graphics and printed and bound
by Courier Stoughton. The cover was printed by Phoenix Color Corp.

Recognizing the importance of preserving what has been written, it is a
policy of John Wiley & Sons, Inc. to have books of enduring value published
in the United States printed on acid-free paper, and we exert our best
efforts to that end.

ISBN 0-471-00087-6

Printed in the United States of America

10   9   8   7   6   5   4   3   2   1

Preface

Once again, I would like to welcome back past users of *Management Mistakes*. You will note that while we have retained some of the most popular classic cases, more changes have been made in this edition than in any previous one. For new users, I hope this book will meet your full expectations and be an interesting and effective learning tool.

As a supplemental text, this book can be used in a great variety of courses, both undergraduate and graduate, ranging from principles of management to strategic management to business policy. It can also be used in courses in business ethics and organizational theory.

The hypothesis of this edition, as in the previous editions, is that notable experiences of major firms can provide powerful learning insights. Through triumphs and troubles, others can learn what works and what does not; which practices to embrace and which to avoid. Thus, important management concepts are fleshed out in real-world scenarios. Using classic as well as current cases of well-known companies, students gain practical knowledge and learn decision-making skills through a series of real-world scenarios.

As a response to positive feedback on the changes to the third edition, we have again included some cases of notable management successes. Many of you have told us that such comparisons of mistakes and successes make for added learning insights.

Although we have classified the cases under the various management functions—such as planning, organizing, leading and controlling, as well as ethical dilemmas—with many situations it is not possible to truly compartmentalize the mistake or the success according to one management function; often, several were involved. We have made a concerted effort also to address the latest management issues, including global applications. Total Quality Management, ethics and social responsibility, non-profit organizations, and customer service. Still, a functional delineation brings order to the subject matter.

NEW TO THIS EDITION

Thirteen new cases have been added to this edition. Many of them are very current, with situations that are still evolving as we go to press. These cases will serve to highlight and integrate the latest in management issues and decisions. New Issue Boxes focus on controversies that have resulted from actions of the companies in question.

LEARNING AIDS

As in the previous editions, a number of learning aids are presented within and at the end of each chapter. Some of these will be common to several cases, and illustrate that certain successful and unsuccessful practices tend to cross company lines.

This edition includes more pedagogical features than previous editions. Updated Information Boxes and Issue Boxes are included in every chapter to highlight relevant management concepts. Learning insights help students see how certain practices cross company lines. Discussion Questions, experiential exercises, and Invitation to Role Play exercises encourage and stimulate student involvement. Invitation To Research suggestions allow students to take the cases a step further, to learn what has happened since the case was written and keeps the book current and up to date. In the final chapter, the various learning insights are summarized and classified into general conclusions.

An Instructor's Manual accompanies this text to provide additional ideas for stimulating class discussion and role plays, as well as teaching suggestions for determining strategies and understanding concepts.

ACKNOWLEDGMENTS

A number of persons have provided encouragement, information, advice, and constructive criticism. In particular, I thank the following reviewers who have given me their valuable suggestions and insights: Vernon R. Stauble, California State Polytechnic University; Donna Giertz, Parkland College; Don Hantula, St. Joseph's University; William O'Donnell, University of Phoenix; Milton J. Alexander, Auburn University; and James F. Cashman, University of Alabama.

Finally, I express my appreciation to Tim Kent, management editor at Wiley, and to Ellen Ford, assistant editor.

Robert F. Hartley

Contents

CHAPTER 1

Introduction

For this fourth edition, we have added 13 new cases, most of these as recent as today's headlines. The older cases that we've kept from previous editions are classics such as the Edsel case and the story of Harley Davidson's battle with Honda.

In accordance with readers' many expressed preferences, we have continued the format of the third edition by examining not only notable mistakes, but also notable successes. We have continued to seek what can be learned—insights that are transferable to other firms, other times, and other situations. What key factors brought monumental mistakes for some firms and resounding successes for others? Through such evaluations and studies of contrasts, we may learn to improve the "batting average" in the intriguing, ever-challenging art of decision making.

We will encounter many examples of the phenomenon of organizational life cycles, with an organization growing and prospering, then failing (just as humans do), but occasionally resurging. Success rarely lasts forever, but even the most serious mistakes can be (but are not always) overcome.

A variety of firms, industries, problems, mistakes, and successes are presented. You will be familiar with most of the firms, although perhaps not with the details of their situations. Although most of the cases are quite recent, a few go back three or more decades. For these classic older cases, the circumstances and the lessons that can be learned are far from dated.

We chose these particular cases to bring out certain points or caveats in the art of management decision making and to give a balanced view of the spectrum of management problems. We have sought to present examples that provide somewhat different learning experiences, where at least some aspect of the mistake or success is unique. Still, we see similar mistakes occurring time and again. The universality of some of these mistakes makes us wonder how much decision making has improved over the decades.

Let us then consider what learning insights we should gain, with the benefit of hindsight, from examining the mistakes and successes of well-known firms.

LEARNING INSIGHTS

Analyzing Mistakes

In looking at sick companies, or even healthy ones that have experienced failures of certain parts of their operations, we may be tempted to be unduly critical. It is easy to criticize with the benefit of hindsight. Mistakes are inevitable, given the present state of the art of decision making and the dynamic environment facing organizations.

Mistakes can be categorized as errors of omission and of commission. *Mistakes of omission* are those in which no action was taken and the status quo was contentedly embraced amid a changing environment. Such errors, which often characterize conservative or stodgy management, are not as obvious as the other category of mistakes. They seldom involve tumultuous upheaval; rather, the company's fortunes and competitive position slowly fade, until years later management suddenly realizes that mistakes having monumental impact have been allowed to happen. The firm's fortunes often never regain their former luster. Examples of companies making such mistakes include IBM, Harley Davidson, and Sears.

Mistakes of commission are more spectacular. They involve bad decisions, wrong actions taken, misspent or misdirected expansion, and the like. Although the costs of the erosion of competitive position coming from errors of omission are difficult to calculate precisely, the costs of errors of commission are often fully evident. The write-offs associated with the Edsel, for example, were estimated to be $100 million in operating losses and another $100 million in unrecoverable investment—big bucks in the 1950s. (The losses would have been far greater except that $150 million of plant and tools were recovered and used in other Ford divisions.) But such costs pale before the hundreds of billions of dollars of losses owing to the excesses in the savings and loan industry, costs borne by the federal government and taxpayers.

Although they may suffer mistakes of omission and commission, companies with alert and aggressive management are characterized by certain actions or reactions when probing their own mistakes or problem situations.

1. Looming problems or present mistakes are quickly recognized.
2. The causes of the problem(s) are carefully determined.
3. Alternative corrective actions are evaluated in view of the company's resources and constraints.
4. Corrective action is prompt. Sometimes this requires a ruthless axing of the product, the division, or whatever is at fault.
5. Mistakes provide learning experiences. The same mistakes are not repeated, and future operations are consequently improved.

Slowness to recognize emerging problems leads us to think that management is lethargic and incompetent or that controls have not been established to provide prompt feedback at strategic control points. For example, a declining competitive position in one or a few geographical areas should be a red flag to management that something is amiss. To wait months before investigating or taking action may mean a permanent loss of business. Admittedly, signals sometimes get mixed, and information may not come as complete as desired, but procrastination cannot be easily defended.

Just as problems should be quickly recognized, the causes of these problems—the "why" of the unexpected results—must be determined as quickly as possible. It is premature to take action before knowing where the problems really lie. To go back to the previous example, the loss of competitive position in one or a few areas may occur because of circumstances beyond the firm's immediate control, such as an aggressive new competitor who is drastically cutting prices to "buy sales." In such a situation, all the competing firms in that area will likely lose some market share, and little can be done except to remain as competitive as possible with prices and servicing. However, closer investigation may disclose that the erosion of business is due to unreliable deliveries, poor quality control, or lost technological advantage.

With the cause(s) of the problem defined, various alternatives for dealing with it should be defined and evaluated and the corrective choice of action made as objectively and prudently as possible. This may require further research, such as obtaining feedback from customers or from field personnel. If drastic action is needed, there usually is little rationale for procrastination. Serious problems do not go away by themselves: They tend to fester and become worse.

Finally, some learning experience should result from the misadventure. A vice president of one successful firm said

I try to give my subordinates as much decision-making power as possible. Perhaps I err on the side of delegating too much. In any case, I expect some mistakes to be made, some decisions that were not for the best. I don't come down too hard usually. This is part of the learning experience. But God help them if they make the same mistake twice. There has been no learning experience, and I question their competence for higher executive positions.

Analyzing Successes

Successes deserve as much analysis as mistakes, although admittedly the urgency is less than with an emerging problem that requires remedial action lest it spread.

Any analysis of success should seek answers to at least the following questions:

Why were such actions successful?

Was it because of the nature of the environment, and if so, how?

Was it because of marketing research, and if so, how?

Was it because of any particular element of the strategy—such as products and/or services, promotional activities, or distribution methods—and if so, how?

Was it because of the specific elements of the strategy meshing well together, and if so, how was this achieved?

Was the situation unique and unlikely to be encountered again?

If not, how can we use these successful techniques in the future or in other operations at present?

ORGANIZATION OF BOOK

We have endeavored to classify the cases under the important management functions of planning, organization, leadership and strategy implementation, control, and, finally, ethical and social responsibility. Admittedly, however, some of the cases involve broader and more pervasive situations and cannot be neatly compartmentalized into, for example, errors of planning or organizing.

Cases in Planning

The first case in the planning section is about the behemoth IBM, the darling of investors for decades. By the early 1990s, IBM was on the ropes, reeling from a surprising lapse in ability to cope with a changed environment.

Genentech, a small pharmaceutical firm, thought it had achieved the ultimate in heart attack pharmacology, and it priced its drug accordingly. Ignoring competing drugs, priced many times less, it stoutly maintained its price and its assertions that a human life was worth any cost. Sales did not meet expectations, but Genentech refused to compromise on its pricing strategy.

The problems of Maytag's Hoover subsidiary in Great Britain almost defy reason and logic. The subsidiary, acting under very loose reins from corporate Maytag, planned a promotional campaign so generous that it was overwhelmed with takers and could neither supply the products nor grant the prizes. In a planning miscue of multimillion-dollar consequences, Maytag had to foot the bill while trying to appease irate customers.

The miscalculation of Coca-Cola in changing the flavor of its traditional and major product shows planning flaws even with the use of extensive evaluation and research. Although the situation eventually worked out, embarrassed executives had to make a major improvisation.

Finally in this section we examine the outstanding success of Southwest Air. It found a strategic window of opportunity in being the lowest cost and lowest price carrier between certain cities. And how it milked this! Now it is threatening major airlines in all their domestic routes.

Organization Cases

We may not always realize the importance of an organization's structure, but flawed organization can cause major problems, whereas the right organization can be a powerful conduit for profitable growth.

The Edsel case could also have been placed under the planning section, because it provides us with the thoughtful realization that even the most detailed planning does not guarantee success. We have placed this case in the organization section because it graphically illustrates the fallacy of creating an organization suited for the most ambitious plans and expectations without sufficient evidence that such expectations are likely to be realized. We also examine the major contrast by the same firm in the space of less than five years—the Mustang. How could the Edsel have been such a failure and the Mustang the most successful new car introduction to that time? Here we have the proof that a firm can learn from its mistakes.

Next we turn our attention to a major factor in retailing since before the turn of the century. For well over one-half century, Sears had been the largest retailer, only recently supplanted by Wal-Mart and Kmart. Sears found itself in danger of losing much more than first place as it struggled to survive in a rapidly changing industry, because it was harnessed with bureaucratic bloat and outmoded policies.

The Campeau case depicts the most famous example of misguided leveraged buyouts (LBOs) using heavy financing. Robert Campeau acquired two major department store corporations, Allied and Federated, through heavy financing in the "raider" tradition of the 1980s. But his greatly expanded organization was too highly leveraged to handle both the operational expenses and the interest costs, and, like a house of cards, began tumbling down. Campeau could not digest what he had swallowed.

Continental Airlines was involved with another opportunistic raider, Frank Lorenzo. His financial wheeling and dealing, his disdain for organization, and his union confrontations brought the airline into bankruptcy twice. Although Continental eventually emerged from bankruptcy, free of Lorenzo, the aftermath was a diminished public image, declining employee loyalty, and competitive vulnerability.

Finally, in this organization section, we examine General Motors' Saturn project, the new tomorrow in U.S. automaking. Relying on a motivated workforce, Saturn has been able to produce cars matching Japanese cars in quality, often priced better, and with trend-setting styling. But profits have mostly eluded it, and some union officials remain critical of the progressive labor-management relationship. But the promise is intriguing.

Cases of Flawed Leadership and Strategy Execution

In the early 1960s, Harley Davidson dominated a static motorcycle industry. Suddenly Honda, a newcomer from overseas, burst on the scene and vastly changed the industry. Harley Davidson's market share dropped from 70 percent to 5 percent in only a few years. The inroads of Honda were a precursor of what was to happen with Japanese imports of all kinds. At the time, Japanese products did not have the image of quality and dependability that they were soon to have, making the quick success of Honda all the more remarkable.

But Harley did revive, as we see in the second case in this section. It did not attempt to meet Honda and the other foreign cycle makers head-on, but rather brought its traditional market for heavy motorcycles into popularity and even prestige. It succeeded at last in creating a mystique for its products.

The A. C. Gilbert Company was unable to handle a crisis. Although this old toymaker should have recognized the environmental factors leading to its crisis long before it did, its greatest mistake was its frenzied reaction, which made matters worse. The case illustrates practically every mistake imaginable, including successive rash decisions in the midst of continued upheaval of the formerly stable organization. In the space of only five years, poor crisis leadership caused the 58-year-old maker of Erector sets and toy trains to fail.

The mind-boggling flaws of an entire industry are described in the savings and loan case. Here the full extent of the debacle is still unraveling, but the final bailout is estimated at over $300 billion. This case represents management's ultimate repudiation of responsibility to its customers and shareholders; personal greed and showmanship became the driving force. Admittedly, management was not alone in culpability: State and federal regulators and a naive, easily influenced Congress must also share the blame. Although the issue is complex, we have focused our attention primarily on flawed managerial leadership and strategy execution.

As the 1980s began, U.S. industry found itself faced with a problem unprecedented in its severity. Foreign firms, especially those of Japan and West Germany, were producing better quality products at less cost than the United States could. Foreign products were invading domestic markets and placing many of U.S. firms at a competitive disadvantage, resulting in the layoff of hundreds of thousands of U.S. workers. In few industries was this invasion of foreign products more severe and disruptive than in the auto and steel industries.

Chrysler in the late 1970s and early 1980s epitomized the dilemma facing many other U.S. firms, although the financial straits of Chrysler, brought on partly by poor management decisions in the past, made its position the more precarious. In this case we examine the background that made such foreign incursions possible and effective, and we describe the situation facing Chrysler's savior, Lee Iacocca, when he took over.

The next case describes the great turnaround of Chrysler at the hands of Iacocca. Unfortunately, Iacocca's success with Chrysler and his resulting fame diluted his concentration on the auto industry. By the late 1980s, Chrysler had lapsed into another looming disaster. An aging Iacocca once more charged to the scene to rescue his company.

The last case in this section describes Sam Walton and his Wal-Mart empire, now the biggest retailer of all. The patterns of success are clearly evident here, and the story of one man's rise to the pinnacle in his chosen field in just a few decades is inspiring indeed. Despite his wealth and prestige, his was still the common touch.

Cases of Flawed Controls

In Part Four we describe three organizations that had serious lapses in maintaining controls and standards and one firm that is the very model of a "tight ship."

United Way of America is a nonbusiness organization. The man who led it to prominence as the nation's largest charity came to perceive himself as virtually beyond authority. Exorbitant spending, favoritism, conflicts of interest—these went uncriticized until investigative reporters for the *Washington Post* publicized the scandalous conduct. Amid the hue and cry, charitable contributions nationwide were drastically reduced.

The next case in this section concerns a product imported from a socialist economy, Yugoslavia. At the time, the Yugo was the lowest priced automobile obtainable in the United States. But the flaws inherent in socialist environments showed up starkly in poor quality, shoddy workmanship, and other problems. Despite the idealogic and political differences between socialist and capitalist work environments, U.S. managers can learn from the Yugo failures.

Days Inn of America has become the nation's largest economy lodging chain. But in the quest for great growth through franchising, Days Inn lapsed in its insistence on adherence to standards. Cleanliness, safety, and security were compromised at some outlets and caused even life-threatening situations to customers.

Although it would seem that maintaining high standards and controls over independent franchises is more difficult than controlling company-owned outlets, McDonald's refutes this notion. Since its beginning, McDonald's has been the epitome of a tightly controlled operation, with the highest standards of cleanliness, product quality and freshness, and customer service. McDonald's has also defied the life-cycle decline that seems to confront almost all firms as they age. It has continued its growth pattern almost unabated for nearly four decades—a remarkable achievement.

Ethical Violations

No firm today can violate social and environmental concerns with impunity. The reputation or public image of a firm can play a crucial role in success and failure. Even more so, the vulnerability to litigation for causing injury can bring any firm to its knees. Even without litigation or governmental intervention, however, the power of special interest groups opposed to certain products or strategies can no longer be ignored. In this last section we examine three cases: A. H. Robins and the Dalkon Shield catastrophe, ethical disputes concerning cigarettes, health clubs, and small loan firms, and finally Johnson & Johnson's successful handling of its Tylenol scare.

When possible, we have depicted the major personalities involved in these cases. Imagine yourself in their position, confronting the problems and decisions they faced at their points of crisis or just-recognized opportunities. What would you have done differently, and why? We invite you to participate in the discussion questions and role-playing episodes appearing at the ends of chapters, as well as the discussion topics in the various boxes within chapters. We urge you to consider the pros and cons of alternative actions in your thoughts and discussions.

QUESTIONS

1. Do you agree that it is impossible for a firm to avoid mistakes? Why or why not?
2. How can a firm speed up its awareness of emerging problems so that it can take responsive action? Be as specific as you can.
3. Large firms tend to err on the side of conservatism and are slower to take corrective action than smaller ones. Why do you suppose this is so?
4. Which do you think is likely to be more costly to a firm, errors of omission or errors of commission? Why?
5. So often we see the successful firm eventually losing its pattern of success. Why cannot success have more durability?

One

PLANNING BLUNDERS

2

IBM: The Giant Tumbles in Coping with Change

On January 19, 1993, International Business Machines Corporation reported a record $5.46 billion loss for the fourth quarter of 1992 and a deficit for the entire year of $4.97, the biggest annual loss in American corporate history. (General Motors recorded a 1991 loss of $4.45 billion after huge charges for cutbacks and plant closings. And Ford Motor Company reported a net loss of more than $6 billion for 1992, but that was a noncash charge to account for the future costs for retiree benefits.) The cost in human lives, as far as employment was concerned, was also consequential, as some 42,900 had been laid off during 1992, with an additional 25,000 planned to go in 1993. In its fifth restructuring, seemingly endless rounds of job cuts and firings had eliminated 100,000 jobs since 1985. Not surprisingly, IBM's share price, which was above $100 in the summer of 1992, closed at an 11-year low of $48.375. And yet IBM had long been the ultimate blue-chip company, reigning supreme in the computer industry. How could its problems have surfaced so suddenly and so violently?

THE ROAD TO INDUSTRY DOMINANCE

"They hired my father to make a go of this company in 1914, the year I was born," said Thomas J. Watson, Jr. "To some degree I've been a part of

IBM ever since."[1] Watson took over his father's medium-sized company in 1956 and built it into a technological giant. Retired for almost 19 years by 1992, he was now witnessing the company in the throes of its greatest adversity.

IBM had become the largest computer maker in the world. With its ever-growing revenues, since 1946 it had become the bluest of blue-chip companies. It had 350,000 employees worldwide and was one of the largest U.S.-based employers. Its 1991 revenues had approached $67 billion, and while profits had dropped some from the peak of $6.5 billion in 1984, its common stock still commanded a price/earnings ratio of over 100, making it a darling of investors. In 1989, it ranked first among all U.S. firms in market value (the total capitalization of common stock, based on the stock price and the number of shares outstanding), fourth in total sales, and fourth in net profits.[2]

During the days of the younger Watson, IBM was known for its centralized decision making. Decisions affecting product lines were made at the highest levels of management. Even IBM's culture was centralized and standardized, with strict behavioral and dress codes. For example, a blue suit, white shirt, and dark tie was the public uniform, and IBM became widely known as "Big Blue."

One of IBM's greatest assets was its research laboratories, by far the largest and costliest of their kind in the world, with staffs that included three Nobel Prize winners. IBM treated its research and development (R & D) function with loving care, regularly budgeting 10% of sales for this forward-looking activity: In 1991, for example, the R & D budget was $6.6 billion.

The past success of IBM and the future expectations for the company with a seeming stranglehold over the technology of the future made it a favorite of consultants, analysts, and market researchers. Management theorists from Peter Drucker to Tom Peters (of *In Search of Excellence* fame) lined up to analyze what made IBM so good. And the business press regularly produced articles in praise and awe of IBM.

Alas, the adulation was to change abruptly by 1992. Somehow, insidiously, IBM had gotten fat and complacent over the years. (In Chapter 12, the case on Harley Davidson, we encounter a similar situation of complacency stemming from long-standing market dominance.) IBM's problems, however, went deeper, as we will explore in the next section.

CHANGING FORTUNES

Perhaps the causes of the great IBM debacle of 1992 started in the early 1980s with a questionable management decision. Perhaps the problems

---

[1]Michael W. Miller, "IBM's Watson Offers Personal View of the Company's Recent Difficulties," *The Wall Street Journal* (December 21, 1992), p. A3.

[2]"Ranking the Forbes 500s," *Forbes* (April 30, 1990), p. 306.

were more deep-rooted than any single decision; perhaps they were a consequence of the bureaucracy that often typifies giant organizations (Sears and General Motors faced somewhat similar problems), growing layers of policies, and entrenched interests.

In the early 1980s, two little firms, Intel and Microsoft, were upstarts, just emerging in the industry dominated by IBM. Their success by the 1990s can be attributed largely to their nurturing by IBM. Each got a major break when it was "anointed" as a key supplier for IBM's new personal computer (PC). Intel was signed on to make the chips, and Microsoft, the software. The aggressive youngsters set standards for successive PC generations and in the process wrested from IBM control over the PC's future. And the PC was to become the product of the future, shouldering aside the giant mainframe that was IBM's strength.

As IBM began losing ground in one market after another, Intel and Microsoft were gaining dominance. In 1982, the combined market value of Intel's and Microsoft's stock amounted to about one-tenth of IBM's. By October 1992, their combined stock value surpassed IBM's; by the end of the year, they topped IBM's market value by almost 50%. See Table 2.1 for comparative operating statistics of IBM, Intel, and Microsoft in recent years. Table 2.2 shows the market valuation of IBM, Intel, and Microsoft from 1989 to 1992, the years before and during the collapse of investor esteem.

Table 2.1 Growth of IBM and the Upstarts, Microsoft and Intel 1983–1992 (in millions)

	1983	1985	1987	1989	1991	1992
IBM						
Revenues	$40,180	$50,056	$54,217	$62,710	$64,792	$67,045
Net income	5,485	6,555	5,258	3,758	(2,827)	(2,784)
% of revenue	13.6%	13.1%	9.7%	6.0%	—	—
Microsoft						
Revenues	$50	$140	$346	$804	$1,843	$2,759
Net income	6	24	72	171	463	708
% of revenue	12.0%	17.1%	20.8%	21.3%	25.1%	25.7%
Intel						
Revenues	$1,122	$1,365	$1,907	$3,127	$4,779	$5,192
Net income	116	2	176	391	819	827
% of revenue	10.3%	0.1%	9.2%	12.5%	17.1%	15.9%

Sources: Company annual statements. Figures from 1992 are estimates from "Annual Report of American Industry" *Forbes* (January 4, 1993), pp. 115–116.

Commentary: Note the great growth of the "upstarts" in recent years, both in revenues and in profits, compared with IBM. Also note the performance of Microsoft and Intel in profit as a percent of revenues.

Table 2.2   Market Value and Rank of IBM, Microsoft, and Intel among All U.S. Companies, 1989 and 1992

	Rank		Market Value ($ millions)	
	1989	1992	1989	1992
IBM	1	13	$60,345	$30,715
Microsoft	92	25	6,018	23,608
Intel	65	22	7,842	24,735

Source: "The Forbes Market Value 500," Forbes Annual Directory Issue (April 13, 1990), pp. 258–259; and Forbes (April 26, 1993), p. 242. The market value is the per-share price multiplied by the number of shares outstanding for all classes of common stock.

Commentary: The market valuation reflects the stature of the firms in the eyes of investors. Obviously, IBM has declined during this period, while Microsoft and Intel have more than tripled their market valuation, almost approaching that of IBM. Yet IBM's sales were $65.5 million in 1992, against sales of $3.3 for Microsoft and $5.8 for Intel.

Defensive Reactions of IBM

As the problems of IBM became more visible to the investment community, chairman John Akers sought to institute reforms to turn the behemoth around. His problem—and need—was to uproot a corporate structure and culture that had developed when IBM had no serious competition.

A cumbersome bureaucracy stymied the company from being innovative in a fast-moving industry. Major commitments still went to high-margin mainframes, but these were no longer necessary in many situations, given the computing power of desktop PCs. IBM had problems getting to market quickly with the technological innovations that were revolutionizing the industry. In 1991 Akers warned an unbelieving group of IBM managers of the coming difficulties: "The business is in crisis."[3] He attempted to push power downward, to decentralize some of the decision making that for decades had resided at the top. His more radical proposal was to break up IBM, to divide it into 13 divisions and give each division more autonomy. He sought to expand the services business and make the company more responsive to customer needs. And, perhaps most important, he saw a crucial need to pare costs by cutting the fat from the organization.

The need for cost cutting was evident to all but the entrenched bureaucracy. IBM's total costs grew 12 percent a year in the mid-1980s, but revenues were not keeping up with this growth.[4] Part of the plan for reducing costs involved cutting employees, which violated a cherished tradition dating back to Thomas Watson's father and the beginning of IBM: a promise never to lay off IBM workers for economic reasons.[5] (Most of the down-

[3]David Kirkpatrick, "Breaking up IBM," Fortune (July 27, 1992), p. 44.
[4]Ibid., p. 53.
[5]Miller, op. cit., p. A4.

sizing was indeed accomplished by voluntary retirements and attractive severance packages, but eventually outright layoffs became necessary.)

The changes decreed by Akers would leave the unified sales division untouched, but each of the new product group divisions would act as a separate operating unit, with financial reports broken down accordingly. Particularly troubling to Akers was the recent performance of the personal computer (PC) business. At a time when demand, as well as competition, was burgeoning for PCs, this division was languishing. Early in 1992 Akers tapped James Cannavino to head the $11 billion Personal Systems Division, which also included workstations and software.

IBM PCs

PCs had been the rising star of the company, despite the fact that mainframes still accounted for about $20 billion in revenues. But in 1990, market share dropped drastically as new competitors offered PCs at much lower prices than IBM; many experts even claimed that these clones were at least equal to IBM's PCs in quality. Throughout 1992, IBM had been losing market share in an industry price war. Even after it attempted to counter Compaq's price cuts in June, IBM's prices still remained as much as one-third higher than its competitors' prices. Even worse, IBM had announced new fall models, and this development curbed sales of current models. At the upper end of the PC market, firms such as Sun Microsystems and Hewlett Packard were bringing out more powerful workstations that tied PCs together with mini- and mainframe computers. James Cannavino faced a major challenge in reviving the PC.

Cannavino planned to streamline operations by slicing off a new unit to focus exclusively on developing and manufacturing PC hardware. By doing so, he would cut PCs loose from the rest of Personal Systems and the workstations and software. This, he believed, would create a streamlined organization that could cut prices often, roll out new products several times a year, sell through any kind of store, and provide customers with whatever software they wanted, even if it was not IBM's.[6] Such autonomy was deemed necessary in order to respond quickly to competitors and opportunities, without having to deal with the IBM bureaucracy.

THE CRISIS

On January 25, 1993, John Akers announced that he was stepping down as IBM's chairman and chief executive. He had lost the confidence of the board of directors. Until mid-January, Akers seemed determined to see IBM

---

[6]"Stand Back, Big Blue—And Wish Me Luck," *Business Week* (August 17, 1992), p. 99.

through its crisis, at least until he would reach IBM's customary retirement age of 60, which would be December 1994. But the horrendous $4.97 billion loss in 1992 changed that, and investor and public pressure mounted for a top management change. The fourth quarter of 1992 was particularly shocking, brought on by weak European sales and a steep decline in sales of minicomputers and mainframes. Now IBM's stock sank to a 17-year low, below $46.

Other aspects of the operation also accentuated IBM's fall from grace: most notably, the decline of the jewel of its operation, IBM's mainframe processors and storage systems.

For 25 years IBM had dominated the $50 billion worldwide mainframe industry. In 1992, overall sales of such equipment grew at only 2 percent, but IBM experienced a 10 to 15 percent drop in revenue. At the same time, its major mainframe rivals, Amdahl Corporation and Unisys Corporation had respective sales gains of 48 percent and 10 percent.[7]

IBM was clearly lagging in developing new computers that could outperform the old ones, such as IBM's old System/390. Competitors' models exceeded IBM's old computers not only in absolute power but in prices, selling at prices of a tenth or less of IBM's price per unit of computing. For example, with IBM's mainframe computers, customers paid approximately $100,000 for each MIPS, or the capacity to execute 1 million instructions per second, this being the rough gauge of computing power. Hewlett Packard offered similar capability at a cost of only $12,000 per MIPS, and AT&T's NCR unit could sell a machine for $12.5 million that outperformed IBM's $20 million ES/9000 processor complex.[8]

In a series of full-page advertisements appearing in such business publications as *The Wall Street Journal*, IBM defended the mainframe and attacked the focus on MIPS:

> One issue surrounding mainframes is their cost. It's often compared using dollars per MIPS with the cost of microprocessor systems, and on that basis mainframes lose. But . . . dollars per MIPS alone is a superficial measurement. The real issue is function. Today's appetite for information demands serious network and systems management, around-the-clock availability, efficient mass storage and genuine data security. MIPS alone provides none of these, but IBM mainframes have them built in, and more fully developed than anything available on microprocessors.[9]

On March 24, 1993, 51-year-old Louis V. Gerstner, Jr., was named the new chief executive of IBM. The two-month search for a replacement for

---

[7]John Verity, "Guess What: IBM Is Losing out in Mainframes, Too," *Business Week* (February 8, 1993), p. 106.
[8]*Ibid.*
[9]Taken from advertisement, *The Wall Street Journal* (March 5, 1993), p. B8.

Akers had captivated the media, with speculation ranging widely. The choice of an outsider caught many by surprise: Gerstner was chairman and CEO of RJR Nabisco, a food and tobacco giant, but Nabisco was a far cry from a computer company. And IBM had always prided itself on promoting from within—for example, John Akers—with most IBM executives being life-long IBM employees. Not all analysts supported the selection of such an outsider. While most did not criticize the board for going outside IBM to find a replacement for Akers, some questioned going outside the computer industry or other high-tech industries. Geoff Lewis, senior editor of *Business Week*, fully supported the choice. He had suggested the desirability of bringing in some outside managers to Akers in 1988:

> Akers seemed shocked—maybe even offended—by my question. After a moment, he answered: "IBM has the best recruitment system anywhere and spends more than anybody on training. Sometimes it might help to seek outsiders with unusual skills, but the company already had the best people in the world."[10]

See the following issue box for a discussion of promotion from within.

INFORMATION BOX

SHOULD WE PROMOTE FROM WITHIN?

A heavy commitment to promoting from within, as had long characterized IBM and other firms, is sometimes derisively called "inbreeding." The traditional argument against this stand maintains that an organization with such a policy is not alert to needed changes, that it is enamored with the status quo, "the way we have always done it." Proponents of promotion from within talk about the motivation and great loyalty it engenders, with every employee knowing that he or she has a chance of becoming a high-level executive.

However, the opposite course of action—that is, heavy commitment to placing outsiders in important executive positions—plays havoc with morale of trainees and lower level executives and destroys the sense of continuity and loyalty. A middle ground seems preferable: filling many executive positions from within, promoting this idea to encourage both the achievement of present executives and the recruiting of trainees, and at the same time bringing the strengths and experiences of outsiders into the organization.

INVITATION TO DISCUSSION

Do you think there are particular circumstances in which one extreme or the other regarding promotion policy might be best? Discuss.

---

[10]Geoff Lewis, "One Fresh Face at IBM May Not Be Enough," *Business Week* (April 12, 1993), p. 33.

ANALYSIS

In examining the major contributors to IBM's fall from grace, we will analyze the predisposing or underlying factors, resultants, and controversies.

Predisposing Factors

Cumbersome Organization. As IBM grew with its success, it became more and more bureaucratic. One author described it as big and bloated. Another called it "inward-looking culture that kept them from waking up on time."[11] Regardless of phraseology, by the late 1980s IBM could not bring new machines quickly into the market, nor was it able to make the fast pricing and other strategic decisions of its smaller competitors. Too many layers of management, too many vested interests, a tradition-ridden mentality, and a gradually emerging contentment with the status quo shackled it—this in an industry that some thought to be mature, but which in reality was gripped by burgeoning change in important sectors. As a huge ship requires considerable time and distance to turn or to stop, so the giant IBM found itself at a competitive disadvantage compared with smaller, hungrier, more aggressive, and above all, more nimble firms. And impeding all efforts to make major changes effective was the typical burden facing all large and mature organizations: resistance to change. The accompanying information box discusses this phenomenon.

Overly Centralized Management Structure. Often related to a cumbersome bureaucratic organization is rigid centralization of authority and decision making. Certain negative consequences may result when all major decisions have to be made at corporate headquarters rather than down the line. Decision making is necessarily slowed, since executives believe they must investigate fully all aspects, and not being personally involved with the recommendation, they may be not only skeptical but critical of new projects and initiatives. More than this, the enthusiasm and creativity of lower level executives may be curbed by the typical conservatism of a higher management team divorced from the intimacy of the problem or the opportunity. The motivation and morale needed for a climate of innovation and creativity is stifled under the twin bureaucratic attitudes "Don't take a chance" and "Don't rock the boat."

The Three C's Mindset of Vulnerability. Firms that have been well entrenched in their industry and that have dominated it for years tend to fall

---

[11]Jennifer Reese, "The Big and the Bloated: It's Tough Being No. 1," *Fortune* (July 27, 1992), p. 49.

INFORMATION BOX

RESISTANCE TO CHANGE

People as well as organizations have a natural reluctance to embrace change. Change is disruptive. It can destroy accepted ways of doing things and familiar authority–responsibility relationships. It makes people uneasy because their routines will likely be disrupted; their interpersonal relationships with subordinates, coworkers, and superiors may well be modified. Positions that were deemed important before the change may be downgraded. And persons who view themselves as highly competent in a particular job may be forced to assume unfamiliar duties.

Resistance to change can be combatted by good communication with participants about forthcoming changes. Without such communication, rumors and fears can assume monumental proportions. Acceptance of change can be facilitated if managers involve employees as fully as possible in planning the changes, solicit and welcome their participation, and assure them that their positions will not be impaired, only changed. Gradual rather than abrupt changes also make a transition smoother, as participants can be initially exposed to the changes without drastic upheavals.

In the final analysis, however, needed changes should not be delayed or canceled because of their possible negative repercussions on the organization. If change is necessary, it should be initiated. Individuals and organizations can adapt to change, although it may take some time.

INVITATION TO DISCUSSION

The worst change an employee may face is layoff. And when no one knows when the next layoff will occur or who will be affected, morale and productivity may both be devastated. Discuss how managers might best handle the necessity of upcoming layoffs.

---

into a particular mindset that leaves them vulnerable to aggressive and innovative competitors. (We will also encounter this syndrome in two later cases, Sears and Harley Davidson, the motorcycle maker.)

The following "three C's" are detrimental to a front-runner's continued success:

Complacency

Conservatism

Conceit

Complacency is smugness—a complacent firm is self-satisfied, content with the status quo, no longer hungry and eager for growth. *Conservatism* when excessive characterizes a management that is wedded to the past, to the traditional, to the way things have always been done. Conservative managers see no need to change because they believe nothing is different today (e.g., "Mainframe computers are the models of the industry and will always be."). Finally, *conceit* further reinforces the myopia of the mindset: conceit for present and potential competitors. The beliefs that "We are the best" and "No one else can touch us" can easily permeate an organization that has enjoyed success for years.

The three C's leave no incentive to undertake aggressive and innovative actions, causing growing disinterest in such important facets of the business as customer relations, service, and even quality control. Furthermore, they inhibit interest in developing innovative new products that may cannibalize—that is, take business away from—existing products or disrupt entrenched interests. (We will discuss cannibalization in more detail shortly.)

RESULTANTS

Overdependence on High-Margin Mainframes. The mainframe computers had long been the greatest source of market power and profits for IBM. But the conservative and tradition-minded IBM bureaucracy could not accept the reality that computer power was becoming a desktop commodity. Although a market still existed for the massive mainframes, it was limited and had little growth potential; the future belonged to desktop computers and workstations. And thus IBM, in a lapse of monumental proportions, relinquished its dominance. The minicomputers first opened up a whole new industry, one with scores of hungry competitors. But the cycle of industry creation and decline started anew by the early 1980s as personal computers began to replace minicomputers in defining new markets and fostering new competitors. The mainframe was not replaced, but its markets became more limited, and cannibalization became the fear.

Neglect of Software and Service. At a time when software and service had become ever more important, IBM still had a fixation on hardware. In 1992 services made up only 9 percent of IBM's revenue. Criticisms flowed:

> Technology is becoming a commodity, and the difference between winning and losing comes in how you deliver that technology. Service will be the differentiator.

> As a customer, I want a supplier who's going to make all my stuff work together.

> The job is to understand the customer's needs in detail.[12]

---

[12]Kirkpatrick, *op. cit.*, pp. 49, 52.

INFORMATION BOX

CANNIBALIZATION

Cannibalization occurs when a company's new product takes some business away from an existing product. The new product's success consequently does not contribute its full measure to company revenues since some sales will be shifted from older products. The amount of cannibalization can range from virtually none to almost total. In the latter case, the new product simply replaces the older product, with no real sales gain achieved. If the new product is less profitable than the older one, the impact and the fear of cannibalization becomes all the greater.

For IBM, the PCs and the other equipment smaller than mainframes would not come close to replacing the bigger units. Still, some cannibalization was likely. And the profits on the lower priced computers were many times less than those of mainframes.

The argument can justifiably be made that if a company does not bring out new products then competitors will and that it is better to compete with one's own products. Still, the threat of cannibalization can cause a hesitation, a blink, in a full-scale effort to rush to market an internally competing product. This reluctance and hesitation needs to be guarded against, lest the firm find itself no longer in the vanguard of innovation.

INVITATION TO DISCUSSION
Assume the role of a vocal and critical stockholder at the annual meeting. What arguments would you introduce for a crash program to rush the PC to market, despite possible cannibalization? What contrary arguments would you expect, and how would you counter them?

In the process of losing touch with customers, the sales force had become reluctant to sell low-margin open systems if it could push proprietary mainframes or minicomputers.

Bloated Costs. As indications of the fat that had insidiously grown in the organization, some 42,900 jobs were cut in 1992, thankfully all through early retirement programs. An additional 25,000 people were expected to be laid off in 1993, some without the benefit of early retirement packages. Health benefits for employees were also scaled down. Manufacturing capacity was reduced 25 percent, and two of three mainframe development labs were closed. But perhaps the greatest bloat was R & D.

The Diminishing Payoff of Massive R & D Expenditures. As noted earlier, IBM spent heavily on research and development, often as much as 10 percent of sales, as shown in Table 2.3. Its research labs were by far the largest and costliest of their kind in the world.

**Table 2.3   IBM Research and Development Expenditures as a Percent of
Revenues, 1987–1991**

	1987	1988	1989	1990	1991
Revenues ($ millions)	$54,217	$59,681	$62,710	$64,792	$67,045
Research, development, and engineering costs	5,434	5,925	6,827	6,554	6,644
Percent of revenues	10.0%	9.9%	10.9%	10.1%	9.9%

Source: Company annual reports.
Commentary: Where has been the significant contribution from such heavy investment in R & D?

And IBM labs were capable of inventing amazing things. For example, they recently developed the world's smallest transistor, 1/75,000th the width of a human hair.

Somehow, with all these R & D resources and expenditures, IBM lagged in transferring its innovation to the marketplace. The organization lacked the ability to quickly translate laboratory prototypes into commercial triumphs. Commercial R & D is wasted without this translation.

CONTROVERSIES

Questionable Decisions. No executive has a perfect batting average of good decisions. Indeed, most executives do well to bat more than 500—that is, to have more good decisions than bad decisions. But, alas, decisions are all relative. Much depends on the importance, the consequences, of these decisions.

IBM made a decision of monumental long-term consequences in the early 1980s. At that time IBM designated two upstart West Coast companies to be the key suppliers for its new personal computer. Thus, it gave away its chances to control the personal computer industry. Over the next 10 years, each of the two firms would develop a near-monopoly—Intel in microprocessors and Microsoft in operating-systems software—by setting standards for successive PC generations. Instead of keeping such developments proprietary (that is, within its own organization) IBM, in an urge to save developmental time, gave these two small firms a golden opportunity, which both grasped to the fullest. By 1992 Intel and Microsoft had emerged as the computer industry's most dominant firms.

And yet the decision still is controversial. It saved IBM badly needed time in bringing its PC to market, and as computer technology becomes ever more complex, not even an IBM can be expected to have the ability and resources to go it alone. Linking up with competitors offers better products and services and a faster flow of technology today, and it seems to be the way of the future.

Former IBM CEO Thomas Watson, Jr., has criticized his successors Frank Cary and John Opel for phasing out rentals and selling the massive mainframe computer outright. Originally, purchasers could only lease the machines, thus giving IBM a dependable cushion of cash each year ("my golden goose," Mr. Watson called it).[13] Doing away with renting left IBM, and John Akers, a newly volatile business, just as the industry position began worsening. Akers, newly installed as CEO, was thus left with a hostile environment without the cushion or support of steady revenues from such rentals. So Watson's argument goes. But the counterposition holds that selling brought needed cash quickly into company coffers. Furthermore, opponents say it is unlikely, given the competitive climate that was emerging in the 1980s, that big customers would continue to tolerate the leasing arrangement when they could buy their machines, if not from IBM then from another supplier whose machines were just as good or better.

Breaking up IBM. The general consensus of management experts was to support Akers' reforms to break up Big Blue into 13 divisions and give them increasing autonomy—even to the point that shares of some of these new Baby Blues might be distributed to stockholders. The idea is not unlike that of Japan's *keiretsu*, in which alliances of companies with common objectives but with substantial independence seek and develop business individually.

The assumption in favor of such breaking up is that the sum of the parts is greater than the whole, that the autonomy and motivation will bring more total revenues and profits. But these hypothesized benefits are not guaranteed. At issue is whether the good of the whole would be better served by suboptimizing some business units—that is, by reducing the profit maximizing of some units in order to have the highest degree of coordination and cooperation. Giving disparate units of an organization goals of individual profit maximization lays the seeds for intense intramural competition, with cannibalization and infighting likely. IBM has embarked on a program of decentralization and internal competition. But will gross profit margins deteriorate even more with such competition? Is the whole better served by a less intensely competitive internal environment?

Intrapreneurship reinforced by *skunkworks* is an approach that some firms have found valuable in bringing an aura of entrepreneurship to large organizations, beset as they are with tendencies toward rigidity and bureaucratic malaise. The following box describes this plan for fostering innovation in large firms.

---

[13]Miller, *op. cit.*, p. A4.

INFORMATION BOX

INTRAPRENEURSHIP AND SKUNKWORKS— PURSUING INNOVATION

Intrapreneurship is the term used to describe the encouragement of entrepreneurial behavior within the large organization. Such a spirit of entrepreneurship—usually only the domain of smaller enterprises—is more conducive to innovative thinking, calculated risk-taking, and quick actions, qualities that are crucial as organizations grow to cumbersome size.

Skunkworks refers to the creation of smaller subunits within the larger corporate structure "where groups of people are allowed to work together in a setting that is highly creative and free of many of the restrictions of large organization."[14]

As an example of the skunkworks concept, Ford Motor Company in late 1989 considered overhauling the Mustang, once a legend but by the 1980s only a fading star. "Team Mustang," a group of about 400 people, scrambled to save this beloved car "on a skinflint budget." In the process they broke rules that previously had governed product development in the rigidly disciplined corporation: They upset the status quo as they vigorously pursued their redesign goal. The result: The Mustang was redone in three years for about $700 million, 25 percent faster and for 30 percent less money than for any comparable new car program in recent years.[15]

In similar fashion, a small group of enthusiastic Apple Computer employees were given separate facilities and permitted to operate free from Apple's normal product development bureaucracy: They set their own norms, and worked without outside interference. They even raised a "jolly roger" over their building as a symbol of their independence. The result? The Macintosh Computer.[16]

INVITATION TO DISCUSSION

Would intrapreneurship or confederations of entrepreneurs within IBM be a viable alternative to breaking up the company into a number of smaller divisions? Do you see any problems with skunkworks?

WHAT CAN BE LEARNED?

Beware of the cannibalization phobia. We have just set the parameters of the issue of cannibalization, that is, how far a firm should go in developing products and encouraging intramural competition that will take sales away from other products and other units of the business. The issue is particu-

---

[14]John R. Schermerhorn, Jr., *Management for Productivity*, 4th ed. (New York: Wiley, 1993), p. 659.

[15]Joseph B. White and Oscar Suris, "How a 'Skunk Works' Kept Mustang Alive—on a Tight Budget," *The Wall Street Journal* (September 21, 1993), pp. A1, A12.

[16]For further information, see Apple Computer *Annual Report*, 1991.

larly troubling when the part of business that is likely to suffer is the most profitable in the company. And yet cannibalization should not even be an issue. At stake is the forward-leaning of the company, its embracing of innovation and improved technology, and its competitive stance. Unless a firm has an assured monopoly position, it can expect competitors to introduce advances in technology and new efficiencies in productivity and customer service.

In general we can conclude that no firm should rest on its laurels, that firms must introduce improvements and change as soon as possible, hopefully ahead of competition—all this without regard to any possible impairment of sales and profits of existing products and units.

Remember the need to be "lean and mean" (sometimes called "acting small"). The marketplace is uncertain, especially in high-tech industries. In such environments a larger firm needs to keep the responsiveness and flexibility of smaller firms. It must avoid layers of management, delimiting policies, and a tradition-bound mindset. Otherwise a big firm is like the enormous vessel that is unable to stop or change course without losing precious time and distance. But how can a big firm keep the maneuverability and innovative thinking of a small firm? How can it remain lean and mean with increasing size?

We can identify certain conditions, or factors, of lean and mean firms:

1. They have simple organizations. Typically, they are decentralized, with decision making moved lower in the organization. This decentralization discourages the buildup of cumbersome bureaucracy and staff, which tend to add both increasing overhead expenses and the red tape that stultifies fast reaction time.

   With a simple organization comes a relatively flat structure, with fewer levels of management than comparable firms. This tendency also has certain desirable consequences. Overhead is greatly reduced with fewer executives and their expensive staffs. But communication is also improved, because higher executives are more accessible, and directions and feedback are less distorted because of more direct communications channels. Even morale is improved because of the better communications and accessibility to leaders of the organization.

2. They encourage new ideas. A major factor in the inertia of large firms is the vested interests of those who see their power threatened by new ideas and innovative directions. Consequently, real creativity is stymied by going unappreciated; often it is even discouraged.

   A firm that wishes to be lean and mean must seek new ideas. To do so requires rewards and recognition for creativity but, even more, acting upon the worthwhile ideas. Few things thwart creativity in an organization more than pigeonholing good ideas of eager employees.

3. Participation in planning is moved as low in the organization as possible. Important employees and lower-level managers are involved in decisions concerning their responsibilities, and their ideas receive reasonable weight in final decisions. Performance goals and rewards should be moved to the lowest possible level in the organization. Such an organizational climate encourages innovation, improves motivation and morale, and can lead to the fast reaction time that characterizes small organizations and often eludes the large.

4. A final factor that characterizes some highly successful, proactive, large organizations as well as small firms is minimum frills—even austerity at the corporate level. Two of our most successful firms today, Wal-Mart and Southwest Airlines, evince this philosophy to the utmost. A no-frills management orientation is the greatest corporate model for curbing frivolous costs throughout an organization.

Beware the "King of the Hill" three C's mindset. As a firm gains dominance and maturity, it must guard against a natural mindset evolution toward conservatism, complacency, and conceit. Usually the C's insidiously move in at the highest levels and eagerly filter down to the rest of the organization. As discussed earlier, this mindset leaves a firm highly vulnerable to competitors who are smaller, hungrier, and anxious to topple the king of the hill.

Although top management usually initiates such a mindset, top management can also lead in inhibiting it. The lean and mean organization is anathema to the three C's mindset. If managers can curb bureaucratic buildup, then the seeds are thwarted. Keys to preventing this mindset are encouragement of innovative thinking throughout the organization and introduction of fresh talent from outside the organization to fill internal positions. A strict adherence to promotion from within is inhibiting.

We can overcome adversity! Perhaps the most valuable lesson that any organization, and its interested publics, can embrace is that adversity is not forever. Firms can come back, as we will describe later. IBM can come back and become a strong competitor. With the computer technology market broadening and evolving, it may never achieve its former dominant position of the 1960s and 1970s—some lost ground may not be regained. But it can prosper again. Management should be capable of learning from mistakes: Mistakes are valuable learning experiences, leading the way to better performance and decisions in the future.

INVITATION

What additional learning insights do you see emerging from the IBM case?

QUESTIONS

1. Assess the pro and con arguments for the 1982 decision to offer Microsoft and Intel a foothold in software and operating systems. (Keep your perspective to that of the early 1980s; don't be biased with the benefit of hindsight.)
2. Do you see any way that IBM could have maintained its nimbleness and technological edge as it grew to a $60 billion company? Reflect on this, and be as creative as you can.
3. "Tradition has no place in corporate thinking today." Discuss this statement.
4. Playing devil's advocate (one who takes an opposing position for the sake of argument), can you defend the position that the problems besetting IBM were not its fault, that they were beyond its control?
5. Giant organizations are often plagued with cumbersome bureaucracies. Discuss how this tendency could be prevented as an organization grows to large size over many years.
6. Which of the 3 C's do you think was most to blame for IBM's problems? Why do you conclude this?

INVITATION TO ROLE PLAY

1. As the new CEO brought in to turn IBM around in 1993, what would you do? (State any assumptions you find necessary, but keep them reasonable. And don't be swayed by what actually happened in 1993. Perhaps better actions could have been taken.) Be as specific as you can, and also discuss the constraints likely to face your turnaround program.
2. You are a management consultant reporting to the CEO in the late 1980s. IBM is still racking up revenue and profit gains, but you detect serious emerging weaknesses. What would you advise management at this time? (Make any assumptions you feel necessary, but state them clearly.) Persuasively explain your rationale.

INVITATION TO RESEARCH

What is the present situation of IBM? Has the great turnaround occurred? What major corrective decisions were made?

3

Genentech:
A Planning Delusion?

A firm thinks it has discovered the magic elixir. In its heady triumph it decides to price this magic potion dearly. After all, how can price be any constraint in the purchase of a life-saving drug for heart attack victims?

A TIME OF TRIUMPH

On a November day in 1987, Genentech, a biotechnology company, has cause to celebrate. Its new heart drug, TPA, has just been approved after some hesitancy by the Food and Drug Administration (FDA) for sale in the United States.

The company goes rather wild. It toasts the approval with champagne under circus tents, it commissions fireworks so massive that the local airport has to be temporarily closed, and its employees and executives stomp to rock and roll music by its biotech band, the Rolling Clones.

Reaching this point of triumph had not been particularly easy. The FDA proved a considerable obstacle. But Genentech management eventually prevailed, although they had to battle unbelievers in the FDA as well as some in the medical community. A major study publicized in March 1985 had indicated that TPA significantly outperformed existing drugs in dissolving deadly blood clots. Based on such compelling evidence, Genentech's management took the strong position that it would be unethical for a doctor not to use the drug to treat heart attacks. And Wall Street analysts enthusiastically endorsed this position, even going so far as to predict malpractice suits for physicians who did not use TPA.

Alas, the FDA did not concur with this enthusiasm. Citing a lack of substantive evidence supporting TPA's effectiveness, it refused to approve the drug in May 1987. But Genentech persevered. The firm submitted further studies alleging that TPA dissolved clots, improved overall heart-pumping action, and extended lives. It exerted strenuous pressure on the FDA with an effective media campaign for TPA.[1] The FDA caved in, and the drug was approved in November. The celebration began.

Management did not rest: Within 15 days, the company held a nationwide teleconference to inform 12,000 physicians, hospital pharmacies, and nurses about this marvelous new drug. Reasoning that a human life was almost priceless, it decided to price TPA at $2200 per dose, a price more than 10 times that of its nearest rival, streptokinase, made by Hoechst AG.

BACKGROUND

Genentech was started by a biologist and an MBA in 1976, with only $500. The two entrepreneurs sought to create the first company to prove the potential of reproducing human proteins through biotechnology. (Biological-based drugs can be as effective as chemical-based drugs but generally have fewer side effects.) Genentech became the first company to commercialize such drugs.

The firm went public in 1980 to a frenzy by investors:

> Genentech . . . elected to sell a million shares at $35 each. This was quite high for a small, untested company. The fever spread swiftly. The financial fundamentals—the multiples, the projections of sales and earnings . . . got trampled as anticipation built. Thirty minutes after the market opened, the underwriters had sold their stock . . . Twenty minutes later the . . . stock hit $89 a share.[2]

Sales grew rapidly. By 1983, sales had reached almost $43 million, with net profits just over $1 million. And the growth continued, as shown in Table 3.1. By 1987 the company was marketing three products: Humulin, a human insulin for diabetes; Roferon, an alpha interferon used to treat leukemia and viruses; and Protropin, a human growth hormone for dwarfism.

These products had rather limited markets. But in 1987 Genentech appeared to have a winner in a new thrombolytic drug, tissue plasminogen

---

[1]R. Rhein, Jr., "FDA Approves TPA Under Pressure," *Chemical Week* 141 (1987), p. 22.

[2]R. Teitelman, *Gene Dreams: Wall Street, Academia, and the Rise of Biotechnology* (New York: Basic Books, 1989), p. 12.

Table 3.1   Genentech Sales and Profits, 1982–1987 (Thousands)

	Sales	Percent Change	Profits	Percent Change
1982	$ 28,838		$ 625	
1983	42,373	46.9%	1,128	80.5%
1984	65,627	54.9%	2,720	141.1%
1985	81,627	24.4%	5,608	105.6%
1986	127,312	56.0%	(353,204)	
1987	218,689	71.8%	42,230	

Source: Company publicly disseminated results.

Discussion: The substantial increases in revenues from year to year indicate a rapidly growing company. Profits seem to be sustaining an even greater year-to-year increase, but the abberration of 1986 destroys the illusion of a firm showing great growth in profits.

activator (TPA), to which it gave the brand name Activase. TPA was a fast-acting agent to clear the clots causing heart attacks. When a clot blocks a vital artery to the heart, the heart muscle is deprived of oxygen and begins to die. Injected through an intravenous drip, TPA can dissolve clots within 30 minutes.

The potential for this new drug seemed awesome. An estimated 1.5 million Americans have heart attacks each year, with approximately 1 million hospitalized.[3] At least one-half of these cases were thought to benefit from clot-dissolving drugs. At a price of $2200 a dose, the market size could be in the neighborhood of $1 billion. Genentech originally evaluated its market at $500 million (purportedly incorporating doctors' conservatism into their estimate).[4]

The major competitor of TPA was streptokinase, made by Hoechst. This older drug was being sold for only $200 a dose. Though effective, it did have certain dangerous side effects, notably allergic reactions and lowered blood pressure. By early 1990 another competing clot-busting drug, Eminase, was introduced by Smith Kline Beecham. Eminase was priced at $1700 a dose, could be injected more easily than TPA, and had longer lasting effects. In Europe Eminase was even administered in ambulances. It also had side effects: possible allergic reactions and lowered blood pressure. But TPA was not without its own side effects, having a possible risk of triggering bleeding in the brain.

[3]E. P. Steinberg, et al., "Cost and Procedure Implications of Thrombolytic Therapy for Acute Myocardial Infarction," *Journal of American College Cardiology* 12 (8) (1988), p. 58A.

[4]Christoph Westphal and Dr. Sherry Glied, "AZT and TPA: The Disparate Fates of Two Biotechnological Innovations and Their Producers," *Columbia Journal of World Business* (Spring/Summer 1990), p. 87.

A MISCALCULATION?

In the euphoria of the sudden FDA approval and the relatively huge market potential, optimism prevailed. The company could see TPA easily contributing one-half of all company sales. And investment analysts saw even more favorable probabilities. The stock price skyrocketed, rising 47 percent in only two weeks, and many employees became rich overnight from their investments in their company's stock.

Genentech did achieve market dominance in its first year, 1988, gaining a 65 percent share of the market for thrombolytic drugs, compared with 30 percent for streptokinase and 5 percent for urokinase. However, sales of TPA were only $189 million, much less than the levels projected. And Genentech's stock fell to one-third its previous level, to the consternation of many employees and other stockholders. In its 1988 annual report, the company gave a tactful explanation:

> For Genentech, 1988 began on the high tide of our successful Activase launch, with initial sales reflecting the enthusiasm of the academic cardiology community, rapid early acceptance and successful distribution. It proceeded more cautiously as this new heart attack therapy emerged into broader medical practice. The modification of historical clinical practice was much slower than anticipated. It takes time and perseverance to establish a whole new way of treating a critical medical condition.[5]

However the company might phrase the miscalculation, the fact remained that it had captured a large part of a disappointingly small market. While sales continued to increase after 1988, the increase was far from phenomenal. Profits also proved to be erratic, as shown in Table 3.2, which shows the operating results after the introduction of TPA in 1987.

What went wrong? Did Genentech get a little too greedy? Did the price prevent the full tapping of a market that it had thought was huge and "in its hand"? The unexpectedly low market growth can be attributed to several factors, all related to TPA's price. Ninety percent of TPA was distributed to hospital pharmacies for use by physicians, and most hospitals stocked the drug. But physicians prescribed clot-dissolving drugs for only about one-third of those patients medically eligible to receive them. Many cardiologists were hesitant to use a new drug, especially one having a measurable risk of a disastrous side effect. And hospital pharmacies, under strong pressures from Medicare and insurance companies to contain costs, could not afford to abandon streptokinase, with its relatively low price of $200 a dose. This

---

[5]*Genentech 1988 Annual Report.*

Table 3.2   Genentech Sales and Profits, 1987–1991—after TPA (Thousands)

	Sales	Percent Change	Profits	Percent Change
1988	$322,759	47.6	$ 20,569	(51.3)
1989	382,210	18.4	43,961	113.7
1990	446,696	16.9	(98,031)	
1991	467,145	04.6	44,322	

Source: Company publicly disseminated results.

Discussion: Genentech's operating results after the introduction of TPA are disappointing. The great breakthrough drug did not contribute well to corporate performance. Sales increases are increasing at a diminishing rate, and profit performance is erratic at best. The huge deficit in 1990 represents a "write-down for certain quantities of Activase (TPA) inventory."

older drug continued to be widely used for Medicare patients; TPA was used more often for privately insured heart attack victims.[6]

Traditional thinking has always held that drugs face an inelastic demand curve (see the information box on p. 35). Perhaps this notion is no longer so valid today.

Was TPA that much more effective than streptokinase at more than 10 times the price? Genentech maintained that it was and that the reluctance to use it was costing lives. But several research studies showed little advantage for TPA, by no means the huge advantage claimed by Genentech.[7] In April 1988, The Ontario Medical Association advised against its use, saying it was too costly.[8]

GENENTECH FIGHTS BACK

Marketers can hardly imagine a scenario worse than this: You have priced your product many times higher than the competition and have supported the mind-boggling markup by extolling unique properties of your product. But then your customers get compelling evidence that your product is no better than its vastly cheaper competitor. This was the dilemma facing Genentech on March 8, 1990. Immediately the stock price fell 1⅛ to 26⅛ before trading was halted on the New York Stock Exchange. Most analysts saw no possibility that Genentech could maintain its $2200 price.

---

[6]Westphal and Glied, *op. cit.*, p. 87.

[7]For example, M. Chase, "Heart Association Targets Uninsured, Poor Patients," *The Wall Street Journal* (November 13, 1991); and Joan O'C. Hamilton, "Genentech: A Textbook Case of Medical Marketing," *Business Week* (August 13, 1990), pp. 96–97.

[8]Westphal and Glied, *op. cit.*, p. 97.

INFORMATION BOX

THE VALIDITY OF AN INELASTIC DEMAND CURVE

The economic concept of price elasticity of demand describes the sensitivity of customers to changes in price. If a small difference in price substantially affects unit sales, the price elasticity of demand is high. Conversely, if demand will be about the same whether a higher or lower price is charged, then the firm faces an inelastic demand for its product. The following diagrams depict this.

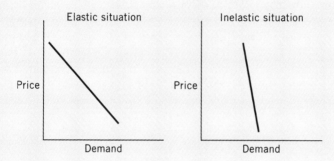

The more horizontal the demand curve, an elastic situation, the more demand is affected by price. In such a situation, a firm will usually opt for low prices and high sales volume. With the more vertical line, the inelastic situation, where demand will not appreciably diminish with a high price, the seller's inclination is to charge a high price. Inelasticity of demand has long been thought to characterize the pharmaceutical industry, with the different drugs holding almost monopoly positions with no exact substitutes available because of each drug's unique properties. The inelastic demand was further buttressed by their necessity for health and even life itself.

The inelasticity of demand and consequent freedom to charge high prices may be eroding today. Publicity about high medical costs and, in particular, drug prices, has been unrelenting. Even physicians, who previously had been rather impervious to concern for prices since they prescribe but do not pay for the products themselves, are becoming more concerned with cost containment. Competition is intensifying in the industry, and although no two drugs are completely alike, differences often are diminishing. Add to this the introduction of generics (i.e., nonbranded drugs priced much lower than branded), and the heady days for drug firms of near monopolies and the vertical inelastic demand curve may be past.

Genentech apparently did not realize or accept this changing market environment.

INVITATION TO DISCUSSION

How can the elasticity of demand be determined? Do you see any problems in this regard?

But four months later, Genentech still had its $2200 price. And although second-quarter sales were off 12 percent from the first quarter, they were ahead of the previous year. How had the company been able to blunt the impact of the supposedly damaging publicity?

Warned in advance of possible negative findings of this European research study, Genentech sought some compromising research findings and found them in two separate American studies by cardiologists at George Washington University and Tulane. These studies concluded that the effectiveness of TPA improved when heparin, an inexpensive anticoagulant that keeps arteries open after TPA initially clears them, was given at the same time as TPA. This was common practice in the United States, but European doctors customarily did not administer heparin for another 12 hours.

Armed with this data, Genentech became aggressive. Just before the March meeting of the American College of Cardiology in New Orleans, it sponsored a symposium in which many physicians left doubting the importance of the European research study and still viewing TPA as superior to streptokinase.

On June 8, 1990, Genentech became a subsidiary of the giant Swiss company Hoffmann-LaRoche. The decision gave Genentech much greater resources for research and development along with considerable marketing expertise (although most would argue Genentech had done fairly well in this regard). The largest independent biotechnology firm was now a subsidiary of a major pharmaceutical corporation.

Genentech's aggressive stance in the marketplace was by no means muted by the merger. The company used patent law to thwart competitors and preserve its market position for TPA. With three patents, Genentech claimed exclusive ownership of natural TPA and all synthetic variations on it, thereby blocking competitors' efforts to develop better synthetic drugs for heart attack victims than the natural version sold by Genentech. *Forbes* headlined an article on this move: "Genentech claims exclusive rights to a chemical in your bloodstream. Could its rather expansive view of patent law be dangerous to your health?"[9]

Did Genentech deserve such patent protection, enabling it to end competitors' research on improved clot-buster variations? Certainly Genentech's TPA was not the panacea, and numerous studies were showing it not meaningfully better than any of the other clot-busters. Still Genentech stubbornly refused to lower its price, even though by 1991 streptokinase cost users less than $100. What had Genentech done to deserve such sweeping patent protection?

Seemingly, not very much. TPA was discovered in the early 1950s and first purified, from human uterine tissue, by a Swedish doctor in 1970. The

---

[9]Gary Slutsker, "Patenting Mother Nature," *Forbes* (January 7, 1991), p. 290.

next year a Belgian research team obtained a U.S. patent for purified human TPA isolated from tumor cells, and Genentech became the exclusive licensee. The labs of Genentech did further work and received two patents for producing TPA by gene splicing or cloning. The techniques for doing so were well known, even at the college level.[10]

Genentech Loses Key Employees

Genentech has a notoriously hard-driving culture, which is not unusual for new high-tech firms. But the company has lost dozens of key employees to start-up firms dealing with even newer technologies.

The latest as of March 1993 was David V. Goeddel, who had been with Genentech for 15 years. A dynamic man, he routinely worked 80-hour weeks. By the time he was 30, he was in charge of molecular biology research and of the team that produced Genentech's first five products, including TPA. He published dozens of scientific articles. Goeddel balanced his hard work with equally rigorous recreation, occasionally climbing major mountains.

At age 41 Goeddel left Genentech to head research at Tularik, Inc., a biotechnology start-up firm he helped found. Whereas Genentech had focused on protein-based drugs using gene splicing, the limitations of such drugs in treating complex diseases such as cancer and AIDS, as well as their need to be injected rather than taken as pills, suggested opportunities for new technologies. And Goeddel wanted to be on the newest cutting edge. Goeddel became the fifth Genentech alumnus to join Tularik. The old corporate structure is cloned there, from having Friday beer bashes to making all employees shareholders.

Arthur D. Levinson, Genentech's vice president for research and development, wryly stated, "We've done well recruiting, and Goeddel's loss won't be devastating. . . . This is a new and uncertain technology, and the way Dave lives is for an adrenalin rush associated with tremendous risks."[11]

ANALYSIS

Genentech's planning strategy can be faulted. Although the company experienced considerable growth, it did not match that of many other high-tech companies, despite what seemed like a blockbuster drug, TPA. Nor did its stock reward investors much, despite the wild rush to buy Genentech shares when they were first offered.

---

[10]*Ibid.*

[11]Joan O'C. Hamilton, "A Biotech Pioneer Goes After Big New Game," *Business Week* (March 22, 1993).

Stubbornness in Maintaining a High Price

Genentech was unbending in its adherence to its $2200 per dose price. It stubbornly maintained that TPA was 50 percent more effective than its nearest competitor, streptokinase, despite significant research studies to the contrary. This rigidity had certain consequences, all negative for the company.

In particular, the high price in the presence of lower priced competing products thwarted the full realization of the market potential. TPA was denied for many Medicare patients because of the cost. Hospital pharmacies and physicians, under pressure for cost containment, were not always eager to use this vastly more expensive option, especially when advantages were not clear-cut. A diminished market potential had a negative impact on operating statistics and stock prices. Furthermore, it invited competitors to come up with something better and cheaper, even though Genentech was temporarily successful in thwarting some of these research efforts.

The justification for the high price was a common one presented by pharmaceutical companies: heavy R & D costs. The company reported spending $200 million over five years to develop TPA.[12] Regardless of whether this number is exaggerated, the fact remains that the basic research leading to TPA did not come from Genentech, as noted earlier. The following issue box discusses recovery of R & D costs.

ISSUE BOX

IS THE RATIONALE OF HIGH R & D EXPENDITURES SUFFICIENT JUSTIFICATION FOR HIGH DRUG PRICES?

Recovery of research and development costs is a reasonable input to any firm's pricing decision, according to the pharmaceutical industry. But this position is not entirely tenable. R & D costs represent sunk costs—that is, outlays that have already been made and which cannot be revoked or canceled. Sometimes such expenditures result in valuable discoveries; sometimes they do not. This is part of the risk of innovation and business decision making: Will the expenditure pay off, or not?

Most firms in a competitive environment cannot afford to incorporate sunk costs into their pricing decisions. They simply cannot price high enough to cover such costs and still be competitive. But the pharmaceutical industry has a predilection for pricing to recover sunk R & D costs. These companies like to use this argument as justification for high margins.

INVITATION TO DISCUSSION
How are R & D costs to be recovered, if not by pricing? Discuss.

---

[12]M. Chase, "Genentech, Battered by Great Expectations, Is Tightening Its Belt," *The Wall Street Journal* (October 11, 1988).

Perhaps Genentech saw image enhancement as justification for the pricing of TPA. We know that a price-quality perception prevails with most consumers (i.e., the higher the price, the better the quality). Does this also apply with medical paraphernalia and drugs? Perhaps. We would like to think our physicians are more sophisticated than the less knowledgeable consumers in this regard—but are they?

The increasing attention given to curbing health costs may be weakening the traditional idea that the most costly is the best. The most expensive product may not be that much better, and frugality may be more prudent. Pricing autocracy in the health industry may be dinosaur thinking.

Undoubtedly another factor, not expressed by Genentech management, was the notion that a new drug—of whatever superior qualities it might be perceived to have—was in a monopoly position. Because of this factor and TPA's unique life-saving qualities, the demand curve was deemed inelastic, independent of price. For who could argue about price when a life in jeopardy might be saved? See the previous information sidelight for the price elasticity of demand discussion as it more recently pertains to the health industry.

The pharmaceutical industry presents a unique marketing situation, one that is virtually unparalleled in any other industry: *The physician who selects and orders a drug is not the customer who pays for it, and the customer usually has no voice in the selection of the drug.* Moreover, once the producing company has established the quality of the product and the company's integrity in the doctors' minds, physicians are more likely to accept future products. Consequently, the acceptability of high drug prices has long held sway. But this is changing. The fact that drug prices in the United States are significantly higher than prices in other countries of the world has received great publicity. Furthermore, when the president of the United States chastises drug firms for unconscionable pricing, the end to unrestrained pricing freedom may be at hand.

Use of Legal Means to Hold Off Rivals

Genentech brought legal action to a new level: to keep rivals from developing competing products. Although it is unclear whether the interests of the general public were well served, it was an effective competitive strategy. But for how long will such a strategy work? The wheels of justice turn slowly, but the many reviews and appeals of verdicts may finally overturn the early broad interpretation of Genentech's patent protection. But even if this happens, the company has given itself substantial breathing room for TPA and its pricing philosophy.

WHAT CAN BE LEARNED?

Beware of rigidity in planning. Genentech has been unbending in its strategy with TPA. Despite numerous threats from lower-priced competing products and controversial research reports, management remained adamant. In so doing, Genentech limited its market potential and very probably its growth in revenues and profits. The moral is clear: Decisions should constantly be reevaluated. If particular planned courses of action are not yielding results up to expectations, then managers should consider other options.

Tread carefully with price/profit opportunism. Pricing to maximize profits, especially in the quasimonopoly situation that arises with many branded drugs, may no longer be a satisfactory strategic plan. With the great emphasis on curbing runaway healthcare costs, and with the concomitant publicity about excess profits in the drug industry, traditional price planning may no longer be tolerated. High profit margins only fuel the critics' fire, reinforcing the perception of drug firms as entirely self-serving and seeking high profits to the detriment of the general public.

Seek to improve public relations. The pharmaceutical industry has a history of abysmal public relations. Over the past half-century, few industries have incurred as much suspicion and skepticisms. Yet no industry has contributed more to human welfare. Although there have been instances of insufficient drug testing—now largely corrected by watchdog governmental agencies—most criticisms have concerned pricing. As described earlier in this chapter, this industry's unique marketing situation—where the customer who pays for the drug has no voice in the product decision—stimulates abuses not possible under more directly competitive conditions.

It is high time that this important industry woke up to the importance of public relations and to the need to nurture its image.

INVITATION

What additional learning insights do you see as emerging from the Genentech case?

QUESTIONS

1. Debate the two positions regarding the pricing and strategic planning for TPA: (a) charging a high price and (b) charging a much lower price. Marshall all the reasons you can for both extreme positions and persuasively defend them.

2. Do you believe that companies like Genentech have a moral obligation to provide low-income patients with free or low-priced drugs? Why or why not?
3. President Clinton castigated the pricing practices of drug firms in his first few months in office. He particularly took issue with the drug firms' defense that they need high profit margins to subsidize their heavy R & D expenditures, alleging that they spend more for advertising and promotion than for R & D. How would you defend the pharmaceutical industry against these charges?
4. What learning insights from the Genentech case do you think would be most beneficial to other firms and other industries?
5. "Even if TPA saves only one life more than its major competitor, streptokinase, its price is justified." Evaluate this statement.
6. "Genentech never did address adequately *who* its customers really were." Evaluate this statement.

INVITATION TO ROLE PLAY

1. Place yourself in the position of Robert A. Swanson, chairman of the board of Genentech. You have been called to Washington to defend your pricing of TPA before a congressional committee investigating high drug prices. How would you defend your $2200 price per dose? Be as persuasive as possible, and prepare to answer critical charges.
2. You are G. Kirk Raub, president and chief executive officer of Genentech. It is 1987 and the FDA has just approved sale of TPA. You disagree with the plans of your boss, Robert Swanson, in the marketing strategy for this drug. Propose a plan different from that actually used by the company. Defend the merits of your plan. (Be as specific as you can and make any assumptions you need to, but keep them reasonable and state them clearly.)
3. You are in charge of U.S. operations for Hoechst, maker of streptokinase, a major competitor of TPA selling at $200 a dose. Design an aggressive strategy to compete with TPA. Be as specific as you can.

INVITATION TO RESEARCH

What is the present situation of Genentech and TPA? Is the $2200 price still holding? Have any new competitors emerged?

4

Maytag:
Bungled Planning in England

The atmosphere at the 1992 annual meeting in the little Iowa town of Newton had turned contentious. As Leonard Hadley faced increasingly angry questions from disgruntled shareholders, a thought crossed his mind: "I don't deserve this!" After all, he had been CEO of Maytag Corporation for only a few months, and this was his first chairing of an annual meeting. But the earnings of the company had been declining every year since 1988, and in 1992, Maytag had had a $315.4 million loss. No wonder the stockholders in the packed Newton High School auditorium were bitter and critical of their management. But there was more. Just the month before, the company had suffered the public embarrassment and costly reparation resulting from a monumental blunder in the promotional planning of its United Kingdom subsidiary.

Hadley doggedly saw the meeting to its close and limply concluded: "Hopefully, both sales and earnings will improve this year."[1]

THE FIASCO

In August 1992, Hoover Limited, Maytag's British subsidiary, launched this travel promotion: Anyone in the United Kingdom buying more than £100

[1]Richard Gibson, "Maytag's CEO Goes through Wringer at Annual Meeting," *The Wall Street Journal* (April 28, 1993), p. A5.

worth of Hoover products (about $150 in American dollars) before the end of January 1993 would get two free round-trip tickets to selected European destinations. For £250 worth of Hoover products, buyers would get two free round-trip tickets to New York or Orlando.

A buying frenzy resulted. Consumers had quickly figured out that the value of the tickets easily exceeded the cost of the appliances necessary to be eligible for them. By the tens of thousands, Britons rushed out to buy just enough Hoover products to qualify. Appliance stores were emptied of vacuum cleaners. The Hoover factory in Cambuslang, Scotland, that had been making vacuum cleaners only three days a week was suddenly placed on a 24-hour, seven-days-a-week production schedule—an overtime bonanza for the workers. What a resounding success for a promotion! Hoover managers, however, were unhappy.

Hoover had not expected more than 50,000 people to respond. And of those responding, management expected that far fewer would go through all the steps necessary to qualify for the free trip and really take it. But more than 200,000 people not only responded but qualified for the free tickets. The company was overwhelmed. The volume of paperwork created such a bottleneck that by the middle of April only 6,000 people had flown. Thousands of others never got their tickets, were unable to get the dates requested, or waited for months before hearing the results of their applications. Hoover established special hotlines to process customer complaints, and these lines were handling 2000 calls a day. But the complaints quickly spread, and the ensuing publicity brought on charges of fraud and demands for restitution.

Maytag dispatched a task force to try to resolve the situation without jeopardizing customer relations any further. But it acknowledged that it was "not 100 percent clear" that all eligible buyers would receive their free flights.[2] The ill-fated promotion was a financially staggering blow to Maytag. It took a $30 million charge in the first quarter of 1993 to cover unexpected additional costs linked to the promotion. Final costs were expected to exceed $50 million, which would be 10 percent of UK Hoover's total revenues. This for a subsidiary acquired only four years before, which had yet to produce a profit.

Adding to the costs were problems with the two travel agencies involved. The agencies were contracted to obtain low-cost space-available tickets and would earn commissions selling "packages," including hotels, rental cars, and insurance. If consumers bought a package, Hoover would get a cut. However, despite the overwhelming demand for tickets, most

---

[2]James P. Miller, "Maytag U.K. Unit Finds a Promotion Is Too Successful," *The Wall Street Journal* (March 31, 1993), p. A9.

consumers declined to purchase the package, thus greatly reducing support money for the promotional venture. Hoover had greatly underestimated the likely response and overestimated the amount it would earn from commission payments.

If the promotion had added greatly to Maytag's and Hoover's customer relations and public image despite cost overruns, the expenditures would seem more palatable. But with all the negative hype, the best that could be expected would be to lessen the worst of the agitation and charges of deception.

Heads rolled. Initially, Maytag fired three UK Hoover executives involved, including the president of Hoover Europe. At the annual meeting, Hadley also indicated that others might lose their jobs before the cleanup was complete. He likened the promotion to "a bad accident . . . and you can't determine what was in the driver's mind."[3]

Receiving somewhat less publicity was another question: Why did corporate headquarters allow executives of a subsidiary such wide latitude that they could saddle parent Maytag with millions of dollars of unexpected costs? Did not top corporate executives have to approve ambitious plans? A company spokesman said that operating divisions were "primarily responsible" for planning promotional expenses. Although the parent may review such outlays, "if they're within parameters, it goes through."[4] This raises the controversy, discussed in the issue box on p. 45, of whether decentralization with its concomitant management by exception can be carried too far.

BACKGROUND ON MAYTAG

Maytag is a century-old company. The original business, formed in 1893, manufactured feeder attachments for threshing machines. In 1907 the company moved to Newton, Iowa, a small town 30 miles east of Des Moines. Manufacturing emphasis turned to home laundry equipment and wringer-type washers.

A natural expansion of this emphasis occurred with the commercial laundromat business in the 1930s, when coin meters were attached to Maytag washers. Rapid growth of these coin-operated laundries took place in the United States during the late 1950s and early 1960s. The 1970s hurt laundromats with increased competition and soaring energy costs. In 1975 Maytag introduced new energy-efficient machines and "home style" stores that rejuvenated the business.

---

[3]Gibson, *op. cit.*, p. A5.
[4]Miller, *op. cit.*, p. A9.

ISSUE BOX

HOW MUCH DECENTRALIZATION AND MANAGEMENT BY EXCEPTION IS ACCEPTABLE?

In a decentralized organization, top management delegates considerable decision-making authority to subordinates. Such decentralization and authority to make decisions can be extensive, or it can be more modest. In the Maytag/Hoover situation, it was evidently extensive. With any decentralization, top management exercises control through management by exception, being apprised only of deviations from expected plans or parameters and variances from expected results.

Extensive decentralization has many advantages: First, top management effectiveness can be improved since time and attention can be freed for the more important matters; second, subordinates are permitted more self-management, which should improve their competence and motivation. But the drawbacks are evident. Parameters within which subordinate managers operate can be so wide that severe miscalculations may ensue. Because top management is ultimately responsible for all performance, including actions of subordinates, it faces greater risks with extensive decentralization and liberal management by exception.

INVITATION TO DISCUSSION
"Because the manager is ultimately accountable for whatever is delegated to subordinates, then extensive decentralization reflects great confidence in subordinates." Discuss.

The Lonely Maytag Repairman

For years Maytag reveled in a marketing coup, with its washers and dryers enjoying a top-quality image thanks to decades of ads in which a repairman laments his loneliness because of Maytag's trouble-free products. Because of this dependability and quality image, Maytag could command a price premium: "Their machines cost the same to make, break down as much as ours—but they get $100 more because of the reputation," grumbled a competitor.[5]

During the 1970s and into the 1980s, Maytag continued to capture 15 percent of the washing machine market and enjoyed profit margins about twice those of competitors. Table 4.1 shows operating results for the period

---

[5]Brian Bremmer, "Can Maytag Clean Up Around the World?" *Business Week* (January 30, 1989), p. 86.

Table 4.1   Maytag Operating Results, 1974–1981
(in millions)

	Net Sales	Net Income	Percent of Sales
1974	$229	$21.1	9.2
1975	238	25.9	10.9
1976	275	33.1	12.0
1977	299	34.5	11.5
1978	325	36.7	11.3
1979	369	45.3	12.3
1980	346	35.6	10.2
1981	409	37.4	9.1
Average net income percent of sales: 10.8%			

Source: Company operating statistics.

Commentary: These years show a steady, though not spectacular, growth in revenues and a generally rising net income, except for 1980. Of particular interest is the high net income percentage of sales, averaging 10.8% over the eight-year period, with a high of 12.3%.

1974 to 1981. Whirlpool was the largest factor in the laundry equipment market, with a 45 percent share, but this was true largely because of sales to Sears under the Sears brand.

Acquisitions

For many years, until his retirement December 31, 1992, Daniel J. Krumm had influenced Maytag's destinies. He had been CEO for 18 years and chairman since 1986, and his tenure with the company encompassed 40 years. In that time the home appliance business had encountered some drastic changes. The most ominous occurred in the late 1980s with the merger mania, in which the threat of takeovers by hostile raiders often motivated previously conservative executives to increase corporate indebtedness greatly, thereby decreasing the attractiveness of their firms. Daniel Krumm was one of these running-scared executives, as rumors persisted that the company was a takeover candidate.

Largely as a defensive move, Krumm pushed through a deal for a $1 billion buyout of Chicago Pacific Corporation (CPC), a maker of vacuum cleaners and other appliances with $1.4 billion in sales. As a result, Maytag was burdened with $500 million in new debt. Krumm defended the acquisition as giving Maytag a strong foothold in a growing overseas market. CPC was best known for the Hoover vacuums it sold in the United States and Europe. Indeed, so dominant was the Hoover brand in England that many people called vacuuming their carpets "hoovering the carpet." CPC also made washers, dryers, and other appliances under the Hoover brand, selling them exclusively in Europe and Australia. In addition, it had six furniture companies, but Maytag sold these shortly after the acquisition.

Krumm had been instrumental in transforming Maytag—the number four U.S. appliance manufacturer behind General Electric, Whirlpool, and Electrolux—from a niche laundry equipment maker into a full-line manufacturer. He had led an earlier acquisition spree in which Maytag had expanded into microwave ovens, electric ranges, refrigerators, and freezers. Its brands then included Magic Chef, Jenn-Air, Norge, and Admiral. The last years of Krumm's reign, however, were not marked by great operating results. As shown in Table 4.2, revenues showed no gain between 1989 and 1992, and income steadily declined.

Trouble

Although the rationale for internationalizing seemed inescapable, especially in view of a recent wave of joint ventures between U.S. and European appliance makers, the Hoover acquisition was troublesome. It was a major brand in England and in Australia, but Hoover had only a small presence in continental Europe. Yet this was the bulk of the market, with some 320 million potential appliance buyers.

The probabilities of the Hoover subsidiary being able to capture much of the European market were hardly promising. Whirlpool was strong, having 10 plants there in contrast to Hoover's two plants. Furthermore, Maytag faced entrenched European competitors such as Sweden's Electrolux, the world's largest appliance maker; Germany's Bosch-Siemens; and Italy's Merloni Group. And General Electric had also entered the market with joint ventures. The fierce loyalty of Europeans to domestic brands raised further

Table 4.2   Maytag Operating Results, 1989–1992

	Revenue	Net Income	% of Revenue
	(000,000)		
1989	$3,089	131.0	4.3
1990	3,057	98.9	3.2
1991	2,971	79.0	2.7
1992	3,041	(315.4)	(10.4)

Source: Company annual reports.

Commentary: Note the steady erosion of profitability, while sales remained virtually static. For comparison with profit performance of earlier years, see Table 4.1 and the net-income-to-sales percentages of this more "golden" period.

questions as to the ability of Maytag's Hoover to penetrate the European market, with or without massive promotional expenditures.

Australia was something else. Hoover had a good competitive position there, and its refrigerator plant in Melbourne could easily be expanded to include Maytag's washers and dryers. Unfortunately, the small population of Australia limited the market to only about $250 million for major appliances.

Britain accounted for one-half of Hoover's European sales, but at the time of the acquisition, its major appliance business was only marginally profitable. This was to change: After the acquisition it became downright unprofitable, as shown in Table 4.3 for the years 1990 through 1992, as it struggled to expand in a recession-plagued Europe. The results for 1993, of course, reflect the huge loss for the promotional debacle. Hardly an acquisition made in heaven.

Maytag's earlier acquisitions also were becoming soured. Its acquisitions of Magic Chef and Admiral were diversifications into lower priced appliances, and sales did not meet expectations. These acquisitions left Maytag's balance sheet and cash flow weakened. See Table 4.4. Perhaps a more serious problem was the fact that Maytag's reputation as the nation's

Table 4.3   Operating Results of Maytag's Principal Business Components 1990–1992

	Revenue (000,000)	*Income*[a] (000)
1990		
North American Appliances	$2,212	$221,165
Vending	191	25,018
European Sales	497	(22,863)
1991		
North American Appliances	2,183	186,322
Vending	150	4,498
European Sales	486	(865)
1992		
North American Appliances	2,242	129,680
Vending	165	16,311
European Sales	502	(67,061)

[a]Operating income (income before depreciation and other adjustments).

Source: Company annual reports.

Commentary: Although these years had not been particularly good for Maytag in growth of revenues and income, the continuing, and even intensifying, losses in the Hoover European operation were troublesome. And this is before the ill-fated early 1993 promotional results.

Table 4.4   Long-Term Debt as a Percent of
Capital from Maytag's Balance Sheets, 1986–1991

Year	Long-Term Debt/Capital
1986	7.2%
1987	23.3
1988	48.3
1989	46.8
1990	44.1
1991	42.7

Source: Company annual reports.

Commentary: The effect of acquisitions, in particular that of the Chicago Pacific Corporation, can be clearly seen in the buildup of long-term debt: In 1986 Maytag was virtually free of such commitments; two years later its long-term debt ratio had increased almost sevenfold.

premier appliance maker became tarnished while General Electric and Whirlpool were attacking the top end of its product line. As a result, Maytag found itself in the third- or fourth-ranked market position in most of its brand lines.

ANALYSIS

Flawed Acquisition Decisions

The long decline in profits after 1989 should have triggered strong concern and corrective action. And perhaps it did, but the action was not effective— the decline continued, culminating in a large deficit in 1992 and serious problems in 1993. As shown in Table 4.2, the acquisitions brought neither revenue gains nor profitability. Perhaps in the rush to fend off potential raiders in the late 1980s, the company bought businesses it might never have considered under more sober times, and perhaps it paid too much for these businesses. Further, these companies cheapened Maytag's proud image for quality.

Who Is to Blame in the UK Promotional Debacle?

Corporate Maytag management was guilty of a common fault in their acquisitions: It gave newly acquired divisions a loose rein, letting them continue to operate independently with few constraints. The attitude that the division's executives should be more knowledgeable about their operations than corporate headquarters can sometimes be misguided confidence. In the UK promotion, Maytag management seemed to have been as derelict as management in England. Planning guidelines or parameters were far too loose and undercontrolled. The idea that subsidiary management could burden the parent with $50 million of unexpected charges borders on the absurd.

Finally, the planning of the UK executives for this ill-conceived travel promotion defies all logic. They vastly underestimated the demand for the promotional offer and greatly overestimated paybacks from travel agencies on the package deals. Yet it took no brilliant insight to realize that the value of the travel offer exceeded the price of the appliance—indeed, 200,000 customers rapidly arrived at this conclusion—and that such a sweetheart of a deal would be irresistible to many consumers at the expense of the company. Was it miscalculation or complete naiveté on the part of executives and their staffs, who should have known better?

How Could the Promotion Have Avoided the Problems?

The disaster resulting from too good of an offer could have been avoided without scrapping the whole idea. A cost-benefit analysis would have provided some guidance as to how much the company should spend to achieve certain benefits, such as increased sales, greater consumer interest, and favorable publicity. The following information box provides a more detailed discussion of cost-benefit analysis as an important planning tool.

A cost–benefit analysis should certainly have alerted management to the possible consequences of various acceptance levels and to the significant risks of high acceptance. However, the company could have set limits on the number of eligible recipients: perhaps the first 1000 or the first 5000. Doing this would have held the costs to reasonably defined levels and avoided the greater risks. The company could alternatively have made the offer less generous, perhaps by increasing the requirements or by reducing the premiums. These more moderate alternatives would still have made an attractive promotion but would have prevented a major, uncontrolled catastrophe.

INFORMATION BOX

COST–BENEFIT ANALYSIS

A cost–benefit analysis is a systematic comparison of the costs and benefits of a proposed action. Only if the benefits exceed the costs should the plan receive a "go" decision. The normal way to make such an analysis is to assign dollar values to all costs and benefits, thus providing a common basis for comparison.

Cost–benefit analyses have been widely used by the Defense Department in evaluating alternative weapons systems. In recent years such analyses have been sporadically applied to environmental regulation and even to workplace safety standards. As an example of the former, a cost-benefit analysis can be used to determine if it is socially worthwhile to spend $X million to meet a certain standard of clean air or water.

Many business decisions can benefit from a cost-benefit analysis. The process provides a systematic way of analyzing the inputs and the probable outputs of particular major alternatives. Although in the business setting some of the costs and benefits are quantitative, these items often should be tempered by qualitative inputs to reach the broadest perspective. Schermerhorn suggests considering the following criteria in evaluating alternatives:[6]

Benefits: What are the "benefits" of using the alternatives to solve a performance deficiency or take advantage of an opportunity?

Costs: What are the "costs" to implement the alternatives, including both direct resource investments and any potential negative side effects?

Timeliness: How fast will the benefits occur and create a positive impact?

Acceptability: To what extent will the alternatives be accepted and supported by those who must work with them?

Ethical soundness: How well do the alternatives meet acceptable ethical criteria in the eyes of multiple stakeholders?

INVITATION TO DISCUSSION
What numbers would you assign to a cost-benefit analysis for Maytag Hoover's plan to offer the free airline tickets? Assume 5000 takers, 20,000 takers, 100,000 takers, then 500,000 takers. (Make any assumptions necessary regarding costs.) What are your conclusions for these various acceptance rates?

WHAT CAN BE LEARNED?

In planning, consider a worst-case scenario. There are those who preach the desirability of positive thinking, of confidence and optimism, be it in personal life, athletics, or business practices. But expecting and preparing for the worst has much to commend it, since a person or a firm is then better able to cope with adversity and therefore make prudent decisions. And if it is deemed that the risks outweigh probable benefits, then the alternative ought to be scrapped or modified.

Apparently the avid acceptance of the promotional offer was a complete surprise: No one dreamed of such demand. Why was it so unreasonable to think that a very attractive offer would meet wild acceptance and to be prepared to set limits to any potential losses?

[6]John R. Schermerhorn, Jr., *Management for Productivity*, 4th ed. (New York: Wiley, 1993), p. 164.

Beware the extremes of decentralization. Although decentralization—that is, moving more authority down into the ranks of the organization—is generally desirable and stimulates better motivation and management development than centralization, it can be overdone. At the extreme, when divisional and subsidiary executives have virtually unlimited decision-making authority and can run their operations as virtual dynasties, corporate management essentially abdicates its authority. Such looseness in an organization endangers cohesiveness; it tends to obscure common standards and objectives; it can even dilute unified ethical standards.

Such extreme looseness of organizational structure is not uncommon with acquisitions, as we noted earlier in the chapter, because of the assumption that the acquired firms were operating successfully before the acquisition and have expertise because of their experience. International operations are often given more freedom of scope than domestic operations simply because executives in the foreign countries are presumed to have more firsthand knowledge of their environment than the parent executives.

Still, there should be limits on how much freedom of scope these divisional and subsidiary executives should be permitted—especially when their operations have not been notably successful. In Maytag's case, the UK subsidiary had lost money every year since it was acquired. One would expect prudent corporate management to ensure tighter supervision under these circumstances.

The power of a cost–benefit analysis. For major decisions executives have much to gain from a cost-benefit analysis. It forces them to systematically tabulate and analyze the costs and benefits of a particular course of action. Managers may find that benefits are too uncertain to be worth the investment in resources or the risk of requiring substantially greater expenditures. If so, the time to come to this realization is before implementing the plan rather than after making substantial commitments.

Without doubt, regular use of cost-benefit analyses for major decisions would improve executives' batting averages for good decisions. Even though some numbers may have to be estimated, especially probable benefits, the process of making this analysis forces decision makers to take a careful look at alternatives and most likely consequences. For more important decisions, input from diverse staff people and executives will bring greater power to the analysis.

INVITATION

What additional learning insights can you add?

QUESTIONS

1. How could the promotion of UK Hoover have been better planned and designed? Be as specific as you can.
2. Given the fiasco that did occur—in particular, the huge, unexpected demand—how do you think Maytag should have responded?
3. Comment on the following statement. "Firing the three top executives of UK Hoover is unconscionable. It smacks of a vendetta against European managers by an American parent. After all, their only 'crime' was a promotion that was too successful."
4. Do you think Leonard Hadley, the Maytag CEO for only two months, should be soundly criticized for the UK situation? Why or why not?
5. Please speculate: Why do you think this UK Hoover fiasco happened in the first place? What went wrong?
6. Evaluate the decision to acquire Chicago Pacific Corporation (CPC). Do this both for the time of the decision, and now—after the fact—as a post mortem. Defend your overall conclusions.
7. Use your creativity: Can you devise a strategic plan for UK Hoover to become more of a major force in Europe?

INVITATION TO ROLE PLAY

1. You have been placed in charge of a task force sent by headquarters to England to coordinate the "fire-fighting" efforts in the aftermath of the ill-fated promotion. There is neither enough productive capacity nor enough airline seats available to handle the demand. How do you propose to handle this situation? Be as specific as you can, and defend your recommendations.
2. As a staff vice president at corporate headquarters, you have been charged to develop policies and procedures companywide that will prevent such a situation from ever recurring. What do you recommend?

INVITATION TO RESEARCH

How was the promotional snafu finally resolved? What was the final impact on company image and profits? Has the European operation been brought into the black yet? How has the stock market price of Maytag changed since early 1993?

5

Coca-Cola's Classic Planning Blunder

On April 23, 1985, Roberto C. Goizueta, chairman of Coca-Cola, made a momentous announcement. It was to lead to more discussion, debate, and intense feelings than perhaps ever before encountered from one business decision.

"The best has been made even better," he proclaimed. After 99 years, the Coca-Cola Company had decided to abandon its original formula in favor of a sweeter variation, presumably an improved taste, which was named "New Coke."

Less than three months later, public pressure brought the company to admit that it had made a mistake and that it was bringing back the old Coke under the name "Coca-Cola Classic." It was July 11, 1985. Despite $4 million and two years of research, the company had made a major planning miscalculation in its estimation of customer acceptance of a product change. How could this have happened with such an astute and successful firm? The story is intriguing and provides a number of sobering insights as well as a happy ending for Coca-Cola.

THE HISTORY OF COCA-COLA

Early Days

Coca-Cola was invented by a pharmacist who rose to cavalry general for the Confederates during the Civil War. John Styth Pemberton settled in

Atlanta after the war and began putting out patent medicines such as Triplex Liver Pills and Globe of Flower Cough Syrup. In 1885 he registered a trademark for French Wine Coca, "an Ideal Nerve and Tonic Stimulant." In 1886, Pemberton unveiled a modification of French Wine Coca which he called Coca-Cola and began distributing it to soda fountains in used beer bottles. He looked on the concoction less as a refreshment than as a headache cure, especially for people who had overindulged in food or drink. By chance, one druggist discovered that the syrup tasted better when mixed with carbonated water.

As his health failed and Coca-Cola failed to bring in sufficient money to meet his financial obligations, Pemberton sold the rights to Coca-Cola to a 39-year-old pharmacist, Asa Griggs Candler, for a paltry $2300. The destitute Pemberton died in 1888 and was buried in a grave that went unmarked for the next 70 years.

Candler, a small-town Georgia man born in 1851, had planned to become a physician but changed his mind after observing that druggists made more money than doctors. He struggled for almost 40 years until he bought Coca-Cola, but then his fortunes changed profoundly. In 1892 he organized the Coca-Cola Company; a few years later he downplayed the therapeutic qualities of the beverage and began emphasizing the pleasure-giving qualities. At the same time, he developed the bottling system that still exists, and for 25 years he almost single-handedly guided the drink's destiny.

Robert Woodruff and the Maturing of the Coca-Cola Company

In 1916 Candler left Coca-Cola to run for mayor of Atlanta. He left the company in the hands of his relatives, who, after only three years, sold it to a group of Atlanta businessmen for $25 million. Asa was not consulted, and he was deeply distraught. The company was then netting $5 million. By the time of his death in 1929, annual profits were approaching the $25 million sale price. The group who bought Coca-Cola was headed by Ernest Woodruff, an Atlanta banker. Coke today still remains in the hands of the Woodruff family. Under the direction of the son, Robert Winship Woodruff, Coca-Cola became not only a household word within the United States but one of the most recognized symbols the world over.

Robert Woodruff grew up in affluence but believed in the virtues of personal achievement and effort. As a young man, he ignored his father's orders to return to Emory College to complete the remaining years of his education. He wanted to earn his keep in the real world and not "waste" three years in school. Eventually in 1911 he joined one of his father's firms, the newly organized Atlantic Ice & Coal Company, as a salesman and buyer. But he and his father violently disagreed again, this time over Robert's purchase of trucks from White Motors to replace the horse-drawn carts and drays of the day. Ernest fired his son and told him never to return home. Robert promptly joined White Motors. At the age of 33, he had become the nation's top truck salesman and was earning $85,000 a year. But then he heeded his father's call to come home.

By 1920 the Coca-Cola Company was threatened by bankruptcy. An untimely purchase of sugar just before prices plummeted had resulted in a staggering amount of borrowing to keep the company afloat. Bottler relations were at an all-time low because the company had wanted to raise the price of syrup, thus violating the original franchise contracts in which the price had been permanently fixed. In April 1923 Robert was named president, and he cemented dealer relationships, stressing his conviction that he wanted everyone connected with Coca-Cola to make money. He instituted a quality control program and greatly expanded distribution: By 1930 Coca-Cola had 64 bottlers in 28 countries.

During World War II, Coke went with the GIs. Woodruff saw to it that every man in uniform could get a bottle of Coca-Cola for a nickel whenever he wanted, no matter what the cost to the company. Throughout the 1950s, 1960s, and early 1970s, Coca-Cola ruled the soft drink market, despite strong challenges by Pepsi. It outsold Pepsi two to one. But this was to change.

BACKGROUND OF THE DECISION

Inroads of Pepsi, 1970s and 1980s

By the mid-1970s the Coca-Cola Company was a lumbering giant, and performance reflected this. Between 1976 and 1979, the growth rate of Coca-Cola soft drinks dropped from 13 percent annually to a meager 2 percent. As the giant stumbled, Pepsi Cola was finding heady triumphs. First came the "Pepsi Generation." This advertising campaign captured the imagination of the baby boomers with its idealism and youth. Pepsi's association with youth and vitality greatly enhanced its image and firmly associated it with the largest consumer market for soft drinks.

Then came another management coup, the "Pepsi Challenge," in which comparative taste tests with consumers showed a clear preference for Pepsi. This campaign led to a rapid increase in Pepsi's market share, from 6 to 14 percent of total U.S. soft-drink sales.

Coca-Cola, in reaction, conducted its own taste tests. Alas, these tests had the same result—people liked the taste of Pepsi better, and market share changes reflected this. As Table 5.1 shows, by 1979 Pepsi had closed

Table 5.1   Coke and Pepsi Shares of Total Soft-Drink Market 1950s–1984

	Mid-1950s Lead	1975 % of Market	Lead	1979 % of Market	Lead	1984 % of Market	Lead
Coke	Better than 2 to 1	24.2	6.8	23.9	6.0	21.7	2.9
Pepsi		17.4		17.9		18.8	

Source: Thomas Oliver, *The Real Coke, the Real Story* (New York: Random House, 1986), pp. 21, 50; "Two Cokes Really Are Better Than One—For Now," *Business Week* (September 9, 1985), p. 38.

the gap on Coca-Cola, having 17.9 percent of the soft-drink market to Coke's 23.9 percent. By the end of 1984, Coke had only a 2.9 percent lead, and in the grocery store market it was now trailing 1.7 percent. Further indication of Coke's diminishing position relative to Pepsi was a study done by Coca-Cola's own marketing research department. This study showed that in 1972, 18 percent of soft-drink users drank Coke exclusively, whereas only 4 percent drank only Pepsi. In 10 years the picture had changed greatly: Only 12 percent now claimed loyalty to Coke, and the number of exclusive Pepsi drinkers almost matched, with 11 percent. Figure 5.1 shows this graphically:

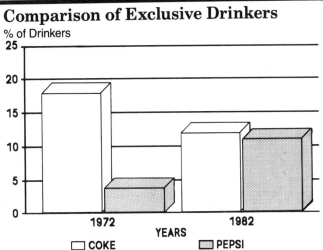

Figure 5.1 Coke versus Pepsi: Comparison of exclusive drinkers.

The fact that Coca-Cola was outspending Pepsi in advertising by $100 million made Coke's deteriorating competitive performance all the more worrisome and frustrating. Coca-Cola had twice as many vending machines, dominated fountains, had more shelf space, and was competitively priced. Why was it still losing market share?

The Changing of the Guard

J. Paul Austin, the chairman of Coca-Cola, was nearing retirement in 1980. Donald Keough, the president for Coca-Cola's American group, was expected to succeed him. But a new name, Roberto Goizueta, suddenly emerged.

Goizueta's background was far different from that of the typical Coca-Cola executive. He was not from Georgia, was not even Southern. Rather, he was the son of a wealthy Havana sugar plantation owner. He came to the United States at age 16 to enter an exclusive Connecticut preparatory school, Cheshire Academy. He spoke virtually no English when he arrived, but he quickly learned the language by using the dictionary and watching movies—and became the class valedictorian.

Goizueta graduated from Yale in 1955 with a degree in chemical engineering and returned to Cuba. Spurning his father's business, he went to work in Coke's Cuban research labs.

Goizueta's complacent life was to change in 1959 when Fidel Castro seized power and expropriated foreign facilities. He fled to the United States with his wife and their three children, arriving with $20. With Coca-Cola he soon became known as a brilliant administrator, and in 1968 he was brought to company headquarters. In 1980 Goizueta and six other executives were made vice chairpersons and began battling for top spots in the company.

Chief executive officer J. Paul Austin, soon to retire because of Alzheimer's disease, favored an operations man to become the next CEO. But he was overruled by Robert Woodruff, the 90-year-old patriarch. In April 1980 the board of directors approved the recommendation of Goizueta for the president. When Goizueta moved on to become chairman of the board in March 1981, Donald Keough succeeded him as president.

Shortly after his promotion, Goizueta called a worldwide manager's conference in which he announced that nothing was sacred to the company anymore, that change was imminent, and that managers had to accept that situation. He also announced ambitious plans to diversify beyond the soft-drink industry.

In a new era of change announced by a new administration, the sacredness of the commitment to the original Coke formula became tenuous, and the ground was laid for the first flavor change in 99 years.

Marketing Research

With the market share erosion of the late 1970s and early 1980s, despite strong advertising and superior distribution, the company began to look at the product itself. Evidence was increasingly suggesting that taste was the single most important cause of Coke's decline. Perhaps the original secret formula needed to be scrapped. And so Project Kansas began.

Under Project Kansas in 1982 some 2000 interviews in 10 major markets were conducted to investigate customers' willingness to accept a different Coke. People were shown storyboards and comic strip–style mock commercials and were asked series of questions. One storyboard, for example, said that Coke had added a new ingredient and tasted smoother; another said the same about Pepsi. Then consumers were asked about their reactions to the "change concept" (for example, "Would you be upset?" and "Would you try the new drink?"). Researchers estimated from the responses that 10 to 12 percent of Coke drinkers would be upset and that one-half of these would get over it, but one-half would not.

Although interviews showed a willingness to try a new Coke, other tests disclosed the opposite. Small consumer panels, or focus groups, revealed strong favorable and unfavorable sentiments. But the technical division persisted in trying to develop a new, more pleasing flavor. By September 1984 the division thought it had done so. The new version was a sweeter, less fizzy cola with a soft, sticky taste due to a higher sugar content from the exclusive use of corn syrup sweetener, which is sweeter than sucrose. This cola was introduced in blind taste tests in which consumers were not told what brand they were drinking. These tests were highly encouraging: The new flavor substantially outperformed Pepsi, whereas in previous blind taste tests Pepsi had always beaten Coke.

As a result researchers estimated that the new formula would boost Coke's share of the soft-drink market by one percentage point. This point would be worth $200 million in sales.

Before adopting the new flavor, Coca-Cola invested $4 million in the biggest taste test ever. Some 191,000 people in more than 13 cities participated in a comparison of unmarked various Coke formulations. The use of unmarked colas was intended to eliminate any bias toward brand names. Fifty-five percent of the participants favored New Coke over the original formula, and New Coke also beat Pepsi. The research results seemed to be conclusive in favor of the new formula.

The Go Decision

Even when the decision was made to introduce the new flavor, a number of ancillary decisions had to be made. For example, should the new flavor be added to the product line, or should it replace the old Coke? Executives thought that bottlers would be opposed to adding another cola. After considerable soul searching, top executives unanimously decided to change the taste of Coke and take the old Coke off the market.

In January 1985 the task of introducing the new Coke was given to the McCann-Erickson advertising agency. Bill Cosby was to be the spokesman for the nationwide introduction of the new Coke, scheduled for April. All departments of this company were gearing their efforts for a coordinated introduction.

On April 23, 1985, Goizueta and Keough held a press conference at Lincoln Center in New York City in order to introduce the new Coke. Invitations had been sent to the media from all over the United States, and some 200 newspaper, magazine, and TV reporters attended the press conference. However, many of them came away unconvinced of the merits of the new Coke, and their stories were generally negative. In the days ahead, the news media's skepticism would exacerbate the public rejection of the new Coke.

The word spread quickly. Within 24 hours, 81 percent of the U.S. population knew of the change, and this was more people than were aware in July 1969 that Neil Armstrong had walked on the moon.[1] Early results looked good; 150 million people tried the new Coke—more people than had ever before tried a new product. Most comments were favorable. Shipments to bottlers rose to the highest percent in five years. The decision looked unassailable. But not for long.

AFTERMATH OF THE DECISION

The situation changed rapidly. Although some objections were expected, the protests quickly mushroomed. In the first four hours, the company received about 650 calls. By mid-May, calls were coming in at a rate of 5,000 a day, in addition to a barrage of angry letters. The company added 83 WATS lines and hired new staff to handle the responses. People were

---

[1]John S. Demott, "Fiddling with the Real Thing," *Time* (May 6, 1985), p. 55.

speaking of Coke as an American symbol and as a longtime friend that had suddenly betrayed them. Some threatened to switch to tea or water. Here is a sampling of the responses.[2]

> The sorrow I feel knowing not only won't I ever enjoy real Coke, but my children and grandchildren won't either. . . . I guess my children will have to take my word for it.

> It is absolutely TERRIBLE! You should be ashamed to put the Coke label on it. . . . This new stuff tastes worse than Pepsi.

> It was nice knowing you. You were a friend for most of my 35 years. Yesterday I had my first taste of new Coke, and to tell the truth, if I would have wanted Pepsi, I would have ordered a Pepsi not a Coke.

In all, more than 40,000 such letters were received that spring and summer. In Seattle strident loyalists calling themselves Old Coke Drinkers of America laid plans to file a class action suit against Coca-Cola. People began stockpiling the old Coke. Some sold it at scalper's prices. When sales in June did not pick up as the company had expected, bottlers demanded the return of old Coke.

The company's research also confirmed an increasing negative sentiment. Before May 30, 53 percent of consumers said they liked the new Coke. In June the vote began to change: More than one-half of all people surveyed said they did not like the new Coke. By July only 30 percent of the people surveyed each week said that they liked the new Coke.

Anger spread across the country, fueled by media publicity. Fiddling with the formula for the 99-year-old beverage became an affront to patriotic pride. As Robert Antonio, a University of Kansas sociologist, stated, "Some felt that a sacred symbol had been tampered with."[3] Even Goizueta's father spoke out against the switch when it was announced. He told his son the move was a bad one and jokingly threatened to disown him. By now company executives began to worry about a consumer boycott.

Coca-Cola Cries "Uncle"

Company executives now began seriously thinking about how to recoup the fading prospects of Coke. In an executive meeting, the managers decided to take no action until after the Fourth of July weekend, when the sales results for this holiday weekend were in. Results were unimpressive. They decided to reintroduce Coca-Cola under the trademark of Coca-Cola Classic.

---

[2]Thomas Oliver, *The Real Coke, the Real Story* (New York: Random House, 1986), pp. 155–156.

[3]John Greenwald, "Coca-Cola's Big Fizzle," *Time* (July 22, 1985), p. 48.

The company would keep the new flavor and call it New Coke. Top executives announced the decision to the public on July 11, walking onto the stage in front of the Coca-Cola logo to make an apology to the public. They never admitted that New Coke had been a total mistake.

This presentation delivered two messages to American consumers. First, to those who were drinking New Coke and enjoying it, the company conveyed its thanks. To those who wanted the original Coke, the message was, "We heard you—the original taste of Coke is back."

The news spread fast. ABC interrupted its soap opera *General Hospital* on Wednesday afternoon to break the news. In the kind of saturation coverage normally reserved for disasters or diplomatic crises, the decision to bring back old Coke was prominently reported on every evening network news broadcast. The general feeling of soft-drink fans was joy. Democratic Senator David Pryor of Arkansas expressed his jubilation on the Senate floor: "A very meaningful moment in the history of America, this shows that some national institutions cannot be changed."[4] Even Wall Street was happy. Old Coke's comeback drove Coca-Cola stock to its highest level in 12 years.

On the other hand, Roger Enrico, president of Pepsi-Cola USA, said, "Clearly this is the Edsel of the '80s. This was a terrible mistake. Coke's got a lemon on its hands and now they're trying to make lemonade."[5] Other critics labeled this decision to change Coke "the blunder of the decade."[6]

WHAT WENT WRONG?

The most convenient scapegoat, according to consensus opinion, was the marketing research that preceded the decision. Yet Coca-Cola spent about $4 million and devoted two years to the marketing research. About 200,000 consumers were contacted during this time. The error in judgment was surely not from want of trying. But when we dig deeper into the research efforts, some flaws become apparent.

Flawed Marketing Research

The major design of the marketing research involved taste tests by representative consumers. After all, the decision point involved a different-

---

[4]Ibid.

[5]Ibid., p. 49.

[6]James E. Ellis and Paul B. Brown, "Coke's Man on the Spot," *Business Week* (July 29, 1985), p. 56.

flavored Coke, so what could be more logical than to conduct blind taste tests to determine the acceptability of the new flavor, not only versus the old Coke but also versus Pepsi? And these results were significantly positive for the new formula, even among Pepsi drinkers. A "go" signal seemed clear.

But with the benefit of hindsight, some deficiencies in the research design were more apparent and should have caused concern at the time. The research participants were not told that by picking one cola, they would lose the other. This turned out to be a significant distortion: Any addition to the product line would naturally be far more acceptable to a loyal Coke user than would be a complete substitution, which meant the elimination of the traditional product.

While three to four new tastes were tested with almost 200,000 people, only 30,000 to 40,000 of these tests involved the specific formula for the new Coke. The research was geared more to the idea of a new, sweeter cola than to the final formula. In general a sweeter flavor tends to be preferred in blind taste tests. This is particularly true with youth, the largest drinkers of sugared colas, and the group that had been drinking more Pepsi in recent years. Furthermore, preferences for sweeter tasting products tend to diminish with use.[7]

Consumers were asked whether they favored change as a concept and whether they would likely drink more, less, or the same amount of Coke if there were a change. But such questions could hardly probe the depth of feelings and emotional ties to the product, and the decisions and plans based on the flawed research were themselves vulnerable.

Symbolic Value

The symbolic value of Coke was the sleeper. Perhaps this should have been foreseen. Perhaps the marketing research should have considered this possibility and designed the research to map it and determine the strength and durability of these values—that is, whether they would have a major effect on any substitution of a new flavor.

Admittedly, when we get into symbolic value and emotional involvement, any researcher is dealing with vague and nebulous attitudes. But various attitudinal measures have been developed to measure the strength or degree of emotional involvement, such as the *semantic differential*, described in the following box.

---

[7]"New Coke Wins Round 1, but Can It Go the Distance?" *Business Week* (June 24, 1985), p. 48.

INFORMATION BOX

MEASURING ATTITUDES—THE SEMANTIC DIFFERENTIAL

An important tool in attitudinal research, image studies, and planning decisions is the *semantic differential*. It was originally developed to measure the meaning that a concept—perhaps a political issue, a person, or a work of art, or in marketing a brand, product, or company—might have for people in terms of various dimensions. As first presented, the instrument consisted of pairs of polar adjectives with a seven-interval scale separating the opposite members of each pair. For example:

Good   —   —   —   —   —   —   —   Bad

The various intervals from left to right would then represent degrees of feeling or belief ranging from extremely good to neither good nor bad to extremely bad.

This instrument has been refined to obtain greater sensitivity through the use of descriptive phrases. The following are examples of such bipolar phrases for determining the image of a particular brand of beer:

Something special —   —   —   —   —   —   —   Just another drink

American flavor   —   —   —   —   —   —   —   Foreign flavor

Really peps   —   —   —   —   —   —   —   Somehow doesn't
you up   pep you up

The number of word pairs varies considerably, but there may be as many as 50 or more. Flexibility and appropriateness to a particular study are achieved by constructing tailor-made word and phrase lists.

Semantic differential scales have been used to compare images of particular products, brands, firms, and stores against competing ones. The answers of all respondents can be averaged and then plotted to provide a "profile," as shown below for three competing beers on four scales (actually, a firm would probably use 20 or more scales in such a study).

In this profile, brand A shows the dominant image over its competing brands in three of the four categories; however, the negative reaction to its price should alert the company to review pricing practices. Brand C shows a negative image, especially regarding the reliability of its product. The old-fashioned image may or may not be desirable, depending on the type of customer being sought; at least the profile indicates that brand C is perceived as being distinctive from the other two brands. Probably the weakest image of all is that of brand B; respondents viewed this brand as having no distinctive image, neither good nor bad. A serious image-building campaign is desperately needed if brand B is to compete successfully; otherwise, the price may have to be dropped to gain some advantage.

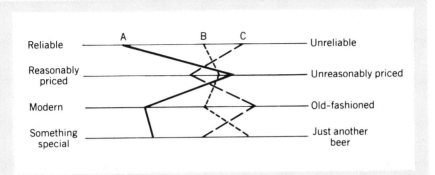

Easy to administer and simple to analyze, the semantic differential is useful in identifying where there might be opportunities in areas presently not well covered by competitors. It is also useful to a well-established firm—such as Coca-Cola—to determine the strength and the various dimensions of attitudes toward its product. Semantic differential scales are also valuable in evaluating the effectiveness of planning changes, such as a change in advertising theme. Here the semantic differential can be administered before and after the campaign, and any changes in perceptions can be pinpointed.

INVITATION TO DISCUSSION

In the example of the three beers, how would you attempt to build up the brand image of beer B? How successful would you expect to be?

Herd Instinct

A natural human phenomenon asserted itself in this case—the herd instinct, the tendency of people to follow an idea, slogan, or concept and to "jump on the bandwagon." At first, acceptance of the new Coke appeared to be reasonably satisfactory. But as more and more outcries were raised—fanned by the press—about the betrayal of the old tradition (somehow Coke became identified with motherhood, apple pie, and the flag), public attitudes shifted vigorously against this perceived unworthy substitute. The bandwagon syndrome was fully activated. It is doubtful that by July 1985 Coca-Cola could have done anything to reverse the unfavorable tide. To wait for it to die down was fraught with danger, for who would be brave enough to predict the durability and possible heights of such a protest movement?

Could such a tide have been predicted? Perhaps not, at least not the full strength of the movement. Coca-Cola expected some resentment, but perhaps it should have been more cautious and considered a "worst case" scenario in addition to what seemed the more probable. Coca-Cola would then have been prepared to react to such a *contingency*.

INFORMATION BOX

CONTINGENCY PLANS

Planning involves resource deployment through the use of budgets. Resources to be deployed include both work force and facilities: the number of people to be involved in the particular aspect of the operation and the amount of money and facilities required to meet planned goals and expectations. Such resource deployment depends on certain assumptions made about both the external and internal environment. When plans are made for major projects, such as new Coke, and resources are committed, the success of the commitment depends greatly on the accuracy of the assumptions that are made. When, as events unfold, it becomes clear that certain assumptions were either overly optimistic or overly pessimistic, then plans and resource deployments need to be revised.

Contingency plans are well used when dealing with a new product or project. Different plans may thereby be developed for the different contingencies, or sets of conditions that may occur. For example, Plan A may assume a certain level of acceptance; Plan B may be developed for better-than-expected circumstances; Plan C may be ready to put to use if early results are discouraging. When such plans are drawn up in advance, a firm is better able to cope with varied outcomes and can either marshal additional resources or cut back to more realistic expectations.

With such contingency plans developed, Coca-Cola would have been better prepared to react to the surprising resistance to its new product. For example, it could have developed plans for different levels of customer acceptance, including the worst scenario that was actually encountered: nonacceptance and public agitation. Although in this case, the decision making under crisis conditions apparently worked out satisfactorily, in another instance it might not have. Carefully thought-out alternative actions generally have a better payoff than decisions made quickly in a crisis situation.

INVITATION TO DISCUSSION
Do you think any contingency plan of Coca-Cola would have anticipated the extent of public agitation? Even if such a worst-case scenario were considered, is it likely that reactions would have been improved? Why or why not?

WHAT CAN BE LEARNED?

Taste is an unreliable preference factor. Taste tests are commonly used in marketing research, but some marketers remain skeptical of their validity. Take beer, for example. Do you know of anybody—despite strenuous claims—who can in blind taste tests unerringly identify which is which among three or four disguised brands of beer? We know that people tend to favor the sweeter in taste tests. But does this mean that such a sweeter flavor will always win out? Hardly. Something else is operating with consumer preference other than the fleeting essence of a taste—unless the flavor difference is extreme. Research and decisions that rely primarily on taste tests tend to be more vulnerable to mistakes.

Brand image is usually a powerful sales stimulant. Advertisers have consistently been more successful by cultivating a desirable image or personality for their brands or the types of people who use them than by standing by such vague statements as "better tasting."

Beware of tampering with the traditional image. Not many firms have a 100-year-old tradition to be concerned with, or even 25, or even 10. Most products have much shorter life cycles. No other product has been so widely used and so deeply entrenched in societal values and culture as Coke.

The psychological components of the great Coke protest make interesting speculation. Perhaps in an era of rapid change, many people wish to hang on to the one symbol of security or constancy in their lives—even if this is only the traditional Coke flavor. Perhaps many people found this protest to be an interesting way to escape the humdrum, by making waves in a rather harmless fashion, and in so doing see if a big corporation might be forced to cry "uncle."

One wonders how many consumers would even have been aware of any change in flavor had the new formula been quietly introduced. But, of course, the advertising siren call of "New!" would have been muted.

So, do we dare tamper with tradition? In Coke's case the answer is probably not, unless it is done very quietly; but, then, Coke is unique.

Tampering with a major product still in high demand may be risky indeed. Conventional wisdom advocates that changes are best made in response to problems, that when things are going smoothly the success pattern or strategy should not be tampered with. This may or may not be a good rule of thumb.

Actually, things were not going all that well for Coke by early 1985. Competitive position had steadily been declining to Pepsi for some years. Vigorous promotional efforts by Pepsi featuring Michael Jackson had increased market share of regular Pepsi by 1.5 percent in 1984, while regular Coke was dropping 1 percent. Moreover, regular Coke had steadily been losing competitive position in supermarkets, dropping almost 4 percent between 1981 and 1985. And foreign business, accounting for 62 percent of total soft-drink volume for Coca-Cola, was showing a disappointing growth rate.[8]

---

[8]"Pepsi's High-Priced Sell Is Paying Off," *Business Week* (March 4, 1985), pp. 34–35; "Is Coke Fixing a Coke That Isn't Broken?" *Business Week* (May 6, 1985), p. 47.

So there was certainly motivation for considering a change. And the obvious change was to introduce a somewhat different flavor, one more congruent with the preference of younger people who were the prime market for soft drinks. We do not subscribe to the philosophy of "Don't rock the boat" or "Don't change anything until forced to." However, Coca-Cola had another option.

Major changes often are better introduced without immediately discarding the present. The obvious alternative was to introduce the new Coke but still keep the old one. The lesson here is, "Don't burn your bridges." Of course, in July Roberto Goizueta brought back the old Coke after some months of turmoil and considerable corporate embarrassment and competitive glee— which soon turned to dismay. The obvious drawback for having two Cokes was dealer resentment at having to stock an additional product in the same limited space and bottler concern at having a more complicated production run. Furthermore, there was the real possibility that Pepsi would emerge as the number one soft drink because of two competing Cokes—and this would be an acute embarrassment for Coca-Cola.

Sheer advertising expenditures does not guarantee effectiveness. Coca-Cola was outspending Pepsi for advertising by $100 million, but its competitive position in the 1970s and early 1980s continued to erode in comparison to Pepsi's. Pepsi's campaign featured the theme of the "Pepsi Generation" and the "Pepsi Challenge." The use of a superstar such as Michael Jackson also proved to be more effective with the youth market for soft drinks than Bill Cosby for Coca-Cola. Any executive has to be left with the sobering realization that the sheer number of dollars spent on advertising does not guarantee competitive success. A smaller firm can still outdo a larger rival.

The power of the media needs to be considered in decisions that are likely to generate widespread interest. The press and broadcast media can be powerful influences of public opinion. With the new Coke, the media undoubtedly exacerbated the herd instinct by publicizing the protests to the fullest. After all, this was news. And news seems to be spiciest when an institution or person can be criticized or found wanting. The power of the press should also be sobering to an executive and ought to be one of the factors she or he considers with certain decisions that may affect the public image of the organization.

INVITATION

What additional learning insights do you see as emerging from the Coca-Cola case?

CONSEQUENCES

Forced by public opinion into a two-cola strategy, the company found the results to be reassuring. By October 1985 Coke Classic was outselling New Coke by better than 2 to 1 nationwide and by 9 to 1 in some markets. Restaurant chains such as McDonald's, Hardees, Roy Rogers, and Red Lobster had switched back to Coke Classic.

For the full year of 1985, sales from all operations rose 10 percent and profits, 9 percent. In the United States, Coca-Cola soft-drink volume increased 9 percent; internationally it rose 10 percent. Profitability from soft drinks decreased slightly, representing heavier advertising expenses for introducing New Coke and then reintroducing old Coke.

Coca-Cola's fortunes continued to improve steadily, if not spectacularly. By 1988 it was producing 5 of the 10 top-selling soft drinks in the country and had 40 percent of the domestic market to Pepsi's 31 percent.[9]

Because the soft-drink business was generating about $1 billion in cash each year, Roberto Goizueta had made a number of major acquisitions, such as Columbia Pictures and the Taylor Wine Company. However, these did not meet his expectations and were disposed of. Still, by 1988 Coca-Cola had a hoard of $5 billion in new cash and debt capacity, and the enticing problem now was how to spend it.

The most successful diversifications were in the soft-drink area. As recently as 1981 there had been only one Coke, and not too many years before, only one container, the 6½-oz. glass bottle. By 1987 only one-tenth of 1 percent of all Coke was sold in that bottle.[10] Classic Coke was the best-selling soft drink in the United States, and Diet Coke was the third largest selling. New Coke was now being outsold by Classic about 7 to 1. Table 5.2 shows the total sales volume of the Coke family.1 percent of all Coke was sold in that bottle.[10] Classic Coke was the best-selling soft drink in the United States, and Diet Coke was the third largest selling. New Coke was now being outsold by Classic about 7 to 1. Table 5.2 shows the total sales volume of the Coke family.

Coca-Cola's future looked bright. Per capita soft-drink consumption in the United States had been rising significantly in the 1980s, as shown in the following table:

---

[9]John H. Taylor, "Some Things Don't Go Better with Coke," *Forbes* (March 21, 1988), pp. 34–35.

[10]Thomas Moore, "He Put the Kick Back into Coke," *Fortune* (October 26, 1987), pp. 47–56.

	Per Capita Consumption	Percent Increase
1980	34.5 gal	
1986	42 gal	22%

Source: Pepsico 1986 Annual Report, p. 13.

The international potential was also great. Per capita consumption outside the United States was only four gallons—yet 95 percent of the world's population lives outside the United States.

CONCLUSION

Some called new Coke a misstep, others a blink. At the time of the fiasco some called it a monumental blunder, the mistake of the century. But it hardly turned out to be that. As sales surged, some competitors accused Coca-Cola of engineering the whole scenario in order to get an abundance of free publicity. Coke executives stoutly denied this and admitted their error in judgment. For who could foresee, as *Fortune* noted, that the episode would "reawaken deep-seated American loyalty to Coca-Cola"?[11]

Table 5.2   1986 Family of Cokes

Kinds	Millions of Cases
Total of one cola, 1980	1,310.5
1986	
Coca-Cola Classic	1,294.3
Diet Coke	490.8
Coke	185.1
Cherry Coke	115.6
Caffeine-Free Diet Coke	85.6
Caffeine-Free Coke	19.0
Diet Cherry Coke	15.0

Source: "He Put the Kick Back into Coke," *Fortune* (October 26, 1987), p. 48.

[11]Ibid., p. 48.

QUESTIONS

1. How could Coca-Cola's marketing research have been improved? Be as specific as you can.
2. When a firm is facing a negative press, as Coca-Cola was with the new Coke, what recourse does the firm have? Support your conclusions.
3. Do you think Coca-Cola would have been as successful if it had introduced the new Coke as an addition to the line and not as a substitute for the old Coke? Why or why not?
4. "If it's not broken, don't fix it!" Evaluate this statement.
5. Do you think Coca-Cola engineered the whole scenario with the new Coke, including fanning initial protests, in order to get a bonanza of free publicity? Defend your position.
6. Would you, as a top executive at Coca-Cola, have "caved in" as quickly to the protests? Would you have "toughed it out" instead?

INVITATION TO ROLE PLAY

1. Assume that you are Roberto Goizueta and that you are facing increasing pressure in early July 1985 to abandon the new Coke and bring back the old formula. However, your latest marketing research suggests that only a small group of agitators are making all the fuss about the new cola. Evaluate your options and support your recommendations to the board.
2. You are the public relations director of Coca-Cola. It is early June 1985, and you have been ordered to "do something" to blunt the negative publicity. What ideas can you offer that might counter or replace the negatives with positive publicity?

INVITATION TO RESEARCH

What is the present situation with Coca-Cola? Is Coke Classic still the big winner? Is New Coke still being produced? Is Coca-Cola winning the battle with Pepsi? How are the two companies doing in the international arena? What is the status regarding recent diversifications of Coca-Cola?

6

Contrast—Southwest Airlines: Finding a Strategic Window of Opportunity

In 1992 the airlines lost a combined $2 billion, matching a dismal 1991, and bringing their three-year red ink total to a disastrous $8 billion. Three carriers—TWA, Continental, and America West—were operating under Chapter 11 bankruptcy, and others were lining up to join them. But one airline, Southwest, was profitable as well as rapidly growing, with a 25 percent sales increase in 1992 alone. Interestingly enough, this was a low-price, bare-bones operation run by a flamboyant CEO, Herb Kelleher. Kelleher had found a niche, a strategic window of opportunity, and oh, how he milked it! See the following box for further discussion of a strategic window of opportunity and its desirable accompaniment, a SWOT analysis.

HERBERT D. KELLEHER

Herb Kelleher impresses people as an eccentric. He likes to tell stories, himself often the butt, and many involve practical jokes. He admits he is sometimes a little scatterbrained. In his cluttered office, he displays a dozen ceramic wild turkeys as a testimonial to his favorite brand of whiskey. He regularly smokes five packs of cigarettes a day. As an example of his zaniness, he painted one of his 737s to look like a killer whale to celebrate the opening of Sea World in San Antonio. Another time, during a flight he had flight attendants dress up as reindeer and elves while the pilot sang Christmas carols over the loudspeaker as he gently rocked the plane. Kelleher

---

INFORMATION BOX

STRATEGIC WINDOW OF OPPORTUNITY AND SWOT ANALYSIS

A strategic window is an opportunity in the marketplace, one that is presently neglected by competitors and one that fits well with the firm's competencies. Strategic windows often last for only a short time (although Southwest's strategic window has been much more durable) before they are filled by alert competitors.

Strategic windows are usually found by systematically analyzing the environment, examining the threats and opportunities it holds. The competencies of the firm, its physical and financial resources, and, not the least, its people resources—management and employees and their strengths and weaknesses—should also be assessed. The objective is to determine what actions might be appropriate for that particular enterprise and its orientation. This is commonly known as a SWOT analysis: analyzing strengths and weaknesses of the firm and opportunities and threats in the environment.

Although SWOT analysis may be a formal part of the planning process, it may also be informal and even intuitive. We suspect that Herb Kelleher instinctively sensed a strategic window in short hauls and low prices. While he must have recognized the danger that his bigger competitors would try to match his prices, he believed that with his simplicity of operation he would be able to make a profit while bigger airlines were racking up losses.

INVITATION TO DISCUSSION
Why do you think the major airlines overlooked the possibilities in short hauls at low prices?

---

is a "real maniac," said Thomas J. Volz, vice president of marketing at Braniff Airlines. "But who can argue with his success?"[1]

The son of a Campbell Soup Company executive, Kelleher grew up in Haddon Heights, New Jersey. He graduated from Wesleyan University and New York University Law School. In 1961 he moved to San Antonio, where his father-in-law helped him set up a law firm, and in 1968, he and a group of investors put up $560,000 to found Southwest. Of this amount, Kelleher contributed $20,000.

In the early years Kelleher was the general counsel and a director of the fledgling enterprise. But in 1978 he was named chairman, although he had no managerial experience, and in 1981 he became CEO. His flamboyance soon made him the most visible aspect of the airline, and he starred in most of its TV commercials. A rival airline, America West, charged in ads that

---

[1]Kevin Kelly, "Southwest Airlines: Flying High with 'Uncle Herb,'" *Business Week* (July 3, 1989), p. 53.

Southwest passengers should be embarrassed to fly such a no-frills airline, whereupon Kelleher appeared in a TV spot with a bag over his head. He offered the bag to anyone ashamed to fly Southwest, suggesting it could be used to hold "all the money you'll save flying us."[2]

Kelleher knew many of his employees by name, and they called him "Uncle Herb" or "Herbie." He held weekly parties for employees at corporate headquarters, and he encouraged such antics by his flight attendants as organizing trivia contests, delivering instructions in rap, and awarding prizes for the passengers with the largest holes in their socks. But such wackiness had a shrewd purpose: to generate a gung-ho spirit to boost productivity. "Herb's fun is infectious," said Kay Wallace, president of the Flight Attendants Union Local 556. "Everyone enjoys what they're doing and realizes they've got to make an extra effort."[3]

THE BEGINNINGS

Southwest was conceived in 1967 on a napkin, according to folklore. Rollin King, a client of Kelleher, then a lawyer, had an idea for a low-fare, no-frills airline to fly between major Texas cities. He doodled a triangle on the napkin, labeling the points Dallas, Houston, and San Antonio.

The two tried to go ahead with their plans but were stymied for more than three years by litigation, battling Braniff, Texas International, and Continental over the right to fly. In 1971 Southwest won, and it went public in 1975. At that time it had four planes flying between the three cities. Lamar Muse was president and CEO from 1971 until he was fired by Southwest's board in 1978. At that point the board of directors tapped Kelleher.

At first Southwest was in the throes of life and death low-fare skirmishes with its giant competitors. Kelleher liked to recount how he came home one day "beat, tired, and worn out. So I'm just kind of sagging around the house when my youngest daughter comes up and asks what's wrong. I tell her, 'Well, Ruthie, it's these damned fare wars.' And she cuts me right off and says, 'Oh, Daddy, stop complaining. After all, you started 'em.'"[4]

For most small firms, competing on a price basis with much larger, well-endowed competitors is tantamount to disaster. The small firm simply cannot match the resources and staying power of such competitors. Yet Southwest somehow survived. Not only did it initiate the cut-throat price competition, but it achieved cost savings in its operation that the larger airlines could not. How long would the big carriers be content to maintain their money-losing operations and match the low prices of Southwest?

---

[2]Ibid.
[3]Richard Woodbury, "Prince of Midair," *Time* (January 25, 1993), p. 55.
[4]Charles A. Jaffe, "Moving Fast by Standing Still," *Nation's Business* (October 1991), p. 58.

In its early years, Southwest faced other legal battles, such as Dallas and Love Field. The original airport, Love Field, is close to downtown Dallas, but it could not geographically expand although air traffic was increasing mightily. A major new facility, Dallas/Fort Worth International Airport, consequently replaced it in 1974. This airport boasted state-of-the-art facilities and enough room for foreseeable demand, but it had one major drawback: It was 30 minutes further from downtown Dallas. Southwest was able to avoid a forced move to the new airport and to continue at Love, but in 1978, competitors pressured Congress to bar flights from Love Field to anywhere outside Texas. Southwest was able to negotiate a compromise, now known as the Wright Amendment, that allowed flights from Love Field to the four states contiguous to Texas. In retrospect, the Wright Amendment forced onto Southwest a key ingredient of its later success: the strategy of short flights.[5]

GROWTH

Southwest grew steadily but not spectacularly through the 1970s. It dominated the Texas market by appealing to passengers who valued price and frequent departures. Its one-way fare between Dallas and Houston, for example, was $59 in 1987 versus $79 for unrestricted coach flights on other airlines.

In the 1980s Southwest's annual passenger traffic count tripled. At the end of 1989, its operating costs per revenue mile—the industry's standard measure of cost-effectiveness—was just under 10 cents, about 5 cents per mile below the industry average.[6] Although revenues and profits were rising steadily, especially compared with the other airlines, Kelleher took a conservative approach to expansion, financing it mostly from internal funds rather than debt.

Perhaps the caution stemmed from an ill-fated acquisition in 1986. Kelleher bought a failing long-haul carrier, Muse Air Corporation, for $68 million and renamed it TransStar. (This firm had been founded by Lamar Muse after he left Southwest.) But by 1987 TransStar was losing $2 million a month, and Kelleher shut down the operation.

By 1993 Southwest had spread to 34 cities in 15 states. It had 141 planes, and each made 11 trips per day. It used only fuel-thrifty 737s and still concentrated on flying large numbers of passengers on high-frequency, one-hour hops at bargain fares (average $58). Southwest shunned the hub-and-spoke systems of its larger rivals and took its passengers directly from city to city, often to smaller satellite airfields rather than congested major

---

[5]Bridget O'Brian, "Southwest Airlines Is a Rare Air Carrier: It Still Makes Money," *The Wall Street Journal* (October 28, 1992), p. A7.

[6]Jaffe, op. cit., p. 58.

metropolitan fields. With rock-bottom prices and no amenities, it quickly dominated most new markets it entered.

As an example of the company's impact on a new market, Southwest came to Cleveland, Ohio, in February 1992, and by the end of the year was offering 11 daily flights. In 1992 Cleveland Hopkins Airport posted record passenger levels, up 9.74 percent from 1991. "A lot of the gain was traffic that Southwest Airlines generated," noted John Osmond, air trade development manager.[7]

In some markets Southwest found itself growing much faster than projected, as competitors either folded or else abandoned directly competing routes. For example, in Phoenix, Arizona, America West Airlines cut back service in order to conserve cash after a Chapter 11 bankruptcy filing. Southwest picked up the slack, as it did in Chicago when Midway Airlines folded in November 1992. And in California, Southwest's arrival led several large competitors to abandon the Los Angeles-San Francisco route, unable to meet Southwest's $59 one-way fare. Before Southwest fares had been as high as $186 one way.[8]

Now cities that Southwest did not serve were petitioning for service. For example, Sacramento sent two county commissioners, the president of the chamber of commerce and the airport director, to Dallas to petition for service. Kelleher consented a few months later. In 1991 the company received 51 similar requests.[9]

A unique situation was developing. On many routes Southwest's fares were so low that they competed with buses and even with private cars. By 1991 Kelleher did not even see other airlines as his principal competitors: "We're competing with the automobile, not the airlines. We're pricing ourselves against Ford, Chrysler, GM, Toyota, and Nissan. The traffic is already there, but it's on the ground. We take it off the highway and put it on the airplane."[10]

Tables 6.1, 6.2, and 6.3 and Figure 6.1 depict various aspects of Southwest's growth and increasingly favorable competitive position. Although total revenues of Southwest are still far less than the four major airlines in the industry (five if we count Continental, just emerging from its second bankruptcy, and described in Chapter 10), its growth pattern presages a major presence, and its profitability is second to none.

Tapping California

The formidable competitive power of Southwest was perhaps never better epitomized than in its 1990 invasion of populous California. By 1992 it had

---

[7]"Passenger Flights Set Hopkins Record," *Cleveland Plain Dealer* (January 30, 1993), p. 3D.
[8]O'Brian, op. cit., p. A7.
[9]Ibid.
[10]Subrata N. Chakravarty, "Hit 'Em Hardest with the Mostest," *Forbes* (September 16, 1991), p. 49.

Table 6.1   Growth of Southwest Airlines: Various Operating Statistics, 1982–1991

Year	Operating Revenues (000,000)	Net Income (000,000)	Passengers Carried (000)	Passenger Load Factor
1991	$1,314	$26.9	22,670	61.1%
1990	1,187	47.1	19,831	60.7
1989	1,015	71.6	17,958	62.7
1988	880	58.0	14,877	57.7
1987	778	20.2	13,503	58.4
1986	769	50.0	13,638	58.8
1985	680	47.3	12,651	60.4
1984	535	49.7	10,698	58.5
1983	448	40.9	9,511	61.6
1982	331	34.0	7,966	61.6

Source: Company annual reports.

Commentary: Note the steady increase in revenues and in numbers of passengers carried. Although the net income and load factor statistics show no appreciable improvement, these statistics are still in the vanguard of an industry that has suffered badly in recent years. See Table 6.2 for a comparison of revenues and income with the major airlines.

become the second largest player, after United, with 23 percent of intrastate traffic. Southwest achieved this position by pushing fares down as much as 60 percent on some routes. The big carriers, which had tended to surrender the short-haul niche to Southwest in other markets, suddenly faced a real quandary in competing in this "Golden State." Some described Southwest as a "500 pound cockroach, too big to stamp out."[11]

The California market was indeed enticing. Some 8 million passengers each year fly between the five airports in metropolitan Los Angeles and the three in the San Francisco Bay area, this being the busiest corridor in the United States. It was also one of the more expensive, because the low fares of AirCal and Pacific Southwest Airlines had been eliminated when these two airlines were acquired by American and US Air.

Southwest charged into this situation with low fares and frequent flights. While airfares dropped, total air traffic soared 123 percent in the quarter Southwest entered the market. Competitors suffered: American lost nearly $80 million at its San Jose hub, and US Air lost money even though it cut service drastically. United, the market leader, quit flying the San Diego—Sacramento and Ontario–Oakland routes where Southwest had rapidly built up service. The quandary of the major airlines was compounded because this critical market fed traffic into the rest of their systems, especially the lucrative transcontinental and trans-Pacific routes. The

[11]Wendy Zellner, "Striking Gold in the California Skies," *Business Week* (March 30, 1992), p. 48.

Table 6.2   Comparison of Southwest's Growth in Revenues and Net Income
with Major Competitors, 1987–1991

	1991	1990	1989	1988	1987	% 5-yr gain
Operating Revenue Comparisons ($ millions)						
American	$9,309	$9,203	$8,670	$7,548	$6,369	46.0
Delta	8,268	7,697	7,780	6,684	5,638	46.6
United	7,850	7,946	7,463	7,006	6,500	20.8
Northwest	4,330	4,298	3,944	3,395	3,328	30.1
Southwest	1,314	1,187	1,015	860	778	68.9
Net Income Comparisons ($ millions)						
American	(253)	(40)	412	450	225	
Delta	(216)	(119)	467	286	201	
United	(175)	73	246	426	22	
Northwest	10	(27)	116	49	64	
Southwest	27	47	72	58	20	

Source: Company annual reports.

Commentary: Southwest's revenue gains over these five years outstripped those of its largest competitors. Although the percentage gains in profitability are hardly useful because of the erratic nature of airline profits during these years, Southwest stands out starkly as the only airline to be profitable each year.

competitors could hardly abdicate California to Southwest. American, for one, considered creating its own no-frills shuttle for certain routes.[12] Could anyone stop Southwest, with its formula of lowest prices and lowest costs and frequent schedules? And, oh yes, its good service and fun?

Table 6.3   Market Share Comparison of Southwest and Its Four Major
Competitors, 1987–1991 (in $ billions)

	1991	1990	1989	1988	1987
Total Revenues: American, Delta, United, Northwest	$29,757	$29,144	$27,857	$24,633	$21,835
Southwest Revenues	$1,314	$1,187	$1,015	$860	$778
Percent of big four	4.4	4.1	3.6	3.5	3.6
Increase in Southwest's market share, 1987–1991:	22%				

Source: Company annual reports.

[12]Ibid.

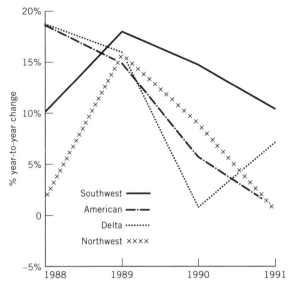

Figure 6.1. Year-to-year percentage changes in revenues, Southwest and three major competitors, 1988–1991.

INGREDIENTS OF SUCCESS

Southwest's operation under Kelleher had numerous distinctive character-istics contributing to its success pattern and its seizing of a strategic win-dow of opportunity, but the key factors appear to be cost containment, employee commitment, and conservative growth.

Cost Containment

Southwest had been the lowest cost carrier in its markets. Even when its larger competitors tried to match its cut-rate prices, they could not do so without incurring sizable losses, unlike Southwest. Nor did they seem able to trim their costs to match Southwest. For example, in the first quarter of 1991, Southwest's operating costs per available seat mile (i.e., the number of seats multiplied by the distance flown) were 15 percent lower than America West's costs, 29 percent lower than Delta's, 32 percent lower than United's, and 39 percent lower than US Air's.[13]

Many aspects of the operation contributed to these lower costs. Because all its planes were a single aircraft type, Boeing 737s, Southwest had low costs of training, maintenance, and inventory. And since a plane earns revenues

---

[13]Chakravarty, op. cit., p. 50.

only when flying, Southwest worked to achieve a faster turnaround time on the ground than any other airline. While competitors take more than an hour to load and unload passengers and to clean and service the planes, about 70 percent of Southwest's flights have a turnaround time of 15 minutes, and 10 percent have even pared the turnaround time to 10 minutes.

In areas of customer service, Southwest curbed costs as well. It offered peanuts and drinks, but no meals. Boarding passes were reusable plastic cards. Boarding time was saved because no seats were assigned. Southwest subscribed to no centralized reservation service. It did not even transfer baggage to other carriers; that was the passengers' responsibility. Admittedly, such customer service frugalities would be less acceptable on longer flights—and this helped to account for the difficulty competing airlines had in cutting their costs to match Southwest's. Still, if the price is right, many passengers might also opt for no frills on longer flights.

Employee Commitment

Kelleher was able to achieve an esprit de corps unmatched by other airlines despite the fact that Southwest employees were unionized. Unlike the adversarial relationship between unions and, for example, Frank Lorenzo at Eastern and Continental Airlines, Southwest was able to negotiate flexible work rules, with flight attendants and even pilots helping with plane clean-up. Employee productivity continued very high, permitting the airline to carry a lean staff. Kelleher resisted the inclination to hire extravagantly when times were good, necessitating layoffs during leaner times, a policy that contributed to employee feelings of security and loyalty. And the low-key attitude and sense of fun that Kelleher engendered helped, perhaps more than anyone could have foreseen. As Kelleher declared, "Fun is a stimulant to people. They enjoy their work more and work more productively."[14]

Conservative Growth

Not the least of the ingredients of success was the conservative approach to growth that Kelleher maintained. He resisted the temptation to expand vigorously (for example, to seek to fly to Europe or get into head-to-head competition with larger airlines with long-distance routes). Even in the company's geographical expansion, conservatism prevailed. The philosophy of expansion was to do so only when enough resources could be committed to go into a city with 10 to 12 flights a day, rather than just 1 or 2. Kelleher called this "guerrilla warfare," concentrating efforts against stronger opponents in only a few areas rather than dissipating strength by trying to compete everywhere.

Even with a conservative approach to expansion, the company showed vigorous but controlled growth. Its debt, at 49% of equity, was the lowest

[14]Ibid.

among U.S. carriers. With an A minus, Southwest also had the airline industry's highest Standard & Poor's credit rating.

WHAT CAN BE LEARNED?

The power of low prices, and simplicity of operation. If a firm can maintain prices below those of its competitors, and do so profitably and without sacrificing quality of service, then it has a powerful advantage. Southwest was able to do this with its simplicity of operation. Competition on the basis of price is seldom used in most industries (although the airline industry has been an exception), primarily because competitors can quickly match prices with no lasting advantage to anyone. As profits are destroyed, only customers benefit, and then only in the short run. The following issue box discusses the controversy of competing on price and delineates the alternative.

ISSUE BOX

PRICE COMPETITION: SHOULD WE ATTEMPT IT?

The great limitation in using price as a competitive weapon is that competitors may retaliate and start a price war. It is not difficult to lower a price and it is not difficult to offer a stripped-down model to match a competitor's low price. Sellers lose out in such a situation, and prices may even settle permanently at a lower level. As a result, most firms—except in new, rapidly growing, and technologically changing industries—find it best to compete on *nonprice* bases rather than face a cut-throat pricing situation.

With nonprice competition emphasis rests on such factors as service, warranties, delivery, quality, and all other efforts to obtain greater product differentiation. A good reputation for quality and dependability, for example, cannot be easily and quickly matched by competitors.

The classic example of the importance of price competition was the 1972 WEO—or, "Where Economy Originates"—campaign of A & P. Amid heavy advertising, A & P began lowering prices on 90 percent of the merchandise in its 4,200 stores. This action resulted in vicious price wars that destroyed the profits of the entire supermarket industry in 1972. But A & P suffered the most: Its net loss for the year was $51.3 million, the worst in the company's modern history. Although it had a small gain in sales and in market share, the results were not lasting.[15]

INVITATION TO DISCUSSION

Although price wars are usually anathema to sellers, customers benefit. On balance, do you see any disadvantages of price wars from the customers' viewpoint?

---

[15]For more detail on the disastrous A & P price campaign, see Robert Hartley, *Marketing Mistakes*, 5th ed. (New York: Wiley, 1992), Chapter 11. Also relevant is Chapter 8 on the Yugo car.

The durability of the cost control of Southwest, however, points out the true competitive importance of low prices. Customers love the lowest price producer *if* the producer does not sacrifice too much quality, comfort, and service. While there was some sacrifice of service and amenities with Southwest, most customers found this acceptable because of the short-haul situation; dependable and reasonable service was still maintained.

The power of a niche strategy. Directing marketing efforts toward a particular customer segment or niche can provide a powerful competitive advantage. This strategy is especially true if no competitor is catering directly to this niche. Such an untapped niche then becomes a strategic window of opportunity.

Kelleher was quick to reveal the niche strategy of Southwest: When other airlines set up hub-and-spoke systems in which passengers are shunted to a few major hubs from which they are transferred to other planes going to their destination, "we wound up with a unique market niche: we are the world's only short-haul, high-frequency, low-fare, point-to-point carrier.... We wound up with a market segment that is peculiarly ours, and everything about the airline has been adapted to serving that market segment in the most efficient and economical way possible."[16] The following information box discusses the criteria needed for a successful niche or segmentation strategy.

Southwest has been unwavering in its pursuit of its niche. While others have tried to copy, none have fully duplicated it. Southwest remains the nation's only high-frequency, short-distance, low-fare airline. As an example of its virtually unassailable position, Southwest accounts for more than two-thirds of the passengers flying within Texas, and Texas is the second largest market outside the West Coast. Now that Southwest has invaded California, some San Jose residents drive an hour north to board Southwest's Oakland flights, skipping the local airport where American has a hub. And in Georgia, so many people were bypassing Delta's huge hub in Atlanta and driving 150 miles to Birmingham, Alabama, to fly Southwest that an entrepreneur started a van service between the two airports.[17]

Unlike many firms, Southwest has not permitted success to dilute its niche strategy. It has not attempted to fly to Europe or to get into head-to-head competition with larger airlines on longer domestic flights. And it has not sacrificed growth potential in curbing such temptations: Its strategy still has many cities to embrace.

Seek dedicated employees. Stimulating employees to move beyond their individual concerns to a higher level of performance, a true team approach,

---

[16]Jaffe, op. cit., p. 58.
[17]O'Brian, op. cit., p. A7.

INFORMATION BOX

CRITERIA FOR SELECTING NICHES OR SEGMENTS

In deciding what specific niches to seek, these criteria should be considered:

1. **Identifiability.** Is the particular niche identifiable so that those persons who constitute it can be isolated and recognized? It was not difficult to identify the short-route travelers, and while their numbers may not have been readily estimated initially, this was soon to change as demand burgeoned for Southwest's short-haul services.

2. **Size.** The segment must be of sufficient size to be worth the efforts to tap. And again, the size factor proved to be significant, with Southwest soon offering 83 flights daily between Dallas and Houston.

3. **Accessibility.** For a niche strategy to be practical, the segment(s) chosen must be such that promotional media can be used to reach it without much wasted coverage. Southwest had little difficulty in reaching its target market through billboards, newspapers, and other media.

4. **Growth potential.** A niche is more attractive if it shows some growth characteristics. The growth potential of short-haul flyers proved to be considerably greater than that for airline customers in general. Partly the growth reflected customers won from other higher cost and less convenient airlines. And some of the emerging growth reflected customers choice of giving up their cars to take a flight that was almost as economical and certainly more comfortable.

5. **Absence of vulnerability to competition.** Competition, both present and potential, must certainly be considered in making specific niche decisions. By quickly becoming the low-cost operator in its early routes, and gradually expanding without diluting its cost advantage, Southwest became virtually unassailable in its niche. The bigger airlines, with their greater overhead and less-flexible operations, could not match Southwest prices without going deeply into the red. And the more Southwest became entrenched in its markets, the more difficult it was to pry it loose.

INVITATION TO DISCUSSION
Assume you are to give a lecture to your class on the desirability of a niche strategy, and you cite Southwest as a classic example. But suppose a classmate asks, "If a niche strategy is so great, why didn't the other airlines practice it?" How do you respond?

---

was one of many of Kelleher's accomplishments. Such an esprit de corps enabled crews to turn planes around in 15 minutes instead of the hour or more it took competitors; it brought a dedication to serving customers far beyond what could ever be expected of a bare-bones, cut-price operation;

and it brought a contagious excitement to the job that was obvious to customers and employees alike.

Having such dedicated employees was not due solely to the nurturing of the extrovertive, zany, and down-home Kelleher, although his personality certainly helped. So did company parties, Kelleher's legendary ability to remember employee names, a sincere company, and Kelleher's interest in the employees. Flying in the face of conventional wisdom, which describes the relationship between management and labor as adversarial with the presence of a union, Southwest achieved its great teamwork while being 90 percent unionized.

Whether such a worker dedication can pass the test of time and the test of increasing size is uncertain. Kelleher himself was 62 in 1993, and retirement looms. A successor will have a different personality, yet it is possible for a large organization to maintain employee commitment. In Chapter 18 we will examine the leadership style of Sam Walton and the growth of Wal-Mart to become the largest retailer.

One factor that encourages a dedicated workforce is company growth. A rapidly growing firm—especially an underdog growing from humble beginnings—has an atmosphere of contagious excitement. Opportunities and advancements depend on growth, and employees can acquire stock in the company and see their shares rising. Success tends to create a momentum that generates continued success, yet we know that eventually all organizations will see slowing growth and possibly even decline. IBM and Sears are witnesses to that scenario.

INVITATION

Can you identify additional learning insights that could be applicable to firms in other situations?

QUESTIONS

1. In what ways might airline customers be segmented? Which segments or niches would you consider to be Southwest's prime targets? Which segments probably would not be?
2. Do you think Southwest employees' dedication will quickly fade when Kelleher leaves? Why or why not?
3. Discuss the pros and cons of expansion of Southwest beyond short hauls. Which arguments do you see as most compelling?
4. Evaluate the effectiveness of Southwest's unions.

5. On August 18, 1993, a fare war erupted. To initiate its new service between Cleveland and Baltimore, Southwest announced a $49 fare (a sizable reduction from the then standard rate of $300). Its rivals, Continental and US Air, retaliated. Before long, the price was $19, not much more than the tank of gas it would take to drive between the two cities—and the airlines also supplied a free soft drink. Evaluate the implications of such a price war for the three airlines.

6. A price cut is the most easily matched strategy, and usually provides no lasting advantage to any competitor. Identify the circumstances when you see it desirable to initiate a price cut and potential price war.

7. Do you think it is likely that Southwest's position will continue to remain unassailable by competitors? Why or why not?

INVITATION TO ROLE PLAY

1. Herb Kelleher has just retired, and you are his successor. Unfortunately, your personality is quite different from his: You are an introvert and far from flamboyant, and your memory for names is not good. What would be your course of action to try to preserve the great employee dedication of the Kelleher era? How successful do you think you will be? Did the board make a mistake in hiring you?

2. Herb Kelleher has not retired. He is going to continue until at least age 70. Somehow, his appetite for growth has increased as he has grown older, and he has charged you with developing plans for expanding into longer hauls—maybe to South and Central America, maybe even to Europe. Be as specific as you can in developing such expansion plans.

   Kelleher has also asked for your evaluation of these plans. Be as persuasive as you can in presenting this evaluation.

INVITATION TO RESEARCH

What is Southwest's current situation? What is its market share in the airline industry? Is it still maintaining a high growth rate? Has its stock continued to climb? Has it expanded beyond its short-haul strategy?

TWO

ORGANIZATIONAL MISHANDLING

CHAPTER 7

From Monumental Failure to Outstanding Success: The Edsel and the Mustang

In the annals of business history perhaps no greater turnaround was ever achieved by one company in the space of a few years than that of the Ford Motor Company in the late 1950s and early 1960s. In the late 1950s, Ford hatched the blunder that to this day has become synonymous with fiascos of monumental proportions—the Edsel. A few years later, in 1962, it developed the most successful new car model ever introduced up to that time—the Mustang.

Did the Edsel mistake result in a tremendous learning experience at Ford? Did the Mustang's success come from simple luck? Or could the success of the Mustang reflect more the genius of the man who was the key force behind the Mustang, Lee Iacocca, a man we know today for his success with Chrysler?

PART A   THE EDSEL—ORGANIZATIONAL INCOMPATIBILITY WITH POTENTIAL

The factors behind the Edsel demise were more than strictly organizational, although an expensive and separate dealer organization was a major contributor. The Edsel case could also have been placed in the section on planning, since the product itself, the name, the way it was introduced, and quality control problems all contributed to its demise. But without the separate and expensive dealer organization, might there still be an Edsel today?

AN EARLIER BLUNDER

Henry Ford introduced the Model T in 1909. It sold initially for $850 and was available in only one color: black. The Model T quickly became a way of life. Ford conducted mass production on a scale never before seen, introducing and perfecting the moving assembly line so that the work moved to the worker. Ford sold one-half the new cars made in this country until 1926 and had more than double the output of his nearest competitor, General Motors (GM). Prices by 1926 had fallen as low as $263. For 17 years the Model T had neither model changes nor significant improvements, except for a decreasing selling price as the company realized more production economies.

By the mid-1920s, however, millions of Americans wanted something fancier, and GM brought out Chevrolet, featuring color, comfort, styling, safety, modernity, and—most of all—a showy appearance. The Model T was doomed.

In desperation Henry Ford altered the Model T: The factory painted it attractive colors; rounded its fenders; lengthened and lowered the body; and slanted the windshield. But still sales declined. Finally, in May 1927, Ford stopped production altogether for nearly a year, laying off 60,000 workers in Detroit while a new car, the Model A, slowly took shape, with a changeover estimated to have cost Ford $100 million. Although the Model A was successful, Ford never regained the lead from GM.[1]

In the 1920s a failure in market assessment was devastating. To some extent, the failure of the Edsel was also due to bad market assessment that led to overly ambitious expectations and organizational planning.

THE EDSEL

The Edsel, Ford's entry into the field of medium-priced cars, was introduced for the 1958 model year in early September 1957. This timing gave it a jump on competitors, who traditionally introduce new models in October and November of the previous years. Ernest Breech, the board chairman of the Ford Motor Company, set the 1958 goal for the Edsel Division at 3.3 to 3.5 percent of the total auto market. In a 6-million-car year, this would be about 200,000 cars. However, the company executives considered this a very conservative estimate and expected to do much better. Ten years of planning, preparation, and research had gone into the Edsel. The need for such a car in the Ford product line appeared conclusive, so Ford spent approximately $50 million for advertising and promotion in the pre-intro-

---

[1]Adapted from Jonathan Hughes, *The Vital Few* (Boston: Houghton Mifflin, 1966), pp. 274–358.

duction and introduction of the car. In the late summer of 1957, the success of the massive venture seemed certain. The company did not expect to recover the $250 million of development costs until the third year, but the car was expected to be operationally profitable in 1958.

Rationale

The rationale for the Edsel seemed inescapable. For some years there had been a growing trend toward medium-priced cars. Such cars as Pontiac, Oldsmobile, Buick, Dodge, DeSoto, and Mercury were accounting for one-third of all car sales by the middle 1950s, whereas they had formerly contributed only one-fifth.

Economic projections confirmed this shift in emphasis from low-priced cars and suggested a continuing demand for higher-priced models in the 1960s. Disposable personal income (expressed in 1956 dollars) had increased from about $138 billion in 1939 to $287 billion in 1956, with forecasts of $400 billion by 1965. Furthermore, the percentage of this income spent for automobiles had increased from around 3.5 percent in 1939 to 5.5 or 6.0 percent in the middle 1950s. Clearly, the economic climate seemed to favor a medium-priced car such as the Edsel.

The Ford Motor Company had been weakest in this very sector. GM had three makes—Pontiac, Oldsmobile, and Buick—in the medium-price class; Chrysler had Dodge and DeSoto to appeal to this market; but Ford had only Mercury to compete for this business, and Mercury accounted for a puny 20 percent of the company's business.

Studies had revealed that every year, one out of five people who bought a new car traded up to a medium-priced model from a low-priced car. As Chevrolet owners traded up, 87 percent stayed with GM and one of its three makes of medium-priced cars. As Plymouth owners traded up, 47 percent bought a Dodge or DeSoto. But as Ford owners traded up, only 26 percent stayed with the Ford Motor Company and the Mercury, its one entry in this price line. Ford executives were describing this phenomenon as "one of the greatest philanthropies of modern business," the fact that Ford up-traders contributed almost as much to GM's medium-price penetration as Chevrolet had been able to generate for GM.[2] The entry of the Edsel seemed necessary, if not overdue.

---

[2] Henry G. Baker, "Sales and Marketing Planning of the Edsel," in *Marketing's Role in Scientific Management*, Proceedings of the 39th National Conference of the American Marketing Association (June 1957), pp. 128–129.

Research Efforts

Marketing research studies on the Edsel covered a period of almost 10 years. Marketers concluded that the personality of the new car (called the "E-car" initially, before the Edsel name had been selected) should position it as the smart car for the young executive or professional family on its way up. Advertising and promotion would stress this theme, and the appointments of the car would offer status to the owner.

Researchers wanted the name for the E-car to fit the car's image and personality, so they gathered some 2000 names, and several research firms sent interviewers with the list to canvass sidewalk crowds in New York City, Chicago, Willow Run, Michigan, and Ann Arbor, Michigan. The interviewers asked what free associations each name brought to mind, but the results were inconclusive.

Edsel, the name of Henry Ford's only son, had been suggested for the E-car. However, Henry Ford's grandsons, the three Ford brothers in active management of the company (Henry II, Benson, and William Clay), were lukewarm to this idea of their father's name spinning "on a million hub-caps." And the free associations with the name Edsel were negative, being "pretzel," "diesel," and "hard sell."

At last 10 names were sent to the executive committee, but none of them aroused any enthusiasm. The name Edsel was finally selected, although it was not one of the recommended names. Four of the 10 names submitted were selected for the different series of Edsel: Corsair, Citation, Pacer, and Ranger.

Search for a Distinctive Style

Styling of the Edsel began in 1954. Stylists were asked to be both distinctive and discreet, in itself a rather tall order. The stylists studied existing cars and even scanned the tops of cars from the roof of a 10-story building to determine any distinguishing characteristics that might be used for the Edsel. Consumer research could provide some information as to image and personality desired but furnished little guidance for the actual features and shape of the car. Groups of stylists considered various "themes" and boiled down hundreds of sketches to two dozen to show top management. Clay and plaster mock-ups were prepared so that three-dimensional highlights and flair could be observed. The final concept was satisfying to all 800 stylists.

The result was a unique vertical front grille—a horse-collar shape, set vertically in the center of a conventionally low, wide front end—push-button transmission, and luxury appointments. The vertical grille of the Edsel was compared by some executives to the classic cars of the 1930s, the

LaSalle and Pierce Arrow. Push buttons were stressed as the epitome of engineering advancement and convenience. The hood and trunk lid were push button; the parking brake lever was push button; the transmission was push button. Edsel salespersons could demonstrate the ease of operation by depressing the transmission buttons with a toothpick.

The Edsel was not a small car. The two largest series, the Corsair and the Citation, were 2 inches longer than the biggest Oldsmobile. It was a powerful car, one of the most powerful made, with a 345-horsepower engine. The high performance possible from such horsepower was thought to be a key element in the sporty, youthful image that was to be projected.

A Separate Division for Edsel

Instead of distributing the new Edsel through established Ford, Mercury, and Lincoln dealers, a separate dealer organization was decided upon, to be controlled by a separate headquarters division. These new dealers were carefully selected from over 4600 inquiries for dealer franchises in every part of the United States. Most of the 1200 dealers chosen were to handle only Edsel, with dual dealerships restricted to small towns. Consequently, there were now five separate divisions for the Ford Motor Company: Ford, Mercury, Lincoln, Continental, and Edsel.

Although establishing Edsel as a separate division added to the fixed costs of operation, this move was thought to be desirable in the long run. An independent division could stand alone as a profit center and should encourage more aggressive performance than if Edsel were merely a second entry in some other division.

The dealer appointments were made after intensive study to learn where to place each dealer in the nation's 60 major metropolitan areas. Population shifts and trends were carefully considered, and the planned dealer points were matched with the 4600 inquiries for franchises. The Edsel was to have the best-located dealer body in the automobile industry. Applicants for dealerships were carefully screened, of course. Guides used in selection included reputation, finances, facilities, management ability, the ability to attract and direct good people, sales ability, proper attitude toward ethical and competitive matters, and type of person to give proper consideration to customers in sales and services.[3] The average dealer had at least $100,000 committed to this agency. Edsel Division was prepared to supply skilled assistance to dealers so that each could operate as effectively and profitably as possible and also provide good service to customers.

[3]Ibid., p. 143.

Promotional Efforts

July 22, 1957, was the kickoff date for the first consumer advertising. It was a two-page spread in *Life* magazine in plain black and white, and it showed a car whooshing down a country highway at such speed it was a blur. The copy read: "Lately some mysterious automobiles have been seen on the roads." It went on to say that the blur was an Edsel and was on its way. Other "preannouncement" ads showed only photographs of covered cars. Not until late August were pictures of the actual cars released.

The company looked beyond their regular advertising agencies to find a separate one for the Edsel. Foote, Cone and Belding was selected, this being one of the two in the top 10 who did not have any other automobile clients. The campaign designed was a quiet, self-assured one that avoided as much as possible the use of the adjective "new," which was seen as commonplace and not distinctive enough. The advertising was intended to be calm, not to overshadow the car.

The General Sales and Marketing Manager, J. C. Doyle, insisted on keeping Edsel's appearance one of the best-kept secrets of the auto industry. Never before had an auto manufacturer gone to so much trouble to keep the appearance hidden. Advertising commercials were filmed behind closed doors, the cars were shipped with covers, and no press people were given photographs of the car before its introduction. The intent was to build up an overwhelming public interest in the Edsel, causing its arrival to be anticipated and the car itself to be the object of great curiosity. Some $50 million was allocated for this introductory period.

THE RESULTS

Introduction day was September 4, 1957, and 1200 Edsel dealers eagerly opened their doors. And most found potential customers streaming in, out of curiosity, if nothing else. On the first day, more than 6500 orders were taken. This was considered reasonably satisfying. But there were isolated signs of resistance. One dealer selling Edsels in one showroom and Buicks in an adjacent showroom reported that some prospects walked into the Edsel showroom, looked at the Edsel, and placed orders for Buicks on the spot.

In the next few days, sales dropped sharply. The first 10 days of October had only 2751 sales, an average of just over 300 cars per day. To sell 200,000 cars per year (the minimum expectation), between 600 and 700 would need to be sold each day.

On Sunday night, October 13, the Ford Motor Company put on a mammoth television spectacular for Edsel. The show cost $400,000 and starred

Bing Crosby and Frank Sinatra, two of the hottest names in show business at that time. Even this failed to cause any sharp spurt in sales. Things were not going well.

For all of 1958, only 34,481 Edsels were sold and registered with the motor vehicle bureaus, less than one-fifth the targeted sales. The picture looked a little brighter in November 1958 with the introduction of the second-year models. These Edsels were shorter, lighter, and less powerful, and they were priced from $500 to $800 less than their predecessors.

Eventually the Edsel Division was merged into a Lincoln-Mercury-Edsel Division. In mid-October 1959, a third series of annual models of Edsels was brought out. They aroused no particular excitement either, and on November 19, 1959, production was discontinued. The Edsel was dead.

Between 1957 and 1960, 109,466 Edsels were sold. Ford was able to recover $150 million of its investment by using Edsel plants and tools in other Ford divisions, leaving a nonrecoverable loss of more than $100 million on the original investment plus an estimated $100 million in operating losses.

WHAT WENT WRONG?

The project was carefully planned and organized. With such a major commitment of work force and financial resources, supported by decades of experience in producing and marketing automobiles, how could this product have failed? Where were the mistakes? Could they have been prevented? As with most problems, there is no one simple answer. The marketplace is complex. Many factors contributed to the demise of the Edsel: among them, poor judgment by people who should have known better (except that they were so confident because of the abundance of planning) and economic conditions outside the company's control. We will examine some of the factors that have been blamed for the Edsel's failure. None of them alone would have been sufficient to destroy the Edsel; in combination, the car did not have a chance.

Exogenous Factors

One article on the failure of the Edsel said, "In addition to mistakes, real and alleged, the Edsel encountered incredibly bad luck. Unfortunately, it was introduced at the beginning of the 1958 recession. Few cars sold well in 1958; few middle-priced cars sold, even fewer Edsels."[4] A dealer in San

---

[4]William H. Reynolds, "The Edsel Ten Years Later," *Business Horizons* (Fall 1967), p. 44.

Francisco summed it up this way: "The medium-priced market is extremely healthy in good times, but it is also the first market to be hurt when we tighten our belts during depression. . . . When they dreamed up the Edsel, medium-priced cars were a big market, but by the time the baby was born, that market had gone 'helter-skelter.'"[5]

The stock market collapsed in 1957, marking the beginning of the recession of 1958. By August 1957, sales of medium-priced cars of all makes were declining. Dealers were ending their season with the second-largest number of unsold cars in history up to that time. Table 7.1 shows total U.S. car sales from 1948 (as the country was beginning production after World War II) until 1960. You can see from this table that 1958 sales were the lowest since 1948.

Table 7.2 shows the production of the major makes of medium-priced cars from 1955 to 1960. Note the drastic drop-off of all makes of cars in 1958, though the trend had been downward since 1955.

The trend was changing from bigger cars to economy cars. American Motors had been pushing the compact Rambler, and, in the year the Edsel came on the market, sales of foreign cars more than doubled. This change in consumer preferences was not solely a product of the 1958 recession, which indicated that it would not reverse once the economy improved. Sales of small foreign cars continued to be very strong in the following years, reflecting public disillusionment with big cars and a desire for more economy and less showy transportation. Table 7.3 shows the phenomenal in-

Table 7.1   U.S. Motor Vehicle Sales, 1948–1960

Year	Units Sold
1948	3,909,270
1949	5,119,466
1950	6,665,863
1951	5,338,436
1952	4,320,794
1953	6,116,948
1954	5,558,897
1955	7,920,186
1956	5,816,109
1957	6,113,344
1958	4,257,812
1959	5,591,243
1960	6,674,796

Source: 1973 Ward's Automotive Yearbook (Detroit: Ward's Communications), p. 86.

[5]"Edsel Gets a Frantic Push," Business Week (December 7, 1957), p. 35.

Table 7.2   U.S. Medium-Priced Car Production, 1955–1959 (units)

	1955	1956	1957	1958	1959
Mercury	434,911	246,629	274,820	128,428	156,765
Edsel			54,607	26,563	29,667
Pontiac	581,860	332,268	343,298	219,823	388,856
Oldsmobile	643,460	432,903	390,091	310,795	366,305
Buick	781,296	535,364	407,283	257,124	232,579
Dodge	313,038	205,727	292,386	114,206	192,798
DeSoto	129,767	104,090	117,747	36,556	41,423

Source: 1973 *Ward's*, pp. 112, 113.

crease in import car sales during this period, a trend that should have alerted the Edsel planners.

Other exogenous factors were also coming into play at the time of the Edsel's introduction. The National Safety Council had become increasingly concerned with the "horsepower race" and the way speed and power were translating into highway accidents. In 1957 the Automobile Manufacturing Association, in deference to the criticisms of the National Safety Council, signed an agreement against advertising power and performance. But the Edsel had been designed to highlight these two features: a big engine with 345 horsepower to support a high-performance, powerful car on the highways. Designed to handle well at high speeds, its speed, horsepower, and high-performance equipment could not even be advertised.

Table 7.3   U.S. Sales of Import Cars, 1948–1960

Year	Units Sold
1948	28,047
1949	7,543
1950	21,287
1951	23,701
1952	33,312
1953	29,505
1954	34,555
1955	57,115
1956	107,675
1957	259,343
1958	430,808
1959	668,070
1960	444,474

Source: Automobile Facts and Figures, 1961 Edition (Detroit: Automobile Manufacturers Association), p. 5; compiled from U.S. Department of Commerce statistics.

Consumer Reports was not overly thrilled about the Edsel. Its 800,000 subscribers read this the first sentence in the magazine's evaluation of the Edsel: "The Edsel has no important basic advantage over the other brands." Negative articles and books regarding the "power merchants" of Detroit were also appearing about this time. John Keats published his *Insolent Chariots*, and the poet Robert Lowell condemned our "tailfin culture."[6]

Marketing Research

The failure of the Edsel cannot be attributed to a lack of marketing research. However, these research efforts can be faulted in three respects.

First, the research efforts directed to establishing a desirable image or "personality" for the new car were not all that helpful. Although they were of some value in determining how consumers viewed the owners of Chevrolets, Fords, Mercurys, and other brands and led the Edsel executives into selecting the particular image for their car, in reality there was an inability to translate this desired image into tangible product features. For example, although upwardly mobile young executives and professionals seemed a desirable segment of consumers for Edsel to appeal to, would heavy horsepower and high-speed performance features attract these consumers? (Many of these consumers were shifting their sentiments to the European compacts about this time, repudiating the "horsepower race" and the chrome-bedecked theme of bigness.)

Second, much of the research was conducted several years before the introduction of the Edsel in 1957. Although demand for medium-priced cars seemed strong at that time, the assumption that such attitudes would be static and unchanging was unwise. A strong shift in consumer preferences was undetected but should have been noticed. The increasing demand for imported cars should have warranted further investigation and even a reexamination of plans in light of changing market conditions. At the very least, this observation should have led to some toning down of optimistic expectations for the Edsel and more conservative sales forecasts and budgets.

The last area where the marketing research efforts can be criticized is in the name itself, Edsel. Here the blame lies not so much with the marketing research, which never recommended the name in the first place, as with a Ford management that disregarded marketing research conclusions and chose the name. Much has been written about the negative impact of the name, and most of this criticism may be unjustified. Many successful cars

---

[6]As reported in John Brooks, *The Fate of the Edsel and Other Business Adventures* (New York: Harper & Row, 1967), p. 57.

on the market today do not have what we would call winning names. For example, the names *Buick, Oldsmobile, Chrysler*, even *Ford* itself lack excitement. A better name could have been chosen—and was, a few years later, with the Mustang, and also the Maverick—but it is doubtful that the name can justifiably be blamed for the Edsel's demise.

The Product

Changing consumer preferences for smaller cars came at about the time of the introduction of the Edsel. Disillusionment was setting in regarding large-sized, powerful cars. However, other characteristics of the car also hurt. The styling, especially the vertical grille, aroused both positive and negative impressions. Some liked its distinctiveness, seeing it as a restrained classic look without extremes. But the horse-collar shaped grille was unappealing to other people.

The biggest product error had to do with quality control. In a failure to adhere to quality standards, cars were released that should not have been. Production was rushed to get the Edsel to market on schedule and also to get as many Edsels as possible on the road so that people could see the car. But many bugs remained. The array of models increased the production difficulties, with 18 models in the Ranger, Pacer, Corsair, and Citation series.

As a result, the first Edsels had brakes that failed, leaked oil, and were besieged with rattles; sometimes the dealers could not even start them. Before these problems could be cleared up, the car had gained the reputation of being a lemon, and this was a tough image to overcome. The car quickly became the butt of jokes.

The Separate Edsel Organization

A major mistake that can be singled out was the decision to go with a separate division and separate dealerships for Edsel. Although this separation was supposed to lead to greater dealer motivation and consequently stronger selling push than when such efforts were diluted among several makes of cars, the cost factors of such separation were disregarded. Having a separate division was expensive and raised breakeven points very high because of the additional personnel and facilities. Furthermore, Ford did not have ample management personnel to staff all its divisions adequately.

Despite the care used in selecting the new Edsel dealers, some of them were underfinanced, and many were underskilled in running automobile dealerships compared to the existing dealers selling regular Ford products.

Other Edsel dealers were "dropouts," or the less successful dealers of other car makers.

An additional source of difficulty for the viability of the Edsel dealers was that they had nothing else to offer but Edsel sales and service. Dealers usually rely on the shop and maintenance sections of their businesses to cover some expenses. Edsel dealers had only the Edsel to work on, and the work on the Edsel was usually a result of factory deficiencies; they could not charge for this work. Dealers quickly faced financial difficulties with sales below expectations and service business yielding little revenue.

Promotional Efforts

Contrary to what could be reasonably expected, the heavy promotional efforts before the Edsel was finally unveiled may have produced a negative effect. The general public had been built up to expect the Edsel to be a major step forward, a significant innovation, and many were disappointed. They saw instead a new-styled luxury Ford, uselessly overpowered, gadget- and chrome-bedecked, but nothing really so very different; this car was not worth the buildup.

Another problem was that the Edsel came out too early in the new car model year—in early September—and had to suffer the consequences of competing with 1957 cars that were going through clearance sales. Not only did people shy away from the price of the Edsel, but in many instances they did not know if it was a 1957 or 1958 model. *Business Week* reported dealer complaints: "We've been selling against the clean-up of 1957 models. We were too far ahead of the 1958 market. Our big job is getting the original lookers back in the showrooms."[7]

Some dealers had complained about too much early advertising; now they were complaining of lack of promotion and advertising in October and November when the other cars were being introduced. At the time when the Edsel was competing against other new models, advertising was cut back; Edsel executives saw little point in trying to steal attention normally focused on new models.

Finally, the following is one of the more interesting explanations for the failure of the Edsel:

> Oral symbolism . . . [was] responsible for the failure of the Edsel. The physical appearance was displeasing from a psychological and emotional point of view because the front grille looked like a high open mouth. . . . Men do not want to associate oral qualities with their cars, for it does not fit their self-image of being strong and virile.[8]

[7]"Edsel Gets a Frantic Push," op. cit., p. 35.
[8]Gene Rosenblum, *Is Your VW a Sex Symbol?* (New York: Hawthorn, 1972), p. 39.

PART B   THE MUSTANG—SIMPLICITY FOR THE GREAT REVERSAL

The Mustang was introduced on April 17, 1964, a little over four years after the Edsel was discontinued. In the first four months that the Mustang was on the market, more Mustangs were sold than Edsels had been sold in their 26-month history. The Mustang ranks as one of the automotive industry's most successful new model introductions.

LEE IACOCCA

Lee Iacocca played a primary role in the success of the Mustang, becoming Ford Division general manager in 1960. He embodied the great American success story. The son of an Italian immigrant, Iacocca saw education as the route to success. He went to Lehigh University and later to Princeton for a master's degree in engineering. "In my day you went to college, not to go into government or to be a lawyer, but to embark on a career that paid you more money than the guy who didn't go. For 32 years I was motivated by money," Iacocca was to say some years later.[9]

Iacocca started with the Ford Motor Company as an engineer trainee in 1946 at $125 a week. As he moved upward through the Ford organization, he transferred to sales, later becoming sales manager, then vice president and general manager of the Ford Division. By 1977 he was the president of the entire Ford Motor Company, earning $978,000. But in July 1978, Henry Ford abruptly fired him. The falling out was attributed to basic disagreement between Ford and Iacocca over the pace of downsizing cars: Iacocca wanted to move fast, whereas Ford was worried about the impact of such additional investment on short-term profits and wanted to move more slowly. Today, Iacocca is best known as the savior of Chrysler.

In addition to being a natural salesman, Iacocca has a genius for assessing the general public's desires for cars. While still a sales manager he noticed that many people were pleading for Ford to bring back the old two-seat Thunderbird. The youth market appeared to Iacocca to show increasing potential, and as his voice began to be heard more in the organization, he was able to push his ideas of a personal car directed to the youth market. He wanted such a car to be inexpensive but peppy and sporty-looking.

THE ENVIRONMENT FOR THE AUTOMOBILE IN 1964

The decade 1954 to 1964 brought big changes to the auto industry. In 1954 Nash and Kelvinator merged with Hudson Motor Car Company to form

---

[9]"Off to the Races Again," *Fortune* (December 4, 1978), p. 15.

American Motors, and Studebaker merged with Packard to form the Studebaker Corporation. The Packard line was discontinued in 1958, and Hudson was dropped in 1959. The Edsel was introduced in late 1957 and dropped in 1959. Import cars were trickling into the United States around 1955 and gaining popularity. By the late 1950s, both Studebaker and American Motors were successfully producing small cars.

In 1960 John F. Kennedy was elected president. His popularity brought with it a new emphasis on youth. Kennedy also inherited a sluggish economy, and this he tried to remedy with tax cuts that increased disposable income. In 1963 he dropped the excise tax on automobiles. The ground was now laid for a greatly stimulated demand for cars.

In 1961 some 23 automakers were fighting for a market of 7,920,00 cars in 1955 (1955 is used as a base comparison year since it was the industry's best year, not exceeded until 1964). The number of makes of cars had been steadily declining since 1921, when 61 competitors were vying for a much smaller market. Some of the well-known makes that failed were

- Packard, after 59 years
- Hudson, after 49 years
- Nash, after 40 years
- Auburn, after 38 years
- Pierce Arrow, after 37 years
- Franklin, after 33 years
- Hupmobile, after 32 years
- Reo, after 32 years
- Stutz, after 24 years

In the early 1960s, the remaining carmakers began introducing many new models: Some 350 different ones were brought to market in 1961 and another 400 in 1962. Consumer preferences appeared to be changing, and the automakers were offering a great assortment, trying to find which would gain acceptance. But the sheer number of choices was leading to customer confusion. Adding to the mess was the introduction of luxury series of Chevrolets, Fords, and Plymouths, while additional models of Pontiacs, Buicks, and Dodges were being brought out at both the high and low ends of their markets. Price overlapping was severe. The top three automakers were also now producing compacts to counter the inroads being made by imports as well as by the American Motors' Rambler compact.

The economy was sluggish in 1961, and economic uncertainties about the Kennedy administration appeared to throttle demand. Many consumers delayed their purchases during the 1961 and 1962 model years, but confidence began building. Dealer stocks at the beginning of the 1963 model year were the lowest since 1957. The year 1963 proved to be a good sales year, with about 7 million cars sold.

The overall economy looked good in 1964. Disposable income was increasing about 5 percent over 1962. Consumer use of credit was burgeoning, and this always augured well for car sales. The growth of two-car families was a particularly optimistic factor, with well over 700,000 expected in 1964. More sobering was the gain made by imports to about 8 percent of the U.S. market. Other lower priced sports cars were also gaining in popularity.

For the most part, carmakers virtually ignored young people's fascination with autos. Cars play an important role both as a symbol and as an instrument of maturity, although such insights had only begun to be recognized in the early 1960s. But now the realization was growing that the 15- to 24-year-old group constituted a vibrant and growing market segment. Demographic studies showed that the number of 20- to 24-year-olds would increase by 54 percent by 1970. In the same period, the 15- to 19-year-old group would grow 41 percent. Both increases were far greater than anticipated gains in total population.

THE MUSTANG

Marketing Research Efforts

After the prodigious marketing research efforts that preceded the Edsel disaster, it would not have been surprising for Ford to give short shrift to marketing research in the succeeding years. But research was used, though on a smaller scale than in the 1950s.

The statistics on demographics, and particularly on the growing youth market, were widely circulated throughout the company. The company received strong indications that older Americans were acquiring more youthful tastes and becoming involved in activities considered youthful for the time, such as golf and tennis. Thus it seemed that the right car might appeal not only to youth but to older people looking for symbols of youth. Additional research revealed that more people were buying sports cars and their accoutrements: bucket seats, zippy engines, and four-speed stick shifts.

Ford management decided to make the Mustang a sports car. Since many of the individuals in the youth market were just getting started in their careers, the new car had to be versatile. It needed to be priced low enough to meet the needs of the young, low-income earner in addition to middle-income groups; it had to have a back seat and a trunk to accommodate small families, and, if possible, it should appeal to the growing number of two-car families. Thus it should be a family car. In sum, the Mustang ought to be all things to all people. These were the conclusions of the research studies. Now these had to be turned into specifications for the styling and engineering departments.

After designs were drawn up, the results from showing the designs to panels of consumers were fed back to product planning, where reevaluations were made of the designated desirable and undesirable design features. After a model of the car was developed, further research investigated how well the design met consumer preferences. An interesting situation developed. In trying to determine the best price for the Mustang, Ford invited 52 couples to view a model of the car. When they thought it was to be priced at $3500 they found a lot of things wrong with the car, but when they were given a price less than $2500, the consumers thought it had great styling and plenty of back seat room.

At this point, with the car now developed and favorable consumer research feedback at hand, Mustang sales were projected at 200,000 units for 1964. Before the official launch date, Ford test marketed the car with strongly positive results.

The Product

The Edsel fiasco was still a sharp and painful memory: The $200 million loss and nine years of "wasted" research soured upper management on any similarly ambitious undertaking. Recognizing managerial prejudices, Iacocca developed the Mustang in three years for only $65 million dollars. The car was pieced together from the Falcon, a compact car, and the Fairlane, a midsize car. It was "cross-sourced"—that is, built from existing stock. The six-cylinder engine and transmission to power the car were taken from the Falcon. Beyond the costs of new body styling, the only other major expense was in designing a suspension system. Iacocca in an interview described the people involved with it as basically "lunching off the rest of the corporation."[10]

The long hood/short deck style of the Mustang was to fascinate buyers through the 1960s and early 1970s. In fact the styling hardly changed during those years. The car came in three basic forms: a hardtop, a convertible, and a semifastback coupe. Convertible sales started at the 100,000 unit annual level but dropped to 15,000 a year by 1969. The notchback hardtop was the sales leader. The coupe, also known as the 2+2, soon overtook the convertible in sales and averaged about 50,000 units annually through 1970.

The standard Mustang engines during the first six months of production were the 170 cubic inch, six-cylinder and the 260 cubic inch, V-8 small block. By fall of 1964, these engines had been bored and stroked to 200 CID and 289 CID, respectively. More powerful engines were added, including large block V-8s by 1970.

---

[10]"Ford's Mustang: The Edsel Avenged," *Forbes* (September 1, 1964), pp. 13–14.

Part of the Mustang's appeal lay in its many options, which enabled a customer to personalize the car. Careful use of the order form could result in anything from a cute economy car to a thundering fast drag racer or a deceptively nimble sports car. Transmission choices included automatics, four-speeds, three-speeds, and stick-overdrive units. Handling packages, power steering, disc brakes, air conditioning, and tachometer and clock packages were also available. A special GT package offered front disc brakes, a full gauge instrument panel, and special gadgets. A variety of interiors were available, along with accent stripes and special exterior moldings.

To position the Mustang in the marketplace and to make it affordable for young people, the base sticker price was set at $2,368 for a six-cylinder hardtop. The price was advertised nationally in virtually all announcement material.

Choosing a name for this new car presented the expected problems: "The name is often the toughest part of a car to get right. It's easier to design doors and roofs than to come up with a name," Iacocca reminisced in his autobiography.[11] Finalists from thousands of suggestions were Bronco, Puma, Cheetah, Colt, Mustang, and Cougar. Finally, Mustang was chosen, named not for the horse but for the famous World War II fighter plane. But it was thought to have "the excitement of wide-open spaces and was American as all hell."

The Promotional Blitz

Ford launched a massive campaign in print and television to promote the Mustang. The intent was to cover as many potential markets as possible in a short period of time. Families, women, and youth were target audiences for Ford's bold introduction of the new model.

On April 2, 1964, barely two weeks before Mustang's debut, Ford began the TV onslaught. Simultaneous programs were purchased on all three networks. During the next month, Mustang commercials were run on 25 different programs on all three networks. The TV coverage placed Mustang commercials in 95 percent of all homes with TV, with an average frequency of 11 messages per home. Color pages were bought in 191 newspapers, in 63 markets. Black-and-white ads were placed in other newspapers, for a total of 2612 newspapers in 2200 markets. Four-page color inserts appeared in *Life, Look, Reader's Digest, The Saturday Evening Post*, and 20 other national magazines.

Additional promotional efforts were more innovative. Ford joined with Alberto-Culver to run a national contest for Command hair dressing: the Command Sports Car Sweepstakes. This brought mention of Mustang on

---

[11]Lee Iacocca, *Iacocca* (New York: Bantam, 1984), p. 69.

radio in 60 to 70 commercials per week in 31 major markets for almost two months. Mustang was also pictured on display material, on 2 million Command packages, and in Alberto-Culver national advertisements.

Ford worked out similar arrangements with other companies, such as AMT Toy Company, Holiday Inn, Sea & Ski Company, Jantzen, and the Indianapolis Motor Speedway. A model Mustang could be purchased for one dollar from AMT Toys. Mustangs were displayed in lobbies of 200 Holiday Inn motels and were featured in their directories and in their national advertising. They were displayed in 15 of the country's busiest airports. At University of Michigan football games, several acres of space were rented, with huge signs proclaiming "Mustang Corral." Sea & Ski introduced a new style of sunglasses called Mustang, and the company's national advertising featured the sports car with the glasses. Major department stores used actual Mustangs as props for some of their displays. Jantzen conducted a Miss Smile contest with the Mustang as its grand prize. The Indianapolis 500-mile race had a Mustang convertible as its pace car for 1964.

Among other things, Ford set up a traffic-building registration contest that offered 1000 prizes, including 25 Mustangs. A 3-million-piece mailing inaugurated the contest.

Four days before the official launching, a hundred reporters participated in a 70-car Mustang rally from New York City to Dearborn, Michigan, some 700 miles. Enthusiastic commentaries in hundreds of magazines and newspapers added to the growing excitement about this new car. A coup of no small moment was the simultaneous featuring of the Mustang on the covers of both *Time* and *Newsweek*.

Results

The Mustang took off. On April 17, Ford dealers were mobbed with customers; one dealer even had to lock his doors against a huge crowd outside. During the first weekend it was on sale, four million people visited dealer showrooms.

Initial expectations were that 75,000 Mustangs would sell during its first year. But optimism was growing, and by the introduction, sales projections were 200,000. A second plant was converted to Mustang production, bringing annual capacity up to 360,000. And still it was not enough; a third plant had to be converted. While people were buying Mustangs in record numbers, most were also ordering from a long list of profitable options, spending an additional $1000. In the first two years alone, the Mustang generated net profits of $1.1 billion.

The first 100,000 units sold in only 92 days. More than 400,000 were sold in the first 12 months. The success of the Mustang brought some production economies. There was no complete assembly-line shutdown for model changes between 1964 and 1965; the 1964 models were still rolling off the line while the 1965 models were being tooled for the next production run.

How long would it last? Ford expected General Motors and Chrysler to enter the market with competitive models, although Ford thought the competitors would need several years to develop a new model. It was not until fall 1966 that Chevrolet introduced a competitor, the Camaro, with styling similar to the Mustang: long hood, short deck, and same length wheelbase. Chrysler followed soon after with the Barracuda. But the Mustang more than held its own, maintaining more than one-half of the market for lower-priced sports cars.

KEYS TO SUCCESS

External

The economic cards were better stacked for the Mustang than for the Edsel. Productivity was increasing by 1964 and, as a result, so was the standard of living. Since wage increases did not outpace changes in productivity, inflation was not a problem. By the mid-1960s there was a build-up of demand for new cars. Table 7.4 shows total U.S. car sales for the period between 1960 and 1970. Up to that time, 1965 was the largest sales year in automotive history. With the luck of perfect timing, the spring introduction in April 1964 enabled the Mustang to take full advantage of the situation. There was less competition from new models, because introductions had taken place in the fall.

Table 7.4   U.S. Motor Vehicle Sales, 1960–1970

Year	Units Sold
1960	7,905,117
1961	6,652,928
1962	8,197,311
1963	9,108,776
1964	9,307,860
1965	11,137,830
1966	10,396,299
1967	9,023,736
1968	10,820,410
1969	10,205,911
1970	8,283,949

Source: *Automotive News 1978 Market Data Book Issues*, p. 10.

Social changes taking place in that period also benefited the Mustang. A national preoccupation with youth and physical fitness accelerated by the late 1960s. The Mustang's image of youth and vitality, reflected even in its name, made it a natural product for this changing environment.

Marketing Research

In contrast to the Edsel researchers, Mustang marketers kept marketing research current. They used several methods to monitor the youth market, including hot rod shows and sponsorship of college campus activities. The hot rod shows gave Ford ideas about car styling, handling, and performance. The youth market was creating its own type of automobiles, which the researchers saw as supporting the need for a personal car. By maintaining presence on college campuses, Ford could see that students bought foreign cars as a display of independence, individualism, and personal taste. Ford researchers concluded that buyer preferences form while young people are college-age, and Ford consequently made a major effort to capture this growing market.

The Product

The Mustang's unique body style—long hood/short deck—appealed to many consumers. Quality control was high. This emphasis on quality became a company-wide policy for all models (although quality never seemed to match that of foreign cars in many people's minds). The Mustang also filled a need in the market for a personalized car: It could be tailored to the individual through the wide choices of models and options. The more options a customer bought, the greater the profit margin, since options typically carry higher markups than basic cars. Furthermore, since production costs were low, even the basic car had a large profit margin. Therefore, record sales were accompanied by above-average profit margins.

Promotion

Virtually every medium was used effectively. The various creative promotional contests helped gain additional attention and conveyed desirable image associations, particularly that of the youthful sports car. Drawings or raffles helped increase traffic flow through dealer showrooms. Promotional efforts had continuity and timing. Information flowed constantly from television to radio, to print, and finally to personal selling. Before long, a Mustang was visible almost everywhere one looked. Knowledge of the Mustang was pervasive throughout the country.

Distribution

This time Ford decided to use its regular dealers to sell Mustangs. By using its existing 6400 dealers, the company avoided the substantial costs of a new division and kept the breakeven point for reaching profitability moderate. (The following box provides a more specific discussion of these issues.)

In addition, the increased traffic that Mustang created brought potential buyers for other Ford models. Many of the operational expenses normally incurred by a new model can be spread over the older models. Dealer reputations were already established with adequate financing and sales and service-center staffing. With a product in great demand, there is no concern about having a sufficiently motivated sales force. Once the sales potential of the Mustang could be seen, any sales force would be highly motivated and enthusiastic. Success feeds on success.

INFORMATION BOX

THE BREAKEVEN POINT

A breakeven analysis is a vital tool in making go/no-go decisions about new ventures. This can be shown graphically as follows: Below the breakeven point, the venture suffers losses (as Edsel did); above it, the venture becomes profitable.

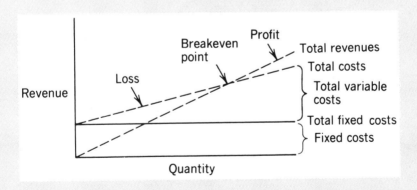

Hypothetical comparison of Edsel (with separate dealer organization) and Mustang (without separate dealer organization):

For this example, let us assume that promotional expenses and other basic operating expenses for the first year are $50,000,000 for both cars. These are fixed costs or overhead that the two ventures will incur regardless of sales.

Assume that the average profit contribution beyond production costs and the other variable costs is $400 per car (actually for the Mustang the profit contribution was considerably higher because of lower production costs and increased sales of more profitable optional equipment). The sales needed to breakeven are

$$\text{Breakeven} = \frac{\text{Total fixed costs}}{\text{Contribution to overhead}}$$

$$= \frac{\$50,000,000}{\$400} = 125,000 \text{ units}$$

But the Edsel had substantial additional fixed costs because of its separate dealer organization. We can estimate these additional costs as follows:

Salary and expenses for 100 field representatives for liaison with 1,200 dealers	$ 6,000,000
Salary and expenses for Edsel organizational staff—management and back-up personnel and facilities	4,000,000
Additional operating expenses—overhead, telephone, postage, etc.	2,000,000
Total Additional Costs	$12,000,000

Therefore, the Edsel breakeven is

$$\frac{\$12,000,000 + \$50,000,000}{\$400} = 155,000 \text{ units}$$

But the actual sales of Edsel were 54,607 units the first year, 26,563 the second year, and 29,667 the last year, far below the breakeven point. The higher fixed costs of the separate dealer organization only exacerbated the situation.

In making go/no-go decisions, these costs can be estimated quite closely. What cannot be determined as surely are the sales figures. Certain things can be done to affect the breakeven point. Obviously it can be lowered if the overhead is reduced, say from $50,000,000 to $30,000,000. Higher selling prices also result in a lower breakeven because of higher per-unit profit (but prices would probably affect total sales quite adversely). Promotional expenses can be either increased or decreased and affect the breakeven point, but they probably also have an impact on sales. But Edsel's drain of a costly separate dealer organization had a major negative impact on the breakeven point and did not appear to have made any positive contribution to sales.

INVITATION TO DISCUSSION
Is it unreasonable to expect a new venture to breakeven the first year? Why or why not?

WHAT CAN BE LEARNED?

Few pairs of successes and failures can match the range of learning insights provided by analysis of the Edsel and the Mustang.

For new ventures, stay flexible and have contingency plans. A major contributor to the Edsel disaster was an unrealistically high sales expectation. Sales forecasting for a new product is hazardous at best. Sometimes sales greatly exceed expectations, as with the Mustang; at other times they may not even come close to achieving expectations. This is one of the calculated risks of decision making in an uncertain environment. If one is too optimistic, production and other resource allocations will be too high, and heavy costs will be incurred. Yet sales expectations that are too low play into the hands of more aggressive competitors who are ready to meet the untapped demand.

In dealing with an uncertain future for a new product, the greatest possible flexibility should be sought. The organization should be prepared for expansion, while not allowing the commitment of resources to bring on disaster if expectations are not realized. This suggests going easy on such things as heavy plant expansion and the accompanying fixed costs until demand is more certain. Contingency plans (discussed in Chapter 5) should be developed for different resource allocations and decisions at varying levels of demand.

Keep the breakeven point as low as possible, especially for new ventures. Edsel's separate dealer organization had a devastating effect on profitability because of the high breakeven point it required. The Edsel could have been sold through existing Ford and Mercury dealers without greatly increasing distribution costs of the new car and without subjecting the dealers to high risks, because they could fall back on sales of their other makes of cars. Edsel's 18 models further increased the breakeven point. While the optimistic sales forecast led to decisions that increased the breakeven point, this need not have been the case, as was shown by the Mustang. Less ambitious organizational and product planning would have lowered the breakeven point.

What can be learned? That optimistic forecasting is bad? That confidently going ahead with an ambitious project is folly? No, not at all. But the decision maker must carefully weigh the risk and reward factors of costly and ambitious decisions. Mistakes *will* be made. The future is never certain, despite research and careful planning. The environment is always changing, whether we consider customer attitudes and preferences, competitive efforts, or such unpredictable factors as foreign-created petroleum shortages and skyrocketing energy prices or the reverse—petroleum gluts and plummeting prices.

When a decision involves high stakes and an uncertain future—which translates into high risks—is it not wiser to approach the venture somewhat conservatively, not spurning the opportunity, but also not committing all resources and efforts until success appears more certain?

It can be argued that with a new model of car—whether the Edsel, or K-cars, or X-cars—the huge start-up investment militates against halfway measures. But separate dealerships need not be established, an array of models can be reduced; even advertising can be more conservatively placed. And the compelling example of the Mustang shows that not all new model introductions need involve gigantic tooling and production costs.

The external economic and social environment is important, and so is luck. Some maintain that luck confounds careful planning and analysis and rewards the intuitive and impulsive. Some even rail against the injustice of raw luck and its rewarding of the unworthy. But let's face it. Luck, opportunism, providential timing—these can be powerful factors in the success of firms and individual careers; but they can also be instruments of disaster.

The Edsel could hardly have been introduced at a worse economic time, with a recession in full force and demand for all cars dropping. The Mustang caught the other swing of the pendulum, with an upward-looking economy and pent-up demand leading to the largest sales volume year in automotive history in 1965. This raises an intriguing question: Would the Edsel have been a success if it had been introduced later, say, in the early 1960s? We would still answer in the negative. Despite a more favorable economy, something else in the environment was playing against the Edsel. Consumer tastes and interests had shifted from the type of car the Edsel represented to smaller, sportier models that the Mustang heralded.

Marketing research does not guarantee successful decisions. Despite being regarded as the mark of sophisticated management, marketing research by no means guarantees a correct decision. Marketing research provided the Mustang planners with insights that aided the success of the car with respect to design acceptability and optimal pricing. But marketing research is no panacea. Consumer statements regarding preferences often can be difficult to interpret and translate into design characteristics of a finished product. And when research is done incorrectly, or research conclusions are biased or self-serving, it may be worse than useless since it may inhibit the reasonable cautions of prudent executives. The millions of dollars spent on marketing research for the Edsel were wasted because research efforts were terminated two years before the car was introduced, at a time when consumer preferences were changing. Dated research is worse than stale news because it may lead to costly decisions that are far off the mark.

Extensive planning does not ensure success. This caveat flies in the face of the common belief—even the gut feeling—that better planning is the key to personal and all other kinds of success. The stark reality, we are forced to concede, is that heavy planning efforts have the same relationship to success as heavy marketing research efforts: They should help improve the decision-making process, but they by no means guarantee correct decisions. Circumstances and opportunities can drastically change between the planning and the realization.

The Edsel case brings reality to the rosy veneer associated with exacting planning. The planning of the Mustang, on the other hand, was done with far less specificity and with years less lead time; while it erred on the side of conservatism, sufficient flexibility had been built into the production planning to cope with success. Does this excoriate extensive planning? Have executives deluded themselves about the benefits of finely honed planning? We hardly want to condemn planning as worthless and a waste of time. Rather, planning ought to be relegated to a more realistic role—along with other popular tools of "sophisticated" management—and concede that it can err. Perhaps moderation in relying on planning and other advanced managerial tools is best—even though in some circles this smacks of heresy.

Poor quality control has a lasting stigma. The first Edsels had many defects; more than most new cars. The reputation for poorly constructed cars soon spread and remained long after the worst flaws had been corrected. Any firm flirts with danger when it allows lax quality control to permit defectives to reach the market. Reputations are long lasting, a fact that can be a significant impediment or a powerful advantage.

Again, sheer advertising expenditures do not guarantee success. As we saw in the Coca-Cola case, great expenditures for advertising did not produce a competitive advantage; again with the Edsel, massive amounts of advertising did not produce the desired results. Ford spent millions of dollars to promote both the Edsel and the Mustang. We might surmise that the Mustang promotional efforts were more effective than the Edsel, especially in attracting a particular segment of consumers, the youth market. In fact, neither promotional campaign can be seriously criticized. There was, however, one key difference. While Edsel advertising brought people into dealer showrooms, what they saw there did not meet their expectations. The Mustang, on the other hand, was appealing both in ads and in physical presence.

Creative advertising, if backed with sufficient expenditures, can induce people to try the product or at least to examine it more closely. But if the product does not meet expectations, there will be no repeat buying or, in the case of cars, no purchase.

INVITATION

Can you identify additional learning insights coming from the Edsel and Mustang experiences?

QUESTIONS

1. How would you have instituted environmental sensors to provide up-to-date information to Ford executives about changing exogenous conditions?

2. How would you respond to the comment that the failure of the Edsel, despite extensive planning (starting 10 years before the product finally was introduced), means that planning too far in advance is futile?

3. List as many pros and cons as possible for having Edsel as a separate division (with separate dealers) rather than as part of an existing division (and dealer organization) such as Lincoln-Mercury. Which of your pros and cons do you consider to be most important (which means that they deserve a higher weighting in the overall analytical process)?

4. How could the Edsel have been a more innovative entry into the medium-priced car market? What features might have made it successful?

5. Was the success of the Mustang attributable more to lucky timing than to any inspired organizational and resource planning?

6. Do you think the Mustang would have been successful if it had been introduced instead of the Edsel but with the Edsel's same timing and strategy? Discuss.

7. It is six months after the introduction of the Edsel. A serious mistake appears to have been made. What corrective action or change in strategy would you advise at this time? Present your recommendations as persuasively as possible. How effective do you think they might have been?

INVITATION TO ROLE PLAY

1. Assume the role of the Ford executive responsible for the Edsel operation. What strategy will you use both in the introductory period and in the subsequent several years to enable Edsel to attain viability and success? Be as specific and complete as you can and be prepared to defend your proposals against other alternatives. Be sure your recommendations are reasonable and practical.

2. As a staff planner for Ford, you have been asked to evaluate the desirability of a luxury addition to the Mustang line. What factors do you think ought to be considered in this $100 million decision, and how will you research and evaluate them?

INVITATION TO RESEARCH

1. Investigate demand for vintage Edsels and Mustangs. What prices can such old cars in good condition command? Can you suggest any learning insights regarding this?
2. In recent years, several Japanese luxury cars have become highly successful with names and dealerships different from their Honda and Nissan roots. General Motors has even introduced the Saturn with separate dealerships and divisional organization. Does the success of such cars disprove blaming the Edsel disaster partly on its separate dealerships? What was the difference?

8

Sears: An Organizational Morass

On January 25, 1993, Sears announced that after 107 years, the company would no longer offer its venerable catalog. In its long history, the catalog had become part of the American heritage, at least that of rural and small-town America. It was known as the "wish book," as its well-used pages spurred the dreams of countless children and their parents and stimulated their aspirations for a better life.

At the time of the announcement, the catalog was a $3.3 billion operation. Yet it was a source of recurring losses in recent years, losses that a reeling giant could no longer sustain. The closing would cost 3,400 full-time and 16,500 part-time jobs.[1]

The reasons given for the catalog's inability to maintain profitability were its own heavy costs of production and operation at a time of declining demand. Perhaps a bigger factor in the demise was the inroads made by Wal-Mart stores in rural small towns (see Chapter 18 for the Wal-Mart case), where consumers could now find a wide variety of goods at lower prices. Yet many other catalogs of all kinds are flourishing. Perhaps the Sears catalog was symptomatic of the problems facing its parent.

---

[1]"History Collides with the Bottom Line," *Business Week* (February 8, 1993), p. 34.

HISTORY

Richard W. Sears founded the R. W. Sears Watch Company in 1886 in Minneapolis. A year later Alvah C. Roebuck joined the company, and the two men moved the company to Chicago. The corporate name, Sears, Roebuck and Company, was formalized in 1893.

In the early years, the chief business was selling watches by mail order to people in small towns and rural areas. The assortment of goods rapidly expanded, and by 1896 a first general catalog of over 500 pages was published. Not until 1925, almost 40 years after the founding, did General Robert E. Wood, then a senior vice president, experiment with a retail store in Chicago. Its success laid the groundwork for the future retail expansion.

Expansion was rapid. By the end of 1927, Sears had 27 stores in operation, three times the number operating in the previous years. In 1931 Sears retail stores' sales exceeded mail-order sales for the first time, contributing 53.4 percent of total sales. And the growth continued, slackening only during World War II. See Table 8.1 for the growth in retail stores for selected years.

General Wood formed a major subsidiary in 1931: Allstate Insurance Company. At first Allstate operated only by mail, but in a few years it set up sales locations in Sears stores. General Wood, in his long tenure at the helm of Sears, also instituted a major store location policy after World War II. Instead of locating additional stores in crowded downtown areas, he

Table 8.1   Number of Retail Stores, 1925–1988

Year	Number of Stores
1925	1
1927	27
1928	192
1933	400
1941	600
1948	632
1970	827
1975	858
1979	864
1985	799
1988	824

Source: Sears annual reports.

Commentary: Note the great growth in the number of stores up until the early 1970s, then a gradual decline, until by the 1980s there were fewer stores than a decade earlier. This reflects the fact that poorly-performing stores were being closed, but it also shows that few new stores were being opened. This cutback occurred despite the fact that retail space of all retailers doubled during the 1970s and 1980s.

pioneered the idea of locating in outlying areas with an abundance of free parking. The expansion continued. Table 8.2 shows sales and income statistics for Sears and its two major competitors from 1938 to 1955. By now Sears was the nation's largest retailer, as it was to remain for over 50 years.

Sears made some important nonretail acquisitions in 1981. Coldwell Banker, the nation's largest residential real estate broker, and Dean Witter Reynolds, the fifth largest U.S. brokerage house, joined the Sears corporation. They set up shop in the rich traffic areas of Sears stores in the same marketing mode as the highly profitable Allstate Insurance subsidiary. In 1985 Sears celebrated its 100th birthday, and a year later, it introduced the soon-to-be-successful Discover credit card.

But trouble was on the horizon for the huge firm and its key retail sector. Its major competitors now were not Ward and Penney but two discounters, Wal-Mart and Kmart. By the end of the 1980s, these competitors would wrest from Sears its long-held position as largest retailer, while Sears struggled to define what its identity should be in a changed environment.

EDWARD A. BRENNAN

The preservation of the traditional greatness of Sears had to loom large in the mind of Edward A. Brennan, chairman and chief executive of the behemoth retail conglomerate, as events unfolded in late 1992. He is a third-generation Sears man and then had for more than a decade guided Sears' somehow faltering destiny. His rise to top position had a legendary quality.

Table 8.2   Sales and Income Statistics for Sears, Ward, and Penney, 1938–1954

	Ward		Sears		Penney	
Years	Sales (000)	Net Income (000)	Sales (000)	Net Income (000)	Sales (000)	Net Income (000)
1938	$414,091	$19,210	$537,242	$30,828	$257,971	$13,799
1942	632,709	22,353	915,058	29,934	490,356	18,058
1944	595,933	20,677	852,597	33,866	533,374	17,159
1946	654,779	22,932	1,045,359	35,835	676,570	35,495
1948	1,158,675	59,050	1,981,536	107,740	885,195	47,754
1950	1,084,436	47,788	2,168,928	108,207	949,712	44,931
1952	1,106,157	54,342	2,657,408	111,895	1,072,266	37,170
1954	999,123	41,195	2,981,925	117,882	1,107,157	43,617

Source: Moody's and company annual reports for respective years.

Commentary: Note the fading of Ward during this period. This reflects the no-growth policy of Ward chairman, Sewell Avery, after World War II. Ward was never again to be a significant factor, as Sears continued to surge ahead as the biggest retailer.

Born in Chicago in 1934 to a family committed to Sears virtually from the company's beginnings—a grandfather had worked beside Richard Sears, the company's founder—Brennan graduated from Marquette University with a degree in business administration in 1955. He joined Sears in 1956, leaving a men's clothing store and taking a drastic pay cut of $4000 to become a salesman in the Madison, Wisconsin, store. His progress was fast. By 1958 he was running the Sears store in Oshkosh, Wisconsin, and by the end of 1959 he was transferred to Sears headquarters in Chicago. In 1967 he again moved to become manager of a store, this time in Baltimore's African-American ghetto, where his performance came to the attention of Edward Telling, the manager of the eastern territory. In 1969 Telling promoted Brennan to one of the biggest stores in the territory and the following year made him assistant general manager of the New York group of stores. Brennan's star continued to rise.

Invariably in his new positions Brennan distinguished himself by converting losing or mediocre operations to top profit generators. He accepted so many transfers that he once owned homes in three cities. In 1977 he became executive vice president of the southern territory, which consisted of 13 groups and 150 stores, and with the promotion he also became a member of the company's board of directors. In 1978 the south moved from third to first among territories in profitability, and on March 12, 1980, Telling, then chairman of the company, named Brennan president of Sears and chief operating officer of the merchandising group.

With this achievement, Brennan was viewed as a 46-year-old "boy wonder" who had vaulted over senior executives, putting in 90-hour weeks as he moved from territory to territory, store to store. (The work ethic of the Brennan family also carried over to his younger brother, Bernard, who after becoming a Sears buyer eventually wound up as head of Montgomery Ward, Sears's long-time merchandising rival.)

Somehow, the success pattern of Brennan, based on hard work and a firm dedication to his company, proved vulnerable in this top corporate job. Perhaps no one could have resurrected the company in the dynamic environment of the 1980s, but perhaps the task could have been better performed by an outsider, someone not part of the glory days of Sears.

The basic thrust of Sears' merchandising policies had historically been to provide standard-quality goods at low prices, thereby appealing to lower- and middle-income America, but several times the company had tried to upgrade and become fashion-oriented for more affluent customers. These attempts had little success; indeed, in the process of such upgrading, Sears risked losing its mainstream customers.

When Brennan took over as president in 1980, his emphasis was on quality, assortment, and service:

We've adopted quality as our number one strategy for the years ahead. . . . The customer also expects to go into a store and find that store fully stocked. The customer wants good service. It's the store that puts all those things together best that will get the best market share.[2]

Brennan continued the centralization of major policy decisions in Chicago and began revamping stores with more aisles, lower ceilings, and better displays. In addition to the house brands, such as Craftsman tools, Kenmore appliances, and Diehard batteries, which had strong consumer acceptance, Brennan introduced such national apparel brands as Levi, Wrangler, and Wilson. Despite these changes, the merchandise group continued to slip in profits and market share.

In Brennan's tenure the financial services areas began contributing the bulk of the growth in sales and profits. The company was close to achieving the goal of meeting both the shopping and financial-services needs of middle America, a strategy sometimes described as "socks and stocks." Revenues of financial services had grown from $9.5 billion in 1982 to $26 billion in 1991. Even more impressive, the profits of financial services had reached $1.1 billion in 1991, far outstripping the merchandising group profits of $485 million. Table 8.3 illustrates the trend in relative profits of these two areas. Despite the profitable growth of financial services, the erosion of the core merchandising business was troubling.

Brennan, who had been elected chairman and chief executive in 1985, by no means ignored the retailing end of the business. He introduced the

Table 8.3   Contribution of Total Net Income of Financial Services and Merchandising Group, 1970– 1991 (millions)

Year	Net Income	*Financial*		*Merchandising*	
		Amount	*%*	*Amount*	*%*
1970	468	125	27	343	73
1975	523	129	25	394	75
1977	838	474	57	364	43
1979	830	549	66	281	34
1982	861	429	50	432	50
1985	1,294	528	41	766	59
1988	1,454	930	64	524	36
1991	1,586	1,100	69	486	31

Source: Sears annual reports.

Commentary: Note the increasingly subordinate role in corporate profits of the merchandising group in recent years, falling to only 31 percent of total in 1991, the lowest level ever.

[2]Joseph Winski, "New President Hopes to Strike Balance at Sears," *Chicago Tribune* (March 17, 1980), p. 10, sec. 5.

first "store of the future" in King of Prussia, Pennsylvania, in 1982, shortly after assuming the presidency. By 1989 all Sears stores fit this more modern prototype. He had tried various programs to promote the clothing end of the business, using supermodel Cheryl Tiegs and tennis star Yvonne Goolagong to spur apparel sales, but had no apparent success. He even tried "everyday low prices," the strategy used by Wal-Mart and Kmart for customers tired of the "sales" game. Sears announced this strategy with much fanfare in 1989, but it also bombed because the high overhead structure of Sears did not allow it to give its customers rock-bottom prices. Despite the disappointments of these strategic ventures, let us note a great potential advantage that retail chain organizations have, as described in the following information box.

INFORMATION BOX

ADVANTAGES OF CHAINS: OPPORTUNITY FOR EXPERIMENTATION

An organization with numerous similar outlets has an unparalleled opportunity for experimenting with all kinds of new ideas in the quest for what strategy might be most productive and compelling. Prospective strategy changes can be tested with a few stores, any promising modifications can be determined, and the success of the strategy can be ascertained from concrete sales and profits results. All this can be done with relatively little risk by involving only a few outlets of the total chain, and the strategy can be adopted throughout the organization only if results look favorable. Such experimentation is hardly possible for a firm with few comparable units, which describes most manufacturers, so the risks in making major strategic changes are greater for such companies.

INVITATION TO DISCUSSION
How would you design an experiment for a chain organization? Be as specific as you can, and make any assumptions necessary.

The great strength of the Sears retail operation had long been its home improvement area (e.g., paint, power tools, siding, hardware, tires). These durable goods accounted for almost 70 percent of Sears' revenues from merchandise. But now even that area was suffering. Such upstart competitors as Home Depot and Builders Square robustly gained market share at Sears' expense.

SEPTEMBER 30, 1992

In a special meeting, Sears directors approved a program to spin off the Dean Witter Financial Services Group, most of its Coldwell Banker real-estate holdings, and 20 percent of its Allstate insurance unit. The moves would reduce Sears' heavy debt by $3 billion. Sears would essentially be taken back to where it was in 1981, when Brennan first assumed the office of president, except that Sears' retail business had since lost its dominance.

The idea of spinning off subsidiaries was nothing new; it had been urged by some shareholders in the past. The assumption behind any such move is that the whole of the company is worth less than the sum of its parts. Therefore, shareholders would benefit. Some estimated that the breakup of the company could bring $80 to $90 a share, versus the low $40s for the entire firm.[3]

Still, the suddenness and the completeness of the directors' decision was surprising, and Sears became the center of focus in the business press. Besides the slowly deteriorating state of the retail business, several other factors probably led to the abrupt decision. In recent months Sears auto centers had received bad publicity about overcharging customers, and Hurricane Andrew had created huge claims for the Allstate unit. On September 25, 1992, Moody's Investors' Services lowered Sears' credit rating.

The decision was described in headlines as a humbling move for Brennan, since he had been the architect of most of the diversification efforts.[4] Despite the plaudits of some investors and a strong $3.375 rise in the stock price the next day, the drop in credit rating raised serious concerns.

Spinning off the healthiest sectors of the business meant that the underperforming retail sector would no longer be buttressed by the same level of financial support. The weaknesses of its operation would be more visible to the public and could not be covered up or hidden in corporate total statistics. With a retail turnaround likely to be slow if it happened at all, Sears made the paradoxical decision to go with its losers and get rid of its winners.

ACCUSATIONS OF FRAUD AT SEARS AUTO CENTERS

On June 12, 1992, national publications reported that the California Department of Consumer Affairs had accused Sears of systematically overcharging auto-repair customers. The agency even went so far as to propose revoking the company's license to operate its automotive centers in the state.

---

[3]Jeff Bailey, "Sears Stock Fails to Show Further Rally," *The Wall Street Journal* (October 1, 1992), p. A4. Also, Robert A. G. Monks, "Sears and the Shareholder," *The Wall Street Journal* (October 1, 1992), p. A16.

[4]Gregory A. Patterson and Francine Schwadel, "Sears Suddenly Undoes Years of Diversifying Beyond Retailing Field," *The Wall Street Journal* (September 30, 1992), p. A1.

The year-long undercover investigation had been prompted by a growing number of consumer complaints, such as the following.

> Ruth Hernandez of Stockton, California went to Sears to buy new tires for her 1986 Honda Accord. The Sears mechanic insisted that she also needed new struts at a cost of $419.95. Shocked, she sought a second opinion, and another auto-repair store told her the struts were fine. Hernandez was livid and she returned to Sears where a sheepish mechanic admitted the diagnosis was wrong. "I keep thinking," Hernandez reflected, "how many other people this has happened to."[5]

The Department of Consumer Affairs found that its agents were overcharged at Sears Centers nearly 90 percent of the time by an average of $233. The department said that repairmen were pressured to overcharge because Sears set punitive sales quotas. "This is a flagrant breach of the trust and confidence the people of California have placed in Sears for generations," said Jim Conran, director of the Department of Consumer Affairs. "Sears has used trust as a marketing tool, and we don't believe they've lived up to that trust."[6]

The Sears case may be the biggest fraud action ever taken against an auto-repair firm. Although the investigation was conducted in California, the findings seemingly represented a much more widespread problem, perhaps involving Sears's 850 auto-repair centers nationwide.

At first Sears vigorously contested the allegations. It called the accusations by California regulators politically motivated and denied any fraud. The company accused regulators of trying to gain support at a time when they were threatened by severe budget cuts. Sears's lawyers held this position for several days, but the crisis intensified, especially a few days later when New Jersey regulators said that they, too, had found overcharges common in Sears shops.

Sears soon adopted a more conciliatory stance, taking out full-page ads in major newspapers. The ads, in the form of a letter from Chairman Brennan, expressed deep concern about the problem and pledged that Sears would satisfy all its customers: "With over two million automotive customers serviced last year in California alone, mistakes may have occurred. However, Sears wants you to know that we would never intentionally violate the trust customers have shown in our company for 105 years." But auto-service sales dropped 15 percent. And this was a division that produced 9 percent of Sears's merchandising group's revenues and which had been one

---

[5]Example taken from Keven Kelly, "How Did Sears Blow This Gasket?" *Business Week* (June 29, 1992), p. 38.

[6]Tung Yin, "Sears Is Accused of Billing Fraud at Auto Centers," *The Wall Street Journal* (June 12, 1992), B1, B6.

of the fastest growing and most profitable business units in recent years, servicing 20 million vehicles in 1991.[7]

WHAT WENT WRONG?

Sears merchandising efforts represent a classic example of nonresponse to a changing environment. While Brennan made some efforts to institute change —stores of the future, brand-name merchandise, and everyday low prices, for example—these tactics were really only surface gestures of little consequence.

Of much more import, Sears allowed aggressive competitors to capture ever more market share. Sears ignored sweeping changes in demographics and shopping habits, under the assumption that the Sears way of doing business was unassailable, but all the while it was losing business: It lost customers to department stores who offered customers more ambience; to discounters and specialty stores (such as Toys "Я" Us, Home Depot, and Circuit City) that focused on a single category of goods but offered huge assortments at low prices; and to Wal-Mart and Kmart stores that offered the widest possible variety of goods at prices that Sears simply could not match.

In its many decades of retail dominance, Sears had built up a bureaucratic organizational structure. This progression is common for organizations as they achieve great size and dominance over decades. The following information box discusses the bureaucratic type of organization.

INFORMATION BOX

THE BUREAUCRATIC ORGANIZATION

The bureaucratic organization is a natural consequence of size and age. Its characteristics include the following:

A clear-cut division of labor

A strict hierarchy of authority

Staffing by technical competence

Formal rules and procedures

Impersonal approaches to decision making[8]

---

[7]Gregory A. Patterson, "Sears's Brennan Accepts Blame for Auto Flap," *The Wall Street Journal* (June 23, 1992), pp. B1, B12.

[8]This section is adapted from John R. Schermerhorn, Jr., *Management for Productivity*, 4th ed. (New York: Wiley, 1993), pp. 311–312.

While such a well-structured organization would appear to be best in many circumstances, it tends to be too rigid. It relies heavily on rules and procedures and as a result is often slow to adapt to change. Red tape usually predominates, as do many layers of hierarchy, an abundance of staff, and overspecialization. Consequently, creativity and initiative are stifled, and communication between upper management and lower operations is cumbersome and often distorted. Perhaps even more serious, a bureaucratic organization, with its entrenched administrators and staff positions, has a built-in high overhead that makes it difficult to compete against low-cost competitors.

A bureaucratic organization does not have to be inevitable as a firm attains large size and dominance, as shown in Table 8.4: A firm can still mold itself as an adaptive organization. But the temptation is otherwise.

INVITATION TO DISCUSSION:
Can you identify the type of person who tends to work best in a bureaucracy? The one who performs worst in this setup?

As a natural consequence of Sears' organization structure, the company failed to respond well to a rapidly changing environment and was burdened with overhead costs so high that it was unable to match the prices of its most aggressive competitors. For example, in 1991 Sears spent 29.2 percent of its revenues on salaries, light bills, advertising, and other routine costs. At the same time, Kmart's expenses amounted to 19.6 percent of its sales, and Wal-Mart's were even less, at 15.3 percent.[9] Sears was left somewhere in between department stores and discount stores. By no means did it offer the ambience and fashion atmosphere of good department stores, and it certainly could not profitably match the prices of its discount competitors. Observers wondered whether Sears had become an anachronism, an impotent throwback to an earlier time, now sadly out of place and competitively most vulnerable.

Table 8.4   Contrasts of Bureaucratic and Adaptive Organizations

Organizational Aspects	Bureaucratic	Adaptive
Hierarchy of authority	Centralized	Decentralized
Rules and procedures	Many	Few
Division of labor	Precise	Open
Spans of control	Narrow	Wide
Coordination	Formal and impersonal	Informal and personal

Source: John R. Schermerhorn, Jr., *Management for Productivity*, 4th ed. (New York: Wiley, 1993), p. 312.

[9]Stephanie Strom, "Further Prescriptions for the Convalescent Sears," *The New York Times* (October 1, 1992), p. D1.

Perhaps Sears let its attention shift too far from its core retail business in its quest for diversification into financial services. Brennan was the second Sears chairman to see the stores as a great vehicle for disseminating certain kinds of consumer services in addition to merchandise. Certainly, the logic seemed inescapable. (See the following issue box.)

In the last decade at least, the basic business of Sears appears to have been relatively neglected, as attention turned more to services. Perhaps this would also have happened without diversification. It could well be argued that the lack of substantial change and innovation in the retail operation resulted from a smug and complacent organization.

During the late 1970s and the 1980s, U.S. store space doubled, yet Sears failed to add retail space in this period. (See Table 8.1 for the trend in number of stores.) Instead, Sears concentrated on closing unprofitable stores and remodeling others. Naturally it lost market share. Its share of sales of

ISSUE BOX

SHOULD RETAILERS DIVERSIFY INTO SERVICES?

Although merchandising of services may seem far afield of traditional retailing and its merchandising of goods, in some ways consumer services are natural areas for expansion. This is especially true for the retailer with a reputation for dependability and a sizable body of loyal customers with active charge accounts. Sears led most retailers in such diversifications. Much of Sears' success in promoting its home repair, appliance servicing, and auto service was due to its image of offering reliability, honesty, and guaranteed satisfaction. Many customers believed these characteristics to be sorely needed in repair industries, where honest work and dependability were usually lacking. People *trusted* Sears. (Unfortunately, their trust received a setback in mid-1992 with the bad publicity about the auto centers).

Financial services—insurance, investments, and real estate—are viewed by many middle-class Americans as just as arcane and subject to abuse as repair services. It seemed natural that a trusting relationship regarding Sears' quality and dependability could be transferred also to this area. And indeed there was a mutual compatibility, as the success of financial services in the Sears organization has proven.

Unfortunately, corporate executives boosted this end of the total operation until late 1992 but allowed Sears' core business to slip, perhaps irretrievably.

INVITATION TO DISCUSSION

On balance, was the Sears' diversification wise?
Given that the core business is not neglected in the promotion of services, do you see any other dangers in such diversification?

department store merchandise in the United States dropped to less than 6 percent from more than 8 percent.[10] Sears catalog sales also stagnated, despite a boom in catalogs of all kinds during this period.

The 1980s was also a time of rapid expansion of specialty stores, stores featuring limited lines of merchandise but great depth within the categories. Some of these stores were highly successful, such as Limited, Gap, and such discount specialty stores as Toys "Я" Us and Kids "Я" Us. Sears dabbled a bit with specialty stores during this period, opening Business Systems Centers, separate paint and hardware stores, a small chain of eye-care products, and one chain of petite women's clothing stores. It also acquired the Western Auto chain of automotive supplies stores. But the efforts seemed too little too late to capitalize on this specialty store trend.

WHAT CAN BE LEARNED?

Neglect core business at your peril. Unless the prospects for a firm's core business are so bleak that resources and efforts need to be shifted, it is a monumental mistake to neglect the core. This core is where the company's expertise is: It is the focal point of the heritage of success. The core should not be neglected in the quest for exciting but often unproven new ventures. Yet Sears was guilty of this: It shifted attention from retailing of goods to merchandising of financial services. While these diversifications were successful, the deemphasis of the flagship part of its business may never be surmounted.

Again, beware the "king of the hill" three Cs mindset. In Chapter 2, on IBM, we encountered this destructive mindset that weakens frontrunners: conservatism, complacency, and conceit. Like IBM, Sears has lost responsiveness to changing conditions because of this pervasive orientation. You may want to review Chapter 2, in which we discussed how a large and mature organization can guard against such a mindset.

Can great size be achieved without becoming a bureaucratic organization? Although a firm naturally evolves into a bureaucratic organization as it becomes larger and more dominant in its industry, it can guard against this tendency. A firm can seek the adaptive organizational structure illustrated in Table 8.4, emphasizing decentralization, minimization of rules and procedures, an open and flexible division of labor, a wide span of control, and informal and personal coordination. With this orientation, a firm can avoid becoming a ponderous organization with high overhead. But it takes a strong

---

[10]Patterson and Schwadel, op. cit., p. A16.

top management commitment, a commitment to minimize the insularity of the executive suite and to stop cultivating ever more staff positions.

INVITATION

What additional learning insights do you see coming from the Sears case?

QUESTIONS

1. Do you think Sears's retail business can be turned around? Why or why not?
2. How would you propose streamlining the Sears bureaucratic organization? Be as specific as you can. If you need to make assumptions, state them clearly.
3. What is your opinion of the Sears auto-repair centers? Do you think their overcharging was less than, worse than, or about the same as that of their competitors? What led you to this opinion?
4. A common practice of repair people in all areas is to replace some parts that are worn but still workable with new parts. This, of course, raises the price of the repair. But is this really such a bad practice? After all, the new parts should assume longer trouble-free use of the car.
5. Overreliance on promotion from within often is more harmful than desirable to an organization. Evaluate the promotion of Ed Brennan.
6. Evaluate the 1993 decision to drop the Sears catalog. What arguments can you see for keeping it?

INVITATION TO ROLE PLAY

1. It is 1980, and you are the staff assistant to the president of Sears. You sense that major shifts in retailing are emerging and that Sears needs to change if it is to keep its market dominance.
   (a) What research would you recommend for tracking competitive thrusts?
   (b) Based on what we know today, what actions should Sears have taken in the 1980s? Do you think these efforts would have been successful in preserving market dominance? Why or why not?
2. You are an executive assistant to Edward Brennan, CEO of Sears. He wants to institute sweeping reforms in the auto-repair operational units. What arguments might you give him not to push the panic

button but to institute only very modest changes? What counterarguments would you expect?

INVITATION TO RESEARCH

What is the current situation with Sears? Is Brennan still the CEO? Have sweeping changes been started? Has the auto-repair business had any more negative publicity?

9

Campeau Corporation— A Raider Finds Indigestion

The 1980s was a time of frenzied takeovers and leveraged buyouts (LBOs). Sometimes the buyers were friendly; more often they were hostile raiders, making their powerful challenges with heavily borrowed funds, usually so-called junk bonds. These provided the lender with high interest, but also with greater risk of default than many other investments.

A major player in the latter 1980s was Robert Campeau, a French Canadian real-estate developer. In May 1988, Campeau scored a major victory over R.H. Macy & Co. in a bitter battle for Federated Department Store Corporation and its prestigious division, Bloomingdale's. Less than two years earlier, he had acquired another major department store corporation, Allied Stores. A retailing empire was his.

He was soon to find these acquisitions too big to swallow.

ROBERT CAMPEAU

Campeau's is an intriguing rags-to-riches story. He grew up as the eighth of 13 children in the mining town of Sudbury, Ontario. His father was an auto mechanic. Robert left school at 14 to help support the family. He swept garage floors at a local mining company.

By 1949 he was a factory supervisor. During his free time, Campeau built a house in Ottawa for his wife and young child. However, instead of moving them in, he sold the place for $3000 profit, doubling his money.

Thus, encouraged, he went on to build 40 more houses that year, and that was the beginning of his road to great wealth.

In the 1950s and 1960s he gained not only his fortune but a reputation as a master builder. He put up 20,000 houses around Ottawa; he was the first to build on Toronto's lakefront, now one of the city's priciest areas; he went on to be a major builder for the Canadian government. He became good friends with Pierre Trudeau, then Prime Minister of Canada, and they frequently went on ski trips.

His ambition led him to attempt several corporate takeovers in Canada, including that of Royal Trustco Ltd., one of Canada's oldest and richest trust companies. All these attempts failed, and he blamed prejudice of British-descent financiers against a French Canadian. So he turned his sights south. With the acquisition of Federated, his empire consisted of 382 department stores.

What kind of boss is Robert Campeau? He has been widely characterized as eccentric, emotional, ego-driven—some call his a mercurial temperament—hardly an easy man to work for. One talented executive, Robert H. Morsky, former vice chairman of the successful Limited Stores, worked with Campeau for only two months before leaving after a clash of egos. Campeau has been known to call employees at 3 A.M. He berates executives publicly, even shrieking at them. He is even accused by former associates of cheating them at golf. One former executive who worked briefly for Campeau characterized him as having an "Ivan the Terrible management style."[1] Naturally, Campeau had trouble keeping competent executives.

The Acquisition Binge

After failing in takeover attempts in Canada, Campeau turned his attention to the United States with a vengeance in 1986. In his quest for major acquisitions, he found an expensive takeover expert and investment banker in Bruce Wasserstein and First Boston Corporation. Allen Finkelson, a partner of a New York law firm was another key player. They found Campeau eager to take risks with little concern for debt accumulation or liquidity constraints.

Although he knew nothing about retailing, Campeau bought Allied Stores Corporation, an operator of such department stores as Jordan Marsh, for $3.4 billion in December 1986. Then, in May 1988, he won the highly publicized 10-week battle to gain Federated and its Bloomingdale's upscale department stores—and paid a premium price of $6.6 billion to do so—in a bidding war with Macy's. In the process he incurred hefty expenses: $167

---

[1]Kate Ballen, "Campeau Is on a Shopper's High," *Fortune* (August 15, 1988), pp. 70–74.

million in golden parachutes and other stock buyouts for former Federated executives; over $200 million in investment banking, legal, and other fees; and $150.5 million for bridge-loan fees and interest to First Boston Corp., and two other investment bankers.

The classic strategy of raiders who are willing to incur mountainous debt to gain the takeover has been to sell off some of the assets, some of the divisions they acquire, and thus pay off a portion of the debt. Thereby, they supposedly should be able to handle the interest payments on the remainder of the debt. Campeau was no different.

By late 1988, he had cut over $6 billion from his debt load by selling certain divisions of Allied and Federated. He raised $1.2 billion by selling Allied's Brooks Brothers and Ann Taylor divisions and Federated's Gold Circle, Main Street, and Children's Place Stores. He wanted to keep the Jordan Marsh and Maas Brothers chains that had produced almost two-thirds of Allied's profits in 1986 before he bought it. Table 9.1 shows his "empire" after his initial pruning of assets. Campeau wanted to retain some of Federated's best stores: Bloomingdale's, Lazarus, Abraham & Straus, Burdines, and Rich's/Goldsmiths. He slashed expenses by $125 million a year at Allied and by $250 million at Federated, mostly by eliminating employees. For example, he eliminated 5000 jobs at Federated alone. By early 1989, further sales of Federated's specialty and discount stores were expected to bring total debt down to $5.6 billion. It appeared that the combined cash flow of Allied and Federated should amount to about twice the $600 million needed for interest payments, a comfortable margin.

Table 9.1   Campeau's Holdings, Summer 1989, after Initial Asset Sales

Allied Stores Corp.:
   Jordan Marsh, 26 stores—Connecticut, Maine, Massachusetts, New Hampshire, New York, Rhode Island
   Maas Brothers-Jordan Marsh, 28 stores—Florida, Georgia
   Stern's, 24 stores—Pennsylvania, New Jersey, New York
   The Bon, 39 stores—Idaho, Montana, Oregon, Utah, Washington, Wyoming

Federated Department Stores:
   Abraham & Straus, 15 stores—New Jersey, New York
   Bloomingdale's, 17 stores—Connecticut, Florida, Massachusetts, Maryland, New Jersey, New York, Pennsylvania, Texas, Virginia
   Burdines, 30 stores—Florida
   Lazarus, 43 stores—Indiana, Kentucky, Michigan, Ohio, West Virginia
   Ralphs Supermarkets, 132 stores—California
   Rich's/Goldsmith's, 26 stores—Alabama, Georgia, South Carolina, Tennessee

Campeau had other plans. He believed that both Allied and Federated could be streamlined by consolidating their backroom operations and by motivating executives through stock options. And he saw the possibility of a *real synergy of real estate and retailing.*

In capitalizing on the possible synergy of real estate and retailing, Campeau planned to open three to five shopping centers annually in partnership with Edward DeBartolo, the shopping center czar, who had originally loaned Campeau $480 million. With Campeau's prestigious stores anchoring such shopping malls, there would be no difficulty attracting other retail tenants. Campeau also planned to expand the Bloomingdale's chain by 17 stores over the coming five years.

INFORMATION BOX

SYNERGY

Synergy is the creation of a whole that is greater than the sum of its parts. Thus, the whole can accomplish more than the total of the individual contributions. In an acquisition, synergy occurs if the two or more entities, when combined, are more efficient, productive, and profitable than they were as individual operations before the merger.

How can such synergy occur? If duplication of efforts can be eliminated, if operations can be streamlined, if economies of scale are possible, if specialization can be enhanced, if greater financial and managerial resources can be tapped—then a synergistic situation is likely to occur. Such an expanded operation should be stronger than any single part that existed.

In theory, the concept of synergism is a mighty stimulus for acquisitions and for the investors who make them possible. But sometimes the combination of efforts causes the reverse: negative synergy, where the combined effort is worse than the sum of individual efforts. If friction arises between the entities, if organizational missions are incompatible, if the new organizational climate creates fearful, resentful, and frustrated employees, then synergy is unlikely. And if greater managerial and financial resources are not realized—if indeed financial resources are depleted because of the credit demands due to the acquisition—then synergy becomes negative. The whole, then, is less than the sum of its parts. This situation is an organizational blunder on a grand scale. Unfortunately, this would prove to be the case with Campeau.

INVITATION TO DISCUSSION

Do you think a typical committee or group has more synergy than the same individuals working alone? Why or why not?

Trouble!

Just 18 months after scoring the major victory over Macy's and obtaining Federated, the dream became a nightmare. By September 1989, Campeau needed cash, a lot of it, and quickly. By now the company was carrying almost $11 billion in short- and long-term debt, and the annual interest burden was more than $1 billion. By December 1 Federated owed $401 million in notes to First Boston Corporation.

The first inklings of trouble were encountered the year before, in November 1988. This was the Christmas season, with its heavy short-term borrowing needs and Campeau's ability to tap previous lenders was petering out. Underwriters at First Boston had failed to sell a $1.5 billion offering of junk bonds for the Federated unit. They had scaled back the offering to $750 million but still could not find sufficient investors and had to keep a large portion of the bonds themselves. These underwriters were "burned," because Federated bonds dropped 20 percent and bonds of Allied Stores declined 45 percent. Other financing by bonds fell through as well, with the public becoming skittish about junk bonds.

But working capital was rapidly depleting at both Allied and Federated stores. At the same time, costs remained high despite Campeau's efforts to reduce overhead. While Campeau was able to weather the Christmas 1988 borrowing needs, now another Christmas season was looming, with most of this merchandise payable in October. The situation was critical if his stores were to have merchandise to sell during the peak selling season. With apparently nowhere else to turn, Campeau finally approached Olympia & York, owned by the wealthy Reichmann family of Toronto, from whom he had already borrowed substantially in his acquisition drives.

The Climax

On September 11, 1989, *USA Today* reported in a cover story that Bloomingdale's, the "jewel" of Campeau's "retail empire," was on the block, up for sale.[2] Indeed, only Bloomingdale's, with its high-fashion image, would return in one shot the kind of cash Campeau needed to meet interest payment deadlines. Analysts estimated that it would sell for $1 to $1.5 billion: None of the other divisions would individually bring in that much. And Bloomingdale's, of all his acquisitions, was the asset Campeau prized the most.

---

[2]Patricia Gallagher, "Bloomie's on Block in Bid to Buy Time," *USA Today* (September 11, 1989), pp. 1B, 2B.

By the end of the week, the headlines trumpeted that Campeau had saved his retail kingdom, that he had convinced the Reichmanns to give him a crucial $250 million loan to keep the corporation afloat. However, to arrange this Campeau had to give up control of the company. An Olympia & York executive, Lionel G. Dodd, was named chair of a four-person committee formed to oversee the restructuring, and Campeau was conspicuously left off the panel. Expectations were widespread that several more divisions, in addition to Bloomingdale's, would be put up for sale.

Outcome

By early 1990 the Campeau Corporation was on the verge of bankruptcy. Reputations and fortunes were being wrecked in the process. Robert Campeau was removed from active participation and relegated to real estate operations. He had lost wealth it took a lifetime to accumulate: nearly $500 million. Most of this fortune represented the paper losses on some 27.7 million shares of rapidly depreciating stock in his company; a good part of these shares had already been seized by creditors for nonpayment of loans. Perhaps as bad as his financial losses was the humiliation of falling from stardom.

The troubles also were enveloping the wealthy Reichmanns, who had badly misjudged the extent of the Campeau problems. Altogether, they were estimated to have invested more than $700 million in Campeau, with this stake largely depreciated.

The First Boston Corporation that had masterminded both Campeau takeovers and loaned its own money to help complete the deals now found itself with a soured reputation as well as hundreds of millions of dollars in losses, losses so substantial that Moody's downgraded its debt rating. Also hurt was Bruce Wasserstein, one of the guiding lights of Campeau's efforts, who now faced a loss of personal prestige and attractiveness as a consultant.

On January 15, 1990, the Campeau Corporation filed for Chapter 11 bankruptcy protection from its creditors.

ANALYSIS

Campeau had expected to meet his precarious financial obligations. What went wrong? Part of the trouble was that cash flow from these big retailers was considerably less than Campeau had expected because of sagging apparel sales nationally. But the day-to-day operations of the stores were also faltering. The layoffs may have cut into muscle as well as fat. Perhaps the pruning of thousands of jobs in order to cut overhead had severely strained management and staff operations. Such upheavals would demoralize any organization: Instead of tending to business, the employees would be fearful of losing their jobs. Even with heavy cutbacks, however, the cost-reduction plans were up to $200 million too optimistic.

Campeau paid far too much for the Federated purchase. A *Wall Street Journal* article claimed that he paid $500 million too much and that this was key to the financial problems.[3] Actually, Campeau had initially offered $4.2 billion for Federated, but he finally won at $6.6 billion.

The first asset sales went smoothly. In the spring and summer of 1988, Campeau sold Bullock's, I. Magnin, Foley's, and Filene's for $2.75 billion, and he spun off and refinanced Ralphs to generate $800 million in cash. But the remaining asset sales fell far short of expectations. Campeau expected to sell Gold Circle, MainStreet, The Children's Place, and assorted real estate for $727 million; instead, these brought only $562 million.

With inadequate asset sales, incomplete cost-cutting, and a grim look for apparel sales, this was a bad time to bring out Federated's $1.5 billion issue of junk bonds. Only $750 million of these were sold at exorbitant costs and interest rates. The stage was set for disaster for Campeau. Obviously, imprudent borrowing was at the heart of Campeau's troubles, but tides were turning against all corporate raiders who had amassed vast fortunes earlier in the 1980s. Many such acquired businesses were deeply in the red, and their huge debt payments were contributing to defaults that were beginning to play havoc on the junk bond market, the major source of marauder financing. The raider strategy of "using somebody else's money to leverage and strip a company to get rich . . . the days of the free ride" were nearing an end.[4]

Retailing presents a rather unique situation for working capital requirements, which makes highly leveraged operations more risky. The Christmas season accounts for one-third of the year's sales and about one-half of the year's profits. But to achieve this requires a heavy inventory buildup, which calls for substantial short-term funds. In addition, Federated and Allied divisions needed money for a number of longer-term projects, such as developing private-label goods (which carry a higher profit margin) and normal remodeling and refurbishing of stores. Then heavy leverage left little cushion for such financial needs. Already in 1989 another department-store takeover, that of Bonwit Teller and B. Altman stores by Australia's Hooker Corporation, had gone into Chapter 11 bankruptcy.

---

[3]Jeffrey A. Trachtenberg, Robert Melnbardis, and David B. Hilder, "An Extra $550 Million Paid for Federated Got Campeau in Trouble," *The Wall Street Journal* (January 11, 1990), pp. A1, A6.

[4]John Greenwald, "The Big Comeuppance," *Time* (December 11, 1989), pp. 74–76.

INFORMATION BOX

TRANSFERABILITY OF MANAGEMENT SKILLS

Are management skills transferable to other companies and other industries? The common belief is that they are, that the successful manager or administrator in one situation will be able to use these skills and talents effectively in other endeavors, even those completely unrelated to the particular industry experience.

But we see a paradox with Campeau. A hugely successful real estate magnate and developer, he acted more like a babe in the woods in his retail empire building. He vastly overestimated his sales and cash flow projections, and he greatly underestimated his ability to pare expenses and sell off assets. He completely miscalculated the substantial financial needs of major retail stores in their buildup of inventories for the peak Christmas selling season, and he practically destroyed a smooth-functioning organization and its morale.

Could it be that there is a limit to the transferability of management skills? Could it be that at least with retailing, the outsider needs a considerable period of adjustment and learning before being able to effectively take the reins? Or could it be that skill as a raider and as a financial manipulator does not prepare one for operational management? Although we can hardly generalize to all individuals and all situations, the Campeau debacle casts some doubts on the cherished notion of complete and easy transferability of managerial skills. Other raiders, such as T. Boone Pickens and Carl Icahn, have also had difficulty in operating their conquests.

INVITATION TO DISCUSSION
Can you formulate some guidelines as to when managerial skills are likely to be transferable and when they are not transferable?

CONTRAST: A & W—A HIGHLY LEVERAGED BUYOUT THAT SUCCEEDED

Lest we conclude that all takeovers involving heavy borrowing are ill-advised, reckless, and imprudent, let us look at a positive justification. A & W Root Beer is part of America's motorized culture, with roadside stands dating back to 1919. But the draft root beer was not sold by the bottle until 1971, when it quickly became the top-selling root beer in the country, surpassing brands such as Hires and Dad's. Still, root beer was not nearly as popular as cola in the competition for shelf space.

In 1983 A & W's root beer syrup business was sold to a group of investors. Along with the concentrate business, the new owners also got Lou Lowenkron, who had come to A & W in 1980 after some 25 years in the soft-drink industry. He quickly found that new ownership did not mean money for expansion, and he thought a golden opportunity was being wasted by not capitalizing on the potentially powerful A & W name.

In 1986, Lowenkron engineered a leveraged buyout for $74 million, with $35 million in junk bonds. The buyout raised A & W's long-term debt to a dangerous 90 percent, but Lowenkron at last had full control of the company. Unlike Campeau and most of the other raiders, he had an intimate knowledge both of the company and of the industry. He quickly made some major moves. First, he introduced a cream soda, A & W's first line expansion in 70 years. Today, A & W holds one-half of the $350 million U.S. cream soda market. Then he bought the rights to three other brands: Squirt, a grapefruit soda; Country Time Lemonade; and Vernors, a spicy ginger drink. Together these three brands by 1989 accounted for more than one-third of A & W's revenues and about 40 percent of operating profit. Along with its beverage, A & W has emerged as the clear leader in niche soft drinks. For 1989 the company's sales surpassed $110 million, more than triple what they were before the buyout; profits reached $10 million, as compared with a small loss in 1986.[5]

What was the difference with Campeau? We see at least three major ways in which the A & W experience differed from that of Campeau and most other raiders:

1. Lowenkron, the leader of the buyout, was highly experienced in that particular industry.
2. He had a personal interest and had developed a real commitment to overcome the deficiencies of the present operation and ownership.
3. He brought innovation and fresh growth to a staid and conservative organization.

We must conclude that although highly leveraged buyouts are risky because of the heavy debt burden, they represent the means for good management to replace ineffective or overly conservative management.

WHAT CAN BE LEARNED?

The Campeau situation is by no means unique. It represents the great infatuation that raiders and investors had with leveraged buyouts and the ready acceptance of junk bond financing that made them possible. The fact that this acceptance of junk bond financing was to sour dramatically by 1989—hastened in large part by the highly publicized excesses of Campeau—

---

[5]For more details, see Edward Giltenan, "Root Beer Gloat," *Forbes* (December 11, 1989), pp. 156–160.

brought the collapse of such high-risk financing sooner than even the most pessimistic experts predicted.

Highly leveraged situations are extremely vulnerable, and this vulnerability does not need worsening economic conditions. During most of the 1980s, many managers, and not just raiders like Campeau, pursued a strategy of debt financing in contrast to equity (stock ownership) financing. Funds for such borrowing were usually readily available, heavy debt had income tax advantages, and profits could be distributed among fewer shares so that return on equity was enhanced. During this time a few voices decried the overleveraged situations of many companies. They predicted that when the eventual economic downturn came, many such firms would find themselves unable to meet the heavy interest burden. Most lenders paid little heed to such lonesome voices and encouraged greater borrowing.

The widely publicized problems of Campeau and the earlier problems of Hooker and other raiders suddenly changed the expansionist lending sentiments. The hard reality dawned that some of these arrangements were fragile indeed, especially when they rested on optimistic projections for asset sales, for revenues, and for cost savings to cover the interest payments. An economic slowdown proved unnecessary to bring down some of these ill-advised speculations.

We have to conclude that, in deciding on a heavy commitment to borrowed funds, managers should use a worst-case scenario in estimating cash flow sufficiency. Commitments that depend on optimistic projections and allow no room for more sobering developments should be shunned.

The synergy of mergers and acquisitions is suspect. As we discussed previously, the concept of synergy says that a new whole is better than the sum of its parts. Theoretically, this would seem possible since operations can be streamlined for more efficiency and since greater management and staff competence can be brought to bear, as greater financial and other resources can be tapped. Yet, we saw no synergy in Campeau's case, and none in Hooker's acquisitions; many other acquisitions lack synergy as well. More often such concentrations incur severe digestive problems—problems with people, systems, and procedures—that take time to resolve. Furthermore, greater size does not always beget economies of scale. The opposite may in fact occur: an unwieldy organization, slow to act, and vulnerable to more aggressive, innovative, and agile smaller competitors. The siren call of synergy is often an illusion.

Retailing presents unique working capital problems. These problems increase the risk of highly margined undertakings. The great seasonality and the substantial buildup of inventory necessary for the Christmas season causes working capital requirements for ordinary operations to present serious problems to highly leveraged situations. Campeau carelessly overlooked this.

Further adding to the seriousness of the liquidity needs, vendors become reluctant to ship needed goods at the first hints that they might not get paid. Any publicity about financial problems can play havoc with getting sufficient merchandise to meet Christmas selling needs—this proved true even for the prestigious Allied and Federated stores. Despite the cash transfusion of the Reichmann brothers, vendors were still concerned about Christmas shipments. A Dun & Bradstreet cautionary note, reported in the December 7, 1989 issue of *The Wall Street Journal*, exacerbated the problem. And a week later, one of the largest factoring companies in the country, Heller Financial, told its clients to stop shipping merchandise to Campeau's retailing operations.[6]

The positive aspects of organizational restructuring for acquisitions are becoming a myth. The idea of restructuring generally means downsizing in raider parlance. Some assets or corporate divisions are sold off, and the remaining organization is streamlined, which usually means lay-offs. The raider can thereby pay off some of the huge debt burden and generate more cash flow to cover the remaining interest payments.

The assumption is that the parts are worth more if sold than the corporation as a whole is valued by investors, as reflected in stock prices. The other assumption is that the organization has gotten fat and inefficient and that people and operations can readily be pruned.

For some years this strategy of restructuring or downsizing seemed to work fairly well, as eager investors bid up the prices of spun-off assets. But the investment mood changed, with disillusionment setting in. Campeau did not anticipate this change and could not sell some of his divisions for the expected prices. Another raider, L. J. Hooker Corp., was not even able to sell its B. Altman department-store chain and had to liquidate it.[7] By late 1989 many raiders in addition to Campeau were mired in debt, saddled with bankrupt companies, and finding, that they could not run companies as efficiently as the bosses they had ousted. Such well-known corporate raiders as Merv Griffin and T. Boone Pickens were among those having a rude awakening.[8]

Not the least of the emerging problems coming from the organizational restructuring of the leveraged buyouts was the demoralization of the organizations involved. Massive layoffs and forced retirements, complete reassignment of people, traumatic personnel and policy changes, and de-

---

[6]Jeffrey A. Trachtenberg, "Campeau Assails Dun & Bradstreet's Advice to Clients Not to Ship It Goods," *The Wall Street Journal* (December 7, 1989): A4; Jeffrey A. Trachtenberg, "Heller Financial Tells Clients to Halt Shipping Their Goods to Campeau Units," *The Wall Street Journal* (December 15, 1989), p. A3.

[7]Barbara Rudolph, "Debacle on 34th Street," *Time* (December 11, 1989), p. 77.

[8]Greenwald, op. cit.

struction of accustomed lines of communication and authority were hardly the inputs needed to preserve stability and motivation. Worse, in many instances the raiders, such as Campeau, began their restructuring and streamlining without sufficient assessment and preparation in their rush to try to free up working capital to meet hefty interest charges. The operational deficiencies of Federated stores after the Campeau takeover illustrate the negative consequences of hasty major "restructuring."

Great success tends to be ephemeral. We often find that great successes are not lasting, that they have no staying power. Somehow the success pattern gets lost or forgotten or is not well rounded. Other times an operation grows beyond the capability of the originator. Hungry competitors are always waiting in the wings, ready to take advantage of any lapse. An agglomeration of factors beset the corporate raiders of the late 1980s, but at least in some instances, the key delimiting factor was this: They could not manage.

The raiders were able to amass the financial strength for their acquisitions but could not handle the operational consequences. Staying power is the name of the game for lasting success. The comet that flares through the sky and dies brilliantly is hardly a lasting success, yet this describes many corporate buccaneers in the 1980s. They were a colorful and awesome presence—and they frightened many boardrooms—but they had awesome *egos*, which could be a strength but also a crucial weakness.

INFORMATION BOX

THE ROLE OF EGO

Reporters in the national press were quick to label Campeau's acquisition thrust as an ego trip, intimating that an inflated ego was behind a reckless expansion binge. Perhaps they were right. Coming from humble beginnings, Campeau—like many other highly successful people—felt an overwhelming drive to be successful. Ego drive, or profound ambition, may be a good thing. It can be the major fuel for hard work, personal advancement, and entrepreneurship. But ego needs to be harnessed: The drive can exceed the bounds of prudence. Immoderate ego can lead to excesses of spending—both personal and corporate spending. At this point ego is no longer a positive factor but a negative and even destructive influence. As with so many things, moderation appears key to most successes.

INVITATION TO DISCUSSION

Would you like to work for an executive with a strong ego-drive? What advantages and disadvantages for you personally would you see in doing so?

INVITATION

What additional learning insights does this case offer?

QUESTIONS

1. Campeau bought good, even the best, properties. How could he have gone so wrong?
2. Discuss the organizational mistakes in this case and how they might have been avoided.
3. Why did the concept of synergy appear to fail in this case?
4. Are management skills transferable to retailing institutions? Discuss.
5. What are the key differences between successful and unsuccessful leveraged buyouts in the present environment?
6. Why does it seem difficult to transfer financial management skills to operational management? Are entrepreneurial skills easily transferable? Are technological and engineering skills transferable?

INVITATION TO ROLE PLAY

1. As a management consultant, how would you advise Campeau on organizational restructuring after his initial acquisitions of Allied and Federated? Do you think these moves would have made any difference? Why or why not?
2. You are the president of Federated Department Stores. Campeau has just acquired your corporation and is threatening to reduce the workforce by 20%. What arguments can you marshal to persuade him to temper his cost-cutting frenzy?

INVITATION TO RESEARCH

What is Robert Campeau's present situation? The Reichmanns'? Federated's? Bloomingdale's?

10

Continental Airlines: Confrontational Destruction of an Organization

On December 3, 1990, Continental Airlines, the nation's fifth-largest airline company, collapsed into bankruptcy for the second time in less than a decade. In 1983 CEO Frank Lorenzo had taken Continental into bankruptcy court in order to abrogate its labor contracts. Now, in 1990, Lorenzo had loaded the airline with so much debt that Chapter 11 bankruptcy offered the only way to survive backbreaking interest payments. Yet Frank Lorenzo *had* achieved one of his objectives: He had destroyed the unions at both Continental and Eastern Airlines (one of his acquisitions).

THE FRANK LORENZO ERA

Lorenzo has proved to be a consummate manipulator, parlaying borrowed funds and little of his own money to an airline empire. By the end of 1986, he controlled the largest airline network in the non-Communist world: only Aeroflot, the Soviet airline, was larger. Lorenzo's network was a leveraged amalgam of Continental, People Express, Frontier, and Eastern, with $8.6 billion in sales—all this from a small investment in Texas International Airlines in 1971. In the process of building his network, Lorenzo defeated unions, shrewdly used the bankruptcy courts to further his ends, and eventually escaped from his own created mess worth $30.5 million. In the wake of his departure, his empire was swimming in red ink, had a terrible reputation, and was burdened with colossal debt and an aging fleet of planes.

Frank Lorenzo was born in New York City in 1940 of parents who had immigrated from Spain. When Frank was 15 years old, he took his first airplane trip, a TWA flight to London, and was so enamored with flying that upon returning he used his savings to buy stock in the company. In 1961 he graduated from Columbia University with a BA in economics. He had helped finance his education by working part-time as a Coca-Cola truck driver, for which he had to be a member of the Teamster's Union. (In later years, he liked to refer to this time as evidence that he did not deserve his antiunion reputation.) He then went on to earn an MBA from Harvard's Graduate School of Business Administration in 1963. During these years he was keenly interested in the biographies of famous entrepreneurs such as Andrew Carnegie and W. Averell Harriman.

Lorenzo's first job was as a financial analyst at Trans World Airlines. In 1966 he and Robert J. Carney, a buddy from Harvard, formed an airline consulting firm, and in 1969 the two put up $35,000 between them to form an investment firm, Jet Capital. Through a public stock offering they were able to raise an additional $1.15 million. In 1971 Jet Capital was called in to fix ailing Texas International and wound up buying it for $1.5 million. Lorenzo became president and CEO of Texas International in August 1972. He restructured the company's debt, eliminated unprofitable routes, added more lucrative routes, and was able to find funds to upgrade the airline's almost obsolete planes. He brought Texas International to profitability by instituting what he called "peanuts fares," offering discounts of as much as 50 percent on some routes.

In 1978 a new era of market competition was thrust on the airline industry when Congress passed the Airline Deregulation Act, a move that freed the airlines from economic regulation. In effect, managers were now free to decide what routes they would serve and what fares they would charge. This brought unaccustomed freedom to the industry, for which Lorenzo seemed well suited. The following issue box discusses the controversy of airline deregulation.

In 1978 acquisition-minded Lorenzo lost out to Pan Am in a bidding war for National Airlines, but he made $40 million on the National stock he had acquired in the takeover attempt. In 1980 he created nonunion New York Air and formed Texas Air as a holding company. In 1982 Texas Air bought Continental Airlines for $154 million.

Lorenzo's Treatment of Continental

In 1983 Lorenzo took Continental into bankruptcy court, filing for Chapter 11. This move permitted the corporation to continue to operate but spared

---

ISSUE BOX

AIRLINE DEREGULATION: BLESSING OR CURSE?

After 40 years of government regulation, the new freedom was a mixed blessing, for the carriers themselves as well as for the general public. The expectations that the public would pay lower prices was fulfilled, at least for the most competitive routes. But price competition also brought with it a maze of special prices and promotional deals with confusing stipulations and instability of prices. Meanwhile, the less competitive routes, usually those to middle-size cities, often experienced not only higher prices than those before deregulation but also diminished service.

Some experts feared that deregulation eventually would lead to monopoly pricing, as competitors were driven from the market. The higher prices to smaller cities appear to reflect this: The cities are not big enough to attract much competition, and prices have risen accordingly.

At first deregulation led to a large increase in the number of airlines, as newcomers challenged the established carriers. Just prior to deregulation there were 36 scheduled carriers; by the peak year 1984 there were 229.[1] Of these, 24 were large, well-known airlines. By 1991 only 13 of these 24 remained, and 6 were operating under conditions of bankruptcy or default. See Table 10.1. The critics of deregulation who feared greater concentration of firms could see their fears realized, as the five strongest airlines controlled approximately 75 percent of the market.[2] The competitive situation was not altogether grim, however, as smaller airlines, such as Air Reno and Miami Air, sought to exploit niche markets of little interest to the major airlines. And Southwest Air was the darling of the industry in the early 1990s, offering prices lower than the major carriers could match on certain routes. (See Chapter 6.)

Table 10.1   Major Scheduled Airlines, 1984 and 1991

1984	*1991*
Air Cal	Alaskan
Air Florida	American
Alaskan	American West[a]
American	Continental[a]
American West	Delta
Continental	Midway[a]

(continued)

[1]Robert M. Kane and Allan D. Vose, *Air Transportation* (Dubuque, Iowa: Kendall/Hunt, 1987), pp. 11–24.

[2]Michael Oneal, Wendy Zellner, and Seth Payne, "Fly the Lucrative Skies of United American Delta," *Business Week* (October 14, 1991), p. 90–91.

Delta	Northwest
Eastern	Pan Am[a]
Empire	Southwest
Frontier	Trump Shuttle[a]
Midway	TWA[a]
New York Air	United
Northwest	USAir
Ozark	
Pacific Southwest	
Pan Am	
People Express	
Piedmont	
Republic	
Southwest	
TWA	
United	
USAir	
Western	

[a]Operating in bankruptcy or default.
Source: Michael Oneal, Wendy Zellner, and Seth Payne, "Fly the Lucrative Skies of United American Delta," *Business Week* (October 14, 1991), p. 91.

INVITATION TO DISCUSSION
On balance, do you think deregulation has been a blessing or a curse? How good has it been for airline passengers? Has it helped the industry?

its obligation to meet heavy interest payments and certain other contracts while it reorganized as a more viable enterprise. The process nullified the previous union contracts, which prompted a walkout by many union workers. Lorenzo earned the lasting enmity of organized labor and the reputation as a union-buster as he replaced strikers with nonunion workers at much lower wages. (A few years later, he reinforced this reputation when he used the same tactics with Eastern Airlines.)

In a 1986 acquisition achievement that was to backfire a few years later, Lorenzo struck deals for a weak Eastern Air Lines and a failing People Express/Frontier Airlines. That same year Continental emerged out of Chapter 11 bankruptcy, and in February 1987, Texas Air shares soared to $51.50, an all-time high. Now Continental, with its nonunion workforce making it a low-cost operator, was Lorenzo's shining jewel. The low bid accepted for Eastern only reinforced Lorenzo's reputation as a visionary builder.

What kind of executive was Lorenzo? Although he is variously described as a master financier and visionary, his handling of day-to-day problems bordered on the inept.[3] One former executive was quoted as saying, "If he agreed with one thing at 12:15, it would be different by the afternoon."[4] Inconsistent planning and poor execution characterized his lack of good operational strength. Furthermore, his domineering and erratic style of managing alienated talented executives. In the decade from 1983 to 1993, nine presidents left Continental.[5]

But it was Lorenzo's handling of his unionized organizations that brought the most controversy. He became the central issue of confrontational labor–management relations, to a degree perhaps unmatched by any other person in recent years. Although he won the battle with Continental's unions and later with Eastern's, he was burdened with a costly strike by Eastern workers and the residue of ill feeling that impeded any profitable recovery during his time at the helm.

The Demise of Eastern Airlines

Eastern had an illustrious history, and the fact that it ended up ignominiously under Lorenzo's auspices perhaps should not reflect too badly on Lorenzo. The seeds of Eastern's downfall had been sown long before.

Eddie Rickenbacker was the most famous ace the United States produced during World War I, shooting down 22 enemy planes and receiving the Distinguished Service Cross, the Congressional Medal of Honor, and the French Croix de Guerre among other decorations. He became president of Eastern Air Lines in 1938 and served as chairman of the board from 1954 to 1963. But this American hero made a bad decision for Eastern at the start of the jet age: He cancelled an order for DC-8 jets, figuring that his airline could still get by with propeller-driven planes. Delta Air Lines picked up Eastern's order and used the new jets to establish air supremacy over Eastern.

Rickenbacker's successors seemed more interested in enjoying lavish perks and adding expensive layers to management than in addressing fundamental problems. A key problem facing Eastern was its largely north–south routes. Such routes brought great seasonality and dependence on wintertime tourists as well as heavy competition on the heavily flown routes between New York and Miami.

---

[3]For example, Todd Vogel, Gail DeGeorge, Pete Engardio, and Aaron Bernstein, "Texas Air: Empire in Jeopardy," *Business Week* (March 27, 1989), p. 30.

[4]Mark Ivey and Gail DeGeorge, "Lorenzo May Land a Little Short of the Runway," *Business Week* (February 5, 1990), p. 48.

[5]Mary Schlangenstein, "Continental Tempering Celebration," *Cleveland Plain Dealer* (April 16, 1993), pp. E1, E2.

In 1976 another famous American became chairperson: Frank Borman, the former astronaut. By now Eastern was a notoriously high-cost airline with militant unions and a lousy reputation for service. Borman succeeded in lowering overhead and persuading employees to make wage concessions. He also moved to lessen Eastern's dependence on north–south routes by opening a hub in Kansas City. But, like Rickenbacker, he made a catastrophic decision.

Borman boldly invested a huge $1.4 billion in new fuel-efficient planes to replace an aging fleet. The timing could hardly have been worse: Eastern was left swimming in debt at the very time when deregulation hit the airline industry in 1978. Deregulation unleashed price competition that left marginal firms vulnerable. New competitors such as People Express launched fare wars on most of Eastern's major routes. Amid soaring losses, Borman attempted to get more pay cuts from the unions, but now the union turned rancorous and unyielding. In this environment of heavy losses and militant unions, the company in 1986 accepted the low offer of Lorenzo, the "union-buster" of Continental.

With tough contract demands and the stockpiling of $1 billion in cash as strike insurance, Lorenzo seemed eager to precipitate a strike that he might crush. He instituted a program of severe downsizing, and in 1989, after 15 months of fruitless talks, some 8500 machinists and 3800 pilots went on strike.

STRUGGLE TO SURVIVE

Lorenzo countered the strike at Eastern by filing for Chapter 11 bankruptcy. He replaced many of the striking pilots and machinists within months. The unions bitterly contested Lorenzo's leadership, and in the atmosphere of a "'holy war' against the infidel," as Eastern's bankruptcy lawyer, Harvey R. Miller, phrased it, the unions unsuccessfully asked the court to remove Lorenzo as Eastern's chairman, claiming that he was pillaging the firm.[6] Striking machinists picketed Continental at Houston and Newark hubs, and Eastern pilots sought to drag Continental into bankruptcy court.

To cover Eastern's growing losses and to appease creditors, Lorenzo sold gates, planes, and the lucrative Eastern shuttle, raising $850 million in cash. By August Eastern was working up to 390 flights daily, with almost 75 percent of seats filled.

At first Continental benefited from the strike at Eastern. Continental planes filled in on the busy New York–Miami routes, and many planes were carrying heavier passenger loads. Furthermore, by cutting back on

---

[6]Vogel et al., *op. cit.*, p. 30.

money-losing flights from the Denver hub and by building up the more profitable routes, such as those to the South Pacific, Continental boosted operating profits to $170 million in 1990 after losing $69 million in 1989 (however, the company still had a substantial net loss in 1990 after non-operating costs). Table 10.2 shows the revenues and net profits (or losses) of Continental and its major competitors from 1987 through 1991.

In the meantime, as Eastern appeared to be successfully weathering the strike and was building up its flights out of Miami, business dropped drastically late in 1989. Suddenly Eastern's planes were flying less than one-half full, and fuel costs were rising. Management slashed fares in order to regain business, and a liquidity crisis lurked in the wings. Then, on January 16, 1990, an Eastern jet sheared the top off a private plane in Atlanta. Even though the accident was attributed to air controller error, Eastern's name received the publicity.

Table 10.2   Performance Statistics, Major Airlines, 1987–1991

	Operating Revenues (millions of $s)				
	1991[a]	*1990*	*1989*	*1988*	*1987*
Continental	$4,031	$4,036	$3,896	$3,682	$3,404
American	9,309	9,203	8,670	7,548	6,369
Delta	8,268	7,697	7,780	6,684	5,638
United	7,850	7,946	7,463	7,006	6,500
Northwest	4,330	4,298	3,944	3,395	3,328
	Percent Gain, 1987–1991				
Delta	46.6%				
American	46.0%				
Northwest	30.1%				
United	20.8%				
Continental	18.4%				
	Net Income (Millions $s)				
Continental	($1,550)	($1,218)	(56)	(310)	(304)
American	(253)	(40)	412	450	225
Delta	(216)	(119)	467	286	201
United	(175)	73	246	426	22
Northwest	10	(27)	116	49	64

[a]Twelve months ending September.
Source: Department of Transportation.

Commentary: Note the operating performance of Continental relative to its major competitors during this period. It ranks last in sales gain. It far and away has the worst profit performance, having massive losses during each of the years in contrast to its competitors, who, while incurring some losses, had neither the constancy nor the magnitude of losses of Continental.

Eastern creditors were now despairing of Lorenzo's ability to pay them back in full. Three options were under consideration: Liquidate Eastern, sell it, or force a merger with Continental. Such a merger would expose Continental to the bankruptcy process. Also still to be resolved were how to fund Eastern's almost $700 million of pension liabilities.

On December 3, 1990, Continental again tumbled into bankruptcy, burdened with overwhelming debt and an unseemly reputation, another contribution of Frank Lorenzo. In January 1991 Eastern finally went out of business.

EMERGENCE FROM BANKRUPTCY, AGAIN

Lorenzo was gone from the scene. In April 1990 the bankruptcy judge for Eastern appointed trustee Martin R. Shugrue to run the airline. Then in August 1990, Lorenzo agreed to sell his interest in the former Texas Air Corp. (now called Continental Airlines Holdings, Inc.) to Scandinavian Airlines Systems for $30.5 million. Hollis L. Harris, a former Delta Air Lines president, replaced Lorenzo as chief executive. Harris faced a daunting task, but at least Lorenzo was gone.

The legacy of Eastern, however, remained. Creditors were claiming more than $400 million in disputed asset transfers between Eastern and Continental, and the federal Pension Benefit Guaranty Corporation wanted $680 million to cover Eastern's unfunded pension liabilities. Harris sought ways to get out from under Lorenzo's huge debt without gutting the company and destroying the customer base. He raised $150 million by selling the Seattle-Tokyo route to American Airlines, made another $50 million by selling the food-service unit, and froze $400 million in debt payments by filing for Chapter 11.

To its credit—the legacy of Lorenzo—Continental was still the lowest cost operator among major U.S. airlines. However, a poor reputation stymied its ability to get high-fare business travelers. This image also made it difficult to find lenders willing to restructure Continental's debt so that it could emerge from Chapter 11. Adding to this difficulty, Scandinavian Airlines Systems, with a 16.1 percent stake in Continental, planned to write down its $106 million investment—not an optimistic sign for would-be lenders.

All airlines were hurt by a sluggish market in 1991, but for Continental the year was a disaster: "We saw it was worse than we thought. We knew we had to change course."[7] The board brought in Robert R. Ferguson III,

---

[7]Mark Ivey, "The Mess at Continental: 'We had to Change Course,'" *Business Week* (August 5, 1991), p. 24.

veteran of Braniff and Eastern Air bankruptcies, to make changes, as the company continued to chew up top executives. The major criticism against Harris was that he had allowed costs to get out of control. He had matched rivals' fare cuts but had refused to order layoffs and other big cost-cutting measures. The rationale? "Everyone figured that after the [Persian Gulf] war, things would bounce back to normal."[8] But they did not, and, furthermore, Continental was still not attracting the full-fare business travelers.

Continental's problems appeared to be solved when it announced on November 9, 1992, that it had agreed to accept a bid by Air Canada and investor group Air Partners. With $450 million from its new partners, it should be able to escape from bankruptcy. Air Canada and Continental boasted to reporters that they would be able to exploit great synergies in route structure, purchasing, and maintenance.[9]

Despite the fact that the infusion of cash would enable Continental to escape from bankruptcy court, analysts questioned the wisdom of such an alliance between two weak entities. Air Canada was highly leveraged and hardly able to supply the resources Continental needed to reinvest in new equipment to keep up with stronger rivals.

On April 16, 1993, Robert Ferguson announced court approval of a reorganization plan enabling Continental to emerge from Chapter 11 protection. Thus the airline became the first carrier to have survived two bankruptcies. However, unlike the 1983–1986 episode, after which it repaid its creditors all they were owed, this time creditors got only pennies on the dollar; in addition, unsecured creditors took a 35.6 percent stake in the airline.[10]

Although Ferguson admitted that it was a leaner and stronger carrier than before bankruptcy—its debt burden of $1.8 billion was far lower than the $3.98 billion it entered bankruptcy with—he cautioned that it faced major internal struggles, a fiercely competitive and financially battered airline industry, and a shaky economy.[11] The firm now had cash reserves of $578 million, but cash might not last long under adverse circumstances, such as fuel price increases.[12] Still, despite its long history of travail, Continental in 1992 was the nation's fifth largest airline, behind American,

---

[8]Ibid.

[9]Andrea Rothman and William C. Symonds, "Continental: A Basket Case Rescued by a Weakling," *Business Week* (November 23, 1992), p. 40.

[10]Bridget O'Brian, "Judge Backs Continental Airlines Plan to Regroup, Emerge From Chapter 11," *The Wall Street Journal* (April 19, 1993), p. A4.

[11]Mary Schlangenstein, *op cit.*, E1, E2.

[12]"Another Chance for Continental," *Cleveland Plain Dealer* (April 19, 1993), p. B6.

United, Delta, and Northwest, and it served 193 airports. Table 10.3 illustrates the gain in market position of Continental and its major competitors form 1985 to 1992.

With the investment by Air Canada, Continental had taken a first step in pursuing global alliances—perhaps eventually with Air France and Germany's Lufthansa—thus joining other U.S. carriers in seeking mutually beneficial alliances. Such megacarriers, whose routes would span continents, could be the wave of the future.

ANALYSIS

The Legacy of Frank Lorenzo

Continental was savaged in its long tenure as a pawn in Lorenzo's dynasty-building efforts. He had saddled it with huge debts, brought it into bank-

Table 10.3 Airline Industry Concentration Changes, 1985–1991

| | Rank | | Market Share | | Percent Increase |
	1985	1991	1985	1991	
American	1	1	13.3%	20.7%	54.8%
United	2	2	12.5	19.7	57.6
Eastern	3	—	10.0	—	—
TWA	4	7	9.6	6.1	(36.5)
Delta	5	3	9.0	17.1	90.0
Pan Am	6	—	8.1	—	—
Northwest	7	4	6.7	12.4	85.0
Continental	8	5	4.9	9.2	87.8
People Express	9	—	3.3	—	—
Republic	10	—	3.2	—	—
USAir	—	6	—	7.5	
American West	—	8	—	2.9	
Southwest	—	9	—	2.5	
Alaska	—	10	—	1.2	
Others			19.4	0.7	

Source: Department of Transportation statistics, reported in Standard & Poor's *Industry Surveys*, Vol. 161, No. 7, Sec. 1 (Feb. 18, 1993), p. A3.

Commentary: Note the increase in concentration of most of the major carriers, with the exception of TWA, during these six years. Continental's increase of 87.8% in market share compares favorably with the other airlines. The increases in market share have occurred primarily due to the exit of weaker competitors, such as Eastern, Pan Am, People Express, and Republic.

INFORMATION BOX

IMPORTANCE OF A POSITIVE CORPORATE CULTURE

A corporate, or organizational, culture can be defined as the system of shared beliefs and values that develops within an organization and guides the behavior of its members.[13] Such a culture can be a powerful influence on performance results:

> If employees know what their company stands for, if they know what standards they are to uphold, then they are much more likely to make decisions that will support those standards. They are also more likely to feel as if they are an important part of the organization. They are motivated because life in the company has meaning for them.[14]

Lorenzo had destroyed the former organizational climate as he beat down the unions. The replacement employees had little reason to develop a positive culture or espirit de corps given the many top management changes, the low pay relative to other airline employees, and the continuous possibility of corporate bankruptcy. Employees had little to be proud of in this organization.

INVITATION TO DISCUSSION

What do you think it would take to build up a more positive organizational climate at Continental? How long would it take?

---

ruptcy twice, left it with aging equipment. Perhaps a greater detriment was a ravished corporate culture. The above information box discusses corporate culture.

A further major impediment was a reputation that could be described at best as tarnished and at the worst as devastated. The reputation gained of a surly labor force had repercussions far beyond the organization itself. For years Continental had had a problem in wooing the better paying business travelers. Being on expense accounts, they wanted quality of service rather than cut-rate prices. A reputation for good service is not easily or quickly achieved, especially when the opposite reputation is well entrenched.

---

[13]Edgar H. Schein, "Organizational Culture," *American Psychologist*, vol. 45 (1990), pp. 109–119.

[14]Terrence E. Deal and Alan A. Kennedy, *Corporate Cultures: The Rites and Rituals of Corporate Life* (Reading, MA: Addison-Wesley, 1982), p. 22.

On another dimension, Continental's reputation also hindered competitive parity. Surviving two bankruptcies does not engender confidence among investors, creditors, or even travel agents. In the second bankruptcy episode, creditors received only pennies on the dollar.

A Sick Airline Industry

Domestic airlines lost a staggering $8 billion in the years 1990 through 1992. Tense fare wars and excess planes proved to be albatrosses. Even when planes were filled, discount prices often did not cover overhead.

A lengthy recession was mostly to blame. Both firms and individuals were motivated to fly more sparingly. Business firms were finding teleconferencing to be a viable substitute for business travel, and consumers, facing diminished discretionary income and the threat of eventual layoffs or forced retirements, were hardly in an optimistic mood. The airlines suffered.

Part of the blame for the red ink scourge lay directly with the airlines—they were reckless in their expansion efforts—yet they do not deserve total blame. In the late 1980s, passenger traffic climbed 10 percent per year, and in response the airlines ordered hundreds of jetliners.[15] The recession arrived just as the new planes were being delivered. The airlines also greatly increased their debt structure in their expansion efforts; the big three, for example—American, United, and Delta—doubled their leverage in the four years after 1989, with debt by 1993 at 80% of capitalization.[16]

In such a climate, cost-cutting efforts prevailed. But how much can be cut without jeopardizing service and even safety? Some airlines found that hubs, heralded as the great strategy of the 1980s, were not as cost-effective as expected. With hub cities passengers were gathered from outlying "spokes" and then flown to final destinations. Maintaining too many hubs, however brought costly overheads. While the concept was good, some retrenchment seemed necessary to be cost effective.

Two concerns had to be worrisome to airlines such as Continental with heavy debt and limited liquidity. First, how fast the country would emerge from recession would affect vulnerability. Second, the insidious risk of fuel price escalation in the coming years was ever present. Despite Continental's low operating costs, external conditions impossible to predict or control could affect viability.

---

[15]Andrea Rothman, "Airlines: Still No Wind at Their Backs," *Business Week* (January 11, 1993), p. 96.
[16]*Ibid.*

WHAT CAN BE LEARNED?

A negative reputation is difficult to overcome. Through most of the Lorenzo years, Continental suffered a negative reputation, especially with the sought-after business travelers, travel agents, and investors. This image was fostered by confrontational employee relations, which led to union-busting, and by two bankruptcies. The consequences were poor customer service, no assurance of continuity of operations, and high risk for investors and creditors.

A poor image is difficult for any firm to overcome. Trust can only be built up over time. The prudent firm is careful to safeguard its reputation and indeed considers it a most valuable asset.

Contradictory and inconsistent strategies are vulnerable. Lorenzo was often described as mercurial and subject to knee-jerk planning, inconsistent marketing, and poor execution.[17] Clearly focused objectives and strategies mark effective firms. They bring stability to an organization and give customers, employees, and investors confidence in undeviating commitments. Admittedly, some objectives and strategies may have to be changed occasionally to meet changing environmental and competitive conditions, but the spirit of the organization should be resolute, provided it is a positive influence and not a negative one.

Issue: Should an organization be nurtured or confronted? Lorenzo used a confrontational and adversarial approach to his organizations and their unions. He was seemingly successful in destroying the unions and hiring nonunion replacements at lower pay scales. As a consequence Continental became the lowest cost operator of the major carriers, but not without some negatives: service problems, questionable morale, diminished reputation.

Would Lorenzo have been better off working with the organization and the unions? No one can say for certain. The machinists' and pilots' unions of Eastern were particularly hostile, yet this attitude may have grown in response to Lorenzo's earlier union busting at Continental. It is generally better to nurture the existing organization, avoiding the adversarial mindset of "them or us" if at all possible. Admittedly this may be difficult—sometimes impossible, at least in the short-run—but it is worth trying. It should result in better morale, motivation, and commitment to the company's best interest. (See Chapter 6 for the Southwest Airlines' approach to organizational relations.)

INVITATION

What other learning insights does the Continental case provide?

[17]For example, Ivey and DeGeorge, *op. cit.,* p. 48.

QUESTIONS

1. Could Lorenzo's confrontations with the unions of Continental and Eastern have been more constructively handled? How?
2. How can replacement workers—in this case pilots and skilled maintenance people hired at substantially lower salaries than their unionized peers at other airlines—be sufficiently motivated to provide top-notch service and a constructive esprit de corps?
3. Lorenzo has been criticized for making too many "knee-jerk" decisions. What is your understanding of this term? Is it so bad? How could this criticism have been overcome?
4. Evaluate the causes and the consequences of frequent top executive changes, such as those Continental has experienced in the last decade.
5. Compare and contrast the Continental strategy with that of Southwest Airlines. What are the pros and cons of the two strategies?
6. "As the weakest player of the major airlines, the pursuit by Continental of global alliances is premature and presumptuous. The company would be better advised to 'stick to the knitting' and concentrate all efforts on improving domestic operations." Discuss.

INVITATION TO ROLE PLAY

1. It is 1993 and Continental is just coming out of its second bankruptcy. You are the staff adviser to the new CEO, Robert Ferguson. He has asked you to prepare a report on improving customer service as quickly as possible. He has also asked you to design a program to inform both business and nonbusiness potential passengers of this new commitment. Be as specific as possible in your recommendations.
2. You are the leader of the machinists' union at Eastern. It is 1986 and Lorenzo has just acquired your airline. You know full well how he broke the union at Continental, and rumors are flying that he has similar plans for Eastern. Describe your tactics under two scenarios:
   (a) You decide to take a conciliatory stance.
   (b) You plan to fight him every step of the way.
   How successful do you think you will be in saving your union?

INVITATION TO RESEARCH

What is the situation with Continental and with the airline industry today? Have things improved or gotten worse? What is your prognosis for the future of Continental?

11

Contrast—GM's Saturn: An Organization Builds on Quality and Customer Satisfaction

In many ways, the Saturn subsidiary of the General Motors' (GM) is a sales and marketing success. It is the first really effective effort by a U.S. automaker to emulate and even surpass Japanese cars, offering low prices, reliability, and good looks. In addition, the Saturn has been the vanguard of enlightened customer service. Sales have exceeded expectations as well as production capability, with customers waiting up to two months for a new Saturn. In an advertising campaign in late 1992, Saturn pleaded with customers not to be discouraged and buy another brand—that a Saturn was worth the wait.

As of early 1993, the Saturn has been at best a dubious success. Although the car was not expected to make money for several years after production started in November 1990, losses have been far higher than anticipated: more than $700 million in 1991.

How can any product possibly be considered even remotely a success with such a profit drain, despite the ever-growing customer satisfaction and sales and the major challenge it presents to Japanese cars? These positives could make Saturn the U.S. car industry's greatest success if GM doesn't miss this window of opportunity.

HISTORY

The beginnings of Saturn stretch to 1982. Originally it represented an ambitious effort by General Motors to make small cars in the United States as cheaply and well as they could be made overseas. Roger Smith, the CEO of GM at the time, called the $5 billion undertaking "the key to GM's long-term competitiveness."[1]

The project represented GM's attempt to rethink every aspect of automaking. It was hoped that production innovations could save $2,000 from the cost of building a subcompact car. Initial plans called for selling 400,000 units yearly.

So important was the project deemed to be in the total GM scheme that by 1985 Saturn had become a new GM subsidiary. A new factory was to be built from scratch, and in the search for a new site, bids flooded in from dozens of states. GM finally chose a site near Spring Hill, Tennessee.

Hardly had work begun on the new factory in early 1986 before some company goals began changing. As new models of lowest price imports began coming in from Korea and Yugoslavia, GM executives abandoned the idea of competing on cost. Now they began targeting the car for the middle of the import pack, where prices were several thousand dollars higher. As a result the car had grown larger, now positioned between subcompacts such as the Chevrolet Cavalier and midsize cars such as the Oldsmobile Ciera. Sales estimates were downsized. A "first-phase" plant was opened with a capacity for 250,000 cars, with a second factory to be added if sales were strong enough.

By early 1987 pessimists were predicting that the Saturn was doomed. Although production was at least several years away, already demand seemed to be slackening for small cars, and GM was experiencing difficulty with high-tech factories. The more optimistic rumors were that GM might try to save face by folding the separate Saturn subsidiary into the Chevrolet or Pontiac division.

INTRODUCTION

As the 1980s drew to a close, GM's share of the U.S. passenger-car market slumped to 33 percent, a loss of 11 points in only five years. At the same time, Japanese car makers had a seven-point gain in market share, to 26 percent. Consumer surveys were even bleaker: A study by J. D. Powers & Associates found that 42 percent of all new-car shoppers would not even consider a GM car.[2] Saturn now began to assume a position of greater importance to GM. Its new fundamental goal was to sell 80 percent of its cars to drivers who otherwise would not have bought a GM car.

---

[1]William J. Hampton, "Will Saturn Ever Leave the Launchpad? *Business Week* (March 16, 1987), p. 107.

[2]James B. Treece, "Here Comes GM's Saturn," *Business Week* (April 9, 1990), p. 57.

Saturn's ascendancy on the eve of its production inauguration had the full support of GM chairman Roger Smith, although his term of office was soon to end. Smith saw the Saturn as having a bigger role than simply appealing to import buyers. He saw it as an example for the rest of GM as to how to reform its own ponderous and tradition-ridden culture. Indeed, Saturn had created an innovative blend of enlightened labor relations, participatory management, and new technology for the latest manufacturing operations. GM was especially interested in the manufacturing and labor breakthroughs that Saturn had initiated. Just as innovative, but not to be recognized for another year or so, was the great change in traditional passenger-car marketing, customer relations, and servicing.

The company was now becoming so optimistic of Saturn's competitiveness that one marketing strategy under consideration was to have dealers place a Honda Civic, a Toyota Corolla, and an Acura Integra in the same showroom with a Saturn and let customers make their own direct comparisons.

Admittedly, the final version of the Saturn was not the 60-mile-per-gallon, $6000 subcompact originally envisioned, but it was a gem nevertheless. Dealers were allowed to drive prototypes at GM's Mesa, Arizona, proving grounds, and they were enthusiastic about the car's power train and handling: "We went 100 miles per hour, and it was still going strong," said a Saturn dealer form St. Louis. "It was going through curves at 75 to 80 that imports couldn't."[3] Another dealer who also sold Hondas remarked that a Saturn, besides having the quickness and nimbleness of a Honda, "doesn't have the vibrations that the current domestic models have."[4]

The first Saturns were ready for sale in November 1990. In that first month, 641 were sold. Sales more than doubled to 1520 by January 1991. The rush was on, limited only by the production capabilities of the single factory. Table 11.1 shows the growth in units sold from the beginning through July 1992. Table 11.2 shows comparative figures of the sales and market share of Saturn to other GM units and also to major Japanese competitors and the total car market for 1991 and 1992. Saturn's surge was awesome.

DEMAND AFTER TWO YEARS

As demand outstripped supply, dealers were staring at empty lots. In July 1992 Saturn dealers sold 22,305 cars—an average of 115 apiece, twice the rate per dealer for the nearest competitor, Toyota.[5] Foreign rivals continued

---

[3]*Ibid*, p. 58
[4]*Ibid*.
[5]David Woodruff, "Saturn," *Business Week* (August 17, 1992), p. 86.

Table 11.1   Selected Monthly Sales, Saturn, November 1990 through July 1992

Month	Units	Percent Increase
November 1990	641	
January 1991	1,520	137.1%
March 1991	3,302	117.7
May 1991	6,832	106.9
July 1991	8,538	25.0
November 1991	8,355	(2.1)
January 1992	10,757	28.7
March 1992	16,757	55.8
May 1992	18,031	7.6
July 1992	22,305	23.7

Source: David Woodruff, "Saturn: GM Finally Has a Real Winner, but Success Is Bringing a Fresh Batch of Problems," Business Week (August 7, 1992), pp. 86–87.

Commentary: Note the steady increase in monthly sales during this time period. Table 11.2 shows further statistics on Saturn's growth. A winner of major proportions for a U.S. automaker seemed to be emerging.

Table 11.2   Saturn Sales and Market Share Comparisons

	August		Year to Date	
	1991	1992	1991	1992
Retail Sales (units):				
Saturn	7,000	12,039	40,858	129,753
All GM Subscompacts	33,387	36,322	224,127	306,952
All Subcompacts	171,089	153,936	1,152,287	1,212,509
Total GM	221,547	198,172	2,012,599	1,992,835
Total Industry	690,442	644,808	5,601,704	5,584,494
Market Share:				
Saturn	1.0%	1.9%	0.7%	2.3%
All GM Subcompacts	4.8	5.6	4.0	5.5
Total Detroit				
Subcompacts	10.0	10.6	8.8	10.0
Total Toyota	5.0	4.3	4.0	4.2
Total Nissan	1.9	2.8	1.9	2.2
Total Honda	4.1	3.5	2.8	2.6
Total Japanese				
Nameplates	13.0	12.3	10.3	10.8
Total Subcompacts	24.8	23.9	20.6	21.7

Sources: Industry statistics.

Commentary: Noteworthy are the substantial Saturn gains, both in sales and market share, from 1991 to 1992 against all other makes, domestic and foreign. Note in particular the market share gains against Japanese competitors: Toyota, Nissan, and Honda. The GM charge for Saturn to take business away from the Japanese imports appeared to be fully realized as 1992 drew to a close, yet Saturn had still to make a profit.

to flood the market with new models, but Saturn was meeting them head on. It had become the highest quality American-made brand, with as few defects as Hondas and Nissans. In customer-satisfaction ratings, according to a survey by J. D. Power & Associates, buyers rated the Saturn ahead of all American-made cars and most imports. Only Lexus and Infiniti—much higher priced cars—were ranked higher. (See Table 11.3.)

The success of Saturn, however, was causing some problems at GM headquarters. To bring plant capacities in line with the demand, GM would have to pump in more money at a time when the auto giant was facing serious financial problems. In 1991 its North American operations had a devastating $7.5 billion loss. Every dollar spent on Saturn meant that struggling divisions such as Chevrolet, which badly needed to update its outmoded models, would receive less. And at a time when GM was closing assembly plants to the anguished consternation of union workers and local governments, the arena was politically not conducive for a still-money-losing Saturn to receive funds to fully capitalize on its burgeoning customer demand.

A GM decision to delay any new investment would seriously jeopardize Saturn. At the end of July 1992, Saturn dealers had only a 10-day supply of cars on hand: one-sixth of normal stock. Dealers worried that customers would switch to competing brands because of unacceptable delays in servicing their orders, which could devastate Saturn's momentum

Table 11.3 1992 Customer-Satsifaction Ratings (Score on J. D. Power's Survey of New Car Buyers)

Lexus	179
Infiniti	167
Saturn	160
Acura	148
Mercedes-Benz	145
Toyota	140
Industry Average	129

Source: J. D. Power's Survey of New Car Buyers, 1992, as reported by David Woodruff, "Saturn," *Business Week* (August 17, 1992), pp. 86–87; and Raymond Serafin and Cleveland Horton, "Automakers Focus on Service," *Advertising Age* (July 6, 1992), pp. 3, 33.

Commentary: Nissan's Infiniti and Toyota's Lexus have established new industry benchmarks for coddling luxury car buyers. Compared with that elite group, Saturn has surprisingly placed a close third by redefining the standard for treatment of buyers of lower priced mass-volume cars. This high rating is credited to Saturn's elimination of price haggling, high commitment to quality-control, and trail-blazing example of replacing 1800 cars after a coolant mixup. Saturn's customer-satisfaction commitment is not lost on Chrysler: All Chrysler brands finished below industry averages, and Chrysler announced a $30 million massive training effort to improve the way its dealerships handle shoppers and owners.

and make it easy for the great GM bureaucracy to downplay an innovative but unprofitable new division.

Several options short of massive new plant investments were possible. GM Chairman Robert C. Stempel, who replaced Smith, thought it possible to up the productivity at the single Spring Hill plant. Saturn President Richard G. LeFauve was rightly concerned about the dangers of pushing too hard for production at the expense of quality. During a visit by Stempel, after production goals had been increased along with the number of defects, line workers staged a slowdown, resulting in an easing of production goals. LeFauve saw a temporary solution in adding a third shift, which could boost capacity by 44 percent.[6]

Rather than adding another plant, LeFauve proposed an additional $1 billion investment in Spring Hill, which would bring its capacity to 500,000 and enable the division to meet demand for new models. Increased production would permit expansion beyond the 195 original Saturn dealers so that all states could be covered.

Saturn executives worried how to keep their value-conscious buyers as the buyers grew older and wanted to upgrade to bigger cars with more comfort and features. Plans for larger cars and new models depended on further GM investment.

Stempel argued that present Saturn buyers would easily move up to existing GM brands that traditionally cater to older buyers, such as Oldsmobile, Buick, and Cadillac. Still, it was doubtful that Saturn buyers would readily fall into such a trade-up mode, given that most of them were former import buyers who would not have purchased a GM product other than a Saturn.

If GM top management could be convinced to expand Saturn, it was more likely that an older plant would be retooled, rather than a new one built from scratch, regardless of the technological advantages a new facility would offer. Rejuvenating an older plant would save several hundred million dollars and would be more palatable to unions and communities that had experienced the trauma of plant shutdowns. The following issue box discusses the decision problems in allocating scarce resources among competing claims.

The unique relations of Saturn with its autoworkers will be described more fully in the next section. All workers were given a voice in management decisions, and 20 percent of their pay was linked to quality, productivity, and profitability. In late 1992 dissident union workers forced a vote on the teamwork-oriented labor contract that had been approved in Novem-

---

[6]Woodruff, *op. cit.*, p. 88.

ISSUE BOX

HOW SHOULD WE PARCEL OUT INVESTMENT FUNDS?

By mid-1992 the GM executive suite was facing a dilemma of mean consequences. Record multibillion-dollar losses had strapped the company financially, yet never before had the demands for additional investment been so compelling. Saturn, although yet to turn a profit, was a bright star that needed substantial additional production facilities to fully tap its potential. But other divisions, ones dating to the beginnings of GM, needed substantial expenditures either to keep them competitive or to bring them back from the brink. Chevrolet in particular needed funds:

> This flagship division of GM two decades ago was selling one-fifth of all cars in the United States. Now its market share had fallen to only 12.1%. Accentuating the seriousness of Chevrolet's decline, it had long served as GM's entry-level division, the one whose customers often "graduated" to bigger, more expensive GM cars. Chevy dealers were convinced that the aging, hard-to-sell cars in their showrooms were the direct result of GM's generosity to Saturn.[7]

How should problems like this be resolved? Should the nascent star receive whatever it takes to fulfill its promise? Should scarce dollars be committed to resurrecting and sustaining deprived divisions? Should some sort of compromise be worked out, satisfying no one but creating the most equitable solution? Stakeholders in such allocation decisions are more than employees and managers; dealers, communities where plants are located, suppliers, and even customers, have a stake.

INVITATION TO DISCUSSION

How would you resolve this dilemma? Explain your rationale, and support it as persuasively as you can.

---

ber 1991 by a 72 percent margin. They claimed that this innovative contract ignored some seniority rights earned at other GM plants. On January 13, 1993, workers voted 2-to-1 to keep their teamwork-oriented labor contract, with the vote "reflecting strong endorsement of the partnership between union and management, which works hand in hand with Saturn's mission, philosophy, and values."[8]

---

[7]Kathleen Kerwin, "Meanwhile, Chevy Is Sulking in the Garage," *Business Week* (August 17, 1992), p. 90–91.

[8]"Saturn Workers Keep Contract," *Cleveland Plain Dealer* (January 15, 1993), p. E1.

INGREDIENTS OF SUCCESS

A New Labor-Management Climate

A large part of Saturn's success has been an enlightened labor–management relationship, one unique among U.S. carmakers in its sharing of responsibility, although a similar approach has been used by Japanese firms.

At first the Saturn plant was conceived as a high-tech operation with robots and automated guided vehicles. But GM's experiences in a joint venture with Toyota Motor Corporation in Fremont, California, suggested that a change in labor–management relations could be more important for productivity and quality.

LeFauve, the president of the new subsidiary, was convinced that factory floor workers could make a difference, and he led the way for GM management and the United Auto Workers to work closely together almost from the beginning. Saturn employees and managers eat in the same cafeterias. Under a "team concept," workers are split into groups of 6 to 15 and are headed by a supervisor chosen jointly by workers and managers. Each team is responsible for meeting its own training and production goals. Workers start at a base pay equal to about 90% of the average pay at GM and other major U.S. automaker plants. Then they earn bonuses if specific production levels and quality targets are met.

In 1988 Saturn began visiting GM plants and UAW halls in search of workers. Recruiters sought current and laid-off workers willing to shed old habits and work as a team. The choice was not easy for some: They would have to quit their union locals and give up all seniority rights, and there would be no going back. Those who accepted the challenge developed a cultlike commitment.

Training was rigorous. New arrivals faced five days of "awareness training" to teach them how to work in teams and build consensus. Beyond that, workers received 100 to 750 hours of training that even included learning to read a balance sheet, since Saturn opened its books internally and wanted employees to know how much their operations were adding to the cost of a car.

Integration of Production

In contrast to other GM assembly plants, Spring Hill went beyond the usual paint shop and body and assembly plant. Its highly integrated facility includes a power train factory that casts, machines, and assembles engines and transmissions. A plastic-molding plant and a shop for assembling the instrument panel and dash into a single unit are also on site. Saturn consequently did not have to rely on key components supplied by factories hundreds of miles away, thus saving on freight costs and shipping delays. Still, some glitches can occur, and a minor delay can shut down the whole operation, but these delays have become increasingly rare.[9]

Quality Control

From the beginning Saturn sought to emphasize quality and freedom from defects. If it was ever to have a chance with its target customers, former buyers of imports, this was essential. The customer-satisfaction ratings (see Table 11.2) confirmed that Saturn had indeed achieved this objective, and while many buyers of imports were skeptical of any American car at first, the durability of Saturn's reputation for quality was converting more and more of them back to an American car.

Buyers' complaints had been quite limited, but Saturn strove to correct those received. Early on there were two recalls: one for defective seats and another for corrosive engine coolant. Some early complaints were of insufficient headroom and noisy, vibrating engines. The company addressed these complaints rather quickly, lowering rear seats half an inch below the initial design, redesigning engine mounts, and adding more insulation under the hood. However, the company's handling of the necessary recalls epitomized a unique approach to customer relations and to the commitment to quality. The information box on p. 166 details an almost unbelievable innovation in the treatment of recalls.

Most often credited for the high quality ratings was the revolutionary labor agreement. This agreement made partners of Saturn's blue-collar and white-collar workers and gave everyone the authority to solve quality problems, from phoning suppliers for corrective action to rearranging machinery to improve quality and productivity. Motivation was spurred by bonuses for meeting specific production levels and quality targets.

Worker comfort was considered in design of the final assembly line, the theory being that less strain on workers translates into fewer mistakes. Consequently, the whole facility was air conditioned. The floor of the assembly line was wood instead of concrete—this being a first in North America—thus making standing all day less tiresome. And the line itself was designed with the worker in mind: Car bodies moved on pallets that could be raised or lowered for the worker's ease, and workers rode with the body they were working on rather than walking to keep up with the body as on other assembly lines.

---

[9]Woodruff, *op. cit.* p. 88.

INFORMATION BOX

RECALL MAGIC IN FOSTERING QUALITY CREDIBILITY

Only a few months after production commenced for the Saturn, the company was forced to send out 1836 letters to customers, telling them that the car's radiator had been supplied with a faulty coolant and that the cars must be recalled. Such recalls are rather common in the industry, and car owners grudgingly put up with the inconvenience, but Saturn's recall was different. It offered to *replace* the cars, not just repair them. Consequently, regardless of odometer readings, each customer was supplied with a brand new Saturn at no cost. One couple, unwilling to wait three weeks for Saturn to deliver a replica of their old car, chose a red model from the lot. It had a sunroof, unlike their old car, but they were given this $530 option for free. Saturn also paid for a rental car for a day and even drove the couple to the rental company's lot.[10] Not surprisingly, Saturn's actions converted the recall into a major coup in customer relations and initiated the image—as no words alone could ever have—of an overwhelming commitment to quality and customer satisfaction.

In the process of handling the recall, Saturn broke other new ground. It publicly named Texaco as the supplier of the bad coolant. When Texaco learned that it would be identified in the Saturn recall, it rushed its explanation to customers: a freak accident, in which a special order of coolant contained too much sodium hydroxide, making it much more caustic and corrosive, especially for Saturn's aluminum engines. In light of the unfavorable publicity focused on the supplier, Texaco prepared to bear the costs associated with this mistake.

Saturn thus placed new responsibilities on its suppliers, that they provide parts meeting specifications without requiring Saturn inspectors to assure quality. At risk was severe damage to a supplier's reputation.

INVITATION TO DISCUSSION

Assess the pros and cons of such drastic handling of recalls in other situations and with other firms. On balance, can we as consumers expect such liberalization in any other recalls of the auto industry?

Dealer Strategy

While the success of Saturn left many dealers with insufficient cars even to come close to meeting demand, dealers had to be pleased when their monthly sales of 115 apiece in July 1992 were twice the rate per dealer of their nearest competitor, Toyota. Saturn had been slow in opening new dealerships, especially with demand outstripping production capability. With only 195 dealers by late 1992, these dealers were virtually assured of no close competition from other Saturn dealers. This strategy of maintain-

[10]James B. Treece, "Getting Mileage from a Recall," *Business Week* (May 27, 1991), p.38.

ing fewer dealers flies in the face of the traditional practice of having many dealerships in each market.

Initially most dealerships were on the east and west coasts, the heart of import demand. California's Santa Clara county imports, for example, had more than 65 percent of the market. Many of the chosen dealers had also sold imports, because Saturn management believed they would know best how to appeal to such buyers.

The decision to concentrate initially on the coasts left some states without any dealerships. It also left the populous midwest undercovered. The midwest was the heart of the "buy American" sentiments, however, and was the area where GM was already strongest. It was believed that aggressive Saturn efforts here could take more sales away from other GM makes than from foreign automakers.

Advertising

The company turned to San Francisco's Hal Riney & Partners for folksy, offbeat advertising. The target customer was similar to a target Honda Civic buyer: median age 33; 68 percent female; 52 percent married; 60 percent with college degrees; 46 percent holding managerial or professional jobs; and with median household income over $40,000.[11] Ads focused on buyers' lifestyles, playing up product themes that baby boomers could easily relate to, such as safety, utility, and value. The approach did much to create an image for Saturn as an unusual car company, and the pricing practices further advanced this theme.

Innovation in Pricing and the Selling Process

Saturn initiated a new approach to pricing and the car-selling process that was a revolution in the auto industry. A variable price policy had long been traditional, with a customer attempting to drive the best bargain possible and in the process participating in an adversarial contest with the car salesperson and his or her sales manager. Since the consumer lacked sufficient knowledge about costs and markups and was often uncomfortable and inexperienced with haggling, many car buyers disliked having to negotiate and were never sure if they were getting a reasonable deal.

Saturn cars carried no rebates and were priced at a set bottom price, with no haggling or negotiating needed or accepted. In late 1992, prices started at $9195, even after an average 8 percent hike for 1993 models. Customers loved the change in automobile retailing, and they knew they were not paying more than a neighbor for the same car.

---

[11]Larry Armstrong, "If It's Not Japanese, They Wouldn't Bother Kicking the Tires," *Business Week* (April 9, 1990), p. 6.

Other automakers began to emulate Saturn. Ford started selling its sub-compact Escort models at one low price. Chrysler was testing the concept. Even Japanese companies were closely watching the acceptance of the innovation. Somehow GM appeared slow to embrace the one-price policy elsewhere in the organization.

Ruling out haggling was only one part of the Saturn innovation in retailing. In formal courses in Spring Hill, managers and salespeople were instructed in low-pressure selling techniques. The theme of the training was that pampering customers could create word-of-mouth advertising that would be particularly effective in such high-priced and even traumatic purchases as cars.

Combining a good product and top-notch service was bound to lead to happy Saturn customers. But good customer relations went even further. Both dealerships and Saturn headquarters followed up with customers to ascertain their satisfaction.

GM'S DILEMMA

The apparent success of Saturn was not a particular cause for rejoicing at corporate headquarters in late 1992. Undoubtedly it would have been if the new venture were profitable, but several years and billions of dollars of new investment were expected to be necessary before Saturn turned the corner. Meanwhile, General Motors faced a serious cash crunch, especially critical after a $7.5 billion loss from North American operations in 1991. At issue was how limited investment dollars should be allocated. (Refer back to the issue box for more discussion of this management dilemma.)

Now that former Chairman Roger B. Smith, who conceived the Saturn project as a laboratory in which to reinvent his company, has retired from GM, the firm's commitment may have cooled. Saturn has initiated some notable innovations in American carmaking, including labor relation changes such as intensive training programs, rewards for high customer satisfaction ratings, and joint responsibility with management. Its no-dicker one-price policy was being emulated by other car makers but not by GM elsewhere in its organization. Its commitment to customer satisfaction became an actuality and not merely talk. And most of all, Saturn achieved—whether permanently or temporarily—quality levels deemed impossible by U.S. firms still bedeviled by defects and by an uncomplimentary image next to foreign imports. Saturn had much to offer its parent. It remains to be seen whether the slow-moving behemoth with its host of entrenched interests will be able to embrace enough of the Saturn innovations for a significant turnaround. It also remains to be seen at this writing whether a myopic devotion to profits might doom the Saturn as a great experiment that failed.

WHAT CAN BE LEARNED?

A good reputation lingers, but it must be zealously safeguarded. Saturn gained a notable reputation for quality, unique among U.S. cars, and one of the best among all cars. Such a reputation for being defect-free is an invaluable asset, both in keeping present customers who are likely to buy another Saturn (provided that appealing new models are forthcoming) and in attracting new customers by word-of-mouth publicity.

However, one of the ironies of a good reputation or public image is that it can quickly be destroyed. In the case of Saturn, if the company lapses a bit on its quality control—especially in pursuit of the profit demands of the parent—then the good reputation will be jeopardized. Then Saturn will reside with the other U.S. cars: just another domestic car unable to compete with the imports in workmanship and quality.

In large firms, politics and profit potential are not always compatible, perhaps to the detriment of the firm. With its untapped and growing consumer demand, Saturn would seem worthy of substantial additional investment by GM. This may not fully come to pass, and corporate pressures may intensify to do more with less. GM now finds itself with limited financial resources and consequent allocation problems. Long-entrenched divisions such as Chevrolet and Oldsmobile are competing with Saturn for needed funds. This intrafirm rivalry has not escaped the attention of the national business press, as noted in a preceding information box.

In the presence of long-established corporate power relations, Saturn, the upstart, may find itself thwarted by internal jealousies and entrenched interests.

Is there a moral here? Perhaps it is that huge organizations have profound difficulty in breaking from their traditional patterns (might we even call these ruts?). For some it may be impossible; for others, great adversity may sweep a new climate of change into a moribund organization.

Imitation is not a dirty word. Many organizations shun imitation; nothing else will do but to be innovators. Executive pride is often at stake. Innovation suggests a leader; imitation denotes a follower.

However, imitation has much to recommend it. Successful practices deserve to be imitated. Adopting such practices lessens risks from striking out on your own and often can hasten profitability.

Saturn represented innovation with General Motors, but most of the Saturn ideas were borrowed liberally from Japan. For example, just-in-time parts shipments were holding manufacturing costs down, but not without some danger of slowing the assembly line. Saturn workers were trying to eliminate bottlenecks and reduce costs, just as workers do at factories run by Toyota and Honda. Management and union relations likewise were

Japanese in style. The result became a commitment to quality unique among U.S. carmakers but imitative of Japanese imports.

INVITATION

What additional learning insights do you see as emerging from the Saturn case?

QUESTIONS

1. What problems might GM management face if its tries to transplant the Saturn concepts to other divisions?
2. Do you fault top management for pressuring Saturn to turn a profit at this critical juncture of its growth? Why or why not?
3. What problems do you see for Saturn in maintaining its quality and customer relations? Can these problems be resolved?
4. Evaluate the Saturn policy of having relatively few dealers, each with a wide sales territory. What pros and cons do you see for this?
5. How do you personally feel about the haggling that is involved in most car purchases? Do you prefer a one-price policy?
6. Compare the Saturn organizational strategy (i.e., separate division, separate dealers) with that of the Edsel (Chapter 7). How do you account for the differences in the success of the two endeavors?

INVITATION TO ROLE PLAY

1. You are a staff assistant to GM CEO Roger Smith in the early 1980s. He has asked you to give a briefing to the executive committee on whether Saturn should be set up as a separate division or as part of Chevrolet. Prepare such a briefing, listing as many pros and cons as you can for such a separate division, your evaluation of their importance, and finally, your recommendation.
2. You are one of the biggest and most successful Chevy dealers, and you are incensed at the investment dollars given Saturn at the expense of Chevrolet. What will you do? How effective do you think you action will be?

INVITATION TO RESEARCH

What is the present situation of Saturn, with regard to production and sales, consumer attitudes regarding satisfaction and quality, the labor force, and top management's commitment?

Three

FLAWED LEADERSHIP AND STRATEGY EXECUTION

12

Harley Davidson: Relinquishing Dominance to a Foreign Upstart

In the early 1960s, a staid and unexciting market was shaken up, rocked to its core, by the most unlikely invader. This intruder was a smallish Japanese firm that had risen out of the ashes of World War II and was now trying to encroach on the territory of a major U.S. firm that had in the space of 60 years destroyed all of its U.S. competitors and now had a firm 70 percent of the motorcycle market.

Yet, almost inconceivably, in half a decade this market share was to fall to 5 percent, and the total market was to expand many times over what it had been for decades. A foreign invader had furnished a textbook example of the awesome effectiveness of carefully crafted marketing efforts. In the process, this confrontation between Harley Davidson and Honda, the challenger, was a harbinger of the Japanese invasion of the auto industry.

HARLEY DAVIDSON: THE OPPORTUNITY UNNOTICED

Historical Background

Harley Davidson motorcycles date back to 1903, when the Harley and Davidson families, in a 10' by 15' wooden shed in the Davidson backyard, built motorcycles in evenings and weekends. Members of both families participated in the endeavor, aided by a few other people, notably Ole Evinrude, who became a well-known manufacturer of outboard motors. The first year they sold four motorcycles, the next year eight. Production continued to increase, aided by a demand that was greater than could be filled, as motorcycles began replacing horses. By 1915 Harley Davidson was producing 180,000 machines a year, and another brand, Indian, joined it in dominating the U.S. two-wheel machine industry. With America's entry into World War I, practically all of Harley Davidson's production went to the military.

However, the boom collapsed with peacetime. The horseless carriage, particularly Ford's Model T, was tough competition. A motorcycle with a sidecar could never provide the comfort and convenience of the Model T, and Ford priced his cars so low that they cost little more than Harley Davidson motorcycles, and sometimes even less. The situation did not improve during the depression years of the 1930s. Rather than making motorcycles inexpensive to appeal to consumers' reduced incomes during the 1930s, Harley Davidson and its major competitors, Indian and Henderson, made motorcycles more luxurious and more powerful—and, of course, more expensive. A deluxe model with a sidecar in 1930 sold for as much as $2000: all the Spartan comfort of two wheels at more than the price of most automobiles.

World War II again buttressed the motorcycle industry, with Harley Davidson alone selling 90,000 machines. But motorcycles played only a minor role in this war, where the emphasis was on other types of motorized equipment. The peacetime booming economy still found the motorcycle industry on the sidelines. Sales increased much less in proportion than did the sales of automobiles. And now motorcycles were being purchased by some of the wrong people—drifters, gangs of hoodlums, and other undesirables.

In 1953 the Indian Motorcycle Company folded. This was the largest motorcycle manufacturer to fail; others, such as Henderson, Yale, Merkel, Minnesota, Pope, and Thor, preceded Indian. Now only Harley Davidson was left to make motorcycles in the United States, where once there had been 114 makers of motorcycles.

The Public's Perception of the Motorcyclist. Over the decades the motorcycle became synonymous with black leather jackets and with deviant and even violent behavior. This perception dates back to the late 1920s and the 1930s, years of hard times and high unemployment, when a gypsy lifestyle was embraced by some as they roamed over the country untethered by job or responsibilities, often dirty, sometimes drunken, always noisy as their machines roared through city streets. Regardless of the number of motorcyclists who actually fit that description, the idea stuck.

The years after World War II reinforced the idea. In 1947 in Hollister, California, a town of 4800 people, a gang on big, black Harley Davidsons rolled into town, converging on the open taverns, and by evening had torn up the town. The outnumbered police, gathering volunteer deputies and aided by vigilante bands of outraged citizens, met them in a pitched battle that left 50 people injured. The episode led to a movie, *The Wild One*, starring Marlon Brando, in which a gang of hoodlum motorcyclists roam the country, contemptuous of law and order, and take over a small town. *The New York Times* reported on the situation:

> A little bit of the surface of contemporary American life is scratched in Stanley Kramer's "The Wild One" . . . and underneath is opened an ugly, debauched and frightening view of a small, but particularly significant and menacing element of modern youth.[1]

In subsequent years, the antics of motorcycle gangs, particularly Hell's Angels, increased the public's negative image of motorcycles. In 1966 a Florida police official was quoted as follows:

> These punks with the cycles and their Nazi trappings have it in for the world—and for everyone in it. They're a menace, a damned serious menace, that's growing bigger every year.[2]

The Invasion. Sales in the United States were around 50,000 per year during the 1950s, with Harley Davidson, Britain's Norton and Triumph, and Germany's BMW accounting for most of the market. By the turn of the decade, the Japanese firm Honda began to penetrate the U.S. market. In 1960 fewer than 400,000 motorcycles were registered in the United States. While this was an increase of almost 200,000 from the end of World War II 15 years before, it was far below the increase in other motor vehicles. But by 1964, only four years later, the number had risen to 960,000; two years later it was 1.4 million; and by 1971 it was almost 4 million.

As we examine in depth in the next section, Honda instituted a distinctly different strategy to expand the demand for motorcycles. The major elements of this strategy were lightweight cycles and an advertising approach directed toward a new customer. Few firms have ever experienced such a shattering of market share as Harley Davidson did in the 1960s. (Although its market share declined drastically, its total sales remained nearly constant, indicating that it was getting none of the new customers for motorcycles.)

Reaction of Harley Davidson to the Honda Threat

Faced with an invasion of its staid and static U.S. market, how did Harley Davidson react to the intruder? They did not react! At least not until far too late. Harley Davidson considered itself the leader in full-size motorcycles.

---

[1] Bosley Crowther, *The New York Times* (December 31, 1953), p. 9:2.
[2] Lee Gutkind, *Bike Fever* (Chicago: Follett Publishing, 1973), pp. 38–39.

While the company might shudder at the image tied in with the product's usage by the leather jacket types, it took solace in the fact that almost every U.S. police department used its machines. Perhaps this is what led Harley Davidson to stand aside and complacently watch Honda make deep inroads into the American motorcycle market. The managers saw no threat in Honda's thrust into the market with lightweight motorcycles. Their attitude was exemplified in this statement by William H. Davidson, the president of the company and son of the founder.

> Basically, we don't believe in the lightweight market. We believe that motorcycles are sport vehicles, not transportation vehicles. Even if a man says he bought a motorcycle for transportation, it's generally for leisure-time use. The lightweight motorcycle is only supplemental. Back around World War I, a number of companies came out with lightweight bikes. We came out with one ourselves. They never got anywhere. We've seen what happens to these small sizes.[3]

Eventually Harley recognized that the Honda phenomenon was not an aberration and that there was a new factor in the market. The company attempted to retaliate by offering an Italian-made lightweight in the mid-1960s, but it was far too late. Honda was firmly entrenched. The Italian bikes were regarded in the industry to be of lower quality than the Japanese bikes. Honda, and toward the end of the 1960s other Japanese manufacturers, continued to dominate what had become a much larger market than Harley Davidson ever dreamed.

WHAT WENT WRONG FOR HARLEY DAVIDSON?

Harley Davidson's error was one of omission. Its problems came not from misguided expansion but from an unwillingness to change anything. The company took no action, made no commitment—a null decision. But to really understand the mistake, we need to probe deeper: Why did management stubbornly stick to this mindset despite the increasing evidence that a vastly greater potential for motorcycles existed? We can identify two impediments to responsive and aggressive leadership.

First was lack of external focus, a lack of alertness to changing environmental conditions. (See the following box for a discussion of an internal versus an external management orientation.) In defense of Harley management, it is not surprising that such an internal focus should prevail. After all, the motorcycle market had not changed appreciably in decades. The second mindset impediment was inexcusable but unfortunately common.

---

[3]Tom Rowan, "Harley Sets New Drive to Boost Market Share," *Advertising Age* (January 29, 1973), pp. 34–35.

INFORMATION BOX

AN INTERNAL VERSUS AN EXTERNAL LEADERSHIP ORIENTATION

Managers can focus primarily on internal factors, such as technology and cost cutting. They subsequently see the key to attracting customers in improving production and distribution efficiency and lowering costs if possible. Henry Ford pioneered this philosophy in the early 1900s with his Model T. Texas Instruments became dominant in pocket calculators and digital watches by improving efficiency and bringing down prices. Harley Davidson was successful for decades with this orientation and the absence of competition. The internal orientation is most appropriate in three situations (with the third one often of unknown risk):

1. Where demand for a product exceeds supply, such as in new technologies and in developing countries
2. Where the product cost is high and the market can be expanded only if costs can be brought down (the situation Texas Instruments faced)
3. Where there is a present lack of significant competition, and no competitive threat is expected either because of severe entry requirements to the industry or because the market is limited. Obviously, Harley Davidson made a major miscalculation here, assuming that the motorcycle market would be forever limited.

An external leadership orientation recognizes the fallacy of the assumption that products will forever sell themselves "if we can only maintain our production and technological superiority." Looking outside the firm to the business environment results in giving major priority to determining customers' needs and wants, assessing how these may be changing as evidenced by shifts in buying patterns, and adapting products and services accordingly. The external focus also permits more responsiveness to other external forces that may be influencers, such as major competitive thrusts, changing governmental laws and regulations, economic conditions, and the like. With such an external orientation, attention will more likely be directed to locating new opportunities brought about by changing environmental conditions—maybe even discovering strategic windows of opportunity (see Chapter 6)—rather than focusing on internal production and technological advances. Such an orientation is geared to meeting and even anticipating change, and, like it or not, the environment for doing business is more and more dynamic today. Externally oriented leaders usually have the advantage over internally oriented managers.

INVITATION TO DISCUSSION

Describe how the SWOT analysis (strengths, weaknesses, opportunities, threats) should force managers into an external focus. (Hint: You may want to review the first box in the Southwest Airlines case.)

The Three C's Mindset of Vulnerability

We have encountered this negative mindset earlier with IBM and Sears, but perhaps Harley Davidson is the foremost example of how destructive it can really be, not in killing a company but in destroying its potential.

Remember, the three C's are complacency, conservatism, and conceit. In the 1950s and into the 1960s, even while Honda was intensifying its American invasion, Harley was complacent. It saw no competitor who might contest its share of the market for large motorcycles; it was the lone survivor and had a comfortable captive market, the police. Not even the bad image continuing to plague the civilian motorcyclist could dent the complacency of Harley.

Harley saw no need to change any strategy from the satisfactory ways of the past: big machines, expensive (profitable) options—aimed at the hard-core cyclist. Harley Davidson never considered the possibility that the market might be far greater than the hard-core users of big, expensive machines.

It must have given Harley managers great satisfaction to think of themselves as the best of the 100-plus former manufacturers of motorcycles. A feeling of self-confidence and a disdain for potential competitors was easy to come by, especially back in the 1950s and early 1960s when the potential competitor was a small Japanese upstart.

Harley, in defense of its conviction that there was no market for lightweight cycles, was quick to cite how it had attempted to introduce them twice and had failed badly both times. It tried once in 1925 and again in 1949. "Therefore, how could the market want these now?"

In retrospect, a major reason for the failures was that it had priced the lightweights only a little below the heavier motorcycles, and most people consequently saw the heavier machines as the better values. But, more than this, Harley should have recognized that no market is static and unchanging. America's tastes were changing by the late 1950s. A greater interest was being shown in smaller cars and in economy of operation. The Edsel also failed in the late 1950s as consumers spurned its high horsepower and size and turned to the smaller and more economical imported cars. The way was paved for an aggressive and ingenious David to confront Goliath and knock him into the dust.

THE HONDA MOTORCYCLE INVASION

Soichiro Honda was the son of a blacksmith. When he was three years old, his father gave him a pair of pliers, which remained his favorite possession. He only went as far as tenth grade in school, but he had great mechanical ability and received his first patent when he was 14. He became an auto mechanic and by the time he was 21 had opened a garage where he became known as the man who could fix anything. By the time he was 27, his garage had grown to the point where he had 50 employees.

Honda was not only a fixer but also a creator. He bolted an old Curtis airplane engine into an auto chassis and had a racing car that nobody could beat. He designed his own piston rings and by World War II had developed the finest piston rings in Japan. His entire output was taken for military vehicles. Near the end of the war, a bomb demolished his factory. He was then 41, with almost no money.

Honda began looking for other ventures. He purchased 500 small war-surplus gasoline engines that had been used to power communications equipment. He mounted these on standard bicycles. While crude and difficult to start, they sold rapidly in a country with little transportation. After the engines were gone, Honda designed and built his own engine and later also began producing frames and wheels. By 1949 his plant was manufacturing all the basic components and was assembling Honda motorcycles. These early cycles could go 45 miles per hour, getting up to 200 miles per gallon of gas. In 1950 Honda produced 3600 motorcycles. In only two years he employed 1000 men in a plant 100 times larger than he had before. In 1959 Soichiro Honda decided to invade the American motorcycle market.

The Japanese Invasion

Honda's introduction of the lightweight motorbike in the United States did not have a very auspicious beginning: Only 167 units were sold during the first year. Motorcycle experts laughed at the puny Japanese machines. But such derision and skepticism were to change quickly. In 1960 sales were 22,100 units, increasing in only five years more than tenfold to 270,000 units in 1965. By 1965 Honda had 80 percent of the expanding U.S. market, and Harley Davidson was still selling about 35,000 units per year.

While Honda enjoyed steady growth after 1965, it was not as dramatic as during the real growth years from 1963 to 1965. Sales increased to 650,000 units by 1974, but market share steadily declined form 80 percent in 1965 to 45.6 percent in 1977. However, this was still the major share of the U.S. market, which Honda now was contesting with other Japanese firms. Market shares for the leading motorcycle makers in 1977 were as follows:

Honda	45.6%
Yamaha	18.9
Suzuki	10.7
Kawasaki	14.4
Harley Davidson	5.7

In few annals of business history had an invader come into an entrenched market and so quickly gained mastery. How could this have happened?

The Invasion Strategy. Soichiro Honda's philosophy has been widely stated:

> If you turn out a superior product, it will be patronized by the public. Our policy is not simply to turn out a product because there is demand, but to turn out a superior product and create a demand.[4]

To move beyond Japan and open up the export market, Honda thought that his machines would need an international reputation and that this could best be gained on the international racing circuit. In June 1954 he went to the Isle of Man to enter his machines in the oldest of the international racing classics. He was shocked to learn that the European competition was fielding models with three times the horsepower of the Hondas. By 1961, however, Honda had won world championships in the 125-cc (cubic centimeter) and 150-cc engine classes.

But it took more than racing trophies to open the U.S. market. At best only a limited number of bikes would have been sold to motorcycle buffs, so Honda moved his attack on the United States and international markets to a different level, a level never before achieved in the industry. Advertising was given the key role in this strategy.

Promotional Strategy. Honda commissioned the Grey Advertising Agency to handle the U.S. promotion. The task assigned was to win social acceptance for the motorcycle and its rider. The basic thrust of the communications strategy was to create a fresh image for the Honda motorcycle and to educate the general public to a new mode of transportation.

Honda wanted to promote the idea that riding a motorcycle is fun. A basic theme of advertising in the early 1960s was "Holidays and Honda days," and "Go happy, go Honda." To promote this theme, Honda had to buck the negative perceptions of motorcyclists as the black-leather-jacketed characters widely publicized in a continuing negative press. Most Americans had never ridden on or driven a motorcycle, and the negative image of motorcyclists stood in the way of Honda, who wanted to attract a large new market.

Social acceptance was finally achieved by heavy promotion of the theme, "You meet the nicest people on a Honda." Early advertisements showed nine totally different kinds of people—old, young, casual, formal—but they all had in common the fact that they were nice, acceptable people riding Hondas. One ad read as follows:

[4]*Journal of Commerce* (November 6, 1965), p. 23.

You meet the nicest people on a Honda. It's largely a question of personality. A Honda is easygoing, dependable. Makes few demands. Prices start at around $215. And it runs all day on a nickel's worth of gas. That's the kind of friend to have. Frugal. How about one in your family? World's biggest seller.

Despite the quiet tone of this ad, it puts over the Honda story through words like "nice," "easygoing," "friend," "family," and "frugal."

Ads with this theme were placed in magazines, network TV, spot radio, newspapers, outdoor farm publications, and direct mail. The media chosen were designed to reach nontraditional bike owners, people who might never have thought of owning any vehicle with less than four wheels. Ads were placed in magazines such as *Life, Look, The Saturday Evening Post,* and *Sports Illustrated.*

People already sold on motorcycles were not overlooked either, as many ads were also placed in magazines for cycle enthusiasts. Commercials were run on the top 40 radio stations favored by young people. Newspapers were used in key markets as well as large space advertising in more than 225 college newspapers, where the message was stressed that Honda had the answer to campus parking problems. Even billboards were used in a unified program to give Honda maximum public exposure.

The major target of the promotional efforts was the young. Honda and Grey Agency believed that with the increasing number of World War II babies growing up, products that would assert their individuality could become popular. The new lightweight bikes of Honda were introduced as such a product (the Mustang was also introduced about this time, riding the youth crest). While it was expected that many parents would oppose the purchase of a motorcycle, it was thought that their resistance could be overcome by the advertising.

The buyers were primarily young men between 16 and 26: college students, young professionals, and others getting started in their white-collar careers. Studies showed that teenagers were becoming the largest group of owners, with 32 percent of the first-time purchasers under age 20.

While there were other factors in the strategy that contributed to the success of Honda, the importance of the advertising campaign can hardly be overemphasized. Honda succeeded in selling the idea that it was smart and sophisticated to ride a motorcycle through the "nice people" advertising. American and European makers alike credited this advertising campaign with sparking the enormous growth of the entire industry. Indeed, in the annals of advertising there are few such examples of the effectiveness of the mass media in radically changing mores and social acceptability in such a short period of time.

The Product Strategy. Honda invaded the U.S. market with small (50 cc), lightweight bikes that could go miles on a thimbleful of gasoline and which could be purchased for less than $300 when most of the other motorcycles cost $1500 and more. Furthermore, a customer had six snappy colors to choose from in three different models at a time when most other motorcycle makers offered no more than two or three models and color choices. The little Hondas could go 55 miles per hour for 180 miles on 30 cents worth of regular gas, and the product quality was impressive. A top executive of a British motorcycle firm examined a Honda machine in 1961 and made a widely quoted statement: "When we stripped the machine, frankly, it was so good it frightened us. It was made like a watch, and it wasn't a copy of anything."[5]

As Honda began to dominate the U.S. market, it expanded the product line, aiming to have a model for every potential rider. By 1965 14 different motorcycles were available, ranging from a light 50 cc to a fast 305 cc. In 1966 a larger 450-cc bike was added to compete with the Harley Davidson models, but the bulk of the Honda sales in 1965 was in the 150-cc and smaller models.

The potential for trade-up sales spurred Honda to offer larger models, and a few years later Honda offered models up to 1100 cc, fully as large as any Harley Davidson. As people traded up to get bikes with more horse-power, they looked to Honda for the larger motorcycles, not Harley Davidson. One study found that 40 percent of those with light machines were buying heavier ones.

Production Advantage. Honda had certain inherent advantages in its effective strategy to invade the U.S. market. Japanese labor was much less expensive than American, contributing to competitively lower production costs. In addition, the size of the Japanese home market afforded a substantial advantage over any American producer. The demand for motorcycles in Japan was in the neighborhood of two million machines a year. This large sales base made it possible to keep production high and unit costs low. Consequently, motorcycles could be exported at prices unmatchable by foreign producers.

Handling Service Problems. A servicing problem emerged as sales began to mushroom. Growth was so rapid that not enough trained mechanics were available. Parts warehouses encountered severe shortages. The problem for a time became so bad that the growth of Honda was jeopardized, creating the potential for a long-term image problem and loss of customer loyalty. To Honda's credit, once the company recognized the problem, it took immediate corrective actions. More mechanics were quickly trained, more parts warehouses were opened, existing warehouses were

[5]Gutkind, *op. cit.*, p. 160.

enlarged, and dealer inventories were maintained at more adequate levels. There was no serious long-term harm to Honda.

Distribution Strategy. Honda continued its innovative approach to the U.S. market in its distribution strategy and choice of dealers. Previously most motorcycle dealers were located on the outskirts of cities, often in seedy neighborhoods where the leather-jacketed crowd felt more comfortable. Dealerships tended to be dirty, noisy, and rather undesirable neighbors. Honda spurned this approach and often located its dealers in the center of town. New York City for some time had a dealer on Madison Avenue, only three blocks from Grand Central Station and its concentration of commuter traffic. By 1965 more than 1500 Honda dealers were located in every state, making the product readily available. Most of these locations were places where the traditional motorcyclist would hardly feel at ease. Honda had 19 percent of a national total of 8000 dealers, and it compared with Harley Davidson's 880 dealers, or 11 percent.

In addition to selling and servicing Hondas, the company offered another plum to dealers as Honda sought to tap a different customer: the person who preferred to rent—at least at first—rather than buying. By 1965 rentals amounted to some $40 million. In addition to providing extra income, many of those who rented eventually bought. Rentals provided a good way to try out a new form of transportation and to determine how easy it was to handle, and how economical and convenient these vehicles really were. The general public would never rent the large, expensive Harley Davidsons, but many were keen to rent the light and easy-to-handle Hondas.

Reactions to Looming Problems. In 1966 total sales of motorcycles slumped. Although Honda sales increased, they were less than projected, and Honda was concerned. The cause was not difficult to pinpoint. Activity in the Vietnam War was increasing, and more 18 to 25-year-olds were being drafted. This group comprised 50 percent of the Honda market. Adding to the problem, banks were becoming more reluctant to finance purchases for draft-age buyers.

Such problems, of course, were external factors in the environment, presumably conditions that Honda or any other motorcycle maker could do little about. But Honda did. Amid a slumping market, Honda actually increased advertising expenditures from $6 million to $7 million. They mapped out a campaign aimed primarily at the undraftables. One such target was women.

And such a natural move this was. The inexpensive, light, easy-to-manage motorbike was attractive for women. They could buy or rent at convenient and comfortable dealerships, where service was no problem.

The image had changed so that housewives, students, young professionals all could feel compatible. More and more women were induced to turn to this new mode of transportation.

Ingredients of Success

The successful incursion of an unknown foreign invader into a long-established traditional market appeared easy. It took only a few years to accomplish. This experience should be sobering for many firms: Competitive entry can be easy for the innovative outsider with a wider perspective who is willing to accept some risks.

Practically everything that Honda did during the 1960s has escaped criticism. All the elements of the strategy seemed to mesh beautifully. There were a few servicing problems during a period of the most rapid growth, but these were quickly identified and corrected. We might question the dogged perseverance of Honda in gearing itself to winning international racing competitions, and doing so successfully. How relevant were such trophies to the consumer Honda was hoping to woo?

Let us examine what appear to be the key ingredients to the Honda success.

Willingness to Attack the Lion. For any upstart firm to challenge an entrenched competitor is perilous indeed. When the newcomer is an unknown foreign firm attempting to gain entry to the home ground of its formidable foe, and when the foe has been well entrenched for decades, and when the entrenched firm has driven out all the other domestic competitors over the years, the chances of any kind of success appear quite small. In this situation a willingness to attack the lion is a key ingredient of success.

Although the attack could have failed, there was sufficient confidence in the planned strategy that the risks were considered worthwhile. This was no reckless and foolish charge; it was carefully crafted, and while the premises that guided it—namely that the market for motorcycles could be greatly expanded to nontraditional users—were unproven as yet, they were reasonable and worth testing.

Identifying the Potential for Expanding the Market. How did Soichiro Honda arrive at his vision of a widely expanded potential market? While we cannot know for sure, we can make some reasonable assumptions. He did not use an extensive marketing research study. Though such might have confirmed what was already known about the characteristics of the present market, it probably would not have uncovered the widened perspective. It might even have discouraged any such efforts to expand the market because of the negative impressions that motorcycles had with the general public and the sheer audaciousness of the idea that the average person could enjoy two-wheel transportation.

Most likely, Soichiro Honda recognized that the light motorcycles he had been manufacturing should be adaptable to commuter traveling in the United States just as they were being used in Japan. While America was a far different country, with less traffic and more affluence, should not economy and ease of transportation and parking also be desirable there? The product was available, and it was far different from existing competitive products.

Such reasoning seems to violate a solid business principle that customer needs and wants should be firmly ascertained and then products developed to best serve these needs and wants. But sometimes there are exceptions to cherished principles.

Effective Use of Advertising. The negative image of the black-leather-jacketed cyclists was erased and a positive image of upwardly mobile youth and common folk substituted. Mass-media advertising was the main force in changing the image and in doing so highlighted one of the best examples we can ever find of the effectiveness of advertising. While the budget used to achieve such results was unheard of for the industry, the $6 or $7 million spent per year was certainly modest by today's perspectives, when a single-minute commercial during a Super Bowl game costs more than $1 million for the air time alone, not counting the production costs.

Complementing and reinforcing the effective advertising campaign was the coordination of all facets of the strategy and operations. The product was light, pretty, comfortable, nonthreatening to ride, and inexpensive; dealers were recruited who were far removed from the dirty and noisy establishments on the outskirts of towns; product quality was emphasized; and servicing was convenient and more hassle-free than generally encountered with automobiles.

Honda was even careful to shy away from words that had a negative connotation. For example, headgear were not called "crash helmets," which conveyed something negative and rather fearful, but were called "safety-wear." And the word "motorcycle" was never used in an advertisement because it was still thought to have a negative image; instead, the Hondas were described as "two-wheeled motoring sport."

Honda was the trailblazer for the Japanese cars that were soon to flood the U.S. market, capitalizing on a growing public image of quality and economy.

WHAT CAN BE LEARNED?

In the space of a few years, a long-standing U.S. industry came to be dominated by the Japanese. This phenomenon was to occur in other industries as well in later years. The skill of the Honda takeover should have warned other smug American industries; but, alas, most of them, if they paid any attention to this struggle, would have considered the results a fluke. After all, in the 1950s people associated most Japanese goods, as well as products made in other Far Eastern countries, to be poorly made with cheap labor and far below the level of American or European-made goods. Honda blazed the trail that changed that misperception.

The "three C's"—complacency, conservatism, and conceit—make a firm particularly vulnerable to competitors.

It is possible for the most unlikely firm to rise and become an aggressive and major factor in an industry. The inclination of the dominant firm in an industry, however, is to underestimate, belittle, or disdain the competition and not even deign to react or respond to the initial puny efforts of the competitor.

The "three C's" attitudes, which originate from top management, can permeate an entire organization—from production workers to sales staff to those who service customers. The consequences are a reduced commitment to consistency of quality, an aloofness to customer needs and concerns, and a lack of innovativeness in seeking new markets and improved products. There is decreased emphasis on pricing for good value and increased focus on maximizing per-unit profits. The foundation is laid for vulnerability to the aggressive competitor "foolish enough" to invade a seemingly static market and its entrenched firm.

What can an organization do to guard against this dangerous syndrome? In general, these are the best tools:

1. **Bring fresh blood into the organization.** This step is applicable to all levels of staff and managerial personnel. New people bring with them diverse experiences that result in new ideas and different perspectives from those who have long been with the organization. However, these new people must be listened to if their presence is to have any impact on the three C's syndrome.

2. **Monitor the environment and be alert to any changes.** Such monitoring can be formal (perhaps through the systematic use of marketing research) or informal. Every executive can do his or her own monitoring. Generally, monitoring takes three directions:

   a. Keep abreast of the latest statistics and other information in industry and general business publications.

b. Obtain feedback from customers, dealers, and sales staff about environmental changes and any unmet needs and possible opportunities and dangers.

c. Be receptive to new ideas from wherever they may come.

In general the executive needs to cast a wide net, to pull in information and ideas from as many diverse sources as possible. Customer feedback is an important source of such monitoring, but it will not often provide the forward-looking insights that may be critical. For example, a survey of Harley Davidson customers, their dealers, and their shops probably would not have yielded much value since most of these customers would not have realized the attractiveness of lightweight motorbikes. Perhaps a better monitoring of dealers, however, might have led Harley Davidson more quickly to recognize the seriousness of the Honda threat.

Receptivity to new ideas is the most important ingredient if desirable changes are to be made. Where an organization has grown accustomed to a certain way of doing business, any changes can be traumatic and unwelcome.

3. **Always keep a strong commitment to customer service and satisfaction.** The successful and dominant firm must especially beware of slipping here. A systematic survey of customers to measure their satisfaction can be a useful tool. The boxed information on the next page describes how customer feedback can be obtained.

4. **Maintain continuing corporate self-analysis.** It is difficult to sell healthy firms on the need for such an analysis; with sick firms the need is more obvious. Such self-analysis should be particularly directed to the business strategy of the firm and should be comprehensive. In particular, answers should be sought for these questions:

What are we doing right?

What could we do better?

Self-analysis needs to be objective. Care must be taken to minimize defensiveness and obstructionism from involved executives. While no one relishes having his or her performance evaluated and scrutinized more closely than before, it is in the best interest of the firm, and of all involved, to detect promptly any deficiencies or any unmet opportunities. A *marketing audit* is the term most often used for such self-analysis.

Any industry or market may have untapped potential, but only an innovative approach can harvest it. The notion of untapped potential may appear unlikely in supposedly mature industries where sales have been on a plateau for

---

INFORMATION BOX

USE OF CUSTOMER SURVEYS FOR MEASURING SATISFACTION

For a retail firm, attitude surveys can be made by interviewing customers leaving the store or department, perhaps those without a package, under the assumption that such people did not find what they wanted or were in some other way not satisfied. Brief questionnaires inviting customer opinions may be inserted in packages or in monthly statements. The samples need not be large. They should, however, be systematic and continuous; otherwise, trends in attitudes go unnoticed, and danger areas may not be spotted until serious erosion of old customers occurs.

More ingenuity may be required by manufacturers to obtain feedback on customer attitudes, but this is not usually difficult. Customers can always be invited to express their opinions and their satisfaction or dissatisfaction. The more serious complaints or the strongest customer feelings will be brought to light.

Direct measures of customer satisfaction have these particular advantages:

1. Trends can be established for customer attitudes, and problems can be detected before they become serious.
2. Goodwill can be gained by continuing efforts of this kind (the company will gain the reputation of "the firm that cares").
3. Time and expense need not be great.
4. Unfulfilled customer needs and wants may be revealed, and these may suggest opportunities to be tapped.

Customer panels can be useful in obtaining clues for various facets of customer satisfaction. Where the panel is used systematically, the firm may detect changes in its customer-satisfaction effectiveness before they become serious. However, these panels of customers suffer from the flaw of not always being representative of customers in general.

A firm can better maintain and improve competitive position if it closely monitors customer satisfaction. Direct measures, as in the surveys described, are far superior to any indirect estimates, such as from profits, sales, and market share. The latter lack sensitivity because many other determinants, such as environmental elements, quality of competition, and economic factors, affect sales, profits, and market share.

INVITATION TO DISCUSSION
Firms often determine customer satisfaction by tabulating the number of customer complaints. Do you see any problems with this?

---

years. Such an industry not only appears to offer no growth potential, but it also appears unlikely to attract new competition. How could any industry offer less growth and be less likely to attract competition than the old motorcycle industry?

Not only stagnant industries may find untapped potential—it can lie anywhere. A growing industry may find new customers other than those presently cultivated and thereby improve its growth rate. Of course, not all companies and industries can discover untapped potential. Perhaps it is out there, but no one recognizes it or is able to develop it. Sometimes unsuspected opportunities can be found in even stranger places than motorcycles.

Church and Dwight was a small, family-owned firm that made Arm & Hammer baking soda. It had the dubious distinction of being a 125-year-old one-product company. Though its baking soda had almost 100 percent market dominance, sales were declining. In 1970 the company conceived the idea of using Arm & Hammer to eliminate foul odors, and it really did absorb them. Church and Dwight began a TV campaign touting the benefits of using Arm & Hammer inside refrigerators. The results of this innovation? In four years, sales doubled and profits tripled.

There is also the classic example of Listerine. An old product, it was originally sold as a mild external antiseptic. Sales were static until in the 1920s, someone came up with the idea of promoting Listerine as a mouthwash.

As these examples illustrate, new potential may lie in two areas:

1. Finding new customers
2. Finding new uses

Honda essentially used the first approach. It modified the conventional motorcycle to make it attractive to entirely different customers. Arm & Hammer and Listerine found success with the second approach: They promoted new ways for old customers to make greater use of the products.

Never assume that things will always stay the same. One of the worst mistakes an executive can make was that made by the leaders of Harley Davidson in assuming the status quo: assuming that things would stay the same, that customers would not develop new wants, that competitors would not change their strategies or aggressiveness, that the business environment would never become more demanding and less tolerant. Specifically, in Harley's experience the unsuccessful attempts to introduce a lightweight cycle in 1925 and 1949 led to management's conclusion that such a product would never succeed. Very likely the concept was ahead of its time in those early years, but by late 1950 it was ripe. Never, never assume that a mistake can never be resurrected; and for that matter, never assume that a present success will always remain so.

Advertising can change an image for the better. It is usually extremely difficult to build up an image, in this case the image of the motorcyclist. But Honda proved that an image can be improved with the right advertising theme.

Usually the effectiveness of advertising is difficult to measure. We can determine the attention-value of certain ads in relation to other ads, but their real impact on sales is more difficult, often impossible, to measure since so many factors affect sales. Competitive efforts and prices, dealer displays and in-stock conditions, customer attitudes, the economy, and even the weather play major roles. Furthermore, thousands of commercial messages compete for the average person's attention. Many of these are screened out and do not even consciously register with an individual. Consequently, greater and greater expenditures are necessary for advertising to have any impact. In the United States, advertising expenditures are over $130 billion a year. Three firms spend over $1 billion a year each. Are these firms getting their money's worth?

Yet Honda, with relatively modest expenditures for advertising, achieved extraordinary impact. The keys, of course, were the uniqueness of the messages, the tapping of latent consumer needs, and the adroit presentation of clean-cut images of the persons who ride Hondas. This is a great example of the effective role advertising *can* play but practically never does. The coordination of the other elements of the strategy with the advertising reinforced the effective image change.

INVITATION

What additional learning insights does this case provide?

QUESTIONS

1. We have suggested that complacency, conceit, and conservatism led to Harley's vulnerability. How could such an organizational flaw have been prevented?
2. Could Honda have successfully entered the market with big motorcycles in 1960?
3. How could Harley have anticipated the competitive incursion of Honda or some similar firm?
4. "A major mistake of Harley leadership was not diversifying into other product categories." Discuss.
5. While conservatism is one of the 3 C's that make a firm vulnerable to competition, is it really all that bad? In what situations might you recommend conservatism?
6. Given the poor image that Japanese products initially had, do you think Honda would have been even more successful using a more "American" brand name? Discuss.

INVITATION TO ROLE PLAY

It is 1962. As one of the senior executives of Harley Davidson, you have been given the assignment of developing plans to counter the competitive thrust of Honda. What strategy do you recommend, and why?

INVITATION TO RESEARCH

You may find it interesting to investigate how Soichiro Honda parlayed his success in invading the U.S. motorcycle market to successful invasion of the automobile market.

13

Contrast—Harley Davidson Fights Back

By the mid-1960s, Harley Davidson was reeling under the onslaught of Honda. The Japanese firm's lightweight cycles had vastly expanded the motorcycle market, but Harley had no part of this as it desperately tried to hang on to its limited market for heavyweight machines. Essentially, it was left at the starting gate as the total market increased almost a hundredfold from 1960 to 1971. Eventually, by the late 1980s, Harley made a comeback. But in 1961, years of travail and mediocrity loomed ahead.

AFTERMATH OF THE HONDA INVASION: 1965 TO 1981

In 1965 Harley Davidson made its first public stock offering. Soon after, it faced a struggle for control. The contest was primarily between Bangor Punta, an Asian company, and AMF, an American company with strong interests in recreational equipment, including bowling. In a bidding war, Harley Davidson's stockholders chose AMF over Bangor Punta, even though the bid was $1 less than Bangor's $23 a share offer. Stockholders were wary of Bangor's reputation of taking over a company, squeezing it dry, and then scrapping it for the remaining assets. AMF's plans for expansion of Harley Davidson seemed more compatible.

But the marriage was troubled: Harley Davidson's old equipment was not capable of the expansion envisioned by AMF. At the very time that Japanese manufacturers—Honda and others—were flooding the market with high-quality motorcycles, Harley was falling down on quality. One company official noted that "quality was going down just as fast as production was going up."[1] Indicative of the depths of the problem at a demoralized Harley Davidson, quality-control inspections failed 50 to 60 percent of the motorcycles produced. Only 5 percent of Japanese motorcycles failed their quality-control checks.[2]

AMF put up with an average $4.8 million operating loss for 11 years before calling it quits and putting the division up for sale in 1981. Vaughan Beals, vice president of motorcycle sales, still had faith in the company: He led a team that used $81.5 million in financing from Citicorp to complete a leveraged buyout. All ties with AMF were severed.

VAUGHAN BEALS

Beals was a far cry from what one might think of as a heavyweight motorcycle aficionado. He had graduated from MIT's Aeronautical Engineering School and was considered a production specialist.[3] But Beals was far more than that. His was a true commitment to motorcycles, personally as well as professionally. Deeply concerned with AMF's declining attention to quality, he achieved the buyout from AMF.

The prognosis for the company was bleak. Its market share, which had dominated the industry before the Honda invasion, now was 3 percent. In 1983 Harley Davidson would celebrate its 80th birthday; some doubted it would still be around by then. Tariff protection seemed Harley's only hope, and massive lobbying paid off. In 1983 Congress passed a huge tariff increase on Japanese motorcycles. Instead of a 4 percent tariff, Japanese motorcycles were now subject to a 45 percent tariff for the coming five years.[4]

The tariff gave the company new hope, and it slowly began to rebuild market share. Key to this renewal was restoring confidence in the quality of its products, and Beals took a leading role in this. He drove Harley Davidsons to rallies, where he met Harley owners, learned of their concerns and complaints, and promised changes. At these rallies a core of loyal Harley Davidson users called HOGs (for Harley Owners Group) were to be trailblazers for the successful growth to come.

Beals had a fellow traveler on his odyssey: Willie G. Davidson, grandson of the company's founder and the vice president of design. Davidson

---

[1]Peter C. Reid, *Well Made in America—Lessons from Harley Davidson on Being the Best* (New York: McGraw-Hill, 1990), p. 10.

[2]*Ibid.*, p. 27.

[3]Rod Willis, "Harley-Davidson Comes Roaring Back," *Management Review* (March 1986), pp. 20–27.

[4]Robert L. Rose, "Vrooming Back," *The Wall Street Journal* (August 31, 1990), p. 1.

was an interesting contrast to the more urbane Beals: His was the image of a middle-age hippie. He wore a Viking helmet over his long, unkempt hair, and a straggly beard hid some of his wind-burned face. With his aged leather jacket, Davidson fit in nicely at the HOG rallies.

THE STRUGGLE BACK

In December 1986 Harley Davidson asked Congress to remove the tariff barriers, more than a year earlier than originally planned. The confidence of the company had been restored, and it believed it could now compete with the Japanese head to head.[5]

Production Improvements

Shortly after the buyout, Beals and other managers visited Japanese plants in Japan and visited Honda's assembly plant in Marysville, Ohio. They were impressed that they were being beaten not by "robotics, or culture, or morning calisthenics and company songs [but by] professional managers who understood their business and paid attention to detail."[6] As a result, Japanese operating costs were as much as 30 percent lower than Harley's.[7]

Beals and his managers tried to implement some of the Japanese management techniques. They divided each plant into profit centers, with managers assigned total responsibility within their particular area, and set up just-in-time (JIT) inventory and materials-as-needed (MAN) systems to control and minimize all inventories both inside and outside the plants. They formed quality circles (QCs) to increase employee involvement in quality goals and to improve communication between management and workers. (See the following information box for further discussion of quality circles.) Another new program, called statistical operator control (SOC), gave employees the responsibility for checking the quality of their own work and making proper correcting adjustments. Beals and other managers made efforts to improve labor relations by showing more sensitivity to employees and their problems and by offering better employee assistance and benefits. They also introduced certain product improvements, notably a new engine and mountings on rubber to reduce vibration. A well-accepted equipment innovation was to build stereo systems and intercoms into the motorcycle helmets.

[5]"Harley Back in High Gear," *Forbes* (April 30, 1987), p. 8.

[6]Dexter Hutchins, "Having a Hard Time with Just-in-Time," *Fortune* (June 19, 1986), p. 65.

[7]John A. Saathoff, "Workshop Report: Maintain Excellence through Change," *Target* (Spring 1989), p. 3.

The production changes between 1981 and 1988 had outstanding results:

Inventory reduced by 67 percent

Productivity up by 50 percent

Scrap and rework down 66 percent

Defects per unit down 70 percent[8]

INFORMATION BOX

QUALITY CIRCLES

Quality circles were adopted by Japan in an effort to rid its industries of poor quality control and junkiness after World War II. Quality circles are worker–management committees that meet regularly, usually weekly, to talk about production problems, plan ways to improve productivity and quality, and resolve job-related gripes on both sides. They have been described as "the single most significant explanation for the truly outstanding quality of goods and services produced in Japan."[9] For example, in 1982 Mazda had 2147 circles with more than 16,000 employees involved. They usually consisted of seven to eight volunteer members who met on their own time to discuss and solve the issues they were concerned with. In addition to making major contributions to increased productivity and quality, they provided employees an opportunity to participate and gain a sense of accomplishment.[10]

The idea—like so many ideas adopted by the Japanese—originated with two American personnel consultants; the Japanese refined the idea and ran with it. Now, American industry has rediscovered quality circles. Some firms have found them a desirable way to promote teamwork and good feelings and to avoid at least some of the adversarial relations stemming from collective bargaining and union grievances that must be negotiated.

Despite sterling claims, quality circles have not always worked out well. Some workers claim they smack of "tokenism" and are more a façade than a practical tool. Some people question how much lasting benefits such circles have once the novelty has worn off and doubt that the time invested by management and workers in quality circles is productive. Few U.S. workers accept the idea of participating in quality circles on their own time.

INVITATION TO DISCUSSION
How would you feel about devoting an hour or more to quality circle meetings every week or so on your own time? If your answer is "No way," do you think this is a fair attitude on your part? Why or why not?

---

[8]Hutchins, *op. cit.*, p. 66.

[9]"A Partnership; to Build the New Workplace," *Business Week* (June 30, 1980), p. 101.

[10]As described in a Mazda ad in *Forbes* (May 24, 1982), p. 5.

In the 1970s the joke among industry experts was, "If you're buying a Harley, you'd better buy two—one for spare parts."[11] This situation had obviously changed, but the change still had to be communicated to and believed by consumers.

Marketing Moves

Despite its bad times and its poor quality, Harley had an almost unparalleled cadre of loyal customers. Company research maintained that 92 percent of its customers remained with Harley.[12] Despite such hard-core loyalists, the company had always had a serious public image problem. It was linked to the image of a pot-smoking, beer-drinking, woman-chasing, tattoo-covered, leather-clad biker: "When your company's logo is the number one requested in tattoo parlors, it's time to get a licensing program that will return your reputation to the ranks of baseball, hot dogs, and apple pie."[13]

Part of Harley's problem had been with bootleggers ruining the name by placing it on unlicensed goods of poor quality. Now the company began to use warrants and federal marshals to crack down on unauthorized uses of its logo at motorcycle conventions, and it began licensing its name and logo on a wide variety of products from leather jackets to cologne to jewelry, including even pajamas, sheets, and towels. Suddenly retailers realized that these licensed goods were popular and were even being bought by a new customer segment undreamed of until now: bankers, doctors, lawyers, and entertainers. This new breed of customers soon expanded their horizons to include the Harley Davidson bikes themselves. They joined the HOGs, but became known as "Rubbies"—Rich Urban Bikers. And high prices for bikes did not bother them in the least.

Beals was quick to capitalize on this new market with an expanded product line with expensive heavyweights. In 1989 the largest motorcycle— the Fat Boy—was introduced, with 80 cubic inches of V-twin engine and capable of a top speed of 150 mph. By 1991 Harley had 20 models, ranging in price from $4500 to $15,000.

The Rubbies brought Harley back to a leading position in the industry by 1989, with almost 60 percent of the super heavyweight motorcycle market; by the first quarter of 1993, this had become 63 percent. (See Figure 13.1.) The importance of this customer to Harley could be seen in the demographic statistics supplied by *The Wall Street Journal* in 1990: "One in three of today's Harley Davidson buyers are professionals or managers. About 60 percent have attended college, up from only 45 percent in 1984. Their

---

[11]Hutchins, op. cit.
[12]Mark Marvel, "The Gentrified HOG," *Esquire* (July 1989), p. 25.
[13]"Thunder Road," *Forbes* (July 18, 1983), p. 32.

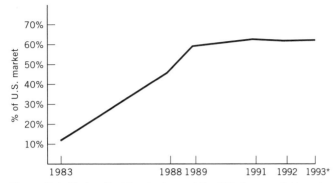

Figure 13.1. Harley Davidson's share of the U.S. heavyweight motor-cycle market, selected years, 1983–1993. (*Sources:* Company reports; R. L. Polk & Company; Gary Slutsker, "Hog Wild," *Forbes* (May 24, 1993), pp. 45–46.

*As of 1st quarter 1993.

median age is 35, and their median household income has risen sharply to $45,000 from $36,000 five years earlier."[14]

In 1989 Beals stepped down as CEO, turning the company over to Richard Teerlink, who had been chief operating officer of the Motorcycle Division. Beals, however, retained his position as chairman of the board. The legacy of Beals in the renaissance of Harley led management writer John Schermerhorn to call him a visionary leader.[15] The information box on p. 198 discusses visionary leadership.

SUCCESS

By 1993 Harley Davidson had a new problem, one born of success. Now it could not even come close to meeting demand. Customers faced empty showrooms, except perhaps for rusty trade-ins or antiques. Waiting time for a new bike could be six months or longer unless the customer was willing to pay a 10 percent or higher premium to some gray marketer advertising in biker magazines.

Some of the 600 independent U.S. dealers worried that these empty showrooms and long waiting lists would induce prospective customers to turn to foreign imports, much as they had several decades before. But other dealers recognized that Beals and company had somehow engendered a brand loyalty unique in this industry, and perhaps in all industries. Assuag-

---

[14]Rose, *op. cit.*, p. 1.
[15]John R. Schermerhorn, Jr., *Management for Productivity*, 4th ed. (New York: Wiley, 1993), pp. 410–411.

INFORMATION BOX

VISIONARY LEADERSHIP

Vision has been identified as an essential ingredient of effective leadership. Having vision characterizes someone who has a clear sense of the future environment and the actions needed to thrive in it.

Undoubtedly, a visionary leader is an asset in a dynamic environment. Such a leader can help a firm grasp opportunities ahead of competitors, revitalize itself, pull itself up from adversity. Schermerhorn states that a visionary begins with a clear vision, communicates that vision to all concerned, and motivates and inspires people in pursuit of that vision. He proposes these five principles of visionary leadership:

1. **Challenge the process.** Be a pioneer—encourage innovation and people with ideas.
2. **Be enthusiastic.** Inspire others through personal example to share in a common vision.
3. **Help others to act.** Be a team player, and support the efforts and talents of others.
4. **Set the example.** Provide a consistent model of how others should act.
5. **Celebrate achievements.** Bring emotion into the workplace and rally "hearts" as well as "minds."[16]

INVITATION TO DISCUSSION

Can you name any visionary leaders? What leads you to think they were visionary? Could some of our acclaimed visionary leaders have been merely lucky rather than prophetic?

---

ing the lack of big bike business, dealers were finding other sources of revenues. Harley's branded line of merchandise, available only at Harley dealers and promoted through glossy catalogs, had really taken off. Harley black leather jackets were eagerly bought at $500; fringed leather bras went for $65; even shot glasses brought $12—all it seemed to take was the Harley name and logo. So substantial was this ancillary business that in 1992 noncycle business generated $155.7 million sales, up from $130.3 million in 1991.

Production

In one sense, Harley's production situation was enviable: It had far more demand than supply. More than this, it had such a loyal body of customers that delays in production were not likely to turn many away to competitors. The problem, of course, was that full potential was not being realized.

[16]*Ibid.*

Richard Teerlink, Beals' successor, expressed the corporate philosophy on expanding quantity to meet the demand: "Quantity isn't the issue, quality is the issue. We learned in the early 1980s you do not solve problems by throwing money at them."[17]

The company increased output slowly. In early 1992 it was making 280 bikes a day; by 1993 production numbers had risen to 345 a day. With increased capital spending, goals were to produce 420 bikes a day, but not until 1996.

Export Potential

Some managers voiced concerns with Teerlink's conservative expansion plans for international operations. The European export market beckoned, and Harleys had become very popular in Europe. The company had promised its domestic dealers, however, that exports would not go beyond 30 percent of total production until the North American market was fully satisfied. Production limits became a major issue when the European big-bike market grew by an astounding 33 percent between 1990 and 1992: Because of its production constraints, Harley could maintain only a 9 to 10 percent share of this market. In other words, it was giving away business to foreign competitors.

To enhance its presence in Europe, Harley opened a branch office of its HOG club in Frankfurt, Germany. This was all it could offer its European fans.

Specifics of the Resurgence of Harley Davidson

Table 13.1 shows Harley Davidson's trend in revenues and net income since 1982. The growth in sales and profits did not go unnoticed by the investment community. In 1990 Harley Davidson stock sold for $7; in January 1993, it hit $39. Its market share of heavyweight motorcycles (751 cc displacement and larger) had soared from 12.5 percent in 1983 to 63 percent by 1993. Let the Japanese have the lightweight bike market! Harley would dominate the heavyweights.

Harley Davidson acquired Holiday Rambler in 1986. The company expected this wholly owned subsidiary, a manufacturer of recreational and commercial vehicles, to be compatible with the existing motorcycle business and to moderate some of the seasonality of the motorcycle business. The diversification proved rather mediocre. In 1992 it accounted for 26 percent of total corporate sales but only 2 percent of profits.[18]

---

[17]Gary Slutsker, "Hog Wild," *Forbes* (May 24, 1993), p. 46.
[18]Company annual reports.

Table 13.1   Harley Davidson's Growth in Revenue and Income
1983–1992 (in millions)

Year	Revenue	Net Income
1982	$210	def. $25.1[a]
1983	254	1.0
1984	294	2.9
1985	287	2.6
1986	295	4.3
1987	685	17.7
1988	757	27.2
1989	791	32.6
1990	865	38.3
1991	940	37.0
1992	1,100	54.0

[a]Deficit.
Source: Company annual reports.
Commentary: The steady climb in sales and profits, except for a pause in 1985, is noteworthy. The total gain in revenues over these 11 years was 423.8%, and income rose more than fifty-fold.

Big motorcycles, made in America by the only U.S. manufacturer, continued to sell. As many as 100,000 people, including 18,000 HOGs, celebrated Harley's 90th anniversary in Milwaukee on June 12, 1993. Hotels were booked solid for a 60-mile radius. Harley Davidson was up and running.

ANALYSIS

One of the first moves Vaughan Beals made after the 1981 leveraged buyout was to improve production efficiency and quality control. This became the foundation for the strategic regeneration moves to come. In this quest he borrowed heavily from the Japanese, particularly in cultivating employee involvement.

The cultivation of a new customer segment for the big bikes had to be a major factor in the company's resurgence. Some analysts were surprised by the fact that affluent consumers were embracing Harley's big, flashy motorcycles. After all, what two groups were less compatible than the stereotyped black-jacketed cyclists and the Rubbies? Perhaps part of the change was due to the fact that high-profile people such as Beals and some of his executives frequently participated in motorcycle rallies and charity rides. Technological and comfort improvements in motorcycles and their equipment added to the new attractiveness. Dealers were also coaxed to make their stores more inviting.

Expanding the product mix not only made Harley-branded merchandise a windfall for company and dealers but also piqued upscale customers' interest in motorcycles themselves. The company was commendably aggressive in running with the growing popularity of the ancillary merchandise and raising well over $100 million in merchandise revenue by the early 1990s.

Some questions remain. How durable is this popularity, both of the big bikes and the complementary merchandise, with this affluent customer segment? Will it prove to be only a passing fad? If so, then Harley needs to seek diversifications as quickly as possible even though the Holiday Rambler Corporation had brought no notable success by 1992. Diversifications often bring disappointing earnings compared with a firm's core business.

Another question concerns Harley's slowness in expanding production capability. Faced with a burgeoning demand, is it better to go slowly, to be carefully protective of quality, and to refrain from heavy debt commitments? This has been Harley's most recent strategy, but it raises the risk of permitting competitors to gain market share in the United States and especially in Europe. The following issue box discusses aggressive versus conservative planning.

ISSUE BOX

SHOULD WE BE AGGRESSIVE OR CONSERVATIVE IN OUR PLANNING?

The sales forecast—the estimate of sales for the periods ahead—serves a crucial role because it is the starting point for all detailed planning and budgeting. A volatile situation presents some high-risk alternatives: Should we be optimistic or conservative?

On one hand, with conservative planning in a growing market, a firm risks underestimating demand and being unable to expand its resources sufficiently to handle the potential. It may lack the manufacturing capability and sales staff to handle growth potential, and it may have to abdicate a good share of the growing business to competitors who are willing and able to expand their capability to meet the demands of the market.

On the other hand, a firm facing burgeoning demand should consider whether the growth is likely to be a short-term fad or a more permanent situation. A firm can easily become overextended in the buoyancy of booming business, only to see the collapse of such business jeopardizing its viability.

Harley's conservative decision was undoubtedly influenced by concerns about expanding beyond the limits of good quality control. The decision was probably also influenced by management's belief that Harley Davidson had a loyal body of customers who would not switch despite the wait.

INVITATION TO DISCUSSION

Do you think Harley Davidson made the right decision to expand conservatively? Why or why not?

WHAT CAN BE LEARNED?

A firm can come back from adversity. Harley Davidson's resurrection almost from the point of extinction proves that adversity can be overcome. It need not be fatal or forever. Many firms are unable to pull themselves around, however, as we will see in the sad case of the demise of A. C. Gilbert Company (Chapter 14).

What does a turnaround require? Above all, it takes a leader who has the vision and confidence that things can be changed for the better. The change may not necessitate anything particularly innovative; it may only involve a rededication to basics, such as improved quality control or an improved commitment to customer service. But such a return to basics requires that a demoralized or apathetic organization be rejuvenated and remotivated. This calls for leadership of a high order. If the core business has been maintained, it at least provides a base to work from.

Preserve the core business at all costs. Every viable firm has a basic core or distinctive position, sometimes called an ecological niche in the business environment. This unique position may be due to its particular location or to a certain product. It may come from somewhat different operating methods or from the customers served. This strong point is the basic core of a company's survival. Though it may diversify and expand far beyond this area, the firm should not abandon its main bastion of strength.

Harley almost did this. Its core—and indeed, only—business was its heavyweight bikes sold to a limited and loyal, though not at the time particularly savory, customer segment. Harley almost lost this core business by abandoning reasonable quality control to the point that its motorcycles became the butt of jokes. To his credit, upon assuming leadership Beals acted quickly to correct the production and employee motivation problems. By preserving the core, Beals could pursue other avenues of expansion.

The power of a mystique. Few products are able to gain a mystique or cult following. Coors beer did in the 1960s and early 1970s, when it became the brew of celebrities and the emblem of the purity and freshness of the west. In the cigarette industry, Marlboro became the top seller from a somewhat similar advertising and image thrust: the Marlboro man. The Ford Mustang had a mystique at one time. Somehow the big Harley Davidson bikes developed a mystique. Harleys appealed to the HOGs and to the Rubbies: two disparate customer segments, but both loyal to their Harleys. The mystique led to "logo magic": Simply put the Harley Davidson name and logo on all kinds of merchandise, and watch the sales take off.

How does a firm develop (or acquire) a mystique? There is no simple answer, no guarantee. Certainly a product has to be unique, but though most firms strive for this differentiation, few achieve a mystique. Image-building advertising, focusing on the target buyer, may help. Perhaps even better is image-building advertising that highlights the people customers might wish to emulate.

Perhaps in the final analysis, acquiring a mystique is a more accidental and fortuitous success than something that can be deliberately orchestrated. Two lessons, however, can be learned about mystiques: First, they do not last forever. Second, firms should run with them as long as possible and try to expand the reach of the name or logo to other goods, even unrelated ones, through licensing.

INVITATION

What additional learning insights can you gain from this Harley Davidson resurgence?

QUESTIONS

1. Do you think Beals' rejuvenation strategy for Harley Davidson was the best policy? Discuss and evaluate other strategies that he might have pursued.
2. How durable do you think the Rubbies' infatuation with the heavy-weight Harleys will be? What leads you to this conclusion?
3. A Harley Davidson stockholder criticizes present management: "It is a mistake of the greatest magnitude that we abdicate a decent share of the European motorcycle market to foreign competitors, simply because we do not gear up our production to meet the demand." Discuss.
4. Given the resurgence of Harley Davidson in the early 1990s, would you invest money in the company? Discuss, considering as many factors bearing on this decision as you can.
5. "Harley Davidson's resurgence is only the purest luck. Who could have predicted, or influenced, the new popularity of big bikes with the affluent?" Discuss.
6. "The tariff increase on Japanese motorcycles in 1983 gave Harley Davidson badly needed breathing room. In the final analysis, politics is more important than management in competing with foreign firms." What are your thoughts?

INVITATION TO ROLE PLAY

1. You are a representative of a mutual funds firm with a major investment in Harley Davidson. You are particularly critical of Vaughan

Beals' visible presence at motorcycle rallies and his hobnobbing with black-jacketed cycle gangs. He maintains that this is a fruitful way to maintain a loyal core of customers. Playing devil's advocate (a person who opposes a position to establish its merits and validity), what arguments will you raise against Beals' practices?

2. As a vice president at Harley Davidson, you believe the recovery efforts should have gone well beyond the heavyweight bikes into lightweights. What arguments do you present for this change in strategy, and what specific recommendations do you make for such a new course of action? What contrary arguments do you expect? How will you counter them?

3. As a staff assistant to Vaughan Beals, you have been charged to design a strategy to bring a mystique to the Harley Davidson name. How would you propose to do this? Be as specific as you can, and defend your reasoning.

INVITATION TO RESEARCH

What is the situation at Harley Davidson today? Has the strategy changed? Has the penetration of the European market increased? Is the mystique still apparent?

14

A. C. Gilbert: Flawed Crisis Management

The A. C. Gilbert Company was not a youngster, having had some 58 years of toy-making experience at the time it failed. For years its name had been respected and well known, and it signified quality.

In a mere five years, all this was to end. Almost incredibly, poor judgment replaced the solid achievements of the past. Managers ignored changing environmental conditions for too long and then substituted rash, frantic decisions for a well-planned, corrective strategy that could have built on the strengths of the company.

BACKGROUND

The A. C. Gilbert Company was the product of one imaginative man's inventiveness and willingness to back his ideas himself rather than selling out. Alfred Carlton Gilbert, after graduation from Yale, established the Mysto Manufacturing Company in 1909 to make the Erector set, which he had perfected. In 1916 this company became the A. C. Gilbert Company. In time his son, A. C., Jr., joined the company as assistant to his father and became president in 1954. In 1961 the senior Gilbert died, and his son became chairman of the board. Gilbert, Jr., was a respected figure in the toy industry, serving as president of the Toys Manufacturers of the United States in 1962 and 1963.

Although the company never became a large firm, it was solidly in the top 10 toy manufacturers in the 1950s, with sales reaching over $17 million. It was strong in science toys—chemistry sets, microscopes, and Erector "engineering" sets—at a time when science was becoming an important national priority. Gilbert had the reputation of a quality toy maker, and its American Flyer trains and Erector sets were known by generations of boys and their parents.

This was the situation as the company entered the 1960s, but the environment for selling toys was changing. The 1960s, with their attendant prosperity, brought a booming toy market, but one that was different from what Gilbert knew. A new promotional medium, television, had become important for toy marketing and was superseding catalogs and window displays. But television was expensive and made the break-even point on toy sales much higher. It also enabled many items, from hula hoops to Batmobiles, to attain quick popularity. The market was changing rapidly, and a firm had to be nimble to tap the sales potential and not be caught with too heavy an inventory when demand was superseded by another fad item.

The toy market was also changing in that traditional toy stores, hobby shops, and department stores were being bypassed for self-service, high-volume supermarkets and discount stores. These new dealers were mainly interested in low-priced, heavily advertised toys with attractive packages that could act as selling tools.

So the successful, well-entrenched company entered the 1960s rather complacent and content with the status quo.

PROBLEMS

Anson Isaacson, president of Gilbert, had a desperate task before him. In April 1966 he was searching frantically among financial circles to raise the money needed to operate another year, after suffering losses of $2.9 million in 1965.

Isaacson had assumed the presidency in June 1964 after A. C. Gilbert, Jr., died. He was a former vice president of Ideal Toy Company, a larger toy maker, and had been brought into the company to straighten out serious sales and profit problems that had been getting worse since 1961.

After three weeks of scouting for financial aid, Anson Isaacson was successful. Pledging most of the remaining unpledged assets of the company, he was able to obtain a loan of $6.25 million; he himself put up $250,000 to show creditors his faith in the company and his confidence in his ability to straighten out the problems. There was one frightening stipulation in the loan agreement, however. The loan was contingent on the company's making a profit in 1966. If Gilbert failed to do so, the loan would be called and the assets liquidated to satisfy the indebtedness. Isaacson was not bargaining from a position of strength and had to accept the condition. Although he did believe that under his management the condition would not pose a particular problem, still it lurked in the background, ominous and threatening.

PRELUDE

Now let us examine how Gilbert had gotten into this mess. The company did not really recognize a problem until the end of 1961, at which time sales dropped from $12.6 million in 1960 to $11.6 million. In 1961 the company counted a mere $20,011 in profits. Gilbert was obviously facing serious problems, and managers hastily devised a program to correct the situation.

In early 1962, with stock prices down, the company became attractive to Jack Wrather, president of a West Coast holding company that owned the "Lassie" and "Lone Ranger" television programs, the Disneyland Hotel, Muzak Corporation (piped-in music), and a boatyard. Wrather acquired a 52 percent interest in the Gilbert Company for some $4 million. He then replaced Gilbert top executives with his own people. Although A. C. Gilbert, Jr., remained as board chairman, his power was substantially lessened.

Wrather's people attributed the 1961 sales drop to two factors: insufficient new products and insufficient advertising. They formulated plans to boost sales to $20 million with the addition of new "hot items" and increased the sales staff 50 percent, assuming that more aggressive selling and more frequent contacts with retailers would lead to increasing sales. After expanding the sales staff, they appointed a new general sales manager and a new director of international sales.

But this strategy proved unsuccessful. In 1962 sales dropped to $10.9 million, with a $281,000 loss. This loss was attributed to the cost of preparing the new, greatly expanded 1963 line and the scrapping of obsolete materials. The company was pinning its great expectations on the 1963 selling season and made a major effort to expand the line. For the first time, the company was offering toys for preschool children and for girls in the 6- to 14-year-old bracket in addition to toys for boys, who had been the traditional market segment. More than 50 new items boosted the line to 307 items, by far the largest in the company's history. The ambitious expansion program seemed fully justified and badly needed; now the market was 35 million boys and girls, instead of just 9 million boys.

Modern Packaging magazine hailed the package revitalization program in 1963.[1] The company had spent upward of $1 million to repackage the entire line. Packages for Erector sets and other long-established toys had been virtually unchanged for many years; now they had an "exciting" new full-color pictorial treatment illustrating the models in action.

The future looked bright at this time, and such an aggressive approach was viewed as badly overdue in an old, conservatively managed family business. Officials confidently predicted record sales and earnings.

It must have been a bitter pill when sales results finally came in (in the toy business, the Christmas selling season is crucial for the year's performance; until the results of this business season are tabulated late in the year, no one really knows how successful a year has been). Incredibly, sales continued to slide in 1963, to $10.7 million; worse, instead of a profit, there was a whopping $5.7 million loss, stemming mostly from huge returns of low-priced toys shipped on a guaranteed sale basis to supermarkets. After Christmas, Gilbert had an inventory of almost $3.5 million in unsold toys.

Corrective Efforts

At this point Jack Wrather decided that a toy-making company needed more expert toy-making experience. He fired most of the top management he had brought in nearly two years before. A. C. Gilbert, Jr., reassumed the presidency, but Anson Isaacson, former Ideal Toy Company vice president, was brought in as chief operating officer and chairman of the executive committee.

In two years losses had reached almost $6 million. This was a terrible drain on a firm whose revenues were not much more than $10 million a year. The company renegotiated loans at higher interest rates, and got major creditors to agree to a delay in payment over a three-year period. After the last several years of profligate expansion of sales staff and product lines, Isaacson began a strong economy drive.

He made a major change in the selling mechanism. In place of company salespeople, he fired the sales staff and switched to manufacturers' representatives. Manufacturers' representatives are independent sales representatives who handle a number of noncompeting lines of various manufacturers and charge a fixed commission, usually 5 or 6 percent on all sales made. They are somewhat less expensive than a company sales force and should be able to contact more dealers. Gilbert had less control over them,

---

[1]"Saving a $500,000 Investment," *Modern Packaging* (August 1963), pp. 97–98.

however, and their customer service for Gilbert could be erratic. In addition, Isaacson made major cuts in factory personnel, reducing administrative and operating expenses from $10 million to $4.7 million for 1964. In June 1964, A. C. Gilbert, Jr., died; Wrather became chairman of the board, and Isaacson, president.

For the 1964 Christmas season, Gilbert Company added 20 new toys to the depleted line. Encouragingly, sales picked up almost 7 percent, to $11.4 million. The company would have registered a profit for the year, but Isaacson insisted on dumping excess inventory to enhance future years' profits, so the company registered a loss of $1.9 million.

The expectations of Isaacson and the Gilbert Company now rested on the fall and Christmas selling season of 1965. This was to be the year the company turned around and reached for its new potential. To this end, the product line was again revamped and a heavy advertising and point-of-purchase display program budgeted. The company committed $2 million for television advertising that centered on a 52-week schedule of Saturday morning Beatles cartoon shows. In addition the Gilbert Company furnished some 65,000 animated displays free to dealers at a cost of $1 million.

Early indications for 1965 were favorable. By July 1 Isaacson predicted a net profit for the year. The order backlog was $12 million in July, and losses for the first 6 months of the year (toymakers characteristically incur losses through most of the year until the peak Christmas business is realized) were only one-half those for the same period in 1964.

Isaacson's optimistic prediction, however, proved wrong. The heavy promotional expenditures did bring sales of $14.9 million, the best since the early 1950s, and a 30 percent increase over the preceding year. However, losses were up to $2.9 million, mostly because of heavy returns on a 007 racing auto set, which was then handled exclusively by Sears, as well as other racing sets. These racing sets turned out to be poorly engineered and constructed, poorly packaged, and overpriced.

As the company's financial condition continued to worsen, Anson Isaacson began his rounds to find the financing necessary to keep the company alive. The multimillion-dollar rescue loan that he finally obtained made virtually all the assets subject to liens to secure such indebtedness and was contingent on the company's making a profit in 1966.

It did not make a profit in 1966. Instead, the announced loss was $12,872,000. The once proud A. C. Gilbert Company went out of business in February 1967. Gabriel Industries acquired certain of Gilbert's assets, including Erector sets and chemistry sets, for about $17 million that went to the financial institutions holding Gilbert's indebtedness.

Figure 14.1 depicts Gilbert's last six years.

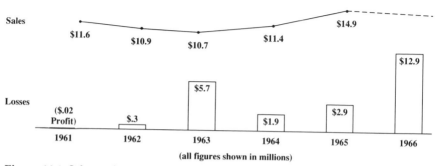

Figure 14.1. Sales and Profits/Losses of Gilbert, 1961–1966.

HOW DID IT HAPPEN?

What role did the frequent top executive changes play in Gilbert's inability to cope with the environmental changes and eventually the crises that overcame it? In particular, did going outside the firm to hire top executives contribute to the demise? The following issue box discusses this controversy: whether outsiders brought in as top executives are more likely to help or hinder an organization in extremis.

We can group the mistakes that Gilbert made into two broad categories: *lack of recognition of the problem* until late and *frantic reactions once the problem was recognized*, resulting in successive mistakes until the end. We will discuss each of these in more detail and identify the specific mistakes under these categories.

Gilbert failed to recognize that the toy environment was changing and that the changes were causing an ever-worsening problem. Diminishing sales from the peak years of the 1950s apparently did not alert the company that there was a problem needing investigation and some adjustment in business strategy.

We have previously noted how major changes in advertising and distribution of toys were occurring and were only belatedly recognized by Gilbert. One change in toy demand that should have been quickly detected was the fact that tabletop slot-car auto racing sets, almost unknown 10 years before, were now outselling toy trains. Gilbert should have been in this market near the outset. Instead, it waited until the mid-1960s to introduce its racing sets. And these sets were poorly engineered, fragile, and overpriced—their returns in 1965 practically scuttled the company.

Not until the end of the 1961 selling season, when the company barely made a profit, did managers become aware of a possible problem. At this point they took frantic and poorly thought-out actions and with the serious loss of 1962, there was no longer any doubt that there was a problem.

ISSUE BOX

ARE EXECUTIVES RECRUITED FROM OUTSIDE MORE LIKELY TO HELP OR HINDER A TROUBLED FIRM?

As the 1990s loomed as a period of corporate turmoil for some of the largest and most prestigious firms in the United States—such as IBM, Eastman Kodak, American Express—many boards of directors sought to recruit outside executives to salvage their operations. IBM is the most widely publicized example, with the board selecting Louis Gerstner, CEO of RJR Nabisco, to orchestrate the revival of the reeling IBM. Not only had Gerstner never worked for IBM, but he was not even familiar with the computer industry. (See Chapter 2.) *Business Week*'s feature article about this was titled "Faith in a Stranger."[2] The board and many analysts saw such unfamiliarity as an advantage in bringing new insights and a fresh perspective to a conservative organization.

The results have been mixed in firms that have gone outside for their top executives. At Eastman Kodak, outsider Christopher J. Steffen resigned as CEO after less than three months on the job. James D. Robinson III was toppled as chief executive of American Express; so was Russell Craig after 14 months at Digital Equipment. One of the shortest tenures of an outsider was Thomas J. Johnson of giant Olympia & York Developments, who lasted only two weeks after becoming president.[3]

The causes frequently are personality problems in meshing with existing senior management. Power struggles may hinder progress on planned agendas for major changes, and sometimes the lack of fit goes far beyond mere personality conflicts.

The Gilbert Company was particularly burdened with the waves of outside executives brought in to institute the planned major changes. Undoubtedly the existing managers were culpable in not recognizing early the drastically changing environment for toys, but their replacements tended to be agents of excessive change, disregarding both the tradition of the company and its resources available for change.

INVITATION TO DISCUSSION

If you were an insider tapped for the presidency of Gilbert and you had a conservative agenda for action, what would you propose? How successful do you think your course of action would have been, compared with more drastic changes?

Managers took desperate actions with the product line, which had remained relatively unchanged for decades. Suddenly, in one year, the line was greatly expanded, including more than 50 new toys directed not only to

[2]Catherine Arnst, "Faith in a Stranger," *Business Week* (April 5, 1993), pp. 18–21.
[3]Joann S. Lublin, "Firms Going Outside for Top Bosses Often Hire Trouble," *The Wall Street Journal* (April 30, 1993), pp. B1, B4.

the traditional target market of 6- to 14-year-old boys but also to girls and preschool children. Furthermore, the toys—lower priced, lower quality, and geared to large-volume sales—were different from what the company had been used to making. This placed great strain on the company's engineering and production capabilities. The almost inevitable result was poorly designed toys of low quality and disappointing customer appeal. The company abandoned its unique niche as a quality toy maker of high-level educational toys and flung itself into the fiercely competitive marketplace against better experienced and mostly larger competitors.

Subsequent actions did nothing to restore the image of the reputable toymaker. A company and brand image is precious; a good image is difficult to develop but easy to destroy.

Toy buyers were critical of the company's product changes and of its packaging:

> Gilbert had a natural in its Erector sets. Instead, they neglected it. They used to offer sets up to $75 packaged in metal boxes. Now the most expensive is only $20, the parts are flimsy, and it's in an oversized cardboard box. They did the same thing to their chemistry sets. You can't store anything in those oversize see-through packages.[4]

Neither did buyers like the new All Aboard series, consisting of landscaped panels that fit together to form a tabletop train layout.

> It's a real good idea, but the quality is poor. The locomotive and cars are cheap and lack detail.[5]

Gilbert's doll series was overpriced, poorly made, and incomplete because the company offered no changes of doll clothes. This was at the time when additional wardrobes were the major appeal of many dolls as well as a source of extra profits.

Incredibly poor timing was the lot of the company in attempting to compete with fad items. For example, in 1965, spy items were especially popular, with spy and secret agent movies and television series having high audience ratings. So Gilbert introduced such spy figures as Man from U.N.C.L.E., James Bond, and Honey West. The only trouble was that they did not reach the market until after Christmas day in 1965, obviously too late for the selling season. Such timing was inexcusable and reflected

---

[4]Art Detman, Jr., "Toymaker, A. C. Gilbert Co., Poor Loser?" *Sales Management* (May 1, 1966), p. 27.
[5]*Ibid.*, p. 28.

drastic problems in the planning and operations of the company; the ground had been laid for this situation in 1964.

Successive errors were piled on each other. After the ill-conceived product line expansion of 1963 that resulted in $5.7 million in losses, an austerity campaign was put in effect in 1964, with major cutbacks made in engineering and production—expenses were consequently reduced more than 50 percent for 1964. But such austerity hardly led to the planning and production efficiencies needed for the quick introduction of fad items.

Other aspects of the austerity were less obvious but consequential. The company switched from having its own sales force to contracting for independent manufacturers' representatives to handle its selling efforts. Although this move was expected to increase dealer coverage while maintaining the cost of selling, dealers did not like the new arrangement: "It used to be that you could call a Gilbert salesman and get service on a problem. Now the reps just want to get the order," disgruntled dealers were saying.[6]

In attempting to widen its distribution to supermarkets, discount stores, and other aggressive promotional retailers, Gilbert made certain concessions that were to cost dearly, such as guaranteeing the sales of its products to some of these demanding outlets. By guaranteeing sales, the company assumed the burden of poor selling efforts, markdowns, and product write-offs of anything unsold after the Christmas season. Guaranteeing sales is usually a last-ditch effort by a new manufacturer trying to gain entry in the marketplace. Offering an unknown brand, such a supplier is totally dependent on retailers and may be forced to accept the conditions demanded by some. Gilbert was not a small unknown firm trying to crack the marketplace. In 1963 it still had a quality image, was widely known, and had good distribution, even though not as wide as desired.

A final dramatic mistake came in 1965. After the austerity of 1964, the company reopened the spigots with a vengeance, adding more new toys, a massive television advertising campaign, and a point-of-purchase display program. Here was a company with sales of just over $11 million, facing the specter of insolvency, budgeting almost 30 percent of sales for a massive promotion effort. The lack of success, resulting from poor judgment of products, distribution, and timing, laid the groundwork for the company's demise. Its image as a reliable producer of high-quality toys was gone. The $6.25 million last-resort financing that Isaacson managed to come up with in 1966 could no longer support the company's efforts to regain a viable niche in the market.

[6]*Ibid.*

Gilbert management had erred profoundly in its crisis management, destroying the company in the process. The following information box offers systematic steps to better cope with crises.

INFORMATION BOX

COPING WITH CRISES

A crisis is an unexpected problem that can lead to disaster unless handled quickly and appropriately.[7] Top management should normally take certain steps in responding to crises or to other major forces dictating change:

1. Gain awareness of a problem
2. Diagnose the cause of the problem
3. Examine alternative solutions to the problem
4. Make a preliminary choice for a new course of action
5. Test the preliminary choice on a small scale before making a permanent choice
6. As a result of the test results or pilot run, either accept and adopt the proposed solution on a wider scale or reject it and consider another alternative.

Effective management is quick to recognize emerging problems, hopefully before they have become serious and are drastically affecting sales and profits. Considerable attention should be given to determining the cause(s) of the problems. This may involve collecting more information, perhaps through a research study or various internal analyses. After determining cause, managers can identify alternative solutions, evaluate their pros and cons in view of the resources of the organization, and select one. If managers have doubts concerning the chosen alternative, they may introduce it on a small scale—perhaps in one or two departments or locations—before proceeding further with it or else testing another alternative.

These, then, are the steps for prudently coping with major change. Crises develop when managers fail to recognize the problem early enough (step one), before sales and profits are drastically affected. The other steps represent the most systematic and effective approach to dealing with it.

INVITATION TO DISCUSSION
How would you answer the objections that going through such a process, especially steps 5 and 6, is too time consuming, that in a crisis situation there is no time for careful testing or pilot runs?

---

[7]Schermerhorn, *op. cit.*, p. 156.

WHAT CAN BE LEARNED?

It does not take long to destroy a company. Perhaps the most important lesson to be learned from Gilbert's experience is that it does not take long for a supposedly healthy and experienced company to come to its end. A series of successive bad decisions coming in the space of a few years can destroy all the gains built up by decades of successful operation.

Firms need to pay close attention to their environment and how it is changing. Gilbert needed to assess changing conditions better and more quickly. Such assessment should have included changes in consumer demand and buying patterns, as well as competitive actions. The changes occurring were not difficult to detect. They were obvious to all—consumers, retailers, and manufacturers alike. But Gilbert continued to operate as if the status quo could be maintained, as if nothing were changing. The lesson is worth repeating: It is important to be constantly alert and responsive to change.

Problems need to be recognized quickly before they reach the crisis stage. In a dynamic environment, problems will inevitably arise. Some may be serious; others are minor or transitory. The seriousness and duration of other problems may be difficult to predict; here, the prudent executive needs at least to consider the worst scenario. A declining market share or competitive position should be a red flag waving that something is amiss that needs to be seriously addressed. What is the cause of the worsening situation? Is it something we need to aggressively act upon? In a time of steadily increasing demand for toys, to have sales remain static or decline strongly suggests something is wrong, even though profitability may not yet be an obvious problem. Gilbert blundered seriously in failing to recognize the changing toy market long before the drastic decline in sales and profits for 1961.

Managers in crisis should guard against reacting without careful analysis of alternatives and their implications. A firm must beware of reacting too quickly, without careful analysis of alternatives. This is the height of misguided crisis management. Problems need to be carefully identified, and probable solutions or adjustments to them weighed in view of the particular strengths and resources of the firm. In Gilbert's case, hasty actions only compounded past mistakes. The whip-sawing was particularly deadly to the company— drastically cutting costs to the bone one year, then in a wild spree budgeting $3 million for advertising and promotional displays at a time when the firm was on the verge of bankruptcy.

At all costs, a firm must zealously guard a quality image. The major strength of the firm was its quality image. In no way should this have been sacrificed to bring out a proliferation of "cheap" new products similar to competitors. By expanding hastily with such products, the company disregarded its production and quality-control capabilities. The flood of poorly made products in one selling season destroyed the quality image that had been built up and maintained for over 50 years. A quality image is difficult to attain, but as we see here, it can be destroyed in only a few months. Maintaining Gilbert's quality image should have been given the highest priority; all decisions should have been made with this in mind.

INVITATION

Do you see any additional learning insights to discuss from the Gilbert fiasco?

UPDATE

Although the Gilbert Company folded, never to return, the Erector set survived. As described earlier, Gabriel Industries, a large toy manufacturer that also makes Tinker Toys, acquired the Erector asset at the liquidation of Gilbert. In 1977 nearly 600,000 Erector sets, ranging in price from $1 for a 45-piece pocket set to $40 for a deluxe 450-piece set, were sold around the world.

In August 1978, CBS purchased Gabriel and its Erector set subsidiary for $27.1 million. The senior vice president of Gabriel made a prediction: "A hundred years from now, I think you'll still be able to buy an Erector set . . . long after everyone here is gone."[8]

QUESTIONS

1. What controls should Gilbert have had to remain alert to changing market conditions? What research would have helped?
2. Do you think Gilbert was right in expanding its target market in 1963? Why or why not?
3. Evaluate the advertising efforts of 1965 and the point-of-purchase display expenditures.
4. Discuss the pros and cons of changing management quickly when adversity sets in.
5. How would you identify a crisis situation at its earliest stage?
6. How would you recommend handling a crisis situation, given that (a) stockholders are small and numerous; (b) the company is family held, and the top executive is family; (c) a few large banks and mutual funds have most of the stock.

---

[8]"The Nuts and Bolts of Erector Set Firm," *Cleveland Plain Dealer* (September 10, 1978), Sec. 2-1.

INVITATION TO ROLE PLAY

1. It is late 1962. As an assistant to the president, what do you advise Gilbert to do when the first drastic decline in profit occurs? Identify the pros and cons of your recommendations, and persuasively present them.
2. As a management consultant, what do you advise at the end of 1963? Again, persuasively present your ideas, identify probable objections, and defend your recommendations.

INVITATION TO RESEARCH

Are Erector sets still available? Who is the manufacturer? What is their quality and attractiveness today?

15

The Savings and Loan Disaster: Leadership Greed on Display

In the 1980s a financial disaster of monumental proportions suddenly emerged on the public consciousness. That it involved the savings of ordinary people and that the long-term consequences would be borne by all taxpayers made it all the more consequential. That it involved management incompetence and violation of depositor and shareholder trust in excesses of spending and lending brought widespread media attention.

Our savings and loan (S & L) industry, the source of home ownership for millions of Americans, was on the verge of total collapse; indeed, hundreds of institutions would go bankrupt. But the savings of the depositors were protected by the federal government and were not at risk, though the government bailout would be the costliest in history.

How could this have happened? What can we learn from it? What management mistakes were made that managers in other times and places, with awareness, can avoid? And what were the keys to success for the S & Ls that survived and prospered during this time?

A SAMPLING OF FIASCOS

Sunbelt Savings

Edwin T. McBirney III was 29 years old when he began his run to a vast fortune in the savings and loan business. The year was 1981. While still in college he had shown unusual business acumen, starting his own business leasing refrigerators to college students. Upon graduation he turned to real estate, becoming a broker and investor in the booming Dallas market.

In December 1981 McBirney formed an investment group that began buying small S & Ls. One of these was Sunbelt Savings, an obscure S & L in Stephenville, Texas. McBirney was to merge these holdings into one large S & L, which he named Sunbelt Savings Association. In less than four years, Sunbelt was the nucleus of a $3.2 billion financial empire. Its growth came mostly from commercial real-estate loans that were so risky that Sunbelt gained the nickname "Gunbelt" for its shoot-from-the-hip lending policies. As one example, Sunbelt lent $125 million (secured only by raw land) to an inexperienced Dallas developer in his twenties who went on to lose $80 million.[1] In its heyday Sunbelt owned mortgage and development service companies, had a commercial-banking division, and made real estate loans to developers from California to Florida.

McBirney and his executives soon were covering Texas in the company's fleet of seven aircraft. McBirney liked to throw sumptuous parties, serving lion and antelope to hundreds of guests at his palatial Dallas home. In 1984 and 1985, Sunbelt paid $1.3 million for Halloween and Christmas galas, including a $32,000 fee to McBirney's wife for organizing the parties. No end seemed to be in sight for these Texas big spenders, but it was just around the corner.

In 1984 the Empire Savings and Loan of Mesquite, Texas, collapsed after funding massive high-risk investments. Its demise raised troubling questions about the entire industry. Edwin Gray, chairman of the Federal Home Loan Bank Board, a regulator of S & Ls, became fearful of a disaster and slammed on the brakes. He forced reappraisals based on current market values, increased capital requirements, limited direct appraisals, and hired hundreds of new examiners and supervisory agents. Appraisers found that the collateral backing billions of dollars of loans had been overvalued by up to 30 percent. Many thrifts had to lower the book value of their loans, reducing their already weak capital positions. Then real estate values plummeted as Texas' economy began collapsing, led by declining oil prices. The domino effect took over as a rash of loan delinquencies led to one foreclosure after another.

Now the excesses of McBirney's heyday came to roost. Hundreds of examiners descended on the Dallas home loan office in the spring of 1986, and the bulk of the Sunbird S & Ls were declared insolvent. While Sunbird itself was spared temporarily, McBirney was forced to resign as chairman by June. Of the foreclosed real estate on Sunbelt's books, only a few million out of its $6 billion portfolio of troubled assets could be sold off. By late

---

[1]Howard Rudnitsky and John R. Hayes, "Gunbelt S & L," *Forbes* (September 19, 1988), p. 120.

1988 the Federal Home Loan Bank Board estimated that it would cost as much as $5.5 billion just to keep Sunbelt alive over the next 10 years.[2]

To add to the insult, a lawsuit filed against McBirney and other insider shareholders charged that nearly $13 million in common and preferred dividends had been taken out in 1985 and 1986, at a time when Sunbelt's capital was rapidly evaporating because of wild expenditures and devaluation of assets.

Shamrock Federal Savings Bank

In Shamrock, Texas, the little savings and loan on the corner went belly up. The collapse of the Shamrock Federal Savings Bank left a bitter pill for this town of 3,000 in the Texas panhandle. It was a common story for many Texas communities: a small-town thrift taken over by an outsider; fast growth followed by sudden insolvency; a trail of incompetent management and soured high-risk ventures in places far beyond the limits of the town. "We made a mistake selling it. We should have kept it under local control, making loans in our community," declared one of the original directors of the town's only savings and loan.

Back in 1977 Phil Cates, a state representative and head of the local Chamber of Commerce, had a vision of a financial institution that would serve Shamrock and other small towns near the Oklahoma line. He started pushing townsfolk to start their own savings and loan association in view of the oil and gas boom that was bringing hundreds of people into the town. Shamrock's two family-owned banks shunned long-term home mortgages and refused to pay competitive interest rates. Cates sold the idea of a local S & L to hundreds of local residents. When the Red River Savings and Loan Association opened in 1979, it had more than 350 stockholders in a town of 2,834. Community pride ran high.

These were the days of S & L deregulation, and small-town thrifts like Red River were hot properties, targets of opportunity for promoters and speculators. One speculator, Jerry D. Lane, offered owners $21 a share, more than double the original price. The townspeople jumped at the opportunity. Lane changed the name to Shamrock Savings Association, and in three years deposits rocketed from $11.6 million to $111.3 million. The thrift's focus shifted far beyond the small town of Shamrock, with offices as far away as Amarillo and Colorado Springs, Colorado. Lane also began buying some of other thrifts' outstanding loans.

Disaster struck in 1987 when the Federal Savings and Loan Insurance Corporation filed a $150 million racketeering suit against Lane and others after the 1985 failure of State Savings of Lubbock, Texas. Lane had been

---

[2]For more detail, see "Why Our S & Ls Are in Trouble," *Reader's Digest* (July 1989), pp. 70–74.

chief executive officer there. Federal regulators had found a pattern common to the S & L industry and would soon find it at Shamrock: making fraudulent loans to developers, concentrating an "unsafe" amount of credit with one client, basing loans on inflated property appraisals, and making them without proper credit documentation. "Loans were made over lunch with a handshake."

Federal regulators closed Shamrock in November 1987; it owed $16.6 million more than it was worth. But its betrayal of the local community occurred before that. The S & L had been conceived to make loans locally for homes and other projects that could help the community, but with its buyout and the shift of emphasis far beyond the local community, its managers had little interest in providing less lucrative but less risky local loans.

Shamrock characterized a large segment of S & Ls, especially in the heady days of the oil boom when Texas and other southwestern states thought there was no stopping the runaway building boom built on the belief that oil prices could only go up. But prices dropped to $14 a barrel in the early 1980s, destroying the cash supports from under commercial real estate projects all across the Southwest.[3]

Lincoln Savings and Loan: Political Scandal

Charles Keating is the former owner of California's Lincoln Savings and Loan. He purchased Lincoln in 1984 and switched it from investing in safe, single-family mortgages to raw land speculation, junk bonds, and huge development projects like the $900-a-night Phoenician Resort in Scottsdale, Arizona.

Keating was a heavy campaign contributor, giving to five prominent U.S. senators: John Glenn, Alan Cranston, John McCain, Donald Reigle, and Dennis De Concini. In total, these influential politicians received $1.3 million from Keating. As his failing S & L came under the scrutiny of the Federal Home Loan Bank Board, which found enough bad loans and shaky business practices to shut it down, he sought help from these senators, and with their help delayed action for two years. During this time the federally guaranteed cost of paying back Lincoln's depositors went up $1.3 billion to $2.5 billion, making this one of the costliest thrift failures.[4]

Keating was eventually convicted of racketeering, fraud, and conspiracy in using the institution's funds and was sent to prison. The senators were reprimanded for their complicity.

So we see in this sampling of S & L blunders a repudiation of any concern for shareholders and employees—high-dollar deals made on the spur of the moment, without investigation, heedless of risks and probable conse-

---

[3]Adapted from "Small Town's Dreams Vanish," *Cleveland Plain Dealer* (August 13, 1989), p. 3C.
[4]Margaret Carlson, "$1 Billion Worth of Influence," *Time* (November 6, 1989), pp. 27–28.

quences. In other words, a wild gambling mentality prevailed with many S & L top executives. Can the responsibility and accountability of the managers be repudiated? The following box explores the responsibilities of managers.

INFORMATION BOX

WHAT IS THE RESPONSIBILITY OF MANAGEMENT?

Managers are well paid. Isn't responsibility for protecting assets a condition for management, even if these assets are somewhat protected by the government? Is there not also a responsibility to the enterprise, that it continue and not be liquidated or merged into extinction? Are not managers custodians of shareholders' trust?

These are some of the troubling questions that arise when management has been completely oblivious to the greater good of the corporation and its shareholders (and depositors). Ancillary questions also arise: Can selfish greed be tolerated in managers who should have our trust and who can hardly afford to abdicate their responsibility? Can recklessness be tolerated? What should be the penalties for fraud?

USA Today opened a "hot line" for the public's responses to the S & L mess. Here is a sampling of responses.[5]

> I don't see how they could have squandered this money and not get prosecuted.

> When I mishandle my money, I have nobody to go bail me out. If [S & Ls] are incapable of handling the trust that was placed in them, maybe they should go belly up.

> The guilty parties to this fraud should be paying off these banks. If a guy owns a $2 million home, it should be auctioned off, and he should be put in jail.

> Every bank that approved big loans over $100,000, when they knew they were shaky, they should be made to pay them back, even if it causes executive hardship.

> They've got to take responsibility for their actions. This makes Watergate look real simple compared to what they've done our country.

In this case, then, we see management mistakes on a grand scale. Perhaps managers guilty of gross misconduct in connection with the public trust should face stronger penalties than simply ouster from a well-paying job with most of their assets intact. What do you think?

INVITATION TO DISCUSSION
As the manager of a failed S & L, you claim that you acted in the best interest of your investors. How could you have foreseen that your high-risk real estate ventures would default? Discuss the acceptability of this defense.

---

[5]Denise Kalette, "Callers Want S & L Cheats Punished," *USA Today* (February 15, 1989), p. B1.

THE FULL FLAVOR OF THE S & L DEBACLE

By 1988, 503 of the nation's 3178 so-called thrift institutions were insolvent. Another 629 had less capital on their books than regulators usually require. In 1987 630 thrifts had lost an estimated $7.5 billion, half again as much as the earnings of all the rest combined.[6] Most of the "terminal" S & Ls got into trouble making risky loans. But fraud also contributed to the failures of nearly 50.[7] More than one-half the troubled thrifts were to be found in Texas, but other sunbelt thrifts were also crashing: Beverly Hills Savings & Loan in California, which had much of its $2.9 billion in assets invested in dicey real estate ventures and junk bonds, closed in 1985; Sunrise Savings & Loan of Florida, with $1.5 billion in assets, was liquidated in 1986; First South Federal Savings & Loan in Arkansas closed in 1986 after 64 percent of its $1.4 billion in loans were found to be speculative. (See Table 15.1 for a sampling of S & Ls on the "deathwatch" as of September 30, 1988.) Still, the worst excesses occurred in Texas, and there were suspicions that some of the insolvent Texas S & Ls were shuffling bum loans from one to another a step ahead of the bank examiners.

Undeniably part of the motivation for taking wild risks with deposits was that individual accounts were insured up to $100,000 by the Federal Savings and Loan Insurance Corporation (FSLIC). But even the resources of this government agency were to be insufficient to cope with the problem without massive congressional appropriations in the billions of dollars.

The lurking danger, of course, was the domino effect. Depositor panic could create a devastating run on the nation's $932 billion in thrift deposits and bring down scores of S & Ls; this would threaten the $14 billion of capital in the 12 regional Federal Home Loan Banks, which would have to supply emergency funds to the thrifts; and emergency funds could potentially

Table 15.1   S & Ls on the "Deathwatch" as of September 30, 1988[a]

State	Thrift	Negative Net Worth (millions)
Texas	Gill Savings, Hondo	($542.7)
	Meridian Savings, Arlington	($387.7)
New Mexico	Sandia Federal, Albuquerque	($482.6)
Arizona	Security S & L, Scottsdale	($351.6)
Arkansas	Savers Federal, Little Rock	($286.5)
California	Westwood S & L, Los Angeles	($222.7)
	Pacific Savings, Costa Mesa	($206.6)
Florida	Freedom S & L, Tampa	($231.6)

[a]This is only a sampling.
Source: SNL Securities, Inc., and Fortune (January 30, 1989), p. 9.

[6]John Paul Newport, Jr., "Why We Should Save the S & Ls," Fortune (April 11, 1986), p. 81.
[7]Robert E. Norton, "Deep in the Hole in Texas," Fortune (May 11, 1987) p. 61.

swamp the FSLIC. The most simple solution would be to write off the insolvent thrifts and pay off their depositors, but this would exceed the original resources of the FSLIC and could cost more then $200 billion. Taxpayers eventually would foot the bill.

HISTORY OF THE SAVINGS AND LOAN INDUSTRY

At first they were called building and loans, and they filled a real need. Before the Great Depression, many commercial banks would not lend on middle-class residential property. Working class people were eventually forced to band together to form cooperative associations to take their deposits and lend those funds out as home mortgages. The Depression saw the failure of thousands of banks and building and loans, and the Roosevelt administration created the two deposit-insurance funds we know today, the FSLIC for S & Ls and the Federal Deposit Insurance Corporation (FDIC), which insures commercial bank deposits.

In the late 1960s, the S & Ls began experiencing some troubles. By law the federally regulated S & Ls were required to make long-term loans with home mortgages, but they borrowed short-term with most of their lendable funds coming from passbook savings accounts. This situation of long-term loans and short-term lendable resources posed no problem at first—until inflation. With this scenario the value of the S & L portfolios, like that of all fixed-rate long-term debt, fell. In 1971 the S & L industry had a negative net worth of $17 billion. When the inflation rate in the 1970s worsened, the industry faced ever larger losses on its loan portfolios.

The environment was changing in other ways as well, In particular, money market mutual funds came on the scene, aided by computer technology. These money market funds accumulated high-yielding financial instruments such as jumbo certificates of deposit (CDs), commercial paper and government notes, and they allowed the small investor to own a piece of the high-yielding package. Technology enabled customers to write checks on these money funds while still receiving high interest. Computers made possible extremely complex bookkeeping for such transactions.

The effect on banks and S & Ls was substantial. Money flowed out of them and into money market funds by the hundreds of billions of dollars. This combined with the double-digit inflation of the late 1970s brought the industry, with its long-term loans at low-interest rates, seemingly to the point of disaster. By 1981 80 percent of the thrifts were losing money, and fully 20 percent were below the minimum capital requirements set by regulators.[8] (See Table 15.2 for a summary of the worsening S & L situation during the 1980s.)

---

[8]John J. Curran, "Does Deregulation Make Sense?" *Fortune* (June 5, 1989) pp. 184, 188, 194.

Table 15.2   Summary of the Worsening S & L Situation During the 1980s

1980–1982: Congress begins phasing out interest-rate limits. Banks and S & Ls are allowed to offer new savings accounts that compete with market interest rates. Federal deposit insurance is boosted from $40,000 to $100,000 per account. Money that flowed out of S & Ls in 1980, when deposit rates were capped at 5.5%, begins flowing back. But the new deposits cost more than S & Ls can earn on the old fixed-rate mortgages made in the 1960s and 1970s at rates as low as 6% and even lower. Now S & Ls are losing billions of dollars, and hundreds fail. The Garn–St. Germain bill is passed in 1982, allowing S & Ls new lending and investment freedom.

Mid-1980s: A lending spree develops, with billions of dollars loaned for apartments, office buildings, and other projects, especially in the booming southwest. Many S & Ls seek high-profit investments to make up for the low rates on old mortgages. In a climate of drastically loosened controls, wild speculation and outright fraud characterize the operations of hundreds of thrifts.

1986: Oil prices plunge, and the Texas economy collapses. The overbuilding is evident as developer loans are defaulted and the properties foreclosed are worth only fractions of building costs. More S & Ls are brought to insolvency. The Federal Savings and Loan Insurance Corporation finds its capital depleted by earlier S & L failures and needs massive infusions of capital. Prospective acquirers are attracted to take over the dead and dying thrifts under most favorable terms.

1988–1989: A massive government bailout is prepared and enacted.

In order to save the thrift industry from a potentially devastating outflow of funds, in 1980 Congress, in the Depository Institutions Deregulation and Monetary Control Act, gradually phased out interest rate ceilings on deposits and allowed S & Ls to make various kinds of consumer loans. Congress also raised the Federal Savings and Loan Insurance Corporation's insurance coverage from $40,000 to $100,000—essentially, the government deregulated the industry. But now a rate war developed among the thrifts, with some paying depositors double-digit interest rates.

Congress acted again in 1982 to remedy the situation, only the remedy led to worse abuses. The Garn–St. Germain Act of 1982 further loosened the restraints on S & Ls, giving them lending powers to write acquisition, development, and construction loans to form development subsidiaries and to make direct investments. If properly handled, the new freedom should have enabled S & Ls to better match assets and liabilities and find a sounder footing. Now they could begin lessening their dependence on mortgage lending and instead seek higher yielding investments. Figure 15.1 shows the decline in mortgage lending by S & Ls over the past 20 years.

By 1982, with constraints of regulation mostly unraveled and a new business environment in place, S & Ls needed to reassess their strategies. More important, they needed to reevaluate their company mission, discussed in the following box.

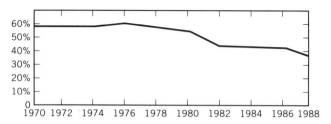

Percent of mortgage debt for one - four family homes held by savings and loans, excluding mortgage securities.

Figure 15.1 Decline in mortgage lending by S & Ls over the last 20 years (*Source:* Federal Reserve).

INFORMATION BOX

WHAT SHOULD OUR MISSION BE?

A company's mission involves a decision: "What business should we now seek to be in?" Such a determination should involve the following factors:

1. Assessing the environment and how it is changing or is expected to change.
2. Appraising competitive factors and how these may be changing.
3. Weighing the particular strengths and weaknesses of the company— what it does best and where it has been deficient.

Mission statements can be too broad—for example, "to make a profit"—or too narrow, focusing on a particular product or service that may become obsolete as technology and customer requirements change. Narrow definitions restrict perspectives and the grasping of different opportunities, just as too broad a definition is useless as a guide for definitive action. An example of a definitive and useful mission statement of a manufacturer is the following:

> The mission is to serve the industry and government with quality instruments used for the primary measurement, analysis, and local control of fluid flow, level, pressure, temperature, and fluid properties. . . . Markets served include instrumentation for oil and gas production, gas transportation, chemical and petro-chemical processing, cryogenics, power generation, aerospace, Government and marine, as well as other instrument and equipment manufacturers.[9]

A company's mission, whether formally stated or merely held in the top executive's mind, can be distorted to a reckless abandonment of former successful and durable practices. It can repudiate community best interest and trust, as we saw with Shamrock and with Sunbelt. Government deregulation in the early

---

[9]John A. Pearce II, "The Company Mission as a Strategic Tool," Sloan Management Review (Spring 1982), p. 17.

1980s provided S & Ls with a vastly expanded arena for doing business. Far too many saw their mission now one of wild growth, unrestrained by cost considerations and risk potential.

INVITATION TO DISCUSSION
Critique this position: "Mission statements are a waste of time. Our executives are going to try to make the most profit they can. That is all investors need be concerned with."

The deregulatory "solution" to S & L problems did not reckon with the unbridled greed that was soon to take place with this greater freedom. It was particularly inviting for schemers and eager speculators in Texas. Previously, Texas regulations had limited lending power of S & Ls to the lesser of the purchase price or the appraised value of any project. But the new federal regulations overrode this requirement, permitting S & Ls to lend 100 percent of appraised value, even if the actual purchase price was much lower. And it was not difficult to find appraisers who would greatly inflate the value of property.

At this point, using federal deposit insurance, the developers got low-rate debt to put into their housing and shopping center developments. If the projects were successful, they made fortunes. If unsuccessful, the Federal Home Loan Bank Board and the Federal Savings and Loan Insurance Corporation absorbed the loss. As Art Soter, a bank analyst at the Morgan Stanley investment banking firm, noted: "What regulators failed to see is that the current system of deposit insurance increases the propensity to take risks."[10]

A further error of deregulation occurred: Equity capital standards were lowered. For years thrifts had to have capital equal to at least 6 percent of their deposits. Then as industrywide losses caused capital to deteriorate— in only two years, 1980 to 1982, the value of capital in the industry fell from $32 billion to less than $21 billion—thrifts were allowed to expand by taking as many deposits as they could.

Brokered deposits soon moved in. These are funds collected by stockbrokers and sent in large amounts to the highest yielding thrifts. With this, there was nothing to slow the growth of the reckless S & L operators. Phenomenal growth was possible, as described in the following example:

American Diversified Savings was a small thrift in a rural town, Lodi, California. In June 1983, it had $11 million in assets. In only 18 months its assets totaled $792 million, mostly from brokered deposits attracted by its high yielding certificates of deposit. The owner, Ranhir Sahni, a former commercial pilot, put the money into his favorite projects: geothermal plants, wind-driven electric generators, as well as a venture to supply local manure to a fertilizer busi-

[10]Curran, *op. cit.,* p. 188.

ness. In 1988, the government had to find $1.1 billion to pay off the depositors and liquidate the thrift.[11]

The seeds for disaster were laid. Washington aggravated the problem and the potential for disaster by failing to hire adequate regulatory staff or to replenish the reserves of the Bank Board or FSLIC. And all this time S & Ls in the southwest continued to slide into bankruptcy.

THE GOVERNMENT BAILOUT

Thus we had a situation of thrifts with billions of dollars of losses, while governmental agencies responsible for them had not nearly the resources to bail out the insolvents. In August 1989 Congress enacted a costly bailout measure and the president signed it. Upward of $166 billion was expected to have to be spent to close or sell hundreds of insolvent S & Ls over the next decade.

An obvious solution was to attract would-be acquirers to take over the dead and dying thrifts and rejuvenate them, so Congress allowed acquirers to use the great bulk of the accumulated tax losses of the previous owners. This decision reduced federal income and other taxes; taxpayers absorbed the losses through a larger deficit, reduced government services, and new taxes. The Federal Home Loan Bank Board made the deal even better: Not only would it guarantee the losses on the nonperforming portfolios, but it also would guarantee the performing portfolios against losses. For example, should interest rates move adversely and lower the value of the performing assets (i.e., those assets still viable and paying interest), the Bank Board would make up the loss if the S & L later found itself not be be liquid. This was a gold mine for acquirers. As *Barron's* noted,

> From the moment an acquirer signed the papers, he would be able to deduct already acquired losses of, say, $1 billion. Against a combined corporate tax rate of about 40%, he would be saving about $400 million in year one. For his out-of-pocket outlay of $50 million, he would have made a return of eight times.[12]

In December 1988 Robert Bass, a 40-year-old Texas billionaire, took over the crippled American Savings and Loan of Stockton, California. This represents perhaps the consummate gilt-edged deal to one of America's richest men.

American Savings was once the largest thrift in the United States, but it got into the same trouble as many others, with brokered deposits and high-risk loans. The Bank Board seized American in 1984 and installed fresh management, but the new team gambled and failed, and the Bank Board eventually granted exclusive bargaining rights to Bass.

---

[11]Curran, *op. cit.*
[12]Described in Benjamin J. Stein, "Steal of the Century?" *Barron's* (February 20, 1989), p. 7.

In the deal American Savings was split into two entities: a healthy S & L with $15.4 billion of good assets and a "bad" one that would liquidate $14.4 billion in sour loans. For a total investment of only $500 million, the Bass Group got 70 percent ownership of the good thrift, a huge, healthy S & L with 186 branches. As another sure thing, more than one-half of this thrift's assets consisted of a $7.8 billion loan to the "bad" S & L that was fully guaranteed by FSLIC to pay a handsome 2 percent more than the cost of the funds. Also as part of the deal, Bass was rewarded with some $300 million in tax benefits.

Taking all this into account, Bass stood to make $400 to $500 million in straight profits over the next four years over his original investment of $500 million.[13]

WAS THE S & L ENVIRONMENT IN THE 1980S IMPOSSIBLE TO MANAGE?

As we have seen, more than one-third of the nation's S & Ls were either insolvent or on the verge of insolvency by 1988. In 1987 the losses were so prodigious for 630 thrifts—$7.5 billion—that these were one-half again as much as the meager earnings of the other 2500.

In such a catastrophic environment, can we find any success stories, any S & Ls that had effectively bucked the trend? The answer is a resounding yes.

Suncoast Savings and Loan Association

Suncoast S & L of Hollywood, Florida, is one of the largest originators and servicers of mortgages in the Southeast. Its strategy has been to reduce the interest rate risk inherent in rate fluctuations. As we have seen before, many of the devastated S & Ls blamed their demise on rising interest rates in which the costs of funds increased while the return remained low because of long-term mortgage commitments.

How did Suncoast reduce such risks? By the purchase and resale of mortgages complemented by its loan-servicing capability. Suncoast and its subsidiaries purchase and originate mortgage loans for resale into the secondary market. In the process of reselling, however, Suncoast retains servicing rights on these mortgages, and these fees comprise a major part of its income. These two activities—purchase and resale of mortgages and loan-servicing capability—are complementary. For example, in declining interest rates, mortgage lending increases as more people buy property during such favorable conditions. But when interest rates rise and loan volume de-

---

[13] Described in S. C. Gwynne, "Help Your Country and Help Yourself," *Time* (February 20, 1989) p. 72.

creases, loan servicing increases in importance as more borrowers hold on to their existing mortgages.

Suncoast gains further risk reduction by contracts in which major Wall Street investment banks purchase mortgage-backed securities on specific dates at agreed-on interest rates and discounts. While this conservative approach is costly, the risk protection from higher interest rates is deemed worth it. The conservative operating strategy caused assets to more than double between 1987 and 1988, with net income rising from 60 cents per share in fiscal 1987 to 98 cents a share one year later. By December 31, 1988, $2.7 billion was serviced in mortgage loans versus $1.1 billion a year earlier. And the return on equity was 14 percent in 1988.[14]

The Boston Bancorp

Boston Bancorp Management consciously decided not to pursue diversification into nontraditional activities, reasoning that the historical focus on retail deposit accounts and home mortgages could be profitable if costs were kept low.

And this Boston Bancorp has done. It limited investment in "brick and mortar," having only four branches serving middle-income communities in metropolitan Boston. A long-established bank-by-mail program eliminated the need for an extensive branch system. Use of funds is primarily in single-family mortgages, commercial mortgages in apartment buildings, and high-quality government obligations and corporate stock—far from risky. With this approach, Boston Bancorp's return on equity has exceeded 18 percent, and it has grown to $1.4 billion in assets.[15]

Austerity has also paid off for other S & Ls—for example, TCF Banking and Savings. When new management took over during the turbulent mid-1980s, the first thing to go was a luxurious suite of executive offices as well as 35 of the association's top brass.[16]

USA Today, in a feature story, described a number of thrifts that bucked the trend and were successful during a time of turmoil in the industry. The common denominator for all of these was *careful growth*, dedicated commitment to pursuing home mortgages rather than commercial deals and brokeraged deposits, and creativity in improving customer service.[17] The following box discusses disciplined leadership and strategy execution.

---

[14]Robert Chaut, "The Well-Managed Thrift: Five Success Stories," *The Bankers Magazine* (July–August 1989), pp. 35 and 38.

[15]*Ibid.*

[16]Harlan Byrne, "Practicing Thrift, Austerity Pays Off for a Midwestern S & L," *Barron's* (September 21, 1987), p. 15.

[17]David Elbert and Harriet Johnson Brackey, "Slow Growth Was the Key to Survival," *USA Today* (February 15, 1989), pp. B1, B2.

INFORMATION BOX

DISCIPLINED LEADERSHIP

Leadership is vulnerable to abuses—abuses in overreaching, in not carefully assessing rewards versus risks in proposals, in operating beyond reasonable means, in simply not keeping a tight rein on costs, and, most important, in failing to guide the organization with the best interests of the stakeholders in mind. Such abuses are especially tempting in times of wild optimism, such as the time of the oil and land booms in the southwest.

Discipline needs to be imposed when the inclination is to run amok. Discipline implies controlled behavior and careful evaluation of actions and opportunities, not growth beyond resources and management capabilities. In the quest for disciplined growth, the executive faces the dual risk of being too conservative. Excessive conservatism may risk missed opportunities and give competitors an advantage, but this stance generally is less risky than jeopardizing the company with too much high-stakes leadership. Continued viability has to receive top priority. Gambling the company is hardly acceptable stakes, even in Las Vegas.

INVITATION TO DISCUSSION
Discuss how disciplined leadership can be imposed on a top executive with wild leanings.

CONCLUSIONS

The S & L industry in the 1980s represents the greatest industry debacle since the Great Depression of the 1930s. The pervasiveness of the disaster engulfed hundreds of savings and loans in all types of communities, from the very small rural towns to the largest cities, from areas of depression to those of the greatest growth. The taxpayers' bill to salvage what can be salvaged will be in the hundreds of billions of dollars.

How could this have happened? Could it have been avoided? What, if anything, can we learn from all this that might be transferable to other situations and other times, that in effect may lessen the probability of such happenings occurring again?

Some have attributed the blame to external circumstances that S & L executives could not control. They were simply victims, these people would lead us to believe. Others blame the government, claiming that in its desire to help the industry during a time of high and increasing interest rates, it promoted dangerous deregulation, permitting S & Ls wide latitude to invest their funds far beyond the traditional home mortgage lending, and relaxed equity restraints. No one could foresee that ballooning oil prices and land values would so abruptly be deflated.

Yet such "excuses" for the debacle rest on unsubstantial foundations. While hundreds of S & Ls failed, more hundreds maintained viability and even showed strength and growth. The common denominator of uncontrollable environmental factors does not hold the valid answer of who or what to blame and how disaster could have been avoided. Furthermore, it was the height of imprudence to expect boom conditions to last.

Where, then, lies the blame? As with most mistakes, management cannot escape primary responsibility. In this case, the fault lay with a management that violated the integrity of the planning function. The violation occurred in two respects: (1) injudicious failure to rein in expenses during a time when the profitable spread of traditional mortgage business was narrowing and (2) a wild spree to highly risky undertakings and investments once the constraints of governmental regulation were loosened. To these one must add a good dash of outright fraud, asset-stripping, and corruption—white-collar crimes. (Of course, the inability of government inspectors to monitor closely enough permitted some of the worst excesses. But we are concerned here with *management* mistakes, not government mistakes.)

WHAT CAN BE LEARNED?

We can draw significant insights from the planning blunders of the sick and dying thrifts and from comparisons of sick and prospering ones.

Adversity creates opportunities. We are left with the growing recognition that adversity—in this case, a supposedly inhospitable environment—can also create opportunities for those who would adjust, adapt, and plan creatively in this environment, even embrace it with gusto—but without reckless abandon. The S & L situation created great opportunities for firms and individuals who had the resources and skill to "rescue" the troubled thrifts, with substantial government largess. And for the healthy competitors, new growth opportunities were also created, albeit the bad image of the failures cast all S &Ls in suspicious light.

The fallacy of aggressive and conservative extremes. Many of the failed thrifts were victims of their own aggressiveness, carried to the extreme of recklessness. If real estate prices and a building boom had continued in the high-growth areas of the south and west, then some of the reckless speculations would have brought above-average payoffs. Unfortunately, a wild house-of-cards philosophy eventually collapses. Excesses can only be tolerated so long in the normal course of events, as has been proven time and again over many centuries. The dangers of a speculative frenzy date back to at least 1634 in Holland, when individual tulip bulbs were bid up to fantastic prices in wild but doomed speculation.

The extremes of conservatism have dangers, too. As we examine in the next learning insight, the environment is in flux; it is constantly changing. Failing to take even minor risks regardless of potential opportunities or to make needed adjustments to a changing business clime can hardly be praised. The extreme example here is the buggy whip manufacturer unwilling to adapt to the new environment of horseless carriages. In general, a middle ground between extreme aggressiveness and ultraconservatism will usually lead to the most durable success.

Any business firm faces a dynamic environment; nothing can be expected to remain constant. This requires some degree of adaptability. A useful perspective of reactions to a changing environment can be gained by considering a continuum of behavior:

Degree of Responsiveness to Environmental Change

Inflexible Unchanging	*Adaptive*	*Innovative*

Thus, a firm can be viewed as occupying a certain point along this continuum: the more conservative and rigid firm toward the left, the more progressive firm that is constantly developing new ideas toward the right.

The terms *adaptive* and *innovative* are somewhat different, although related. We will consider them as different degrees of responsive behavior on the same dimension. *Innovative* may be defined as originating significant changes, implying improvement. *Adaptive* implies a better coping with changing circumstances, but a response somewhat less significant than an innovative reaction.

In a sense the failed thrifts were adaptive to a changed environment, that of greater deregulation. They adapted by forsaking any plans of judicious expansion in favor of a free-wheeling strategy of high risks and opportunism. Then they found themselves unable to cope with the suddenly menacing environment of drastically falling real estate prices and a newly concerned regulatory climate.

Austerity wins out over high living. Nowhere is the contrast of high living and lack of cost constraints compared with relative austerity more evident than here. Reckless spending is a trap. Admittedly, when things are gong well, when prospects seem boundless, the temptation is to open the floodgates of spending, at both the corporate and the personal level.

On the one hand, many of the failed thrifts were guilty of wild spending. Conspicuous examples of this were lavish entertainment, grand facilities, fleets of airplanes, even expensive art collections.[18]

---

[18]For example, see Martha Brannigan and Alexandra Peers, " S & L's Art Collection, Ordered to be Sold, Faces Skeptical Market," *The Wall Street Journal* (October 18, 1989), pp. 1, A12.

On the other hand, we have examples of firms that owe their viability to their austerity. They kept themselves lean, controlled costs, and were able to survive and prosper and even be in position to take over their extravagant competitors.

Whereas some would argue that lavish spending created a public image of great success and prosperity, thus winning new business, a more sober appraisal would be one of foolish waste. Lack of cost restraints is incompatible with effective management and should not be tolerated by shareholders or creditors.

A government "crutch" is a destructive delusion. The knowledge that depositors' accounts were insured up to $100,000 by the Federal Savings and Loan Insurance Corporation undoubtedly motivated some of the reckless investments and other dealings of the failed thrifts. That the government would foot the cost of any speculations that turn sour and would bail out depositors seemed a siren call for some executives. But those who felt entirely shielded by this governmental crutch were to learn to their dismay that while depositors were protected—at great cost to the government and taxpayers—they, the management, faced ouster and even the possibility of legal prosecution.

The shifting tides of politics and the effects on legislation and regulation bring a threat of being "blindsided" to those who rely too much on government support and protection. And the government has no great history of sound legislation: Witness the S & L legislation of the early 1980s that was designed to save the S & Ls but which in reality presented temptation for doom that many found impossible to resist.

INVITATION

Can you add any additional learning insights?

QUESTIONS

1. Would you recommend changing an S & L's mission in the early 1980s, with most government restraints relaxed? If so, how would the mission change?
2. How would you respond to an S & L executive who carefully pointed out to you that if land and oil prices had not collapsed without warning, his portfolio of high-interest loans would have brought great profitability to the firm?
3. Evaluate the following statement. "S & Ls no longer serve a useful purpose, and they should be phased out."

4. A thin line seems to exist between aggressive opportunism and out-right fraud. Where do you think the line should be drawn? Or are both to be criminally condemned?
5. Would you conclude that Edward McBirney's greatest flaw was that he liked ostentatious high living? Why or why not?
6. After the examples described in the case, would you conclude that an "edifice complex" (i.e., an inclination to build prestigious physical facilities) is ill-advised and even, from the viewpoint of an investor, something to encourage divestment?

INVITATION TO ROLE PLAY

1. You are the controller of a medium-sized S & L in the mid-1980s. Your CEO is a flamboyant individual who has just announced his intention of building a new home office on a rather lavish scale. He claims this is necessary to convey the desired image of the firm. Develop a systematic analysis to disprove his idea.
2. You are the top executive of an S & L in a medium-sized town in the mid-1980s. Despite the federal deregulation, you have continued to lend conservatively. Your competitor down the street has acted much more aggressively. Accordingly, he is paying depositors considerably higher interest rates than you can. Your firm is suffering, and the board is exhorting you to "loosen up." Without the benefit of hindsight, what would you do?

INVITATION TO RESEARCH

What is the state of the S & L industry today? What was the final bailout cost?

16

Chrysler Corporation, Early 1980s: "Can We Even Survive?"

On May 11, 1982, a headline in the business section of the Cleveland *Plain Dealer* stated, "Steel Imports Surge Aids Port." The article noted that a shipment of foreign steel was being unloaded on Cleveland docks the same day that domestic steel mills were reporting their lowest operating rate within recent memory. As many as 20 more ships carrying steel imports were expected to arrive in the next 30 days. The article further observed that the scene of imports unloading was nettling a domestic steel industry with 100,000 workers laid off and more than 30,000 on short work weeks.

In industry after industry, U.S. firms were finding it difficult to compete successfully against foreign competitors, not only in domestic markets but also in foreign markets. Business publications were calling for a reindustrialization of America,[1] which no one saw as being easy or quickly accomplished. No industry was more beset by foreign competition and by an inability to match foreign productivity and attractiveness of foreign-made products than the auto industry, and Chrysler was the most grievously beset.

IACOCCA TO THE RESCUE?

In November 1978 Lee A. Iacocca became president of the ailing Chrysler Corporation, at one time the fourth-largest industrial corporation in the

---

[1] For example, *Business Week* (June 30, 1980), entire issue.

United States. Iacocca brought to the enterprise and its hopes for survival his proven abilities of salesmanship, image building, and cost cutting, but many doubted that he would be able to save the company—indeed, whether anything could. There was doubt that the entire U.S. auto industry could be saved, short of governmental subsidization.

Iacocca embodied the great American success story. In an earlier era, this would have been dubbed a Horatio Alger tale, after the prominent fiction writer of rags-to-riches stories early in this century. Iacocca was the son of an Italian immigrant. He saw education as the route to success, and he went to Lehigh University and then on to Princeton for a master's degree in engineering. "In my day you went to college, not to go into government or to be a lawyer, but to embark on a career that paid you more money than the guy who didn't go. For 32 years I was motivated by money," said Iacocca.[2]

Iacocca started with the Ford Motor Company as a trainee in 1946 at $125 a week. As he moved upward through the Ford organization, he was responsible for introducing the trend-setting Mustang in 1964 (only a few years after the Edsel debacle) and later the Maverick, Pinto, and Fiesta. By 1977 he was president of Ford, earning $978,000 that year. Then, in July 1978, Henry Ford abruptly fired him. The falling out has been attributed to basic disagreement between Ford and Iacocca over the pace of downsizing cars: Iacocca wanted to move fast, whereas Ford was worried about the impact of such additional investment on short-term profits and wanted to move more slowly.

After Iacocca left Ford, John J. Riccardo, chief executive of Chrysler, offered him the presidency. In accepting this job, Iacocca turned down a dozen jobs that offered more money. But he was after a place in automotive history: "I might not only save a blue-chip company and 200,000 jobs, but also help the Big Three become an honest Big Three."[3]

THE CHRYSLER DILEMMA

Chrysler had long been the weakest of the Big Three automakers. Although a multibillion-dollar firm, it was smaller, less well financed, and less talented than General Motors (GM) and Ford. It had suffered major reversals in the early 1960s, in 1970, and in 1974 and 1975. The monumental problems affecting the very viability of the company in the later 1970s and early 1980s had their roots in the recession of 1974/1975. At that time, a severe drop in sales forced the company to make massive cuts in capital spending and,

---

[2]"Off to the Races Again," *Fortune* (December 4, 1978), p. 15.
[3]*Ibid.*

perhaps more serious, in engineers and designers. Delays in introducing new models and quality problems resulted. For example, Chrysler compacts Volare and Aspen were introduced in 1976 and subsequently went through eight recalls for defects. Many Chrysler fans who had been loyal through generations turned to other makes.

In 1978 Chrysler lost $205 million. By 1979 problems worsened as gasoline prices rose sharply and the public began demanding small, fuel-efficient cars. Although Chrysler had some success with its subcompact Omnis and Horizons, losses were over $1 billion, and the future of the company was in doubt.

Lobbying in Washington

Iacocca turned to Washington to bail out the company. He sought federal loan guarantees of $1.2 billion. Chrysler's lobbying had irresistible bipartisan appeal in a coming election because of the concentration of Chrysler workers and parts suppliers in such key states as Michigan, Ohio, Indiana, and five other states. The Carter administration strongly supported the loan-guarantee legislation, and Congress finally authorized not $1.2 billion, but $1.5 billion. Chrysler immediately drew on $800 million to help it weather the coming months.

But Chrysler's problems continued, and its actual sales for 1980 were far worse than had been predicted, with the deficit an unbelievable $1.7 billion. Although the blame could be laid on such externals as a recession and mushrooming interest rates that affected consumers and dealers alike, the failure of the widely touted K-car was crucial.

The K-Cars

The Dodge Aries and the Plymouth Reliant were introduced in September 1980 with great fanfare. These were front-wheel drive compacts, somewhat roomier and a bit more fuel efficient than GM's X-cars, introduced 18 months before. It was expected that sales would be about 70,000 for the introductory months of October and November 1980 and 492,000 for all of 1981. Instead, only 34,273 units sold in the first 2 months, and by the end of November, dealers had a 98-day supply of K-cars. GM, in contrast, had a 54-day supply of its older and virtually unchanged X-cars. Ford's new subcompacts, the Lynx and Escort, had also done considerably better than the K-cars during this period. The poor showing of the K-cars could not be blamed solely on external factors. Chrysler had tried to price the K-car close to the X-car; it also loaded most cars with every conceivable option, consequently bringing the price from the basic $6100 car to about $8000.

The disappointment of the K-car introduction did not end Iacocca's troubles. By 1980, even the Omnis and Horizons that had done well the year before began to lose their luster. Chrysler had estimated sales of these cars at 394,000 for all of 1980; by the end of November, only 222,814 had been sold, and dealers' inventories had risen to a 134-day supply. Even Iacocca's hopes to reenter the luxury-car market were facing disappointment. The Imperial was again introduced—for the first time since 1976—with heavy advertising, even using Frank Sinatra to plug it. But sales of 1885 cars in October and November were less than one-half the forecast.

Iacocca's Defensive Moves

Iacocca's reaction to these disasters was to offer rebates of $380 to $1200 a car in December 1980 and in early 1981. An ambitious cost-cutting program was also announced that would save the company $1 billion in 1981. This involved four things:

1. A wage freeze for blue-collar workers.
2. A 5-percent reduction in prices charged by suppliers for 90 days and a freeze for the rest of 1981.
3. A $575-million cut in investment in new-plant capacity and new-product development.
4. A request for lenders to convert $572 million in debt to preferred stock, thereby reducing interest payments by $100 million a year.

Then Chrysler went back to the loan-guarantee board for $400 million.

Although the Chrysler dilemma was unique and more serious than for other U.S. automakers, it was nonetheless symptomatic of the sorry straits confronting a major U.S. industry that had not adequately coped with foreign competition.

The U.S. Auto Industry 1970 to 1980

In the 1970s U.S. automakers' share of the domestic U.S. market fell from 85 percent to 70 percent; in other words, by 1980 imports had captured almost 30 percent of the market, double that of a decade earlier. Import inroads intensified in the latter part of the 1970s. Table 16.1 shows the market share of all imports as well as the units sold of the five leading imports from 1977 through 1980.

The vulnerability to imports came partly form Detroit's failure to build sufficient small-car capacity. American companies ignored the fact that many customers were returning to the idea of simple and efficient transportation. (This was the very idea that Henry Ford had pioneered with his Model T seven decades earlier.) When oil price increases made big cars all but obsolete, the foreign firms were ready and able to step in. Japan alone had a 22 percent share of the U.S. auto market by 1981. Only three years earlier, Japanese imports were 12 percent. As we can see from Table 16.1,

Table 16.1   Import Inroads in the U.S. Auto Market—1977 to 1980

	1980	1979	1978	1977
Total units sold—all makes	8,760,937	10,356,695	10,946,104	10,825,235
Total imports units sold	2,469,180	2,351,053	1,946,094	1,976,512
Market share of imports (%)	28.2%	22.7%	17.8%	18.3%
Leading imports (units sold):				
Toyota	582,204	507,816	441,800	493,048
Datsun	516,890	472,252	338,096	388,378
Honda	375,388	353,291	274,876	223,633
VW	90,923	125,100	216,709	260,704
Mazda	161,623	156,533	75,309	50,609

Source: *Automotive News*, 1981 Market Data Book Issue.

sales volumes in 1980 were below a recession-level 9 million cars, and this included the major share carved out by imports. U.S. automakers incurred some $5.5 billion in red ink in 1980 and 1981. About 2400 dealerships folded in these two years. The president of the 20,000-member National Automobile Dealers Association asserted that "dealers are holding on by their used-car departments."[4]

Another aspect contributing to Detroit's problems was a growing perception by the U.S. consumer that American-made cars were inferior in quality and workmanship to foreign-made, especially Japanese-made, cars. This perception was most difficult to overcome. Although Ford and Chrysler heavily advertised the improved quality of their cars, consumers remained skeptical. Some experts predicted that three years of good word-of-mouth endorsements from happy owners would be needed to overcome the prejudices against the quality of U.S. cars.[5]

With Japan putting out appreciably better cars than U.S. carmakers seemed able to, according to public perception, more and more companies focused on Japanese management techniques and, in particular, on their management/worker relations, which seemed to provide both consistent quality and high productivity. See the following box for a discussion of the Japanese style of leadership.

Sticker Shock

Detroit was blaming all its problems on high interest rates and the discouraging effect they were having on consumer willingness to buy high-ticket items. A consumer survey by the Survey Research Center of the University of Michigan, however, revealed that high car prices, not interest rates, were the biggest reasons for consumers' not planning to buy a new car.

[4]"Detroit's Struggle to Survive," *Business Week* (January 11, 1982), pp. 62–63.
[5]"Why Detroit Still Can't Get Going," *Business Week* (November 9, 1981), p. 110.

INFORMATION BOX

JAPANESE MANAGEMENT–WORKER RELATIONS

In the opinion of almost all experts, Japanese management was superior to U.S. management simply because Japanese firms could produce products of dependable quality, whereas U.S. firms could not. What was the secret of Japanese success, and was it adaptable to American workers?

Hallmarks of the Japanese system, as far as leadership was concerned, seemed to lie in the working relationships between Japanese employees and managers. Essentially, these represented loyalty: loyalty of workers to the company and of the company to its workers. The major manifestations of this have been the following:

- *Lifetime Employment.* With this long-term employment philosophy, the worker grows and matures with the company rather than being laid off or leaving for other opportunities.
- *Broad Career Experience But Slower Promotions.* Japanese managers have been trained to become generalists rather than specialists.
- *Shared Information.* Japanese firms have emphasized information sharing with their workers and lower managers to a much greater extent than most U.S. firms.
- *Collective Decision Making.* Decisions are made by consensus to a much greater extent that in U.S. firms. Thus, responsibility can be shared and a team spirit created.
- *Quality Emphasis.* Quality, as well as an organizational quest for continuous improvement, has been emphasized throughout the organization. Workers have been expected to work together to solve quality problems.[6]

INVITATION TO DISCUSSION
How applicable are these attributes to the American workplace and workers? Do you see any incompatibilities?

Figures compiled by the National Automobile Dealers Association put the average selling price of a U.S.-made new car at $8900 by late 1981. Ten years before, the average price had been $3730. In the single year from 1980 to 1981, prices rose more than $1000. Even GM's Vice Chairman, Howard Kehrl, conceded, "If there's any sales problem, it's getting people to recognize that a very high-quality small car is not cheap."[7] The term "sticker shock" began to be heard and when a potential customer saw car prices 70 percent or more higher than the last car he or she bought, it became easy to delay buying a new car.

---

[6]Schermerhorn, *op. cit.*, pp. 62-63.
[7]"Why Detroit Still Can't Get Going," *Business Week* (November 9, 1981), p. 110.

Detroit's eagerness to embrace high prices was nothing new. Neither should there have been surprise at consumer reluctance to purchase at prices that were significantly higher than prices a few months before. The same thing happened earlier in the 1970s. For 15 months, from 1973 to late 1974, Detroit automaker repeatedly increased the selling prices of their cars. This was a time of burgeoning inflation, with material and labor costs rising sharply. New government standards for safety and pollution control added other costs, and the automakers themselves were incorporating more expensive equipment, such as radial tires.

In this period the average price of a new car increased by $1000, and sales plummeted 25 percent. Automakers began offering cash rebates for a limited time to reduce massive inventories of unsold cars, but the damage had been done. The auto industry led the rest of the nation into a severe recession.

Did the U.S. automakers learn from this? Apparently not. Much the same thing was happening in late 1980 and 1981, when new economy-efficient cars were introduced to compete with foreign imports but at prices that were far from "economy." By June 1981 used car sales were running 19 percent above the previous year while domestic new car sales continued to plummet.

Detroit tried to ease buyers from their sticker shock by offering rebates, lower than market interest rates on new car purchases, and some rollbacks of prices (see the following box). But these were only temporary incentives, and they tended to borrow sales from future months when the rebates and

---

INFORMATION BOX

REBATES

A rebate is a promise by a manufacturer to return part of the purchase price directly to the purchaser. The rebate is usually given to consumers, although it can be offered to dealers instead in the expectation that they will pass some or all of the savings along to consumers.

Obviously the objective of a rebate is to increase sales by giving purchasers a lower price. But why not simply reduce prices? The rebate is used instead of a regular markdown or price reduction because it is less permanent than cutting the list price. Rebates can be quite effective in generating short-term business, But they may affect business negatively once the rebate has been lifted.

INVITATION TO DISCUSSION

Do you see any dangers with rebates from the manufacturer's viewpoint? As a consumer, would you prefer a rebate or a price reduction, or does it make any difference?

other concessions ended. Even worse, the on-again, off-again bargains appeared to confuse some buyers, whereas others were convinced that special deals were a routine part of car purchasing: Demand dried up drastically during those periods when no concessions were in effect.

In defense of their higher sticker prices, Detroit maintained that the front-wheel drive they had adopted for most cars produced high retooling costs. And, with sales volume down, it became essential to squeeze as much profit as possible from every car. But the elasticity of demand could not accept higher prices, whatever the rationale, and demand dried up as sticker prices increased.

OPTIONS FOR CHRYSLER

By the end of 1980, the situation for Chrysler seemed bleak indeed, with sales declining badly and losses becoming astronomical; as shown in the following table:

	1978	1979	1980
Sales (millions)	$13,618.3	$12,001.9	$9,225.3
Losses (millions)	$204.6	$1,097.3	$1,709.7

Source: Chrysler annual reports.

At this point, several options seemed available to Chrysler if it were to survive:

1. It could greatly pare its product line and limit itself only to the small cars that seemed to comprise most of the market demand. By so doing, the full-size and intermediate car lines would be discontinued, and their factories either permanently closed or converted so that they could produce front-wheel-drive subcompacts.

2. Large chunks of the company could be sold off, such as the parts-making operation, which had been running in the red because of underutilization. Some or all of its profitable units, such as the military tank business, Chrysler Financial Corporation, and its electronics division, might also be sold to provide funds needed to support the remaining auto operation.

3. The various lines of cars might be merged into a single nameplate. Thus, Chrysler-Plymouth and Dodge lines could be pared, thereby simplifying assembly, reducing inventory of duplicate parts, and concentrating selling efforts.

4. It could augment its lines with "niche" cars that would be so distinctive they could command a high price and yield a good profit,

even on low sales volume. This strategy had revived BMW, the German sports car manufacturer.[8]

5. An affiliation might be established with another auto maker, such as Volkswagen. This might provide Chrysler with needed cash as well as a product line expanded with foreign-designed cars. Unfortunately, Chrysler was hardly an attractive property for a foreign suitor. Although it had about $2 billion in tax losses that would shield future profits from taxes, it had a colossal drawback in its debt burden: $1.2 billion in guaranteed loans, almost $1 billion in other debts, and $1.2 billion in unfunded pension liabilities.

6. Chapter 11 bankruptcy was the ultimate option. This would not necessarily lead to the company's demise and liquidation. Under Chapter 11 a company continues to operate but has court protection against creditors' lawsuits while working out a plan for paying its debts. However, Iacocca was convinced that such a reorganization under the Federal bankruptcy code would quickly lead to total collapse, with car sales screeching to a halt as a result of what is termed the *orphan syndrome*. When potential customers fear that a firm may collapse, they see warranties as worthless; they suspect that dealers might not be around to handle problems, that resale value of cars will drastically decline, and that parts may become harder to find as years go by. Consequently, only a few diehard loyalists might still be induced to buy. To some extent, the orphan syndrome was already affecting Chrysler because of its widely publicized difficulties.

Most of the preceding options were deemed unworkable by company executives. Paring down to a profitable core, as American Motors had attempted to do, was ruled out because it was thought that Chrysler dealers needed a full line of cars if it was to compete effectively with Ford and GM. In early 1982, however, Chrysler did sell its subsidiary, Chrysler Defense Corporation, to General Dynamics for about $350 million. This division produced the main tank for the U.S. Army, the M-1, and the sale provided a cash cushion against further operating losses.

Iacocca and Chrysler were determined to maintain their role as a full-line auto manufacturer and to hang on doggedly until better times. One analyst criticized, "The problem is not that there aren't any alternatives, but rather the man at the helm . . . Lee's in a race to show Henry (Ford) what he can do. And in the process, he's likely to become a General Custer."[9]

---

[8]"Could Bankruptcy Save Chrysler?" *Business Week* (December 24, 1979), p. 70.
[9]*Ibid.*, p. 72.

WHAT WENT WRONG AT CHRYSLER?

Chrysler's basic problem had long been inadequate capital, aggravated by an acquisitions binge in the 1960s and early 1970s. Many of these acquisitions turned out to be lemons and had to be sold at losses to raise cash in the late 1970s. For example, Chrysler acquired European car companies in an attempt to build a foreign operation that could provide a sales cushion for the periodic downturns of the U.S. market. However, only failing companies were acquired: Simca in France and Rootes Motor Ltd. in Britain. These companies turned into cash drains, siphoning off funds needed at home.

Lacking the capital and some of the creative talents of Ford and GM, Chrysler's products tended to be not innovative but imitative—that is, "me-too" types of cars. Such cars, lacking in prestige and advanced styling, often had to be sold at lower prices than competing cars, and Chrysler had to be satisfied with lower profit margins. This situation was hardly likely to improve soon. For example, GM spent $8 billion in 1981 on plant and equipment; this was more than Chrysler planned to spend in six years.

The current problems stemmed more directly from 1970, when Lynn Townsend, then chairman, decided to squeeze the most out of existing plants and product lines rather than build for the future. Although the strategy seemed sound at the time for a cash-poor company, unforeseen world events sabotaged it. Notably, the Arab oil embargo brought a new emphasis on economy and high mileage, and federal legislation made increased mileage standards mandatory. In 1970 subcompact cars accounted for only 3 percent of the U.S. market, and Townsend opted not to compete with the Vega and Pinto compact cars introduced in 1970 by GM and Ford. Instead, he chose to concentrate on restyling the more profitable big cars, in a $250 million model change. Just a few months later, the oil embargo destroyed the market for gas-guzzling big cars. Chrysler did not have the smaller cars consumers were desperately seeking. The two losing years of 1974 and 1975 brought the severe cutbacks in capital spending and in talented personnel that were to affect future operations.

John Riccardo, Townsend's successor, made another decision in 1975 that was to augment the company's disadvantage. Facing the prospect of costly new federal braking and noise rules, and recognizing—again— the limited cash resources, Riccardo decided to drop the profitable, heavy-duty truck business and instead focus on vans and pickups. Sales of these products were the first to soften at the threat of fuel disruption and higher prices.

Can we fault Chrysler's management for failing to anticipate an oil embargo that was to bring gas lines and burgeoning prices, so that demand for big cars, vans, and the like all but dried up? Could any reasonable person have predicted such a situation? And can we fault Chrysler management for not having the same options available as the larger competitors with vastly superior financial resources? Where do we draw the line between prudent decisions and myopic ones?

The issue is complicated? And perhaps Chrysler's management was a victim of circumstances. Perhaps the same can be said for GM and Ford management, and for that of the steel companies and the other industries vulnerable to foreign competition, yet some of the blame was simply an unwavering embracing of short-term profit objectives. Such objectives induce a firm to postpone plant modernization, to emphasize the most profitable products (in the case of U.S. automakers, and especially Chrysler, this meant big uneconomical cars, or small cars so loaded with expensive options that they cost as much as big cars), to cut back on research and development expenditures, and to seek maximum per-unit profit, even if this meant increased inflation, failure to meet the needs of consumers, and lack of competitiveness with foreign firms.

Chrysler blamed a lot of its troubles on costly government regulations imposed in the 1970s. For example, auto emission standards, fuel economy goals, and a passive seat belt or air-bag systems were estimated to have cost Chrysler $1 billion extra in 1979 and 1980. Being the smallest of the major automakers, it had fewer units to spread such costs over and was thus more seriously affected than GM and Ford. The Reagan administration brought a loosening of some of the regulations. As the information box indicates, many regulations are extremely controversial, with different points of view creating almost irreconcilable issues.

INFORMATION BOX

SCRAPPING AUTO BUMPER STANDARDS

On May 14, 1982, the federal government scrapped requirements that automobile bumpers must withstand a 5 MPH crash without causing damage to the vehicle. Automobiles thereafter were required to have bumpers that protect the vehicle only in crashes of up to 2.5 MPH, with the possibility of later reduction to below 2.5 MPH for some types of autos.

The bumper requirement had been highly criticized by the automobile industry as being unnecessary and adding $35 to $50 to the cost of a vehicle. On the other hand, consumer advocate Ralph Nader called the decision a "surrender to General Motors" that he claimed would cost motorists $400 million a year in added insurance premiums and repair costs. Industry experts confirmed this, estimating that insurance premiums could rise by 10 to 20 percent with the permission of weaker bumpers.[10]

In a pluralistic society in which many different interest groups are vying for legislation and regulations favorable to their position, it is impossible to satisfy all interests. However, in the early 1980s, the pendulum seemed to be swinging back to the side of management as it attempted to overcome foreign inroads.

INVITATION TO DISCUSSION

As a consumer, what is your position regarding government safety regulations for cars? How much more are you willing to pay for greater safety features? Do you think all consumers feel the way you do about safety?

WHAT CAN BE LEARNED?

We can draw some generalizations from the Chrysler problems that apply to the whole U.S. auto industry as well as to such U.S. industries as steel, rubber, machine tools, and consumer electronics. The problems of Chrysler and the other Detroit automakers were symptomatic of problems facing other American industries as the 1970s were ending: A substantial part of American industry was just not able to compete effectively against aggressive foreign competition, particularly the Japanese. A new assessment of American management philosophies seemed indicated, and a painful reevaluation of traditional ways of doing things and criteria for decision making seemed essential if America were to regain its industrial dominance and maintain American jobs.

Perhaps the major lesson to be learned is that Americans are not insulated from competition although we invented mass production and were originally in the vanguard of sophisticated management techniques. Nothing is guaranteed forever. The environment changes. Traditional ways of doing things can be vulnerable to fresh ideas and need to be constantly appraised. We can learn from foreign competitors, just as they, for decades, have learned from us.

Table 16.2 shows the key industries hardest hit in the U.S. market by foreign competitors. This table shows the extent of foreign inroads in certain key industries from 1960 to 1980 (as we saw earlier, by 1981 the auto industry was in even worse shape, with imports in one year jumping from 22.7 percent to 28.2 percent of total U.S. auto sales). Although foreign inroads in the auto industry have received the most publicity, certain other industries have suffered even more—the trend over the last several decades has been disturbing indeed.

---

[10]"U.S. Auto Bumper Standard Scrapped," *Cleveland Plain Dealer* (May 15, 1982), p. 4-A.

Table 16.2   Foreign Inroads in Key Industries in the U.S. Market, 1960–1980

	Percentage of Total Industry Sales by Imports	
Industry	*1960*	*1979*
Autos	4.1%	22.7%
Steel	4.2	14.0
Electrical components	0.5	20.1
Farm machinery	7.2	15.3
Consumer electronics	5.6	50.6
Footwear	2.3	37.3
Metal-cutting machine tools	3.3	26.4
Textile machinery	6.6	45.5
Calculating and adding machines	5.0	43.1

Source: Commerce Department.

U.S. DISADVANTAGE IN PRODUCTIVITY

Productivity in the United States has been a nagging concern. It has been slipping relative to foreign industries and by so doing has made many foreign products more attractive for cost and quality than U.S. goods. The usual measure of productivity is output per hour—that is, how much an American worker produces in an hour compared, say, to a Japanese or German worker. The calculation is made by dividing total output of goods and services by the number of hours or number of workers used to produce the goods. From 1966 to 1976, the United States had the lowest growth rate in productivity of the top 11 Western industrial nations.[11]

Productivity directly affects cost. In 1978 Japanese car companies had a $700 cost advantage per car over their U.S. counterparts. In other words, because of their greater productivity, Japanese carmakers could manufacture a car for $700 less than U.S. carmakers could. Serious as this competitive disadvantage was to American firms, the difference had widened by 1981 to $1500 per car.[12]

Strong pressures began building to make American cars more competitive by reducing labor costs; with U.S. carmakers facing billion-dollar deficits and with worker layoffs increasing, unions began making some concessions. But such efforts only chipped away at Japan's big manufacturing cost advantage. Limiting Japan's imports through quotas was another

[11]Thomas W. Gerdel, "America's Dilemma of Poor Production," *Cleveland Plain Dealer* (January 19, 1981), p. 1-D.

[12]"Why Detroit Still Can't Get Going," *Business Week* (November 9, 1981), p. 109.

often-mentioned recourse, but some feared that quotas might prompt Japan to shift efforts toward larger, more expensive models, an area where U.S. carmakers were not as severely challenged as with small cars. The prospect that Japan might soon be competing against Detroit's entire product line struck fear in the industry.

FACTORS IN U.S. PRODUCTIVITY PROBLEMS

Fingers of blame for U.S. productivity problems pointed in all directions. Although some of the problems were interrelated and due to multiple causes, for the sake of simplicity we will examine them under lack of sufficient investment in productive facilities, short-term profit-maximizing managerial goals, and adversarial (rather than cooperative) relationships of business with labor and with government.

Lack of Adequate Investment in Productive Facilities. Outdated plants typify some U.S. industries. A major example is the steel industry. U.S. firms were still building open-hearth furnaces in the late 1950s, whereas the Japanese were building more modern plants that used the basic oxygen process, a process that, ironically, was a U.S. invention. The U.S. agricultural machinery industry in all practicality excluded itself from growing markets in developing countries by concentrating on making big and expensive machinery appropriate only for the U.S. market. For example, no American firm still makes a farm tractor under 35 horsepower. The failure of the U.S. machine tool industry to meet domestic market needs because of a reluctance to build enough capacity to serve the needs of the market in periods of peak demand simply invited foreign competition. And in consumer electronics, as we all know, most TVs, radios, stereos, and the like are now made by the Japanese; in 1960 about 95 percent of these products were supplied by domestic manufacturers. The Japanese secret: not so much lower labor costs, but superior technology and management.

Along with the sag in investment in modern plant and equipment, compared especially with Germany and Japan, has been a decline in research and development spending since the mid-1960s. This has caused the United States to lag behind in applying technology to commercial products. For example, robots were an American invention, but now Japan has taken the lead in applying robots to a variety of manufacturing processes.

Government regulations and a punitive tax system that penalized savings have also been blamed for a reluctance to invest in capital equipment. And, undeniably, our society in recent decades has been more oriented to spending than to savings—interest payments on loans are fully tax deductible, whereas interest on savings is taxed as ordinary income. The last 15 years have seen a heavy imposition of regulations dealing with environmental protection, safety, health, equal employment, energy efficiency, and the like. Such regulations and the bureaucracy that interprets and enforces them have sometimes placed major obstacles in the way of investing in new plants and even in maintaining present ones. For example, the Environmental Protection Agency has forced some industries, such as steel, to invest millions of dollars that might have gone to modernizing facilities in pollution control devices.

Faltering investment in productive facilities has also been blamed on the huge increase in the service industries, such as health and social services, which have absorbed resources that might have gone into productive areas. Others have blamed the deteriorating rate of productivity on a shortage of engineers and too many bureaucrats, staff people, and lawyers. Even the introduction of computer technology and sophisticated office systems has been blamed. These accoutrements of modern business management have been seen by some as soaking up resources that might have been better used in more directly productive facilities and also in providing more information to management than is really needed: That is, they have placed more people in paper-shuffling roles rather than in more productive activities and in the process have added greatly to the overhead burden.

Short-sighted Management

Major reasons for the decline of U.S. industry must point more directly to management deficiencies. A major orientation of American managers has been and continues to be maximizing profits. Performance is measured by reaching profit objectives, and promotion and compensation are tied to it. The executive who does not achieve profit goals is unlikely to advance very far. Is it any wonder that all levels of executives are thinking about profits and how to get more of them? And what, really, is wrong with this? The answer lies in what kind of profits we are talking about: short-term immediate profits, or profits over the longer run. Long-range goals have tended to be sacrificed for short-run profits—in Chrysler, the rest of the U.S. auto industry, the steel industry, and many other industries as well. Consequently, if heavy investments are needed in research, retooling, and other efforts to reach long-term goals, they tend to be postponed because such programs hurt profits in the short run.

The fallacy of such short-sighted strategies can be clearly seen. The auto industry's postponement of the need to develop high-quality, fuel-efficient vehicles that the car-buying market really wanted gave a big chunk of this business to the imports. Likewise, the steel industry postponed for decades the shifting of production from outmoded facilities and then lacked the capital to do so. (There are exceptions to this. Standard Oil of Ohio [Sohio] made huge investments in Alaskan oil development, even to the point of facing formidable debts a decade before any returns from the investment could be expected. Eventually, the payoff came, and Sohio was flooded with profits: It earned $1.2 billion on sales of $7.9 billion in 1979.)

Adversarial Relationships of Business

Some of the blame for poor productivity is laid at labor's door. Some people maintain that lazy workers who take too many coffee breaks and who have lost their forebears' zeal for work are to blame, not only for poor productivity with its high costs but also for an uncaring attitude toward quality. Sometimes this is seen as resulting from the growth of unions, with their emphasis on seniority at the expense of capability. Unions have been criticized as too greedy, too uncaring, too rigid in adhering to old ways that curb efficiency and protect the status quo. Usually, collective bargaining has taken place in an adversarial rather than a cooperative environment. This contrasts sharply with the labor-management situation in Japan, where most workers stay with the same firm for life and enjoy almost a family relationship—certainly one of teamwork and cooperation toward common objectives.

Management is certainly far from blameless in its labor relations, in the acceptance of inflationary wage settlements, and in the tolerance of mediocre quality. It has often been the easier course of action to make contract concessions and pass the inflationary costs on to customers by raising prices rather than suffer a lengthy strike. The productivity and competitiveness of domestic industries have slowly diminished. Now the challenge is to develop a framework within which labor and management can work together toward a common objective. Both have a stake in the competitive productivity of U.S. industries, because not only profits but jobs are truly at stake. Management has the challenge to offer new incentives to motivate workers to higher levels of productivity.

Government has also tended to take an adversarial stance toward U.S. business. As we have noted before, regulation has tended to be obstructive, even though some regulation is clearly needed. But an explosion of regulations placed on business to achieve social goals, such as equal employment, a cleaner environment, and a safer workplace, have undeniably diverted vast amounts of capital from more productive avenues. A teamwork approach, a spirit of more cooperation, and a less adversarial and litigious relationship may be essential if U.S. productivity is to be competitive. Japan and West Germany certainly have, for the most part, a harmonious and supportive relationship of government and business.

QUESTIONS

1. What incentives would you propose to motivate workers to higher productivity?
2. Discuss in what ways the Japanese worker differs from the typical U.S. worker. (You may need to do some research on this.) How do these dissimilarities affect management-labor relations in the two countries?
3. What suggestions do you have for reducing the adversarial relationship that U.S. business often has had with labor and with government?
4. Why do you think a "Buy American" campaign has never had wide consumer appeal? What would it take to make such a campaign more effective?
5. "The American work ethic makes us vulnerable to certain foreign competitors, such as Japan and Western Europe. We have to face reality." Evaluate this statement.

INVITATION TO ROLE PLAY

1. You are a respected management consultant. How will you persuade top management of the need for a commitment to long-range profitability objectives, rather than short-term profit goals, throughout the organization? What difficulties do you see in getting a full-fledged commitment? How will you reconcile differences of opinion?
2. Place yourself in Iacocca's position. You have just taken over the top job at Chrysler and find the situation even worse than you expected. You realize that the only chance the company has to survive reasonably intact is at least a billion-dollar bailout by the federal government. What arguments will you use to persuade Washington decision makers? What opposing arguments do you expect, and how will you counter them?

INVITATION TO RESEARCH

How satisfied was Iacocca with the eventual bailout? What were his major conclusions about the whole episode? Do you agree with him?

17

Contrast—Chrysler's Great Turnaround

Some said Lee Iacocca performed a miracle at Chrysler. Some said he should be president of the United States. Iacocca brought Chrysler to profitability by 1983 and to a strong performance for the most of the decade. Like a phoenix, the reeling number three automaker had been given new life and respectability.

THE GREAT STAKE IN THE K-CARS

During the darkest days, the hopes for the K-car—the Dodge Aries and the Chrysler Reliant—sustained Iacocca and the Chrysler organization. This front-wheel drive vehicle with only four cylinders afforded great fuel economy—25 miles per gallon in the city and 41 on the highway—and at the same time was roomy enough to seat a family of six. In contrast to other rather flimsy-looking compacts on the market at the time, the K-car appeared strong and solid. Although GM had an older X-car aimed at the economy market, it was not on par with the K-car. Chrysler managers believed they had a superior and attractive product aimed at an important segment of the market, and they saw it as Chrysler's last hope, or as Iacocca put it, "the light at the end of the tunnel" and "the last train in the station; if we failed here, it was all over."[1]

---

[1]Lee Iacocca, *Iacocca* (New York: Bantam Books, 1984), pp. 251–252.

But Chrysler made a mistake. Introduced in October 1980, the cars were an acute disappointment. Production problems and limited supplies prevented a strong launch in dealer showrooms. The major mistake, however, was high pricing, even though the base price, $5880, was well below the principal domestic competitor, GM's Citation hatchback, at $6270. With survival at stake, Chrysler had sent out most of its early K-cars loaded with expensive options—air conditioning, automatic transmissions, velour upholstery, and electric windows—that added several thousand dollars to the price. As a result, the car aimed at the economy market was no longer a low-priced car.

To its credit, Chrysler quickly recognized the problem. Interviews with people leaving dealer showrooms without placing orders confirmed their disappointment in not seeing the good buys they had expected. By the end of 1980, Chrysler was producing more basic models, and sales improved. But now the economy threatened the comeback of the company.

By December 1980 the prime rate soared to 18.5 percent; two months earlier it had been 13.5 percent. Cars, houses, furniture, and appliances were all unsalable. To try to spur sales during this time of almost unparalleled high interest rates, Iacocca led the auto industry in offering refunds to customers based on the difference between 13 percent and the prevailing interest rate at the time of purchase.

1981

Because of the slow start for the K-cars, Chrysler began 1981 in very bad shape. It had to go back to Washington to draw another $400 million in loan guarantees (see Chapter 16 for more details of the government bailout of Chrysler). The consequent bad publicity devastated company sales, as many potential customers, fearing that Chrysler would go out of business and not honor its warranties or be able to supply parts, switched to competitors. Throughout 1981 survival "was never more than a week-by-week proposition."[2]

In the darkest days of 1981, Iacocca proposed a merger with Ford. Since Ford at the time had nothing equivalent to Chrysler's K-car, such a merger seemed reasonable, with both firms standing to benefit. Obstacles loomed, however, including the personality question. Henry Ford had fired Iacocca from the presidency of Ford in 1978. Could he and Iacocca work together now? Another problem concerned antitrust laws: Would such a merger of the number two and three automakers violate restraint of trade and lessening competition laws? This problem seemed easier to resolve. Preliminary talks with Washington about such a merger were promising,

---

[2]*Ibid.*, p. 256.

especially since Chrysler was on the brink of failing. If the merger went through, the Ford/Chrysler combination would have 75 percent of the U.S. sales of General Motors. Thus, the giants would be competing on close to equal footing.

The merger did not come to pass: Ford top management turned it down. We can only speculate whether Henry Ford, although retired, vetoed the idea, or whether Ford top management shuddered at the thought of an aggressive Iacocca again being part of the organization.

As the bitter year of 1981, with its high interest rates and terrible economy, dragged to an end, Chrysler faced another crisis on November 1: It was down to its last million dollars, though it normally spent $50 million a day. In desperation the company persuaded most of its suppliers, including all the major ones, to extend credit terms. Iacocca sweated out meeting payrolls:

> There were times when I said: "God, we need to ship a thousand more cars to get this much cash or we can't meet . . . a $50 million payroll on Friday." Day by day, it was that close, and oh, the numbers were so big.[3]

In the end, the K-cars saved Chrysler. With their looks, fuel economy, and comfort, and now with the right balance of basics and options, consumers continued to buy them in tough economic conditions. *Motor Trend Magazine* gave Chrysler a boost when it named the Aries and the Reliant cars of the year for 1981. But even with the K-car, Chrysler staggered to a $478.5 million loss for 1981.

1982 AND 1983—REBIRTH

By 1982 Iacocca had Chrysler poised for a recovery. By paring costs and improving efficiency, he had reduced the break-even point from 2.3 million cars and trucks to only 1.1 million. He had reduced the work force from 160,000 in 1979 to 80,000 in 1982 and had closed or consolidated 20 of the 60 plants. More than 1000 dealers were gone. Iacocca had brought many new executives into the company: Of the top 28 officials, 15 had come on board in the previous four years. With the greatly reduced breakeven point, any sales beyond the 1.1 million would generate $2500 profit per vehicle.[4]

The economy still lagged for most of 1982, however, improving only near the end of the year. Car sales moved up along with the economy, and by the end of the year the company had eked out a modest operating profit, although net profit had not quite crept out of the red. Still, Chrysler had weathered the storm. Iacocca was a hero.

[3]*Ibid.*, p. 262.
[4]"Can Chrysler Keep Its Comeback Rolling?" *Business Week* (February 14, 1983), p. 134.

The following year, 1983, the company made an operating profit of $925 million—the best in Chrysler's history—and a net profit of $302 million, or 2.3 percent of sales of some $13 billion. The good times were to continue. As shown in Table 17.1, the company rose from the depths to rack up impressive gains in revenues and profits until it again encountered problems in the late 1980s. Table 17.2 shows the comparative net profit percentage figures of Chrysler, General Motors, and Ford during these years. Figure 17.1 shows the percentage growth in revenues of Chrysler compared with GM and Ford from 1984 to 1992.

With the turnaround recognized, Iacocca moved swiftly to secure more financial resources. In spring 1983 he made a new stock offering, and it was gobbled up. Originally, plans were to sell 12.5 million shares, but demand proved so strong that the company issued 26 million shares. The entire offering was sold out within the first hour, at a market value of $432 million. Investors now were salivating at the chance to participate in the greatly improved prospects of Chrysler. Although additional stock offerings dilute the value of each outstanding share, investors in their optimism disregarded this, as the stock price was bid up from $16⅝ at the time of the offering, to $25 a few weeks later, and soon to $35.

Now awash in funds, Chrysler paid off $400 million—one third of the government loan guarantee—after the stock sale. Just a few weeks later, Iacocca paid back the entire loan, seven years before it was due. Many viewed this as rash, giving up over $800 million in cash so soon after the firm was practically at death's door. But the well-publicized payback had great psychological value for the company, its investors, and its present and

Table 17.1   Chrysler's Sales and Profit Performance 1980–1988 (in millions)

	Sales	*Net Profit*	*Percent Profit to Sales*
1980	$8,600	($1,772)	−20.6%
1981	9,972	(555)	−5.6
1982	10,045	(69)	−0.7
1983	13,240	526	4.0
1984	19,573	1,496	7.6
1985	21,255	1,635	7.7
1986	22,586	1,404	6.2
1987	26,277	1,290	4.9
1988	35,473	1,143	3.2

Source: Company public records.

Commentary: In these years we see a big increase in revenues, with sales rising more than fourfold from 1980 to 1988. The return to profitability is significant too, with five consecutive years of profits well over a billion dollars, although the growth of profits to match the growth in sales does not happen. Table 17.4 for the years immediately after 1988 shows Chrysler's situation again worsening, but then also turning around.

Table 17.2   Comparison of Chrysler, General Motors, and Ford on Net Profit Margin, 1983–1988

	Chrysler	General Motors	Ford
1983	4.0%	5.0%	4.2%
1984	7.6	5.4	5.6
1985	7.7	4.1	4.8
1986	6.2	2.9	5.2
1987	4.9	3.5	6.5
1988	3.2	3.8	5.7

Source: Industry statistics.
Commentary: Note how much more profitable, as a percentage of sales, Chrysler can be in good years compared with its domestic competitors. Also note its deteriorating profitability condition by the late 1980s, especially compared with Ford.

potential customers. It conclusively showed the confidence that Iacocca had for Chrysler's future.

1984—ANOTHER COUP

The K-car saved Chrysler in the dark days. In 1984 another innovation added fuel to the rejuvenation of Chrysler: the T115 minivan. At the time it was an entirely new product, bigger than a station wagon but smaller than a van. It held seven passengers, had front-wheel drive, got 30 miles to a gallon, and fit into a normal garage.

Coming just a few years after the near demise of the company, such an innovation seemed a miracle: Where did Chrysler find the resources for such a project? The minivan was not born from scratch but had been first

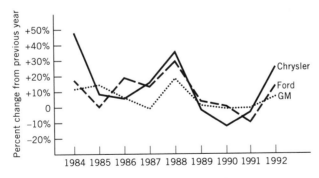

Note the greater peaks and valleys of Chrysler's performance.

Figure 17.1. Comparison of Chrysler, General Motors, and Ford year-to-year percent changes in revenues, 1984–1992. (*Source:* Company Public records.)

conceived at Ford in 1974. Iacocca fell in love with the prototype and predicted a market of 800,000 a year, but Henry Ford would not approve it.
Now at Chrysler Iacocca could have a little retribution for being fired by
Ford. Still, in 1980, Iacocca had to find $500 million to turn out this minivan
that he and Harold Sperlich, who had helped design the Mustang at Ford
and who had also come to Chrysler, had wanted to build at Ford. In a
famous quote, Iacocca said during the difficult days when the minivan idea
surfaced: "The hell with what people say. Somehow we'll find a way to do
it. For God's sake, let's not forget we're here to do cars."[5]

Favorable publicity abounded. *Connoisseur* magazine selected it as one
of the most beautiful cars ever designed. *Fortune* called it one of the 10 most
innovative products of the year, and car magazines featured it on their covers, even months before it went on sale. Chrysler's four minivan nameplates
began selling at a sustained rate of 30,000 per month.

THE NITTY GRITTY OF PRODUCTIVITY IMPROVEMENT

Basic production efficiencies occurring by the early 1980s paved the way for
the revival. Richard Dauch, a former Big Ten football player, was an agent
of change. Iacocca lured him away from Volkswagen in 1980, promising
that he could modernize each plant when a new model was launched.
Dauch's role model was Vince Lombardi: "Inspire 'em with speeches, but if
they do not produce—kick tail and take names."[6]

At the start of the 1980s, the auto industry was ravaged by foreign
competition, particularly the Japanese. No automaker had it worse than
Chrysler: Its quality was in the pits at the same time that production costs
were the highest in the industry. Part of the problem was aged plants: For
example, Dodge Main was built in 1910 and was eight stories tall, with an
assembly line snaking ponderously from floor to floor amid half-assembled
cars awaiting repairs or cannibalization for parts. Part of the problem was a
heedless rush for production at any cost.

Dauch first worked to improve the most obvious deficiencies: squeaks
and rattles. This meant adhering to tight specifications. In five years he
quadrupled the number of robots and the computers that control them. He
transformed the assembly line and introduced just-in-time inventory, under
which parts arrive only as they are needed and in the order in which they
will be used. By 1987 Dauch had invested $1.2 billion in new paint shops to
give Chrysler products the finest finishes in the industry.

[5]John B. Judis, "Myth vs. Manager," *Business Month* (July 1990), p. 26.
[6]Alex Taylor III, "Lee Iacocca's Production Whiz," *Fortune* (June 22, 1987), p. 36.

He worked assiduously to promote quality thinking among his employees, working closely with United Auto Workers officials. He increased the training of all workers, gave them more say about overtime and vacations, and eliminated time clocks. In return he got greater flexibility in scheduling and gained a reputation as tough but fair.

The result was a solid increase in productivity. The production lines by 1987 could deliver 8000 cars and trucks a day, versus 4500 in 1981. The number of labor-hours required to build a vehicle went from 175 to 102. Absenteeism and friction declined sharply.

In other efforts to improve productivity, supplier relations were scrutinized and less efficient suppliers weeded out. Those remaining faced new specifications for quality, costs, and delivery. Car designs and especially number of options were simplified. For example, at one time Chrysler offered an unbelievable 19 million possible combinations of color, trim, and accessories; Dauch reduced this number to 42. Customers still had ample options, and manufacturing costs were reduced by $100 a car.[7]

A major move to reduce production costs and decrease the break-even point for profitability was the basic K-car single platform strategy. As the company moved into the latter 1980s it was still using one basic engine, transmission, and underbody structure, but it had developed eight new models differentiated by sheet metal and distinctive market identities.

The idea of the single platform was born of desperation: Chrysler could not afford all-new models. The engineering was so clever, however, that most customers were unaware of the basic commonality. General Motors, on the other hand, was producing 19 distinct body structures for its 175 models, and most of these were so similar that GM was often criticized for its look-alike cars. Still, how much longer could Chrysler continue selling its clones? Critics were becoming vocal against this long-lasting strategy, and sales of some models were beginning to suffer.

The payoff of the efforts at increasing productivity were monumental. After being lowest in quality and highest in costs in 1982, by 1986 Chrysler was near the top in reliability, durability, and fit-and-finish. It was credited with making a profit per vehicle of $1057 in 1986, while Ford made $847 and GM, only $157.[8] In the process, the competitive position of Chrysler as shown by its market share improved significantly, as shown in Table 17.3.

Iacocca had done it. He had resurrected a desperate company in the depths of the worst recession in half a century. By 1984 he was the author of the best-selling nonfiction hardcover book ever, his own autobiography, selling almost six million copies and staying on top the best-seller lists for a

[7]*Ibid.*, p. 40.
[8]*Ibid.*, p. 36.

Table 17.3   Chrysler Market Share, 1983–1988

Year	Percentage of U.S. Car/Truck Market
1983	9.2%
1984	9.5
1985	11.2
1986	11.5
1987	10.8
1988	11.2

Source: Industry statistics.

Commentary: We see a significant improvement in competitive position during these years, although the growth trend stops in 1987.

year. He was the star of Chrysler's television commercials. He was a charismatic talk-show guest, an authentic American hero, even the object of a "draft Iacocca for President" movement. One of his greatest honors was being appointed by President Reagan to oversee the restoration of the Statue of Liberty—this for the son of Italian immigrants who had come through Ellis Island. What kind of a leader was Iacocca? See the following box for a more detailed discussion of his leadership style.

INFORMATION BOX

IACOCCA'S LEADERSHIP STYLE

A super salesperson, charismatic, politically skilled, decisive—these characteristics have been commonly attributed to Iacocca. He was also a demanding boss, quick to fire subordinates who didn't measure up to his standards. Still, his personality engendered strong loyalty in his colleagues, with many of his managers following him to Chrysler from Ford. Unlike many top executives, he did not demand conformity, but even encouraged disagreement and eccentricity, seeing this as fuel for creativity. Also unlike most top executives, he readily abandoned organizational chains of command to solicit opinions of junior executives, auto dealers, line workers, and even union officials.

Iacocca was hardly a humble man, and his firing by Henry Ford was probably due to a bitter power struggle between two proud men, each unwilling to back down or compromise. Eventually Iacocca's management focus at Chrysler became diluted as his attention shifted to other interests, and some critics did not treat him kindly.

Possibly one of his greatest strengths was his adaptability. If a strategy was not working out, such as his diversifications, he could cut his losses. And in the late 1980s, in the face of strong opposition from his younger designers, Iacocca backed away from his position on styling issues.

INVITATION TO DISCUSSION

In commenting on his future successor, Iacocca noted: "Somebody suggested
. . . that I hire General Norman Schwarzkopf. He's a brilliant strategist and a
hard worker . . . He knows objectives and he must know people, and he sure
would have discipline. What else does an executive need?"[9] Discuss.

TROUBLE AGAIN, LATE 1980S AND EARLY 1990S

After Iacocca's resurrection of Chrysler in the early 1980s, by 1988 the company was hurting again. Still using the K-car frame, which was aging, it had
to make cash rebates up to $2500 to entice buyers. Even trucks sales were
faltering; the Dodge Ram, for example, had not been changed since 1962. To
a large extent this reflected capital deprivation: Sufficient money was not
invested in new car and truck designs.

Admittedly, the company had brought out a variety of nameplates;
some 66 models were marketed during the 1980s. This was twice as many
as Ford, which was twice as big. But Chrysler's many models led to customer confusion, and all these new nameplates, even including the popular
minivan, used the same basic platform developed for the K-car in 1980. So
whether a $10,000 Shadow or Sundance or a $28,000 Chrysler Imperial, the
basic foundation had the same engine, suspension, and underbody parts.
Unfortunately, the press caught on and started denigrating Chrysler.

At the same time, the company was having serious problems assimilat-
ing the 1987 acquisition of American Motors Corporation (AMC) for $757
million. The crown jewel of the buyout was the Jeep line of sport-utility vehicles, selling at a steady 150,000 or so units annually. These units appealed to
younger, more affluent buyers than the older, lower income customers of
Chrysler. Still, the company found itself saddled with the great inefficiencies that had bedeviled AMC. Payrolls burgeoned, AMC's retired workers
brought unfunded pension liabilities of $384 million, and legal claims from
Jeep rollover accidents added another $1.4 billion burden. The aged AMC
plants in Kenosha, Wisconsin and Toledo, Ohio, depressed Chrysler's overall
efficiency. In 1988 the Kenosha plant had to be closed, at a cost of more than
$100 million. The AMC acquisition brought Chrysler's break-even point up
from 1.2 million units a year to 1.6 million. Table 17.4 shows Chrysler's
operating performance in the latter 1980s and the 1990s. Table 17.5 shows
the net profit percentages of Chrysler and its domestic competitors.

---

[9]Alex Taylor III, "Can Iacocca Fix Chrysler—Again," *Fortune* (April 8, 1991), p. 53.

Table 17.4   Chrysler's Operating Performance, 1989–1992 (in millions)

	Sales	Net Profit	Percent Profit to Sales
1989	$34,922	$315	0.9%
1990	30,620	68	0.2
1991	29,370	(665)	(2.3)
1992	36,897	430	1.2

Source: Company public records.

Commentary: Here we see a new sales and profit decline and the beginning of a major and probably more durable turnaround in 1992.

The Iacocca Contribution to the Relapse of Chrysler

After Iacocca brought Chrysler back from the very brink of disaster in the 1982–1984 period, his attention wandered from carmaking. In addition to his personal distractions—his best-selling autobiography, his charisma as a public figure, and his political ambitions—he succumbed to the wheeling and dealing machinations that characterized much of the 1980s. He went on an acquisitions binge.

Instead of investing Chrysler's newfound wealth in new models and improved production facilities, Iacocca found other uses for this money. To begin with, he was obsessed with the share price of Chrysler stock. It seemed a vast injustice to him to see growth stocks such as Xerox trading at price/earnings ratios of 15 to 20 while Chrysler's ratio was under 5. The prevailing climate of the time suggested that diversifications through acquisitions was the key to better Wall Street acceptance. Therefore, if Chrysler could become more than an auto company, its fortunes should soar.

Iacocca began his quest to boost Chrysler stock by spending $1.9 billion to buy up company stock, thus spreading the profits over fewer shares of stock. Then he moved on to acquisitions. Chrysler already owned 24 percent of Mitsubishi, and now he wanted other foreign relationships. He bought a 3.5 percent share in the Italian car company Maserati and began

Table 17.5   Comparison of Chrysler, General Motors, and Ford on Net Profit Margins, 1989–1992

	Chrysler	General Motors	Ford
1989	0.9%	3.4%	4.4%
1990	0.2	(1.6)	0.9
1991	(2.3)	(4.1)	(2.6)
1992	1.2	(0.5)	(0.5)

Source: Industry statistics.

Commentary: While Chrysler faltered badly at the end of the 1980s, it was not alone by 1990. By 1992 only Chrysler had made it back into profitability.

the joint development of a luxury sports car, the TC. In 1986 he upped Chrysler's stake to 15.6 percent, with the option to purchase full control. In early 1987 he bought another Italian sports-car maker, Lamborghini, and later that year he made the major purchase of American Motors Company.

Iacocca made other acquisitions outside the car business, the business that was so unfavorably judged by investors. He bought four rental car companies—Dollar, General, Snappy, and Thrifty—to serve as captive customers for Chrysler's fleet sales. His purchase of Gulfstream Aerospace for $637 million gave him a measure of revenge: He had never quite gotten over his resentment of the government's loan guarantee board, which had forced him to sell the company's jets in order to get the vital loan guarantees. He even expanded into defense contracting with the 1987 purchase of Electrospace Systems, a small defense electronics firm.

In 1987 Iacocca reorganized Chrysler as a holding company with three subsidiaries: Chrysler Motors, Chrysler Financial, and Chrysler Technologies. He considered moving corporate headquarters from the Detroit suburbs to Manhattan and was also seriously considering acquiring the E. F. Hutton brokerage house.

In his spending frame of mind, Iacocca allotted more than $1 billion to the construction of a new Technology Center in Auburn Hills, Michigan. This state-of-the-art facility would house Chrysler's design and research operations.

He eventually tired of his diversification efforts, especially since they uniformly turned out to be unprofitable. He sold Gulfstream in 1990 for a good profit but could not sell Electrospace owing to defense cutbacks. The worst money loser was Maserati, on whose TC sports car he squandered more than $200 million.

The upshot of this spending and acquisition binge was that they diverted Iacocca's attention and resources from the heart of Chrysler's operation, the development of new models to compete in the mid-size and full-size sector of the auto market. The old K-car design, dating back to 1980, was long overdue for replacement.

ANOTHER COMEBACK, 1992 AND 1993

With Chrysler faltering again, an aging Iacocca turned his full attention back to the car business seven years after retiring his company's horrendous bank debt. He and top company executives made a long-overdue five-year commitment in 1988 to concentrate $15 billion on four high-visibility and potentially profitable new models of cars and trucks. Regardless of the economic climate, these were to receive top priority: a 1991 minivan, the 1993 Jeep Grand Cherokee, the 1993 LH sedans, and the 1994 T300 full-size pickup. To try to pay for the project, Iacocca had to unload some of his prior purchases and find other funding. The schedule was met, and now Chrysler's viability seemed assured.

Fearful that the company might not survive until the new models came out, especially if a recession were to occur before then, Iacocca instituted a far-reaching austerity program to cut $3 billion from the company's $26 billion annual operating costs. Product development was totally reorganized and streamlined. He enlisted the suggestions of outside suppliers in the slimming operation and trimmed budgets for marketing and advertising, dealer relations, and health care. Perhaps most important, Iacocca wanted a climate of cost containment to permeate the organization at all levels. Some 24 percent of the white-collar work force had already been eliminated since 1987, with the reduction of 3000 more jobs scheduled for 1991. The number of vice presidents was reduced to 23 from 36, and layers of management—the levels of executives that separate the CEO from the factory floor—were reduced to 9 from the previous 11 (see the following box for a discussion of the implications of management layers, and the concomitant span of control). The number of board members dropped from 18 to 13. Most management consultants were eliminated, as well as white-collar training programs, including Dale Carnegie courses. Even secretaries became "as scarce as rain in Baja."[10]

INFORMATION BOX

LEVELS OF MANAGEMENT AND THE TRADEOFF WITH SPAN OF CONTROL

The more levels of managers there are between the top executive and the lowest workers, the more higher executives are insulated from rank and file workers. Such insulation and distance frustrates communication and impedes rapport, damaging the morale of the workers. It promotes a "them versus us" attitude. Perhaps the greatest disadvantage is that overhead costs rise substantially with each layer: high-salaried executives, their staffs, their offices, and other perks. Yet in large organizations, many layers of management are seen as necessary if the span of control is to be reasonable.

One of the major principles of organization holds that the span of control—the number of subordinates reporting to an executive—should be small enough that employees can be properly supervised. A number of factors can affect the optimum span. Obviously, a more experienced and able executive with competent subordinates and stable and similar operations can handle a wider span. But there is a limit to how many subordinates one person can supervise effectively. General conclusions are that higher management can supervise from four to eight subordinates, whereas the span can reach eight to 15 or more at the lower management levels. A span that is too wide will normally be narrowed by adding one or more management levels, as shown in the following diagram.

[10]*Ibid.*, p. 52.

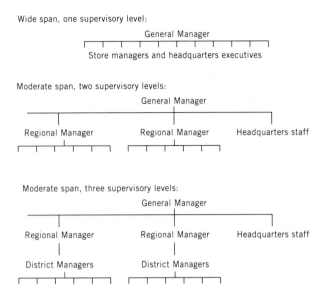

Computers have made it possible to widen spans and reduce the number of levels because they provide timely and abundant operating data. In a time of austerity, so-called "flat" organizations (i.e., ones with few management levels, such as Wal-Mart and Southwest Airlines) have become models of effective organizational structures. The tradeoff is that workers in such flat organizations are less directly supervised. Sometimes, however, this is not so bad. Workers and lower-level managers are given the opportunity to act more independently, which can increase job satisfaction and even advancement potential.

INVITATION TO DISCUSSION
What are some likely consequences of the growing trend toward flat organizations?

Iacocca was prescient. In the last three months of 1990, Chrysler's car and truck sales to dealers dropped 7.2 percent, which should have pushed the company into the red for the year. Instead, the company registered a small profit for 1990, although it racked up a $665 million loss in 1991. Still, Chrysler was able to survive that loss unscathed and still launch its new models on schedule in 1992. Then things improved greatly, with a $430 million profit in 1992. See Table 17.4. By 1993 the company was riding high. Now Chrysler's share price was reflecting optimistic investor sentiments as it reached into the $40s by mid-1993, up from around $14 in early 1991.

Iacocca retired December 31, 1992, with a job well done. As he said on TV, "When it's your last turn at bat, it sure is nice to hit a home run."[11] Robert J. Eaton, formerly with GM of Europe, replaced Iacocca as Chrysler chairman.

THE JAPANESE PRESENCE

The Japanese invasion of the U.S. auto market has been phenomenal and has left U.S. carmakers reeling. Somehow Detroit had trouble adjusting its thinking to combating the Japanese incursion; instead it wanted governmental protection, fighting to keep Japanese cars out.

In 1981 the auto industry received voluntary import restrictions, but the Japanese had already gained 20 percent of the U.S. car market. By 1982 Honda alone sold 195,000 made-in-Japan Accords, this being the fourth most popular car in the United States. Under pressure, Japan agreed to limit auto shipments to the United States to 1.68 million cars a year.

As we have seen with Chrysler (it also took place with the other U.S. automakers), the windfall profits between 1984 and 1988 were not committed to the core business, but were instead dissipated. Automakers spent profits in diversifications having little relationship with the core business, as Iacocca did, and in acquisitions of small, prestigious, unprofitable European automakers.

To their sorrow, the import restraints had two dire consequences for U.S. carmakers. First, Japanese manufacturers circumvented the import ceiling by assembling cars in U.S. plants. Honda led in this process, but soon other firms followed. By 1990 the Japanese were building 1.2 million cars and trucks in the U.S.

The second consequence was upscale Japanese autos. With restrictions on the number of cars, the Japanese moved to more expensive models, thus maximizing the profit on each car shipped. Honda's Acura led the way in 1985 and was quickly followed by other luxury makes that successfully took highly profitable sales from U.S. carmakers.

During the 1980s, U.S. firms scurried behind whatever protectionism they could muster; they repudiated the idea that they could compete nose-to-nose with the Japanese. This began to change by the 1990s.

By the early 1990s, Japanese firms had more than 30 percent of the U.S. car market, but problems were surfacing for them. In particular, the value of the Japanese yen had risen 65 percent between 1985 and 1990. This meant that Japanese cars would normally be that much more costly to customers than U.S. cars. However, Japanese manufacturers tried to counter this by cutting costs and keeping prices competitive without damaging the quality of their output.

[11]Alex Taylor III, "U.S. Cars Come Back," *Fortune* (November 16, 1992), p. 85.

The Japanese marketing strategy for their luxury cars was awesome. For example, Toyota introduced the Lexus in 1989, positioning it against the best of the Europeans, such as the Mercedes, BMWs, and Jaguars, and against domestic Cadillacs and Lincolns. Lexus dealers were given as much as $7000 profit per car as incentive to lure customers with ultimate attention and service. Backed with great quality control, within months the Lexus had established itself as "the thinking man's luxury car," providing great performance without hassle, and unsurpassed maintenance.

By the early 1990s, U.S. carmakers finally began to recognize that they could compete against the Japanese and even win. Part of the optimism stemmed from some economic problems that Japan was facing at home, but part also resulted from a long-overdue realization that U.S. workers could make cars nearly on a par with the Japanese in quality and quality control.

As the country moved into 1993, the business press was trumpeting the troubles in Japan and the opportunity for U.S. firms. Indeed, statistics bore out a resurgence. In 1992 Detroit gained nearly two points of market share, with a 72 percent share of the market for cars and light trucks. The light truck segment in particular was Detroit's coup. This segment had grown to a record 41.6 percent of all vehicles produced in 1992, as consumers replaced sedans with pickups, minivans, and sport-utility vehicles. And of this growing and lucrative market, Detroit gained 4 percent in market share in 1992, to a whopping 91 percent of the market.[12]

Meantime, Japanese producers, in order to maintain a reasonable semblance of profits, were forced to raise their U.S. auto prices by 6.7 percent in 1992, versus Detroit's mere 1.2 percent. The problems in Japan worsened; by 1993 they were the worst since 1974, during the oil shock. Major firms were having record losses, and Nissan became the first major Japanese manufacturer to announce a plant shutdown. Lifetime job tenure was being abandoned. The book *Honorable Poverty* had become a best seller.[13]

U.S. automakers appeared to have learned an important lesson, one that had eluded them for the previous two decades of competition with Japan. They were holding prices down, they were bringing out new products faster, and they were paying more attention to quality standards in production. In addition, they were testing out intriguing new marketing ideas, notably no-haggling selling (see the following issue box), and offering standard packages of popular options at attractive prices.

---

[12]Kathleen Kerwin, "Is Detroit Pulling up to Pass?" *Business Week* (January 11, 1993), p. 63.

[13]Robert Neff, "Fixing Japan," *Business Week* (March 29, 1993), pp. 68–74. For the effect of this situation on the workforce, see Karen Lowry Miller, "Stress and Uncertainty: The Price of Restructuring," *Business Week* (March 29, 1993), p. 74; also "Unemployment in Japan Doubly Hard on Workers," from *The New York Times*, reported in *Cleveland Plain Dealer* (May 22, 1993), p. E2.

ISSUE BOX

TO HAGGLE OR NOT TO HAGGLE OVER THE PRICE OF A CAR?

Traditionally, we have expected to haggle, or negotiate, over the price of a vehicle, whether new or used. It was the naive consumer indeed who did not try to get a better price than the one on the sticker. Invariably some customers would drive harder bargains than others, and some dealers were more eager to "deal" than others. But did most consumers really like this "challenge" of trying to best a car salesperson and the sales manager? And how could you really be sure that you had gotten the best deal?

Some car dealers—and one make of car, the Saturn—are currently testing the waters with no-haggling selling, in which a uniformly low price is offered to all customers with no further negotiation or haggling accepted. (With trade-ins, of course, some negotiation is still possible.) This breaking away from the traditional is the source of some controversy. Although many customers like the idea of not having to haggle, which can be traumatic for novices, others feel that they are not getting as good a price. Still, the very fact that it is being tested suggests that the U.S. auto industry is becoming more innovative and possibly more in tune with customer preferences.

INVITATION TO DISCUSSION
How do you feel about no-haggling car buying? Why do you feel this way? What has been your previous experience in car purchasing?

Lest U.S. carmakers become too satisfied with their recent inroads against the Japanese, they apparently still have a considerable way to go to match the quality of Japanese cars. The widely watched J. D. Power & Associates quality survey listed the following cars as the top 10 for 1993:[14]

Rank	Model
1	Lexus LS 400
2	Lexus SC 300/400
3	Infiniti J30
4	Infiniti Q45
4	Toyota Camry
6	Acura Legend
6	Ford Crown Victoria
8	Lexus ES 300
9	Toyota Paseo
10	Buick Park Avenue
10	Toyota Corolla
10	Toyota Tercel

[14]J. D. Power & Associates, as published in Neal Templin, "Toyota Is Standout Once Again on J. D. Power's Quality Survey," *The Wall Street Journal* (May 28, 1993), pp. B1 and B5.

Embarrassingly, Chrysler was not in the top 10, despite its widely heralded new LH sedans. It also experienced another setback when Japan recalled more than one-half the Chrysler vehicles sold in Japan from 1989 to 1993 because of possible brake failure.

ANALYSIS

In the great Chrysler comebacks, we are impressed with the *thin line* that can exist between failure and even total loss of a company and solid success and glittering acclaim. A few "ifs" dramatize this thin line:

If Iacocca had not been able to sell Washington on giving Chrysler the $1.5 billion loan guarantee, the "bailout," would the company have survived? The federal assistance was no foregone conclusion; indeed, many in Washington were opposed to it. Without the badly needed funds, the company may not have survived intact.

If the K-car had not proven to be an outstanding success, it is unlikely that the company could have remained viable, even with the federal guarantee. Iacocca himself admitted that the K-car was the company's final chance. Not only did the K-car provide needed sales and profits in the early 1980s, but it served as the basic structure for succeeding models into the next decade, enabling Chrysler to generate the cash flow to sustain the company and its options.

If Iacocca's cost cutting in the early 1990s had cut into too much bone and muscle, the weakened Chrysler would have been unable to take advantage of the surge to come a few years later. And again, as with the K-car, all the chips were resting on the market acceptance of a few new models. This was a risky situation, but Chrysler had few other choices.

By the mid-1980s, surrounded by success and wide acclaim, Iacocca forgot his focus. Instead of investing the new plentiful financial resources in new prototypes and models and updating plant and equipment, he squandered billions of dollars on unwise diversifications and other endeavors. This dilution of resources and focus almost redestroyed the company.

Along with the squandering of company financial resources, Iacocca also abandoned his own whole-hearted commitment to Chrysler. Other roads beckoned, and he left company operations in lesser hands as he pursued the life of a popular public figure. Fortunately for Chrysler and its employees, creditors, and investors, he was still around and able to come back to save the company again after he had led it astray.

This brings us to one of the interesting anomalies of great leaders: their inconsistencies of performance. After highly successful decisions and actions, they tend to let up, to rest on their laurels. Perhaps the reason may be that they have overcome the great challenge and have lost interest in the more mundane. They seek new challenges, ones for which they may not be as capable or certainly not as experienced.

WHAT CAN BE LEARNED?

The captain must pilot. After saving Chrysler, Iacocca left it to a number of "strong-willed, highly ambitious mavericks who had been derailed from the fast track at other companies."[15] Gerald Greenwald, Bennett Bidwell, and Robert Lutz came from Ford. Iacocca promoted Sperlich, who had preceded him at Chrysler from Ford and who was instrumental in developing the K-car, to be the company's president. The four senior executives began feuding, with a particularly bitter struggle between Sperlich, the engineer, and Greenwald, the numbers man. Iacocca backed Greenwald and lost his brilliant product designer. By the time Iacocca recovered the helm, the company was in disarray and badly behind in new product planning.

Delegation is the mark of the good executive, but it can be overdone. When several executives are competing for the top spot, such delegation has been likened to a kingdom without a king, with the various lords, formerly working together for the king, fighting among themselves for the throne.[16]

A winning hand eventually succumbs. Chrysler had a winning hand with its K-car, and this success lasted for some years. Eventually and inevitably the K-car became superseded and outmoded. Unfortunately, Chrysler did not recognize this vulnerability in time and almost self-destructed for the second time in less than a decade. The lesson should be clear: A winning strategy or a successful product cannot last forever. Times change, innovations make for obsolescence, competitors match and surpass, and customers grow tired. Chrysler and Iacocca eventually recognized the fallacy of K-car durability and reacted, but it was close.

Spread your risks. Chrysler and Iacocca represent the ultimate gamble: staking everything on one roll of the dice, in this case on the K-car and later on the LH. Fortunately, the gamble paid off. But what if it had not? The company then would probably have folded. Admittedly, with the K-car, Iacocca had little choice. There were no resources left for spreading risks. Just as the gambler stakes everything, so Iacocca risked Chrysler's fortunes. He became a hero because he won. Prudence, however, suggests that management should avoid the "all or nothing" decision: The stakes are too great and the risks too uncertain for such a gamble.

INVITATION

What additional learning insights can you gain from the Chrysler roller coaster?

---

[15]Judis, *op. cit.,* p. 30.
[16]*Ibid.*

QUESTIONS

1. Do you think Chrysler could have survived without the government bailout? Why or why not? Playing the devil's advocate (one who takes an opposing position for the sake of determining the validity), offer arguments why Chrysler should not have received such assistance.
2. "Iacocca was not a great manager. He simply lucked out." Discuss.
3. Defend the acquisitions of Iacocca in the mid-1980s, particularly the four rental car companies, Lamborghini, the airplane company, and the stake in Maserati. While admittedly these did not work out profitably, with the benefit of hindsight, were the decisions all that bad at the time?
4. During some of Chrysler's worst days, Iacocca seriously considered merging Chrysler with Ford, but Ford top executives would not consent. Given that the federal government would have approved, list what you see as the pros and cons of such a merger, (a) from the viewpoint of the companies involved and (b) from the perspective of the general public.
5. Is stock price the best indicator of a corporation's worth?
6. Do you think Iacocca has built the foundation for Chrysler to be reasonably secure and an ever-growing presence in the U.S. auto industry? Array your pro and con arguments and defend your conclusions.

INVITATION TO ROLE PLAY

1. How could Iacocca have better handled his stewardship of Chrysler? Place yourself in his shoes in the 1980s.
2. You are the confidant of Hal Sperlich, the gifted developer of the Mustang for Iacocca at Ford and later of the K-car and the minivan at Chrysler. It is 1986, and your boss is fighting for a new car platform to replace the aging K-car platform. But Greenwald and his accounting and finance cronies oppose this as an unacceptable waste of company resources. What persuasive arguments can you marshall for Sperlich to try to win this key controversy? What course of action do you recommend that he take?

INVITATION TO RESEARCH

How is Chrysler faring as we move beyond the early 1990s? Is Iacocca still a powerful voice? Have the Japanese rebounded from their hard times? Has the U.S. auto industry been able to gain ground on foreign automakers?

18

Contrast—Wal-Mart: Leading to Retailing's Biggest

In March 1992 Sam Walton passed away after a two-year battle with bone cancer. Perhaps the most admired businessman of his era, he had founded Wal-Mart Stores with the concept of discount stores in small towns and had brought it to lofty stature as the biggest retailer in the United States—ahead of the decades-long leader, Sears, ahead of another great discount-store success, Kmart, and ahead of a charging J.C. Penney Company.

THE EARLY YEARS OF SAM WALTON

Samuel Moore Walton was born in Kingfisher, Oklahoma, on March 29, 1917. He and his brother James, born three years later, were reared in a family that valued hard work and thrift. They grew up in Missouri in the depths of the Great Depression.

By the time Sam had entered eighth grade in Shebina, Oklahoma, he was already exhibiting the character traits that would dominate his future life: quiet and soft-spoken, but a natural leader who became class president and captain of the football team. He even became the first Eagle Scout in Shebina's history.

At the University of Missouri, Sam excelled in academics and athletics. He worked his way through college by delivering newspapers, working in a five-and-dime store, lifeguarding, and waiting tables at the university.

After his graduation in 1940, Sam went to the J.C. Penney Company and became a management trainee at the Des Moines, Iowa, store. There he applied his work ethic, competed to become Penney's most promising new man, and became imbued with the Penney philosophy of catering to smaller towns and having "associates" instead of employees or clerks. He also met J. C. Penney himself and was intrigued with his habit of strolling around stores and personally meeting and observing customers and sales-people. After 18 months Walton left Penney's to enter the U.S. Army, but what he had learned in the Penney store in Des Moines was to shape his future ideas.

GROWTH OF WAL-MART

Sam Walton was discharged from the Army in August 1945. By chance he stumbled on an opportunity to buy a Ben Franklin variety store franchise in Newport, Arkansas, and he opened it a month later. The lease arrangement with the building's owner did not work out, so he eventually relocated in Bentonville, Arkansas, in 1950. During the 1950s and early 1960s, Walton increased the number of Ben Franklin franchises to 15. In the winter of 1962 he proposed at a Ben Franklin board meeting that the company should aggressively turn its efforts to discounting, citing the great potential of dis-count stores. The company refused to consider such an innovative idea, so Sam and his brother went ahead anyway and opened a Discount City in Rogers, Arkansas, in 1962; they opened a second store in Harrison, Arkan-sas, in 1964. The company was incorporated as Wal-Mart Stores on October 31, 1969, and became a publicly held company a year later. In 1970 Walton also opened his first distribution center and general office: a 72,000 square foot complex in Bentonville, Arkansas. By 1972 Wal-Mart was listed on the New York Stock Exchange.

In 1976 Walton severed ties with Ben Franklin in order to concentrate on the expansion of Wal-Mart. His operations had extended to small towns in Arkansas, Missouri, Kansas, and Oklahoma.

The essence of Walton's management philosophy during these build-ing years was that of an old-fashioned entrepreneur; Walton personally roamed through his own stores, as well as those of competitors, always looking for new ideas in mass-merchandising (i.e., maximizing sales at attractive prices).

But rather than confronting the major retailers—department stores, chains such as Penney's and Sears, and the strong discounters such as Kmart—he confined his efforts to the smaller cities, ones deemed to have insufficient market potential by the major retailers. He saw these towns as a strategic window of opportunity, untapped by competitors. (Review the Southwest Airline case for a similar seizing of a strategic window.)

Growth accelerated. By the end of 1975 Walton had 104 stores with nearly 6000 employees and annual sales of $236 million, which generated $6 million net profit. The next year, the number of stores had increased to 125, employees to 7500, and sales to $340 million, with $11.5 million in profit.

Table 18.1 compares the growth of sales and number of stores of Wal-Mart with that of Kmart, its major competitor, from 1980 to 1990, the decade in which Wal-Mart forged ahead to become the biggest retailer. By the end of fiscal 1991, Wal-Mart had 1573 stores in 35 states.

Some of these new stores were Wal-Mart SuperCenters, considerably larger than the regular Wal-Marts, having a warehouse-style food outlet under the same roof as the discount store. While such food stores carried items comparable to products in a regular urban supermarket, the assortment and service were superior to those in most direct competitors in the smaller cities. And the key motivation for adding food stores to the general merchandise discount store was the greater frequency of customer shop-

Figure 18.1   Comparison of Growth in Sales and Number of Stores, Wal-Mart and Kmart, 1980–1990

	Kmart		Wal-Mart	
	Sales (millions)	Number of Stores	Sales (millions)	Number of Stores
1980	$14,204	1,772	$ 1,643	330
1981	16,527	2,055	2,445	491
1982	16,772	2,117	3,376	551
1983	18,597	2,160	4,667	642
1984	20,762	2,173	6,401	745
1985	22,035	2,332	8,451	859
1986	23,035	2,342	11,909	980
1987	25,627	2,273	15,959	1,114
1988	27,301	2,307	20,649	1,259
1989	29,533	2,361	25,810	1,402
1990	32,070	2,350 ·	32,602	1,573

Source: Company annual reports.

Commentary: Several of these statistics are of particular interest. The comparison of the sales from 1980 to 1990, slightly more than one decade, of Wal-Mart and Kmart, show the tremendous growth rate of Wal-Mart, starting at little more than 10% of Kmart sales figures to forge ahead by 1990. And Kmart was no slouch during this period.

  Second, Wal-Mart achieved its leadership in total sales with almost 800 fewer stores than Kmart had. This means that Wal-Mart's stores were achieving much higher sales volume than Kmart's, a fact that is further borne out by the statistics in Table 18.3.

ping: Customers shop weekly for groceries, and such patronage exposes them to the other merchandise in the discount store far more frequently than would otherwise be the case.

Wal-Mart by now was also opening another category of stores: Sam's Wholesale, also known as Sam's Clubs. First introduced in 1984, by 1991 there were 148. This wholesale club concept came about as regular discount stores seemed to be reaching saturation in some locations. The wholesale warehouse went a step further in discounting.

Sam's Club stores are large, ranging up to 135,000 square feet. Each store is a membership-only operation, with qualified members including businesses and individuals who are members of certain groups, such as government employees and credit union members. Although the stores are huge, they carry less than 5 percent of the items carried by regular discount stores. Assortments are limited to fast-moving home goods and apparel, generally name brands, with prices 8 to 10 percent over cost but well under those of discount stores and department and specialty stores. Sam's Clubs provided the initial entry for Wal-Mart into the big metropolitan markets that it had avoided in most of its great growth.

In December 1987 Wal-Mart opened its newest merchandising concept, Hypermart USA, in Garland, Texas, a suburb of Dallas. The hypermart offers a combination of groceries and general merchandise in over 200,000 square feet of selling space. The stores also include a variety of fast-food and service shops, such as a beauty shop, shoe repair, and dry cleaners. Thus, a mall atmosphere is created to achieve one-stop shopping.

In spite of optimistic beginnings, the hypermarket idea was not as successful as expected. A scaled-down version was the SuperCenter. Plans were suspended for building more hypermarkets in favor of the super-center concept.

For a comparison of sales and profitability of Wal-Mart with Kmart, Sears, and Penney, see Table 18.2. Note that profitability comparisons include operating profit as a percentage of sales and the more valid measure of profitability, the return of equity (i.e., the return on the money invested in the enterprise). From this table we see that the growth of Wal-Mart in sales and profitability compared with its nearest competitors is awesome. Table 18.3 shows another operational comparison, this time in the average sales per store for Wal-Mart and Kmart. And again, the comparison shows the great growth performance of Wal-Mart.

The Future

Sam Walton received the Medal of Freedom from President Bush on March 17, 1992. Unfortunately, he did not live long to enjoy this high honor

Table 18.2 10-Year Comparison of Gross Revenues, Percentage of Operating Margin, and Return on Equity for Wal-Mart and Its Competitors[a]

	Wal-Mart			Kmart			Sears			J. C. Penney		
Year	Gross Revenue	% Operating Profit Margin	Equity Return %	Gross Revenue	% Operating Profit Margin	Equity Return %	Gross Revenue	% Operating Profit Margin	Equity Return %	Gross Revenue	% Operating Profit Margin	Equity Return %
1981	$2,445.0	5.6	25.6	$16,527.0	2.2	9.0	$27,357	7.2	8.2	$11,860	7.5	13.2
1982	3,376.3	7.8	25.4	17,040.0	4.3	10.1	30,020	8.8	10.1	11,414	8.3	13.3
1983	4,666.9	8.3	26.6	18,878.9	6.0	16.7	35,883	9.7	14.4	12,078	8.7	13.1
1984	6,400.9	8.5	27.5	21,095.9	6.7	15.4	38,828	10.5	14.1	13,451	7.8	11.4
1985	8,451.5	7.2	25.6	22,420.0	6.2	14.4	40,715	9.5	11.5	13,747	7.7	9.8
1986	11,909.1	7.1	26.6	23,812.1	5.7	14.5	44,282	9.1	10.4	15,151	8.6	11.0
1987	15,959.3	6.8	27.8	25,626.6	5.8	15.7	48,439	8.5	12.1	15,747	9.1	14.6
1988	20,649.0	6.4	27.8	27,301.4	6.5	16.0	50,251	9.2	3.0	15,296	8.3	20.4
1989	25,810.7	6.5	27.1	29,532.7	5.8	6.5	53,794	9.2	10.6	16,405	9.2	18.4
1990	32,601.6	6.0	24.1	32,070.0	5.4	14.0	55,971	7.4	7.0	16,365	2.4	15.6

[a]Gross revenue is in $ billions.

Source: Company annual reports.

Commentary: The comparison with major competitors shows Wal-Mart far exceeding its rivals in revenue growth. The operating profit percentage exceeds Kmart's for most years, but Sears and Penney look better here. However, the true measure of profitability is return on equity, and here Wal-Mart shines: It indeed is a very profitable operation, while offering consumers attractive prices.

Table 18.3   Average Sales Per Store, Wal-Mart and Kmart, 1980–1990

	Kmart	Wal-Mart
1980	$ 8,015,801	$ 4,978,788
1981	8,042,338	4,979,633
1982	7,922,532	6,127,042
1983	8,609,722	7,269,470
1984	9,554,533	8,591,946
1985	9,448,970	9,838,184
1986	9,835,611	12,152,040
1987	11,274,527	14,325,852
1988	11,833,983	16,401,111
1989	12,508,682	18,409,415
1990	13,646,808	20,726,001

Source: Computed from Table 18.1.

Commentary: The great increase in sales per store for Wal-Mart is particularly noteworthy. In 1980 Wal-Mart's average store's sales was hardly one-half that of an average Kmart. By 1990 the average Wal-Mart store was generating more than 50% more sales than an average Kmart.

bestowed on him (among many honors, such as Man of the Year, Horatio Alger Award in 1984, and "Retailer of the Decade" in 1989); he died of cancer nine days later, on March 26, 1992.

David Glass, 53 years old, assumed the role of president and chief executive officer. Glass was known for his hard-driving managerial style. He had gained his retail experience at a small supermarket chain in Springfield, Missouri, and had joined Wal-Mart as executive vice president for finance in 1976. He had been named president and chief operating officer in 1984, while Sam Walton had kept the position of chief executive officer. About the transition of executives, Glass had said

> There's no transition to make, because other principles and basic values he (Walton) used in founding this company were so sound and so universally accepted. . . . We'll be fine as long as we never lose our responsiveness to the customer.[1]

Whether a new generation can continue the successful growth efforts of Wal-Mart, now entering the tougher competitive environment of larger metropolitan areas, remains to be seen, but the prospects seem positive.

---

[1]Susan Caminiti, "What Ails Retailing," *Fortune* (January 30, 1989), p. 61.

INGREDIENTS OF SUCCESS

Management Style and Employee Orientation

Sam Walton cultivated a management style that emphasized individual initiative and autonomy over close supervision. He constantly reminded employees that they were vital to the success of the company, that they were essentially "running their own business," that they were "associates" or "partners" in the business, rather than simply employees.

In such employee relations philosophy, he borrowed from James Cash Penney, the founder of the J. C. Penney Company, and his formulation of the "Penney idea" in 1913. This Penney idea also stressed the desirability of constantly improving the human factor, of rewarding associates through participation in what the business produces, and of appraising every policy and action as to whether it squares with what is right and just.

Walton emphasized bottom-up communication, thereby providing a free flow of ideas from throughout the company. For example, the "people greeter" concept (described in the following information box) was implemented in 1983 as a result of a suggestion received from an employee in a store in Louisiana. This idea proved so successful that it has since been adopted by Kmart, some department stores, and even shopping malls.

Another example of listening to employees' ideas came when an assistant manager in an Alabama store ordered too many marshmallow sand-

---

INFORMATION BOX

GREETERS

All customers entering Wal-Mart stores encounter a store employee assigned to welcome them, give advice on where to find things, and to help with exchanges or refunds. These "greeters" also thank people exiting from the store, while unobtrusively observing any indications of shoplifting.

Staffing exists and entrances is not uncommon by retailers; what makes Wal-Mart's greeters unique is their friendliness and patience. Wal-Mart has found that retirees supplementing pensions usually make the best greeters and are most appreciated by customers. As noted earlier, the greeter idea originated as a suggestion from an employee (associate): Sam Walton liked the idea, and it became a company-wide practice.

INVITATION TO DISCUSSION

Do you personally like the idea of having a store employee greet you as you enter and leave an establishment? On balance, do you think the greeter idea is a plus or a minus? Explain.

wiches, or Moon Pies. The store manager told him to use his imagination to sell the excess, so John Love came up with an idea to create the first World Championship Moon Pie Eating Contest. It was held in the store's parking lot. The event was so successful that it is now held every year, drawing spectators not only from the community but from all over Alabama and surrounding states.[2]

Wal-Mart has a profit-sharing plan dating back to 1972 in which all associates share in a portion of the company's yearly profits. As one celebrated example of the benefits of such profit sharing, Shirley Cox had worked as an office cashier earning $7.10 an hour. When she decided to retire after 24 years, the amount of her profit sharing in 1988 was $220,127.[3] In addition, associates may participate in the payroll stock purchase plan in which Wal-Mart contributes part of the cost.

The Sam Walton philosophy of business and management was to create a friendly, "down-home" family atmosphere in his stores. He described it as a "whistle while your work philosophy," one that, as he saw it, stressed the importance of having fun while working because you can work better if you enjoy yourself.[4] He was concerned about losing this attitude or atmosphere: "The bigger Wal-Mart gets, the more essential it is that we think small. Because that's exactly how we have become a huge corporation—by not acting like one."[5]

Another incentive is given to all employees in stores that manage to reduce shrinkage (that is, the loss of merchandise due to shoplifting, carelessness, and employee theft). Employees are given $200 each a year if shrinkage limits are met. This causes associates to become detectives by watching shoppers and each other. In 1989 Wal-Mart had a shrinkage rate of 1 percent of sales, below the industry rate of 2 percent.[6]

A rather unusual way of making employees feel vital to the Wal-Mart operation is information sharing, which amplifies the idea that employees are associates of the business. Management shares the good news and the bad news about the company's performance. In each store managers share operating statistics with employees, including profits, purchases, sales, and markdowns. Every person, from assistant managers to part-time clerks, see

[2]Example described in Don Longo, "Associate Involvement Spurs Gains (Wal-Mart Employees Are Encouraged to Suggest Ideas for Promotions)," *Discount Store News* (December 18, 1989), p. 83.

[3]Example cited in Vance H. Trimble, *Sam Walton: The Inside Story of America's Richest Man* (New York: Dutton, 1990), p. 233.

[4]*Ibid.*, p. 105.

[5]*Ibid.*, p. 104.

[6]Charles Bernstein, "How to Win Employee and Customer Friends," *Nation's Restaurant News* (January 30, 1989), p. F3.

this information on a regular basis. The result: Employees tend to think of Wal-Mart as truly their own company.

Not the least of the open and people-oriented management practices fostered by Sam Walton is what he called MBWA, Management By Walking Around. Managers, from store level to headquarters, walk around the stores to stay familiar with what is going on, to talk to the associates, and to encourage associates to share their ideas and concerns. Such interactions permit a personal touch usually lacking in large firms but so far still dominant as Wal-Mart grows large.

And how have unions fared in such an environment? Not surprisingly, they have had no success. Walton argued that in his "family environment," associates had better wages, benefits, and bonuses than any union could get for them. In addition, the bonuses and profit sharing were inducements far better than those a union could negotiate. As partners in a business operation, how could employees turn to a union?

State-of-the-Art Technology

Sam Walton's decentralized management style led to a team approach to decision making. But this approach would have been difficult to achieve without a heavy commitment to supporting technology. A huge telecommunications system permits Wal-Mart executives to broadcast and communicate to store managers. In addition, home-office management teams, using the company's 11 turboprop planes, fly to various stores to assess their operations. Coming back to headquarters for Friday and Saturday meetings, they assess any problems and coordinate needed merchandise transfers among stores. Through the use of a six-channel satellite, messages can be broadcast to all stores, and a master computer tracks the company's complex distribution system.

Small Town Invasion Strategy

Adopting a strategy similar to that of the J. C. Penney Company of more than half a century before, Wal-Mart shunned big cities and directed its store openings to smaller towns where competition consisted only of local merchants and small outlets of a few chains, such as Woolworth, Gamble, and Penney.

These merchants typically offered only limited assortments of merchandise, had no Sunday or evening hours, and charged substantially higher prices than they would charge in the more competitive environments of larger cities. Other larger retailers, especially discounters, had shunned such small towns as not offering enough potential to support the high sales volume needed for the low-price strategy.

But Wal-Mart found potential in abundance in these small-town markets, as customers flocked from all the surrounding towns and rural areas for the variety of goods and the prices. (In the process of captivating small town and rural consumers, Wal-Mart wreaked havoc on the existing small-town merchants. See the following issue box for a discussion of the sociological impact of Wal-Mart on small town America.) The company honed its skills in such small towns, isolated from aggressive competitors, and found enough business to become the world's largest retail enterprise. Then, flexing its muscles, it began moving confidently into the big cities, whose competitors were as fearful of Wal-Mart as had been the thousands of small-town merchants.

ISSUE BOX

IMPACT OF WAL-MART ON SMALL TOWNS

In most of its growth years, Wal-Mart pursued a policy of opening stores on the outskirts of small rural towns, usually with populations between 25,000 and 50,000. Attractive both in prices and assortment of goods, its stores often became beacons in drawing customers from miles around. Wal-Mart also was likely to be the biggest employer in the town, with 200 to 300 local employees.

But the dominating presence of Wal-Mart was a mixed blessing for many communities. Small-town merchants were often devastated and unable to compete. Downtowns in many of these small towns became decaying vestiges of what perhaps a few months previously had been prosperous centers. But consumers benefited.

Wal-Mart brought tradeoffs and controversy: Was rural America better or worse off with the arrival of Wal-Mart? On balance, most experts saw the economic development brought on by Wal-Mart as more than offsetting the business destruction it caused. But few could dispute the sociological trauma.[7]

INVITATION TO DISCUSSION

What is your assessment of the desirability of Wal-Mart coming into a rural small town? How might your assessment differ depending on your particular position or status in that community?

---

[7]For more discussion of the impact of Wal-Mart, see Karen Blumenthal, "Arrival of Discounter Tears the Civic Fabric of Small Town Life," *The Wall Street Journal* (April 14, 1987), p. 1 ff.; Hank Gilman, "Rural Retailing Chains Prosper by Combining Service, Sophistication," *The Wall Street Journal* (July 2, 1984), p. 1 ff.

Controlling Costs

Sam Walton was a stickler for holding costs to a minimum in the quest to offer customers the lowest prices. Cost control started with Wal-Mart vendors. Wal-Mart has gained a reputation of being hard to please, of constantly pressuring its suppliers to give additional price breaks and cooperative advertising.[8] In further efforts to buy goods at the lowest possible prices, Wal-Mart has attempted to bypass middlemen and sales reps and buy all goods direct from the manufacturer. In so doing, a factory presumably would save money on sales representatives' commissions of 2 to 6 percent of the purchase order and thus be able to pass this savings on to Wal-Mart. Understandably, this has aroused a heated controversy by groups representing sales representatives.

Wal-Mart has been able to achieve great savings in distribution. Its sophisticated use of distribution centers and its own fleet of trucks enable it to negotiate lower prices when it buys in bulk directly from suppliers. More than three-fourths of the merchandise sold in a Wal-Mart store is processed through one of the company's 16 distribution centers. Each center serves 150 to 200 stores with daily delivery. For example, the distribution center in Cullman, Alabama, is situated on 28 acres with 1.2 million square feet. Some 1042 employees load 150 outbound Wal-Mart trailers a day and unload 180. On a heavy day, laser scanners will route 190,000 cases of goods on an 11-mile conveyor.[9]

Each warehouse uses the latest in optical scanning devices, automated materials-handling equipment, bar coding, and computerized inventory. With all of the stores using the satellite network, messages can be quickly flashed between stores, distribution centers, and corporate headquarters in Bentonville, Arkansas. Hand-held computers assist store employees in ordering merchandise. The result is a distribution system that provides stores with on-time delivery at the lowest possible cost. By using the most advanced technologies, Wal-Mart's distribution expenses are only 3 percent of total sales, which is about one-half that of most chains.[10]

Wal-Mart has previously been able to achieve great savings in advertising costs compared with major competitors. Although discount chains typically spend 2 to 3 percent of sales for advertising, Wal-Mart has been able to hold advertising to less than 1 percent of sales. Much of this difference reflects low media rates in most of its markets, the smaller towns. As Wal-Mart moves into larger metropolitan markets, the advertising cost advantage may diminish.

[8]Toni Apgar, "The Cash Machine," *Marketing and Media Decisions* (March 1987), p. 82.
[9]John Huey, "America's Most Successful Merchant," *Fortune* (September 23, 1991), p. 54.
[10]*Facts about Wal-Mart Stores*, Company publication (Bentonville,Arkansas, n.d.), p. 4.

Finally, Wal-Mart's operating and administrative costs reflect a spartan operation that is rigidly enforced. A lean headquarters organization and a minimum of staff assistants compared with most other retailers completes the cost-control philosophy and reflects the frugal thinking of Sam Walton that dates back to his early days.

"Buy American" and Environmental Programs

As foreign manufacturers increasingly began taking market share away from American producers—and in the process, destroying some American jobs—sentiment began mounting for import restrictions to save jobs. And as the amount of imports grew, so did the trade deficit, with consequences not fully understood by most people but generally understood to be something very bad. However, the idea of restricting free world trade is highly controversial: Many experts question whether tariffs, quotas, and other restrictions are in the general best interest. Some say the best scenario is to induce American consumers to "buy American," or at least to give preferential treatment to products produced in this country by American workers; such a policy would eliminate import restrictions but enhance consumer support of American workers and factories.

In March 1985 Sam Walton became very concerned with what seemed to him to be a serious national situation. He sent a message to his buyers to find products that American manufacturers have stopped producing because they couldn't compete with foreign imports. This was the beginning of Walton's "Buy American" program, which had the long-range objective of strengthening the free enterprise system. The program is essentially a cooperative effort between retailers and domestic manufacturers to reestablish the competitive position of American-made goods in price and quality.

This program showcased the power of the huge retailer. Magic Chef, 3M, Farris Fashions, and many other manufacturers joined Walton's crusade, as Wal-Mart pledged to support domestic production for items ranging from film to microwave ovens to flannel shirts and other apparel.

Wal-Mart has been a leader in challenging manufacturers to improve their products and packaging in order to protect the environment. As a result, manufacturers have made great improvements in eliminating excessive packaging, converting to recyclable materials, and eliminating toxic inks and dyes.

The company participates in Earth Day events, with tree plantings, information booths and videos to show customers how to improve the environment. It has also been active in fund raising for local environmental groups, and in "adopt-a-highway" programs, in which store personnel volunteer at least one day every month to collect trash and clean up local highways and beaches.

WHAT CAN BE LEARNED?

Take good care of people. Sam Walton was concerned with two groups of people: his employees and his customers. By motivating and even inspiring his employees, he found that customers were also well served. Somehow in the exigencies of business, especially big business, this emphasis on people tends to be pushed aside. Walton made caring for people common practice.

By listening to his employees, by involving them, by exhorting them, and by giving them a real share of the business—all the while stressing friendliness and concern for customers—Walton fostered a business climate unique in almost any large organization. In addition to providing customers with the friendliest of employees, his stores also offered honest values and great assortments and catered to the concerns of many middle-income Americans for the environment and American jobs.

Go for the strategic window of opportunity. Strategic windows of opportunity sometimes come in strange guises. They always represent areas of overlooked or untapped potential business by existing firms. But in the formative and early growth years of Wal-Mart, no window could ever have seemed less promising than the one Sam Walton milked to perfection and to great growth. Small towns and cities in many parts of rural America were losing population and economic strength, partly because of the decline in family farms and the accompanying infrastructure of small businesses. It was therefore not surprising that the major discount chains focused their growth efforts on large metropolitan areas. Although many small cities had Penney's and Sears outlets as well as such other chains as Woolworth, Gamble, and Coast to Coast stores, these were usually small stores, often old, marginal, and rather in the backstream of corporate consciousness. This retail environment was one of small stores with limited assortments of merchandise and relatively high prices.

In this environment Sam Walton seized his opportunity. He saw something that no other merchants had: that the limited total market potential meant a dearth of competition. He also saw that the potential was far greater than the population of the small town and its immediate surrounding population. Indeed, a large Wal-Mart store in a rather isolated rural community could draw customers from many miles away.

Do such windows of opportunity still exist today? You bet they do for the entrepreneur with vision, an ability to look beyond the customary, and the courage to follow up on his or her vision.

The marriage of old-fashioned ideas and modern technology can be a potent strategy. Sam Walton embraced this strategy with more success than any other entrepreneur in modern business, and he made it work throughout his organization, despite its growth to great size. In the forefront of retailers in the use of communications technology and computerized distribution, he still was able to motivate his employees to offer friendly and helpful customer services to a degree that few large retailers have been able consistently to achieve.

Other firms can benefit from the example of Wal-Mart in cultivating homespun friendliness with awesome technology, and competitors are trying to emulate. The particular difficulty that many are finding, however, is in achieving consistency.

Showing environmental concern can pay dividends. Today, as perhaps never before, many people are concerned about the environment, and it seems high time that we have such concern, while much of the environment can still be salvaged and protected from the abuses of a modern industrial age. Given such sentiment, the firm that takes a leadership position for environmental protection stands to benefit from improving customer relations and, not the least, from positive media attention.

Another issue important to many Americans involves foreign inroads to the detriment of many U.S. manufacturers and jobs. Regardless of the great controversy over the desirability of free trade, many middle-class Americans have applauded the leadership of Wal-Mart in its widely publicized "Buy American" policy.

What is the moral for other businesses? Be alert to the increasing concerns of the public, and where possible, act on them to achieve a leadership role.

INVITATION

Can you identify additional learning insights that could be applicable to firms in other situations?

QUESTIONS

1. How might you attempt to compete with Wal-Mart if you were
   (*a*) a small hardware merchant?
   (*b*) a small clothing store for men?
   (*c*) a Woolworth?
2. Do you think Wal-Mart is vulnerable today, and if so, in what way? If you do not think it is vulnerable, do you see any limits to its growth?
3. Why do you think the hypermarket idea failed to meet expectations? Was Wal-Mart too quick to table expansion plans for its hypermarkets?
4. What weaknesses do you see Wal-Mart as either having now or potentially? How can the company overcome them?

5. Wal-Mart is now entering urban areas. What new challenges does this present? Will Wal-Mart need to change? Can "the Wal-Mart way" work only in rural and exurban areas?
6. Can discounting go on forever? What are the limits to growth by price competition?
7. Discuss Wal-Mart's business practices (especially in regard to unions, invading small towns, and supplier relations) in terms of their ethical ramifications for the industry and for society. Should students be encouraged to emulate these practices?

INVITATION TO ROLE PLAY

1. Assume the role of a top executive at Kmart. You have seen Wal-Mart's phenomenal growth to the point that it now is the biggest retailer, surpassing your own company. Admittedly most of this growth has come in smaller communities where you were not present. Now Wal-Mart is invading your turf. How will you counter this competitive thrust of the world's most successful retailer? Be as specific as you can. (If both Kmart and Wal-Mart stores are operating in your community, you may want to visit both and analyze their strengths and weaknesses.)
2. You are the principal adviser to David Glass, who has replaced Sam Walton as chief executive. What advice do you give Glass for continuing the successful growth pattern now that the charismatic founder is no longer present to inspire the organization? Be as specific as you can, and make assumptions if necessary, but spell them out.

INVITATION TO RESEARCH

Has Wal-Mart faltered since Sam Walton's death? Are there any ominous signs on the horizon?

Four

ATROPHIED CONTROLS

19

United Way:
Where Were the Controls?

The United Way, the preeminent charitable organization in the United States, celebrated its 100-year anniversary in 1987. It had evolved from local community chests, and its strategy for fund-raising had proven highly effective: funding local charities through payroll deductions. The good it did seemed unassailable.

Abruptly in 1992, the persona of honesty and integrity that United Way had built was jeopardized by investigative reporters' revelations of free-spending practices and other questionable deeds of its greatest builder and president, William Aramony. A major point of public concern was Aramony's salary and uncontrolled perks in a lifestyle that seemed inappropriate for the head of a charitable organization that depended mostly on contributions from working people.

In 1993 another paragon of not-for-profit social enhancement organizations came under fire: the venerable Girl Scouts. Multimillion-dollar profits of Girl Scout cookies were found to be used mostly to support a sprawling bureaucracy instead of the Girl Scout troops that provided the labor in the first place.

We are left to question the operations and lack of controls of our major charitable and not-for-profit entities. Business firms have to report to shareholders and creditors, but not-for-profit organizations have been permitted to operate largely without the checks and balances that characterize most other organizations.

THE STATURE AND ACCOMPLISHMENTS OF THE UNITED WAY

For its 100th anniversary, then President Ronald Reagan summed up what the United Way stood for:

December 10, 1986

United Way Centennial, 1887–1987
By The President Of The United States Of America
A Proclamation

Since earliest times, we Americans have joined together to help each other and to strengthen our communities. Our deep-roots spirit of caring, of neighbor helping neighbor, has become an American trademark—and an American way of life. Over the Years, our generous and inventive people have created an ingenious network of voluntary organizations to help give help where help is needed.

United Way gives that help very well indeed, and truly exemplifies our spirit of voluntarism. United Way has been a helping force in America right from the first community-wide fund raising campaign in Denver, Colorado, in 1887. Today, more than 2,200 local United Ways across the land raise funds for more than 37,000 voluntary groups that assist millions of people.

The United Way of caring allows volunteers from all walks of life to effectively meet critical needs and solve community problems. At the centennial of the founding of this indispensable voluntary group, it is most fitting that we Americans recognize and commend all the good United Way has done and continues to do.

The congress, by Public Law 99-612, has expressed gratitude to United Way, congratulated it, and applauded and encouraged its fine work and its goals.

NOW, THEREFORE, I RONALD REAGAN, President of the United States of America, by virtue of the authority vested in me by the Constitution and laws of the United States, do hereby proclaim heartfelt thanks to a century of Americans who have shaped and supported United Way, and encourage the continuation of its efforts.

IN WITNESS WHEREOF, I have hereunto set my hand this tenth day of December, in the year of our lord nineteen hundred and eighty-six, and of the Independence of the United States of America the two hundred and eleventh.

Ronald Reagan

Organizing the United Way as the umbrella charity to fund other local charities through payroll deduction established an effective means of fund-raising. It became the recipient of 90 percent of all charitable donations. Employers sometimes used extreme pressure to achieve 100 percent participation of employees, which led to organizational bonuses. The United Way achieved further cooperation of business organizations by involving their executives as leaders of annual campaigns, amid widespread publicity. It would consequently cause such an executive acute loss of face if his or her own organization did not go "over the top" in meeting campaign goals. A local United Way executive admitted that "if participation is 100 percent, it means someone has been coerced."[1]

For many years, outside of some tight-lipped gripes of corporate employees, the organization moved smoothly along, with local contributions generally increasing every year and with the needs for charitable contributions invariably increasing even faster.

The national organization, United Way of America (UWA), is a separate corporation and has no direct control over the approximately 2200 local United Way offices. Most of the locals voluntarily contributed one cent on the dollar of all funds they collected, however, and in return, the national organization provided training and promoted local United Way agencies through advertising and other marketing efforts.

Much of the success of the United Way movement in becoming the largest and most respected charity in the United States was due to the 22 years of William Aramony's leadership of the national organization. When he first took over, the United Ways were not operating under a common name. He built a nationwide network of agencies, all operating under the same name and using the same logo of outstretched hands, which became nationally recognized as the symbol of charitable giving. Unfortunately in 1992 an exposé of Aramony's lavish lifestyle and questionable dealings led to his downfall and burdened local United Ways with serious difficulties in fund-raising.

WILLIAM ARAMONY

During Aramony's tenure United Way contributions increased from $787 million in 1970 to $3 billion in 1990. Aramony built up the headquarters staff to 275 employees and increased his headquarters budget from less than $3 million to $29 million in 1991. Of this amount, $24 million came from the local United Ways, with the rest coming from corporate grants, investment income, and consulting.[2] Figure 19.1 shows the organizational chart as of 1987.

---

[1]Susan Garland, "Keeping a Sharper Eye on Those Who Pass the Hat," *Business Week* (March 16, 1992), p. 39.

[2]Charles E. Shepard, "Perks, Privileges and Power in a Nonprofit World," *The Washington Post* (February 16, 1992), p. A38.

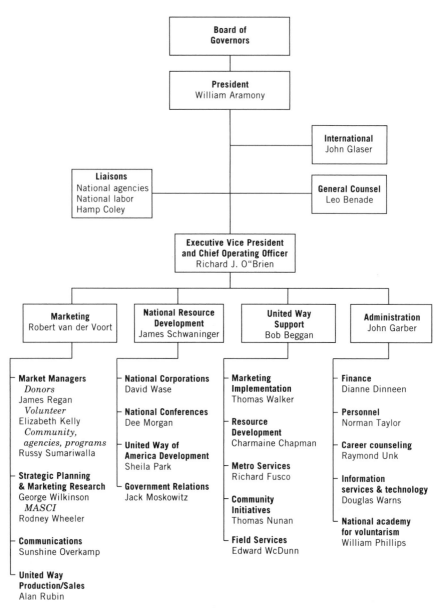

Figure 19.1

Aramony moved comfortably among the most influential people in our society. He attracted a prestigious board of governors, including many top executives from America's largest corporations, but only three of the 37 came from not-for-profit organizations. The board was chaired by John

Akers, chairman and CEO of IBM. Other board members included Edward A. Brennan, CEO of Sears; James D. Robinson III, CEO of American Express; and Paul J. Tagliabue, commissioner of the National Football League. The presence of such top executives on the board brought United Way prestige and spurred contributions from some of the largest and most visible organizations in the United States.

Aramony was the highest paid executive in the charity field. In 1992 his compensation package was $463,000, nearly double that of the next highest paid executive in the industry, Dudley H. Hafner of the American Heart Association.[3] The board fully supported Aramony, regularly giving him 6 percent annual raises.[4]

Investigative Disclosures

The Washington Post began investigating Aramony's tenure as president of United Way of America in 1991, raising questions about his high salary, travel habits, possible cronyism, and dubious relations with five spin-off companies. In February 1992 it released the following information on Aramony's expense charges:[5]

- Aramony had charged $92,265 in limousine expenses to the charity during the previous five years.
- He had charged $40,762 on airfare for the supersonic Concorde.
- He had charged more than $72,000 on international airfare that included first-class seats for himself, his wife, and others.
- He had charged thousands more for personal trips, gifts, and luxuries.
- He had made 29 trips to Las Vegas between 1988 and 1991.
- He had expensed 49 journeys to Gainesville, Florida, the home of his daughter and a woman with whom he had had a relationship.
- He had allegedly approved a $2 million loan to a firm run by his chief financial officer.
- He had approved the diversion of donors' money to questionable spin-off organizations run by long-time aides and provided benefits to family members as well.
- He had passed tens of thousands of dollars in consulting contracts from the UWA to friends and associates.

[3]Shepard, "Perks, Privileges, and Power," A38; and Charles E. Shepard, "United Way of America President Is Urged to Resign," *The Washington Post* (February 27, 1992), p. A1.
[4]Joseph Finder, "Charity Case," *The New Republic* (May 4, 1992), p. 11.
[5]Shepard, "Perks, Privileges, and Power"; Shepard, "President Is Urged to Resign"; Kathleen Teltsch, "United Way Awaits Inquiry on its President's Practices," *The New York Times* (February 24, 1992), p. A12 (L); Charles E. Shepard, "United Way Report Criticizes Ex-Leader's Lavish Lifestyle," *The Washington Post* (April 4, 1992), p. A1.

United Way of America's corporate policy prohibited the hiring of family members within the actual organization, but Aramony skirted the direct violation by hiring friends and relatives as consultants and within the spin-off companies. He paid hundreds of thousands of dollars in consulting fees, for example, to two aides in vaguely documented and even undocumented business transactions.

The use of spin-off companies provided flexible maneuvering. One of the spin-off companies Aramony created to provide travel and bulk purchasing for United Way chapters purchased a $430,000 condominium in Manhattan and a $125,000 apartment in Coral Gables, Florida, for Aramony's use. Another of the spin-off companies hired Aramony's son, Robert Aramony, as its president. Loans and money transfers between the spin-off companies and the national organization raised questions. No records showed that the board of directors had been given the opportunity to approve such loans and transfers.[6]

CONSEQUENCES

When the information about Aramony's salary and expenses became public, reaction was severe. Stanley C. Gault, chairman of Goodyear Tire & Rubber Co., asked, "Where was the board? The outside auditors?"[7] Robert O. Bothwell, executive director of the National Committee for Responsive Philanthropy, said, "I think it is obscene that he is making that kind of salary and asking people who are making $10,000 a year to give 5 percent of their income."[8] At this point let us examine the issue of executive compensation. Are many executives overpaid? The following issue box addresses this controversial topic.

As a major consequence of the scandal, some United Way locals withheld their funds, at least pending a thorough investigation of the allegations. John Akers, chairman of the board, noted that by March 7, 1992, dues payments were running 20 percent behind the previous year, saying "I don't think this process that the United Way of America is going through, or Mr. Aramony is going through, is a process that's bestowing a lot of honor."[9]

---

[6]Shepard, "Perks, Privileges and Power," p. A38.

[7]Susan Garland, op. cit., p. 39.

[8]Felicity Barringer, "United Way Head Is Forced out in a Furor over His Lavish Style," *The New York Times* (February 28, 1992), p. A1.

[9]Felicity Barringer, "United Way Head Tries to Restore Trust," *The New York Times* (March 7, 1992), p. 8L.

ISSUE BOX

EXECUTIVE COMPENSATION: IS IT TOO MUCH?

A controversy is mounting over multimillion-dollar annual compensations of corporate executives. In 1992, for example, the average annual pay of CEOs was $3,842,247; the 20 highest salaries ranged from over $11 million to a mind-boggling $127 million (for Thomas F. Frist, Jr., of Hospital Corporation of America).[10]

Activist shareholders, including some large mutual and pension funds, began protesting pay practices, especially for top executives of firms that were not doing well financially. New disclosure rules imposed in 1993 by the Securities and Exchange Commission (SEC) spotlighted questionable executive pay practices. In the past complacent board members, themselves well paid and often closely aligned with the top executives of the organization, condoned liberal compensations, but this may be changing. The major argument supporting high executive compensations is that compared with salaries of some entertainers and athletes, they are modest. And are not their responsibilities far greater than those of any entertainer or athlete?

In light of the for-profit executive compensations, Aramony's salary was modest. And results were on his side: He made $369,000 in basic salary while raising $3 billion; Lee Iacocca, on the other hand, made $3 million while Chrysler lost $795 million. Where is the justice?

Undoubtedly Aramony, as head of a large for-profit corporation, could have earned several zeros more in compensation and perks, with no raised eyebrows. But is the situation different for a not-for-profit organization, when revenues are derived from donations of millions of people of modest means? This is a real controversy. On one side, shouldn't a charity be willing to pay for the professional competence to run the organization as effectively as possible? But on the other side, how do revelations of high compensation affect the public image and fund-raising ability of such not-for-profit organizations?

INVITATION TO DISCUSSION

What is your position regarding Aramony's compensation and perks, relative to the many times greater compensations of for-profit executives?

In addition to the decrease in dues payments, UWA was in danger of having its not-for-profit status revoked by the Internal Revenue Service due to the relationship of loans made to the spin-off companies. For example, it loaned $2 million to a spin-off corporation of which the chief financial officer of UWA was also a director, which is a violation of not-for-profit corporate

[10]John A. Byrne, "Executive Pay: The Party Ain't Over Yet," *Business Week* (April 26, 1993), pp. 56-64.

law. UWA also guaranteed a bank loan taken out by one of the spin-offs, another violation of not-for-profit corporate law.[11]

The adverse publicity benefitted competing charities, such as Earth Share, an environmental group. United Way, at one time the only major organization to receive contributions through payroll deductions, now found itself losing donations to other charities able to garner contributions in the same manner. All the building that William Aramony had done for the United Way as the primary player in the American charitable industry was now in danger of disintegration because of his uncontrolled excesses.

On February 28, amid mounting pressure from local chapters threatening to withhold their annual dues, Aramony resigned. In August 1992 the United Way board of directors hired Elaine Chao, the Peace Corps director, to replace Aramony.

Elaine Chao

Chao's story is one of great achievement for one aged only 39. She is the oldest of six daughters in a family that came to California from Taiwan when Elaine was 8 years old. She did not know a word of English. The family prospered through hard work. "Despite the difficulties . . . we had tremendous optimism in the basic goodness of this country, that people are decent here, that we would be given a fair opportunity to demonstrate our abilities," she told an interviewer.[12] Chao's parents instilled in their six daughters the conviction that they could do anything they set their minds to, and all the daughters went to prestigious universities.

Elaine Chao earned an economics degree from Mount Holyoke College in 1975, then went on for a Harvard MBA. She was a White House fellow, an international banker, chair of the Federal Maritime Commission, deputy secretary of the U.S. Transportation Department, and director of the Peace Corps before accepting the presidency of the United Way of America.

Her salary is $195,000, less than one-half of Aramony's. She has cut budgets and staffs: no transatlantic flights on the Concorde, no limousine service, no plush condominiums. The board of governors has been expanded to include more local representatives and has established committees on ethics and finance. Still, Chao has no illusions about her job: "Trust and confidence once damaged will take a great deal of effort and time to heal."[13]

---

[11]Shepard, "Perks, Privileges, and Power"; Charles E. Shepard, "United Way Chief Says He Will Retire," *The Washington Post* (February 28, 1992), p. A1.

[12]"United Way Chief Dedicated," *Cleveland Plain Dealer* (March 28, 1993), p. 240A.f.

[13]Ibid.

Local United Way's Concerns

In April 1993, for the second time in a year, United Way of Greater Lorain County (Ohio) withdrew from the United Way of America. The board of the local chapter was still concerned about the financial stability and accountability of the national agency. In particular, it was concerned about Aramony's retirement settlement. The national board and Aramony were negotiating a significant "golden parachute" retirement package in the neighborhood of $4 million.

News of this triggered the Lorain County board's decision to again withdraw from UWA. There were other reasons as well for this decision. The national agency was falling far short of its projected budget because only 890 of the 1400 affiliates that had paid membership dues two years before were still paying. Roy Church, president of the Lorain agency, explained the board's decision: "Since February . . . it has become clear that United Way of America's financial stability and ability to assist locals has been put in question. The benefit of being a United Way of America member isn't there at this time for Lorain's United Way."[14]

Elaine Chao's task of resurrecting United Way of America would not be easy.

See the following information box for a discussion of a related example of nonprofit callousness to its parties.

ANALYSIS

Executives' lack of accountability of expenditures was a major contributor to the UWA's problems. This lack of controls encouraged questionable practices, since there was no one to approve or disapprove, and it made executives, especially Aramony, vulnerable to great shock and criticism when their practices became known. The fact that voluntary donations were the principal source of revenues made the lack of accountability all the more scandalous. The situation was not greatly different for the Girl Scouts. For a for-profit organization, looseness of controls affects primarily stockholders; for a major charitable organization, it affects millions of contributors, who see their money being squandered with no controls and no compunction.

Where controls and financial reporting are deficient, and where a system of checks and balances is lacking, two consequences tend to prevail, neither one desirable or totally acceptable. The worst case scenario is outright "white-collar theft," when unscrupulous people find it an opportunity for personal gain. The absence of sufficient controls and accountability can make even normally honest persons succumb to some temptation.

[14]Karen Henderson, "Lorain Agency Cuts Ties with National United Way," *Cleveland Plain Dealer* (April 16, 1993), p. 7C.

INFORMATION BOX

ANOTHER CONTROVERSY: GIRL SCOUTS AND THEIR COOKIES

The main funding source for the nation's 2.6 million Girl Scouts is the annual cookie sale, estimated to generate $400 million in revenue.[15] The practice goes back some 70 years, although in the 1920s the girls sold homemade cookies. Now each regional council negotiates with one of two bakeries that produce the cookies, sets the price per box, which ranges from $2 to $3, and divides the proceeds as it sees fit. Typically, the Girl Scout troops get 10 to 15 percent, the council takes more than 50 percent, and the rest goes to the manufacturer.

Criticisms have emerged and received public attention regarding the dictatorial handling of these funds by the councils. There are 332 regional councils in the United States, each having an office and a paid staff overseen by a volunteer board. Some councils have dozens of employees, with most serving mainly as policy enforcers and supervisors. At the troop level, volunteer leaders, often women with daughters in the troop, guide their units in the true tradition of scouting, giving their time tirelessly. For the cookie drives, the girls are an unpaid sales force—child labor, as critics assail—that supports a huge bureaucratic structure. Little of the cookie revenue comes back to the local troops.

The bureaucracy does not tolerate dissent well. *The Wall Street Journal* cites the case of a West Haven, Connecticut, troop leader, Beth Denton, who protested both the way the Connecticut Trails council apportioned revenue and the $1.6 million in salaries and benefits paid to 42 council employees. After she complained to the state attorney general, the council dismissed her as leader.[16]

Admittedly, the individual salaries in the bureaucracy were not high by corporate standards or even by not-for-profit standards. Council administrators' salaries ranged up to about $90,000. Perhaps more disturbing was that volunteer leaders saw no annual financial statements of their council's expenditures and activities.[17]

INVITATION TO DISCUSSION
Evaluate the council's position that annual financial records of their council's activities should be entirely confidential to full-time staff.

Second, insufficient controls tend to promote a mindset of arrogance and allow people to play fast-and-loose with the system. Aramony seemed to fall into this category with his spending extravagances, cronyism, and other conflict-of-interest activities. (Some of the Girl Scout Councils, too,

---

[15]Ellen Graham, "Sprawling Bureaucracy Eats up Most Profits of Girl Scout Cookies," *The Wall Street Journal* (May 13, 1992), p. A1.

[16]Ibid., p. A4.

[17]Ibid.

perceived themselves as aloof from the dedicated volunteer troop leaders, tolerating no criticism or questioning, dictating and enforcing all policies without consultation or participation, and preventing scrutiny of their own operation.)

The UWA theoretically had an overseer: the boards, similar to the board of directors of business corporations. But when such boards act as rubber stamps, where they are closely in the camp of the chief execu-

---

ISSUE BOX

WHAT SHOULD BE THE ROLE OF THE BOARD OF DIRECTORS?

In the past, most boards of directors have tended to be closely allied with top executives and even composed mostly of corporate officials. In some organizations today this is changing, mostly in response to critics concerned about board tendencies to support the status quo and perpetuate the "establishment."

More and more, opinion is shifting to the idea that boards must assume an active role:

> The board can no longer play a passive role in corporate governance. Today, more than ever, the board must assume an activist role—a role that is protective of shareholder rights, sensitive to communities in which the company operates, responsive to the needs of company vendors and customers, and fair to its employees.[18]

Incentives for more active boards have been the increasing risks of liability for board decisions as well as liability insurance costs. Although the board of directors has long been seen as responsible for establishing corporate objectives, developing broad policies, and selecting top executives, these duties are no longer viewed as sufficient. Boards must also review management's performance—acting as a control mechanism—to ensure that the company is well run and that stockholders' interests are furthered. And, today, they must ensure that society's best interests are not disregarded.

But the issue remains: To whom should the board owe its greatest allegiance—the entrenched bureaucracy or the external publics? Without having board members representative of the many special interests affected by the organization, the inclination is to support the interests of the establishment.

INVITATION TO DISCUSSION

Do you think a more representative and activist board will prevent a similar scenario from damaging United Way in the future? Why or why not?

---

[18]Lester B. Korn and Richard M. Ferry, *Board of Directors Thirteenth Annual Study* (New York: Korn/Ferry International, February 1986), pp. 1–2.

tives, they are not really exercising control. This appeared to be the case with United Way of America during the "reign" of Aramony; similarly, as discussed in a preceding box, with the regional councils of the Girl Scouts, many of the volunteer boards appear to have exercised little or no control.

Certainly a board's failure to fulfill its responsibility is not unique to not-for-profits. Corporate boards have often been notorious for promoting the interests of the incumbent executives. Although this is changing today, it still prevails. See the preceding issue box for a discussion of the role of boards of directors.

WHAT CAN BE LEARNED?

Beware the arrogant mindset. A leader's attitude that he or she is superior to subordinates and even to concerned outsiders is a formula for disaster, both for an organization and even for a society. Such an attitude promotes dictatorship, intolerance of contrary opinions, and an attitude that "we need answer to no one." We have seen the consequences with William Aramony: moving over the edge of what is deemed by most as acceptable and ethical conduct, assuming the role of the final authority who brooks no questions or criticisms. The absence of real or imagined controls or reviews seems to bring out the worst in people. We seem to need periodic scrutiny to avoid falling into the trap of arrogant decision making devoid of responsiveness to other concerns. The Girl Scout bureaucracy's dealings with its volunteers corroborates the inclination toward arrogance and dictatorship in the absence of sufficient real controls.

Checks and balances—controls—are even more important in not-for-profit and governmental bodies than in corporate entities. For-profit organizations have "bottom-line" performance (i.e., profit and loss performance) as the ultimate control and standard. Not-for-profit and governmental organizations do not have this control, so they have no ultimate measure of their effectiveness.

Consequently, not-for-profit organizations should be subject to the utmost scrutiny of objective outsiders. Otherwise, abuses seem to be encouraged and perpetuated. Often these not-for-profit organizations are sheltered from competition, which usually also demands greater efficiency. Thus, without objective and energetic controls, not-for-profit organizations have a tendency to get out of hand, to be run as little dynasties unencumbered by the constraints that face most businesses. Fortunately, investigative reporting and increasing litigation by allegedly abused parties today act as the needed controls for such organizations. In view of the revelations of investigative reporters, we are left to wonder how many other abusive and reprehensible activities have not as yet been detected.

Nonprofits are particularly vulnerable to bad press. Nonprofits depend on donations for the bulk of their revenues. Unlike most businesses, they depend on people to give without receiving anything tangible in return. Consequently, any hint or semblance of waste or misdealings with donated money can quickly dry up contributions or cause them to be shunted to other charities.

With governmental bodies, of course, their perpetuation is hardly at stake with bad publicity, but the administrators can be recalled, impeached, or not reelected with enough adverse publicity.

INVITATION

Can you add to these learning insights?

QUESTIONS

1. How do you feel, as a potential or actual giver to United Way campaigns, about the "high living" of Aramony? Will these allegations affect your gift giving? Why or why not?

2. What prescriptions do you have for thwarting arrogance in not-for-profit and/or governmental organizations? Be as specific as you can, and support your recommendations.

3. How do you personally feel about the coercion that some organizations exert for their employees to contribute substantially to the United Way?

4. Given the information supplied in the box about the dictatorial relationships between Girl Scout councils and the local volunteers, and recognizing that such anecdotal information may not be truly representative, what do you see as the pros and cons of Girl Scout cookie drives? On balance, is this fund-raising effort still desirable, or might other alternatives be better?

5. Even in the absence of government regulation, should a charity be more forthcoming with its financials in the same manner as a publicly-held company? Is a charity in essence a publicly-held company, if we consider its stakeholders?

6. Should persons electing to work for non-profits demand salaries commensurate with those in the for-profit sector? Or does working for non-profits carry rewards other than salary? What are they? How much are they worth?

7. Should charitable organizations have paid, full-time staffs, or should they be run and staffed by volunteers and by people paid modest stipends?

INVITATION TO ROLE PLAY

1. You are an adviser to Elaine Chao, who has taken over the scandal-ridden United Way. What advice do you give her for quickly restoring the confidence of the American public in the integrity and worthiness of this preeminent national charity organization?

2. You are a member of the board of governors of United Way. Allegations have surfaced about the lavish lifestyle of the highly regarded Aramony. Most of the board members, being corporate executives, see nothing at all wrong with his perks and privileges. You, however, feel otherwise. How will you convince the other members of the board of the error of condoning Aramony's activities? Be as persuasive as you can in supporting your position.

3. You are the parent of a Girl Scout who has worked assiduously to sell hundreds of boxes of cookies. You now realize that the efforts of your daughter and thousands of other girls is primarily supporting a bloated central and regional bureaucracy, and not the local troops. You feel strongly that this situation is an unacceptable use of child labor. Describe your proposed efforts to institute change.

INVITATION TO RESEARCH

What is United Way's situation today? Are local agencies contributing to the national? Have donations matched or exceeded previous levels? Has Elaine Chao restored confidence? Did William Aramony receive his multi-million-dollar severance package?

20

The Yugo:
A Socialist Fiasco in a
Competitive Environment

The Yugo was introduced in the U.S. market with what seemed a significant differential advantage: It was the lowest priced car available in
America. The Yugo, as the name implies, was a product of Yugoslavia,
then an Eastern European Socialist republic. Its failure in the United States
typifies the problems that socialist firms have competing in Western capitalist markets. The particular orientation of socialist firms and their work
forces—which emphasizes protected jobs and uniformity of status—makes
it difficult to compete in the harsher climate of private enterprises and a
market economy.

Although the flaws of socialism are apparent in this case and can be
given major blame for Yugo's troubles, we find learning insights of broader
applicability.

THE DECISION

In early 1985 Malcolm Bricklin, 46, had raised $10 million and formed a
company called Yugo America. He planned to import the Zastava Yugo 55,
a small, boxy, front-wheel-drive car from Yugoslavia and to put it on sale in
the northeastern United States by summer for a startling $3990. At the time
the average sticker price was $11,500, and Yugo would cost about $1000 less
than the next cheapest car on the market, the Suzuki Sprint, which Chevrolet was selling in some western states. The low-end market had recently

been neglected by the Japanese because of import quotas that had encouraged them to export higher priced cars to the United States.

Bricklin was an entrepreneur, and Yugo America was a subsidiary of his Bricklin Industries. To date he had no history of success in the auto industry. On the contrary, Bricklin had tried unsuccessfully to sell the Subaru 360, another minicar, back in 1969. He had later started a factory in Nova Scotia to build a sports car that bore his name, but that venture also failed. Two strikes already. But there would be a third strike to come: More recently he had taken over the import and sale of the foundering Fiat X1/9 and Spider sports cars. He even changed the Fiat nameplate to the more glamorous Bertone and Pininfarina nameplates, and still the cars did not sell.

Undaunted by his past failures, Bricklin thought he at last had a real gem of an opportunity with his Yugo. He envisioned the Yugo, if promoted right, to have a potential 1 million customers in the United States. But he was fearful of emphasizing "cheap": "People don't want anything cheap," he said. "It has to be perceived as a smart buy, like getting something real good on sale."[1]

With what seemed like shrewd wisdom, he turned to Leonard Sirowitz, a New York ad man who had created many memorable Volkswagen Beetle ads in the 1960s. Sirowitz saw an "uncanny" parallel between the highly successful Beetle and the Yugo. The Beetle was homely; it was the cheapest car on the road at the time; and it was marketed not to the blue-collar worker but to the 1960s equivalent of the yuppie. At that time Sirowitz's ads had turned the public's fascination from chrome and tail fins and gas guzzlers to the character and frugality of the VW Beetle. He accepted the Yugo advertising challenge.

Sirowitz had something else going for him. In the 1960s he had been instrumental in overcoming the American public's suspicions of unfamiliar foreign products. In that decade, "made in Japan" raised serious questions about quality. His ads had helped Sony sell its portable TVs and had played a major role in changing the perception of Japanese products of all kinds from low quality to high quality.

In 1985 it appeared that the image of the Yugo would need similar doctoring. Because it was a then communist country, Yugoslavia's image was more akin to breadlines and shoddy consumer goods than to quality. Yet Bricklin and Sirowitz reasoned that the Yugo should be a dependable product for U.S. streets and highways. For five years it had been produced by Yugoslavia's leading car manufacturer, Zavodi Crvena Zastava, mostly for domestic consumption, where it appeared sturdy enough to survive notori-

---

[1]Jaclyn Fierman, "Can a Beetle Brain Stir a Yearning for Yugos?" *Fortune* (May 13, 1985), p. 73.

ously rough Yugoslavian roads. Already, Bricklin's Yugo America had spent $1.5 million to get the car ready for U.S. emissions and safety tests and had sent a nine-foot telex to the factory requesting detailed cosmetic changes.

The factory knew of the stakes in this U.S. introduction. The country was in desperate need of dollars to meet its foreign debt payments as well as import needs. The trade deficit in 1985 had been significantly increased by Yugoslavia's large purchases of airliners from Boeing and McDonnell Douglas. Debts to Western banks now totaled $24 billion, and the Yugo could provide the key to reducing that debt. The factory stood to make up to $2800 for each car sold. (Yugo America expected to earn $200 to $300 per car.)

Because of the importance of this venture, the Zastava factory developed two assembly lines: one for cars slated for domestic consumption, and the other for cars slated for exportation. The best and most experienced workers were assigned to this second production line. The factory was thus able to assure Bricklin that only cars of superb quality would find their way to the U.S. market.

Crvena Zastava had been making automobiles for about 30 years, mostly under license from larger auto firms in other countries. The Yugo was essentially a Fiat front-wheel-drive design dating back to the early 1970s. In 1984 the company turned out only 171,000 cars and exported 47,000 of these to Europe, Africa, and the Middle East. That year the U.S. market promised a rich opportunity. But the 130-year-old Serbian conglomerate, which also made weapons, looked even beyond the U.S. market: It planned to quadruple its exports by 1989 to worldwide markets.

Of the million potential customers that Bricklin saw for the Yugo, he envisioned that some would normally purchase used cars but would now be induced to buy a new car costing less than many used cars do. He saw another large potential group of purchasers to be suburbanites who needed a second or even a third car for basic transportation around town. He thought other purchasers would include those who had been shocked out of the new car market by the average $11,500 sticker price. Altogether, Bricklin expected that sales would reach at least 100,000 units a year near term, then 250,000 after several years—not as great as the heady days of the Beetle, one of the best-selling cars in history, but still a satisfactory showing for both Yugo America and Yugoslavia.

ACTION

By November 1985 overwhelming demand for the cars convinced Bricklin to cancel a planned $10 million ad campaign. His dealers had already received more than 8000 orders since August. Shipments were running far behind demand, as only 1558 had been shipped. At the current rate, the company would receive 100,000 orders by August 1986, although it planned to import only 40,000 cars this first year. The company could earn $16 million its first year, and Bricklin was now planning a public stock offering. His sales projections reached 70,000 cars for model year 1987 and 250,000 for model year 1988. He planned to continue selling the Yugos each year for under $4000, including such extras as power brakes. Cheap labor kept the prices low: Yugoslav workers earned only $1 an hour.

Despite the early success, Bricklin believed that Yugo needed a full range of cars to be competitive. Consequently, he planned to expand the product line from 1986 to 1991 to include larger autos. The basic Yugo GV was a four-passenger two-door hatchback with a 1.1 liter, four-cylinder engine. By June 1986 he planned to introduce a GVS model, which added sports trim to the GV model. By June 1987 the GVX was to be introduced, which would have a larger engine for better performance. In June 1988 a convertible was to be introduced for the youth market. Also planned for 1988 was the Yugo 103, a larger four-door hatchback. By 1989 the Yugo 104 was planned, this being an upscale notchback sedan the size of the Honda Accord. And shortly after this, the TCX was planned to be introduced—a two-seat, four-wheel-drive sports car to sell for under $10,000. With such a broad product line, Bricklin felt assured of Yugo's success.

Except for slower-than-expected deliveries from Yugoslavia, which the factory assured him would be corrected, no problems loomed. Bricklin and his Yugo had apparently found a strategic window, one that had been abandoned by the Japanese, and he was prepared to make the most of it. As a final coup, in a December issue, *Fortune* magazine's fifth annual roster of products of the year listed the low-priced Yugo as one of the top seven.[2]

STORM CLOUDS

By early 1986, competition was beginning to emerge in the low-priced car sector. These cars were termed *minis*—cars selling for under $6000 fully equipped and with engines smaller than 1.2 liters. One industry group, J. D. Power and Associates, predicted that sales of cars priced below $6500 would account for about 12 percent of the total U.S. market by 1991. The three principal competitors for 1986 appeared to be Chevrolet's Sprint (expected to sell 60,000 at $5380); South Korea's Hyundai, which was already selling Canada's most popular import, the $4800 Pony; and Yugo. But the $3990 price of the Yugo still seemed the dominant force in this minicar market.

However, two widely publicized reports appearing in February and March of 1986 brought serious image problems to Yugo, and even jeopar-

---

[2]"Products of the Year," *Fortune* (December 9, 1985), pp. 106–112.

dized its viability in the competitive U.S. market. That the sentiment regarding the Yugo could change from highly positive to seriously negative shows the risks in competing in a capitalistic market and the need for reliable products.

The February 1986 *Consumer Reports (CR)* gave a scathing criticism of the Yugo. First of all, *CR* noted that it was virtually impossible to buy a Yugo for $3990. Dealer preparation charges, destination charges, and other essential add-ons would most likely bring the price to about $4650. The following is quoted directly from *CR*:

> Is low price sufficient justification for buying the Yugo? We don't think so. Overall, the Yugo scored below every other small car we've tested in recent years. It's heavy for its size, and though its tiny engine revs willingly enough, it delivers weak performance and unimpressive fuel economy. Handling was competent and braking was very effective, but comfort, ride, shifting, heating, and the design of the controls were below par.
>
> Our Yugo was a sorry sample indeed. We note 21 defects attributable to sloppy assembly or incomplete dealer preparation. Oil dripped from the engine and coated the underbody as we drove. When it contacted the hot exhaust system, the car filled with acrid smoke. Despite several attempted repairs by the dealer, with "factory" assistance, the oil continued to leak, and the car continued to smoke and smell. The clutch chattered. The brakes squealed, and every so often they dragged so badly that we could barely coax the car to 45 mph on level pavement. The speedometer clicked. The hood became loose. The reception of the official Yugo radio was so poor that we played tapes most of the time. The rear-window washer quit. The ignition switch had to be replaced. And two bolts holding the transmission were loose.[3]

The report further described this as a dated car, painfully reminiscent of Fiats of a decade earlier. Serious questions were raised as to the safety of such a small car. After additional denunciations, the *CR* article concluded: "If $4400 is the most you can spend on a car, we think you'd get better value from a good used car than a new Yugo."[4]

The issue box on p. 308 presents the issue of responsibility for quality.

As if this critical commentary by *Consumer Reports* was not enough, a month later the results of federal crash tests hit the news media. The National Highway Traffic Safety Administration, in releasing the results of the tests for 1986, said that the two-door hatchback Yugo had run up the worst scores of all the cars tested.[5]

---

[3]"How Much Car for $3,990?" *Consumer Reports* (February 1986), pp. 84–86.
[4]Ibid.
[5]Reported, among other media, in "Yugo Results Poor in Crash Tests," *The Washington Post* (March 13, 1986), p. E1.

ISSUE BOX

RESPONSIBILITY FOR QUALITY

Because products have become more complex and the assembly line has divorced workers from the pride of making something from start to finish, problems with defects and poor quality have become widespread. No other industry has received the critical attention to quality problems that the auto industry has. As we know, U.S. carmakers have confronted an invasion of quality imports, especially from Japan. As they doggedly tried to rise above their image of poor quality, some companies looked for someone to blame for the persistence of poor-quality products.

Management blamed workers for their indifference, and the phrase, "Beware the Monday car" became widely accepted. But some workers pointed the finger at management:

> I don't believe it is inherent in human nature to do a lousy job. . . . We on the line take our cue from those in the home office. If they don't really care about quality, they can't expect us to either.[6]

Workers blamed overemphasis on production and poor management for all such problems.

In Yugoslavia similar blaming predominated, but on a larger scare. The socialist work ethic, for both managers and laborers, promoted disavowing any customer orientation and disregarding worker efficiency and productivity. Decades of this work ethic made competition with capitalist firms difficult.

INVITATION TO DISCUSSION

U.S. managers and union officials have long given lip service to the need for better quality, but talk does not seem enough. What suggestions do you have for instilling a real commitment to quality in an organization? Be as specific as you can.

CONSEQUENCES

In June 1986 Bricklin postponed indefinitely a first public offering of common stock. Sales, which had been rather modestly estimated at 40,000 for the year, did reach 35,900, but this was by no means a robust picture. Hyundai's Excel, a South Korean import, was the big winner in minicars that year, racking up 168,882 sales. This was a record for a first-year imported car. The previous record dated back to 1958, when the French Renault Dauphine sold 48,148.

---

[6]Martin Douglas, "Auto Workers Can Only Do as Well as Head Office Permits." In *Management for Productivity*, ed. John R. Schermerhorn, Jr. (New York: Wiley, 1984), p. 441.

For 1987, Yugo increased the advertising budget to $20 million, up from $13 million in 1986, and introduced several new models. While Yugo sales rose modestly in 1987 to 48,812, this was still far below the projections of 70,000.

Bricklin Industries obtained the sole U.S. distributorship for another small foreign car in early 1987, this time the Proton Saga from Malaysia. Bricklin estimated he could sell 100,000 Sagas during the initial year in the United States and 250,000 a year within five years. He planned to spend $10 million to modify the car for the American market. It would sell for $5000 to $8000, with the U.S. debut planned for early 1988. This car would complement the Yugo line and provide dealers with a more extensive offering, as well as an alternative to the faltering Yugo.

In an attempt to improve Yugo's severely eroded quality image and to increase sales, the company offered a 12,000 mile or 1-year warranty package as part of the 1988 strategy. The warranty covered all parts and labor costs for wear items and adjustment items. A 4-year or 40,000-mile warranty covered labor and parts for the engine and transmission. More models were to be introduced, including a convertible and a sporty model. Yugo boosted its advertising and promotional budget to $48 million for 1988, and a new TV ad campaign emphasized toughness and reliability. The theme line was, "The toughest, most dependable cars a little money can buy."

Despite these efforts, 1988 was not a good year. Projections back in 1985 had been for 250,000 sales by 1988. And actually sales started out fairly strong, but by the latter part of the year, monthly sales were running at less than one-half the previous year's pace and were to reach a total of only 32,000. Table 20.1 shows the projections and actual sales for the Yugo during these years.

In mid-1988 Bricklin sold out his interest in the parent firm, Global Motors, to an investment banking firm. He had invested heavily in trying to adapt the Proton Saga to the U.S. market, which forced him to delay the introductions of badly needed additional Yugo models.

On January 30, 1989, Yugo America filed for bankruptcy along with its parent, Global Motors, listing assets of $30.5 million and liabilities of $49.9

Table 20.1   Expectations and Actual Sales of the Yugo

	Expected Sales	Actual Sales
	(units)	
1986	40,000	35,959
1987	70,000	48,812
1988	250,000	32,000
1989	250,000	10,500

million. The filing was a response to threats by an Ohio liquidator to dump several thousand Yugos on the market below wholesale cost. The Ohio firm had taken the cars as part of a complicated financial arrangement Global had undertaken to raise enough cash to continue operations.

The financial difficulties were triggered by the sudden sales collapse in 1988. While lack of new and more attractive models was certainly a factor in this sales decline, an increasing number of lenders were showing reluctance to finance the risky first-time buyers attracted to the car.

Zastava Bails out Its American Distributor

Most of the original Yugo management team was now gone. Recognizing the need to try to continue to penetrate the U.S. market, Zastava, the Yugoslavian producer, now invested capital to keep Yugo America afloat while it readied a new GVC convertible and all-new subcompact hatchback models that it hoped would be more attractive to the American consumer. It announced that it would honor all car warranties. Yugo America at the time of the bankruptcy filing owed its dealers $2.5 million in rebates and reimbursements for warranty repairs going back three months. Zastava tried to help the 260 remaining dealers sell 16,000 unsold 1988 Yugo cars. It planned to build more 1989 cars if demand exceeded the supply. The manufacturer intended to concentrate on 1990 models, which were to include a convertible, automatic transmission for some models, and the Yugo 103, a four-door model with a larger fuel-injected engine than the Yugo GV.

Yugo America emerged from Chapter 11 bankruptcy in December 1989, thanks to the intervention of Zastava. It was now a wholly owned subsidiary of the Yugoslavian manufacturer. Sales for 1989 had been virtually nonexistent, with only 10,500 cars sold. The subsidiary was still $125 million in debt, and under the terms of its reorganization plan, creditors were told that partial payments on the debt would be resumed only if U.S. sales rose to 20,000 a year. Two new models were planned for early introduction, both having larger and more sophisticated engines. Plans were to launch a $10 million advertising campaign to help revive sales, with major emphasis on its low prices.

A major problem was to woo back dealers who had dropped the Yugo cars after the company filed for bankruptcy-law protection in January 1989. The number of dealers at the beginning of 1990 was 185, down from 350 two years before. "We probably need 270 dealers in the United States for the brand to be viable," said John A. Spiech, Yugo's new president and chief executive officer.[7] A one-quarter page ad aimed at recruiting dealers

---

[7]Jacqueline Mitchell, "Yugo America Sets $10 Million for Ads to Revive Car Line," *The Wall Street Journal* (January 8, 1990), p. B3.

appeared on January 23, 1990, in *The Wall Street Journal*. The message of the advertisement: "Yugo Is Here to Stay. . . . Permanently."

In April 1993 Yugo America ceased operations and filed a Chapter 7 bankruptcy liquidation petition, ending seven years in the United States. The company blamed the civil war in the former Yugoslavia for preventing its parent, Zavodi Crvena Zastava, from providing sufficient financial backing and a regular supply of cars and parts to the U.S. market. But sales had hardly been robust: Only 2941 Yugos were sold in 1992.[8]

ANALYSIS

We have examined other cases—notably the Edsel and Gilbert—in which poor quality proved an albatross, something not to be overcome. How does the Yugo differ from the earlier cases? It shows graphically the deficiencies of firms in socialist economies and their particular vulnerabilities in competing in Western markets. The contrasts of Eastern and Western management styles and work ethics are stark and worth describing. We can learn from the institutionalized limitations of Eastern European firms.

The Socialist Business Environment

The bureaucratic central planning that characterized socialist communist countries—though it minimized unemployment, maintained relative income equality, and provided housing and health care and even higher education for the most promising—did not present the spur for efficiency that capitalism does. Workers and managers alike had little incentive and experience in initiative and innovative thinking.

The result limited consumer choice. Since there was little competition, products were functional and not stylish; there was nothing to motivate improving them or innovating; and the products were often poor quality, defective, and otherwise third-rate by Western standards. Factories and stores were bogged down with more workers than needed, with workers unconcerned about doing a good job or grooming themselves for advancement. With income equality endemic in the goals of socialism, the compensation of the top executive of a firm might be no more than three or four times that of the lowliest worker. Consequently, incentives for managers were meager compared to those in capitalist firms. Management skills have lagged in such an environment and have been further thwarted by the dependence on bureaucratic central planning.

---

[8]Gregory A. Patterson, "Importer of Yugos to the U.S. Files for Liquidation," *The Wall Street Journal* (April 21, 1993), p. C16.

Not even the best workers were permitted pay increases or incentive bonuses. In such an atmosphere of egalitarianism, why should any person work harder than his or her peers, who could hardly be fired no matter how poorly they worked? For decades socialist workers have known no other work ethic than simply spending their time on the job in the easiest way possible. An adage jokingly repeated throughout Eastern Europe asserted "They pretend to pay us and we pretend to work." While the self-interested pursuit of profits provides powerful incentives for individual efforts and drives resources toward their higher paying use in capitalist societies, this condition did not exist under socialism a few years ago.

If you had visited a factory in an Eastern European country (and while changes are forthcoming as these countries grapple with discarding the communist mantle, it may take years for widespread changes to take place in the work ethic and managerial competence), you would have found far too many workers, many of them in thinly disguised idleness. A typical retail store would have more employees than customers. And in the ingenuity of requiring the most employees possible, a simple sales transaction might involve three or four different stations and their separate workers.

Is it any wonder that such firms had difficulty competing against Western firms? Is it so surprising that Yugo cars, despite the two separate assembly lines, were merely representative of the built-in inefficiencies of socialist economies?

Given the inability of most socialist products to compete in Western markets with attractive product features, technological superiority, or quality, the only option was competition on the basis of lowest price. Actually, competing in world markets as the lowest-price producer was not even possible for most such firms because of the inefficiencies due to the socialist policies of full employment, no layoffs, and no incentives. Even with low-priced labor, socialist factories were not low-cost producers. But in order to get badly needed Western currencies, a socialist government, such as the former Yugoslavia's, could subsidize export production and assist in the costs so that these products could indeed be offered at the lowest prices in export markets.

Yugo was the lowest-price new car available in the United States. Was this a strong competitive advantage? Unfortunately, it promised no lasting advantage. A low price, if effective in winning customers, can be easily matched or countered by competitors. In Yugo's case, while it stubbornly maintained the lowest price, it had a growing number of competitors—both foreign and domestic—who entered the scene with technologically superior cars of better quality priced only modestly more than the Yugo.

Low price, then, is highly vulnerable as a competitive advantage. An advantage based on other considerations—such as dependability, quality, technological advances, styling, even the glamour of a respected foreign brand—is not so easily countered by competitors.

Were Domestic Deficiencies Also Evident?

So far we have blamed the producer for the problems besetting the Yugo. But should Bricklin and Yugo America be exonerated from all blame? We think not. Their expectations were far too rosy for an unknown car from an unproven manufacturer in a socialist country. A longer trial period with more careful attention to the warranty and servicing work by fewer well-chosen dealers might have saved the Yugo from its devastating quality image. It never overcame this poor image. Undoubtedly, Bricklin was surprised at the poor quality of the cars and their technological obsolescence. But he should have given defect prevention top priority. In his haste to expand, he assumed away such possible problems and laid the ground-work for the future difficulties of the Yugo.

Quality Control

Given that the Zastava factory was soon aware of the quality problems—which Yugo America should have been protesting—could not improved quality control standards have corrected the situation before it got out of hand and permanently damaged the image of the car? We discuss the concept of Total Quality Management in the information box on p. 314. We need to recognize that for a complex product such as a car, quality control can be costly if it is done so thoroughly that few defects are passed on. In the absence of more careful and motivated workers, however, quality control standards should have been exhaustive.

The U.S. dealers should also have assumed more responsibility for quality control. After all, the final preparation and servicing was done by dealers before delivery to customers; a more systematic and thorough examination of each car before delivery should have uncovered many of the worst and most immediate defects. Each dealer should have had a knowledgeable service department, both for the preparation stage and for later, when customers brought back the cars to be serviced and to have any newly discovered problems fixed.

Worker Motivation

Finally we come to worker motivation. Could not the factory, despite its socialist setting, have developed better employee motivation? The separate assembly line should have been a source of worker pride for those so selected. Apparently this was of no consequence, nor was any other type of motivation evident. But even in socialist countries, where pay scales are rigid with no incentive for superior performance, other methods of motivation are possible, such as recognition, token honors and awards, and more prestigious assignments.

INFORMATION BOX

TOTAL QUALITY MANAGEMENT (TQM)

The purpose of quality control is to minimize or eliminate defects before the customer is exposed to them. In addition to safeguarding a quality image, effective quality control can reduce waste and rejects. The phrase Total Quality Management (sometimes also referred to as Total Quality Control) today is generally used to describe the commitment to quality principles in all aspects of the operation and to meeting customer needs by doing things right the first time. Thus, TQM involves *quality assurance*, that is, the prevention of defects. In this quest, management is willing to examine the whole system, including technologies and people, in order to ascertain the keys to consistent quality attainment.

This broad perspective in looking at quality control has come into prominence with the success of the Japanese in bringing a new level of quality to all kinds of products. Interestingly, the Japanese advances in the achievement of consistent quality were introduced by an American consultant, W. Edwards Deming, more than four decades ago. He taught the Japanese these principles:

1. Tally defects.
2. Trace them to the source.
3. Make corrections.
4. Record what happens afterward.

Employee involvement in quality is essential to TQM's success. And this has led to quality-control circles of employees dedicated to ever-improving their own quality of work. Even more important is higher management dedication and commitment, encouragement, and tangible reward for employees' contribution to quality maintenance.

The problems of the Yugo suggest the inability of the manufacturer to wholeheartedly embrace the concept of quality control, much less TQM. This attitude was fostered by the conditioning of the domestic customers from decades of past experiences: to expect poor quality under socialism and to accept it as a way of life, with little complaint. Such conditioning thrived in an absence of aggressive domestic competition.

INVITATION TO DISCUSSION

We have just insinuated that part of the pervasive socialist phenomenon of poor quality is due to the fact that customers were conditioned to accept it as a way of life. But is it fair to partially blame customers? Discuss.

CONCLUSION: CAN A SOCIALIST FIRM COMPETE IN A CAPITALISTIC MARKETPLACE?

The Yugo typifies the serious weaknesses in the socialist/communist firm. With a few rare exceptions, it also typifies the strategy of most such firms when they try to export to Western countries: They compete as the lowest priced brand in their class. Is change likely? While Eastern Europe is frenetically trying to reshape itself to a market-oriented economy, this will require a considerable process of adjustment.

The biggest problem in such an adjustment may well be in engineering technology. In many socialist industries this lags Western firms by one to three decades. Catching up may be a long, slow process. Still, efficiency should be improved and worker motivation increased. Yet, this also will be difficult with workers steeped in the socialist work ethic. But it can be done, as the following example of Hungarian workers exposed to Western management shows:

In the Fall 1988, Levi Strauss, in a joint venture with four Hungarian firms, opened a factory for making blue jeans in a town of 40,000 in southern Hungary. This proved to be a model of what could be accomplished by Western management and socialist workers. Under the agreement, Levi Strauss had total control over production and marketing, and as a joint venture the factory was exempt from many of the restrictions that other Hungarian employers faced.

Motivational tactics included wages more than twice the average for Hungarian garment workers, and the work force achieved production levels considered remarkable by Hungarian experts, and even by Western observers. The workers, most of them young women with no previous garment experience, were approaching the world production record for the 51 plants operated by Levi Strauss worldwide. Wages were based directly on how much an employee produced. In the clamorous neon-lit sewing room, the pace appears breakneck. No one stands idle, amazing Hungarian economists and managers.

Three workers have been fired, this being so unusual that it caused a scandal that reached national news. Three-month contracts can be terminated if employees work at less than 60 percent efficiency. Some of the workers complain that they're treated like slaves, and others that no one could last more than four or five years at the pace. But high compensation spurs them on.

By contrast, a neighboring knitwear factory is beset with the problems common to much of Hungarian industry: a huge, outmoded plant producing low-quality goods; a badly paid, sluggish work force; and a top-heavy organization (of 600 employees, one-quarter work in the office). The value of production per employee is one-tenth that at the Levi Strauss factory.[9]

How long will it take to change a decades-long work ethic? Under the right circumstances, perhaps not as long as some think.

---

[9]Compiled from several sources, including Alexandra Shelley, "Hungary Sees Profit in Levi's," *International Herald Tribune* (May 15, 1989), pp. 1, 13.

WHAT CAN BE LEARNED?

While the problems of the Yugo emanate mostly from a different environment and depict the weaknesses of socialism, American managers can learn from these difficulties.

A poor-quality image is haunting. This insight is nothing new, but perhaps repetition is needed since so many firms repeat this mistake of underestimating the importance of quality, dependability, and a reputation for such quality. As noted before, a bad reputation cannot easily be overcome. It lingers powerfully, even when the problem is corrected. And this posits the fundamental maxim: A firm's reputation for quality and dependability must be safeguarded at any cost. To lose this, as Edsel and Gilbert did, and as Yugo has more recently, is a burden that cannot be escaped easily or quickly and which may be life threatening to the product and the enterprise.

A competitive advantage based on lowest price is the most vulnerable and the most easily countered. It is not difficult to lower a price. It is not difficult to introduce a stripped-down model to match a competitor's low price. It *is* difficult to counter competitive strengths such as good service, dependable quality, style, or technological features. Consequently, any brand or firm that attempts only to be competitive on the basis of lowest price has but a short-term and tenuous advantage.

Worker and management motivation can be an advantage or a major obstacle. On the one hand, an organization of highly motivated executives and workers has a distinct competitive advantage. We would expect such a firm to have better productivity, alertness to ideas for improvement, and strong continuing efforts to maintain or improve quality. On the other hand, a poorly motivated workforce cannot be relied on for consistently defect-free output, will not give maximum effort for good productivity, and will not contribute new ideas and innovativeness.

Motivation does not solely or even optimally depend on compensation; people are motivated, often more so, by other factors. Individuals are motivated by many different things, of which compensation is but one. Recognition, good working conditions, opportunity for advancement—these are only a few of the things that motivate people. Even the fairness and competence of the supervisor can be a powerful factor in motivating workers to their best efforts. (See the following box for a more detailed discussion of worker motivation.)

It is true that firms in socialist countries lack some of the motivational tools that capitalist firms enjoy, but other means of motivation are available if management recognizes the desirability of motivating the workforce to its best efforts.

INFORMATION BOX

WORKER MOTIVATION

Motivation refers to how strongly an individual wants to do his or her job well; it refers to the desire to succeed. Much research has focused on motivation, and a number of theories have developed. Its importance in the workplace is undeniable. How to achieve it consistently is the challenge.

In our society we know that motivation varies greatly among individuals. Some persons are self-starters; others are motivated by certain job-related factors such as money, working conditions, an understanding supervisor, status, and even harsh criticism. Motivation for assembly-line workers, especially when unionized, has presented particular challenges. Exceeding the group norm for speed and careful work may not be acceptable, but efforts can certainly be made to increase the group norms through worker participation, empathetic and nonadversarial management, and encouraging a team attitude toward company objectives. Certainly pride in the company, the job, and the products is worth seeking.

Motivation is a complex topic and an everlasting challenge, but certain practical management tactics help:

Pride and identification with the company can be fostered, so that company goals become individual goals.

Employees' self-esteem can be enhanced by inviting their participation in solving problems, publicly recognizing accomplishments, and explaining the importance of what they are doing.

A feeling of security can be promoted by building a work environment that reduces uncertainty, often best achieved by keeping communications channels open regarding any pending changes.

Just and empathetic supervision encourages a nonadversarial atmosphere of fairness.

Could the workers in a socialist economy be motivated to be more productive and conscientious? While management faces constraints in the use of incentive pay, promotional opportunities, and the ability to discipline and terminate under most circumstances, could not workers be motivated in other ways to do a superior job? For example, could not their sense of pride have been stimulated by the opportunity to produce for the U.S. market? If "only the best" were chosen for this assembly line, could not that have been a source of pride, of teamwork, of commitment to the firm and to the country?

INVITATION TO DISCUSSION

Analyze the desirability of cultivating an elite work group to, for example, "produce for export markets." What do you see as pros and cons? Why do you suppose this was ineffective with the Yugo?

The route to dependable quality takes great effort and constant follow-up. The temptation is to skimp on quality control because it is expensive: As discussed in an earlier box, quality control is no panacea. Both the inspections and the pulling out of defective products are costly and time consuming. Giving only a small sample of the output careful inspection hardly prevents defective products from going out, but to inspect every item may be an unreasonable alternative. And quality control still does not get at the cause of any difficulties so that these can be corrected; for this, a quality assurance program or TQM must be put in place.

The firm wanting to safeguard its quality reputation may need to use more expensive and strict quality control standards and TQM procedures. Despite the higher costs, safeguarding an image and lessening future complaints and costly handling of returned goods may mandate greater controls. The issue becomes one of short-term cost savings versus longer-term benefits in image and adjustment costs. Too many firms have erred in the direction of short-term cost considerations at the expense of long-term customer satisfaction and loyalty.

INVITATION

Can you add additional learning insights?

QUESTIONS

1. Would increasing the warranty have helped Yugo's problems? Why or why not?
2. How could Yugo America have tackled its image problem of cheap and poor quality in 1990?
3. While we are given only sketchy information about the communist factory, Zastava, what do you think might have been done to improve worker performance given the constraints of no incentive pay and very limited disciplinary powers?
4. Let us make an assumption: The communist factory, Zastava, has somehow been able by 1990 to correct its quality problems; its cars are now fully competitive with other makes in the U.S. market. Given this scenario, would you expect the Yugo to survive and prosper? Why or why not?
5. How would you attempt to instill pride in a communist workforce?
6. Discuss the desirability of a lowest-price strategy.

INVITATION TO ROLE PLAY

Place yourself in the position of Bricklin in 1985. You have the contract as sole importer of Yugo cars to the United States. What will you do to eliminate or minimize the quality-control problems of the foreign import? Be as specific as you can, and defend your reasoning.

INVITATION TO RESEARCH

Most of the bankruptcies that we encounter are Chapter 11 filings, which Yugo America filed in 1989. How is a Chapter 7 filing different? What protection, if any, do customers of such a bankrupt firm have as to warranties, parts, and repairs?

21

Days Inns—Disavowing Standards for the Sake of Growth

A DISASTER

On a June morning in 1991, two men drowned in a swimming pool outside the Days Inn in Orange, Texas. One had jumped in to save the other, who seemed paralyzed and unable to save himself. But the rescuer also became paralyzed, and the two men drowned with their arms entwined. The cause? The pool was electrified.

Guests had complained about electric shocks in the water as early as 1990, but apparently management did nothing to correct the situation except to turn off the underwater lights in the pool. In June 1991 managers turned the job of fixing the pool lights over to a new member of the maintenance crew, Ahimuto Masuda Almazon, who claimed he knew something about wiring.

After the disaster, Roger Owens, an electrical engineer, examined the pool facilities on behalf of attorneys representing the plaintiffs. He found such a tangle of corroded wires that "any backyard mechanic would have seen something was wrong."[1]

Investigators found a broad pattern of neglect in the motel. The kitchen was infested with cockroaches, air conditioners were always breaking down, plumbing was unreliable, carpeting and wallpaper needed replacing,

---

[1]Kevin Helliker, "Errant Electricity in a Days Inn Pool Killed a Guest and a Good Samaritan," *The Wall Street Journal* (May 26, 1992), p. A10.

and the roof leaked; and yet a Days Inns inspector had given the motel 421 out of 500 possible points on the company's quality-assurance review, which was a grade of "B."[2] Except for the serious electricity leakage, the problems at the Orange outlet appeared rather typical of the entire Days Inn franchised chain and its neglect of basic housekeeping and maintenance standards.[3]

BACKGROUND

The neglect had not always been standard. Days Inns was founded in 1970 by Cecil B. Day, a man of high moral principles. Day prohibited alcohol on premises, kept a chaplain on call 24 hours a day at each outlet, and maintained a security department that was one of the best in the lodging industry. To ensure high and consistent standards, the company owned at least one-half of its motels and granted franchises only sparingly, rejecting about 90% of applications.

In 1984 things changed when the company was acquired in a leveraged buyout. The new owners had one goal only: to achieve the most rapid growth possible and to do this by accepting practically anyone as a franchisee. See the following information box for a discussion of franchising.

THE BUYOUT AND THE TURNABOUT

In 1984 Cecil B. Day's estate sold Days Inns for $570 million to an investment group led by Henry Silverman, then CEO of Reliance Capital Group. As was common in the leveraged buyout days of the 1980s, little cash was used in this purchase—only $30 million. More than $500 million was raised by junk bonds (see Chapter 9, the Campeau case, for more discussion of junk-bond financing and its problems).

Silverman now embarked on a policy of rapid growth that transformed the once-cautious and tightly controlled chain. He developed a franchise-sales team and offered hefty financial incentives for signing new franchisees. Some of the team members earned commissions in the hundreds of thousands of dollars.

The number of outlets quadrupled after the 1984 buyout. The 1300th outlet opened in Ashland, Ohio, in 1992,[4] and the company expected to add

---

[2]Ibid.
[3]Ibid.
[4]"Opens 1,300th Hotel, in Ashland, Ohio," *Hotel and Motel Management* (September 7, 1992), p. 66.

INFORMATION BOX

FRANCHISING

Franchising is a contractual arrangement in which the franchisor extends to independent franchisees the right to conduct a certain kind of business according to a particular format. While the franchising arrangement may involve a product, a more common type of franchise provides a service rather than a product. The major contribution of the franchisor is a carefully developed, promoted, and controlled operation. Franchise operations depend on similar physical facilities and external signs to identify their far-flung outlets. Important to franchise operations are prescribed standards and procedures to ensure uniform offerings and service.

A firm realizes two major advantages in expanding through franchised outlets rather than company-owned units. First, expansion can be very rapid, since the franchisees put up some or most of the money. Almost the only limit to growth is the need to screen applicants, to find suitable sites for new outlets, and to develop the managerial controls necessary to ensure consistency of performance. Second, people normally operate the outlets conscientiously because franchisees are entrepreneurs with a personal stake, not hired managers. However, as we see in this case, not all Days Inns franchisees had a long-term, customer-service commitment; some were interested in "milking" the operation with minimal expenditure for maintenance and upkeep. And the franchisor was lax in enforcing adherence to specific standards of performance and maintenance—in other words, Days Inn had very loose controls.

INVITATION TO DISCUSSION
Given the short-term, profit-maximizing objective of some of Days Inns franchisees, how could the franchisor have enforced stricter controls and standards? What is the downside of such strict enforcement? Where should the line be drawn?

---

130 additional properties over the next five years.[5] Only about one-third of the growth now came from new motels; the rest came from conversions, existing properties that became Days Inns. Some of these older buildings were 30 years old and had been independent motels or members of other chains that had needed heavy renovation if they were to continue to belong to their old franchises. Silverman's salespeople targeted older Holiday Inns, in particular, and some 75 shifted to Days Inns. For example, the Days Inn in Flagstaff, Arizona, was a former Holiday Inn. At 25 years of age it faced

---

[5]"Expects to Add 130 Properties over Next 5 Years," *Business Travel News* (April 6, 1992), p. 16.

expulsion unless it did a million-dollar overhaul, so it joined Days Inns for a modest expenditure.

In addition to lowering upkeep and renovation standards, the Days Inns franchisor reduced its commitment to safety. Before the 1984 buyout, a vice president of security headed a department with dozens of employees and a budget of more than $1 million. New franchisees received two days of safety training, and managers and owners were briefed on the need for periodic lock changes and employee background checks.[6]

Silverman reduced the security department to an office of one person. Although the company kept no records on crime statistics, anecdotal evidence suggests that crime at the inns greatly increased. In 1988, for example, a nine-year-old girl was sexually molested in a hallway. The building had neither security guards nor locked side entrances to make it safer. Three weeks later an eight-year-old girl was kidnapped from the same motel and raped. In another Days Inn, in Orlando near Disney World, 10 thefts were reported in 1984 while it was a company-owned outlet; in 1988, after it became a franchise, 80 thefts were reported, and it became the most theft-ridden motel in the city, according to police.[7]

Under Silverman the 120 company-owned outlets were sold to franchisees, so that Days Inns no longer owned a single motel. Now it merely sold its signs, sold its reservation and marketing services, and collected as royalty fees 6 to 10 percent of the revenues of every inn.

The change in management and the liberalization of standards and controls brought great inconsistencies to the chain. Some motels were well-run and even equivalent to those of higher-priced chains. But others were not, as the Orange, Texas, unit proved. Customer satisfaction with the Days Inns chain plummeted. A survey of 1600 travelers in 1991 rated Days Inns next to last among 17 midpriced chains in physical appearance and room quality. Another survey of 100,000 travelers ranked Days Inns last among 11 chains in guest satisfaction.[8] Concomitant with the poor survey ratings, the occupancy rates fell from about 70 percent in 1984 to 56 percent in 1992, almost 10 percentage points lower than those of similarly priced chains such as Hampton and Red Roof.

In 1989 Silverman sold the chain to Tollman-Hundley Lodging, Inc., the largest franchisee, for about $765 million. This deal included the assumption of $620 million of debt. Silverman and his investors left with a profit of $125 million. Tollman-Hundley soon found the $700 million of

---

[6]Kevin Helliker, "How a Motel Chain Lost Its Moorings After 1980s Buy-Out," *The Wall Street Journal* (May 26, 1992), p. A10.

[7]Ibid.

[8]Ibid.

high-interest debt it incurred in the purchase overwhelming, so in 1991 it sought refuge from creditors by filing for Chapter 11 bankruptcy protection. The story of wheeling and dealing does not end there. Reenter Henry Silverman. Now specializing in distressed hotel chains, he arranged the purchase of the Ramada and Howard Johnson lodging chains in 1990 for Blackstone Capital Partners. Then, early in 1992, he led Blackstone in acquiring the principal assets of Days Inns out of bankruptcy proceedings for $269 million debt-free, less than one-half the 1984 buyout price.[9] Now Silverman could run the three chains.

In December 1992 the company, now named Hospitality Franchise Systems, went public in an initial public offering led by underwriters Merrill Lynch, Salomon Brothers, and the Nikko Securities Company. The shares immediately began trading on the New York Stock Exchange.

HOSPITALITY FRANCHISE SYSTEMS

Hospitality Franchise Systems (HFS) became the world's largest hotel franchisor, as measured by number of hotel rooms. Table 21.1 shows the number of units and the number of rooms of the three systems controlled by HFS as of September 30, 1992.

Based on the number of rooms, Days Inns was the third largest individual lodging firm in the United States and the largest in the economy segment (average nightly room rates were less than $46). Ramada was the fourth largest lodging firm in the United States, targeted for the middle market segment with room rates generally at $46 to $70 per night. Howard Johnson, the 12th largest U.S. lodging chain, was also middle market, focusing primarily on the leisure travel market. In February 1993 HFS announced

Table 21.1   Outlets and Rooms of HFC Affiliates, 1990–1992

	1990	*1991*	*1992*
Days Inns			
Hotels	1,094	1,216	1,312
Rooms	128,071	133,053	138,618
Ramada			
Hotels	508	549	586
Rooms	84,302	92,206	96,651
Howard Johnson			
Hotels	436	510	543
Rooms	53,825	59,498	60,714

Source: Public records.

[9]Howard Rudnitsky, "Triple Dipper," *Forbes* (November 25, 1991), pp. 171–172.

an agreement to acquire the Super 8 Motels' franchise business, which would give HFS about 1000 more properties with close to 60,000 rooms.

The earnings of HFC were derived primarily from annual franchise royalty fees that were based on a percentage of annual gross room revenues of the hotels (currently these range from 4 to 5 percent for royalty fees, with an additional 3 to 4.5 percent for marketing and reservation fees). In addition, standard franchise agreements required initial fees of $20,000 to $38,000.

For these fees the franchisor provided a national reservation system, national advertising, group sales, quality standards and inspections (of questionable strictness, as we have seen), training programs, volume purchasing, and some other support services.

Silverman

What sort of person was Silverman, this man who figured in a decade of Days Inns maneuvering? He was enamored with Cuban cigars so rare that for years he could get them only from a Lebanese arms merchant friend, who allegedly got them through high-level governmental contacts in Cuba. His Park Avenue apartment once belonged to the legendary Walter Chrysler. At his country house in Bedford Hills, New York, he was a neighbor of Carl Icahn, a notorious corporate raider. And, of course, he drove a Bentley.

Silverman was celebrated as a deal maker. He described deal making as "like going to war, without the bloodshed. . . . You say 'jump,' and legions of lawyers and bankers and investment bankers and accountants and consultants and PR guys and everybody else sort of jumps." Tollman blamed Silverman for the financial bath he and Hundley took in acquiring Days Inns in 1989. (Their default in late 1990 enabled Silverman and his Blackstone Group to reacquire the company for hundreds of millions less in 1992.) Silverman maintained that he told Tollman, "You guys were not naive babes. Don't tell me you didn't know what the debt was."[10]

THE LODGING INDUSTRY

The lodging industry suffered in the late 1980s and 1990s from excessive construction: About 7000 hotels with 900,000 rooms were built in the 1980s. The incentive was favorable tax legislation and easy access to capital from lenders, the same spurs that led to the great merger mania and the savings and loan excesses.

During its great growth of the 1980s, the lodging industry evolved into numerous chains, as entrepreneurs recognized the attractiveness to con-

---

[10]Andrea Rothman, "Fast Talk, Fat Cigars, and Big Deals—in the '90s," *Business Week* (August 19, 1991), pp. 90–91.

sumers of standardized lodging. In particular, consumers liked chains for their computerized reservation systems and ensured amenities.

In expanding, a firm had three basic alternatives: (1) It could own and operate the units itself, (2) it could manage properties owned by someone else, or (3) it could franchise or license its name and method of operation to another party, the franchisee. While many lodging firms used more than one of the options, HFS limited itself to franchising and shunned company ownership of any outlets.

The Competitors

Holiday Inn is the largest hotel chain worldwide, with almost 1700 Inns and almost 329,000 rooms. Holiday Inn has been fully owned by the British company, Bass PLC, since January 1990. In the United States, Manor Care has seven hotel chains, with the largest operating under the Comfort Inn, Quality Inn, Econo Lodge, and Rodeway Inns names. Nearly all of these are franchises.

Marriott is the largest operator of U.S. hotel rooms, mostly owned or managed by the parent company, with four chains: Marriott, Courtyard, Residence Inn, and Fairfield Inn. Other large U.S. brands include Hilton, French company Accor S.A.'s Motel 6, ITT's Sheraton, and privately owned Hyatt. Table 21.2 lists the 10 largest economy/limited service lodging chains in the United States as of April 27, 1992.

Effects of Saturation on Days Inns

Having too many hotel and motel rooms—lodging saturation—adversely affected the entire industry. Days Inns was particularly vulnerable. Table 21.3 shows the occupancy rate of Days Inns for 1990 through 1992 and lists

Table 21.2   Largest Economy/Limited Service U.S. Lodging Chains by Number of Rooms, 1992

Days Inns of America	134,000 rooms
Motel 6	72,800
Comfort Inns	68,700
Super 8 Motel	53,300
Econo Lodge	51,400
Travelodge	39,500
Hampton Inns	36,800
La Quinta Motor Inns	27,100
Hospitality International	25,100
Red Roof Inns	23,300

Source: Industry public records.

Table 21.3   Occupancy and Average Room Rates, Days Inns, 1990-1992

	1990	1991	1992
Occupancy	57.2%	54.5%	56.8%
Room rate	$44.40	$44.14	$44.54

Source: Company public reports.

the average room rate. The average room occupancy rate for the industry in 1992 was 61.7 percent, up from the year-earlier 60.1 percent.[11]

Although we do not know the break-even point for Days Inns related to occupancy rate, the below-industry average suggests two things: (1) Days Inns appears to have substantially overbuilt relative to industry potential, and (2) its below-industry-average performance suggests vulnerability to competition. We suspect the latter item also reflects the sacrifice of rigid standards in the pursuit of growth. Sheer number of rooms does not a success make. In the lodging industry climate in the early 1990s, we would expect some marginal firms to succumb.

Clearing the industry of marginal operators makes the situation more attractive to those remaining. Days Inns, with its dominance in the economy/limited service sector, may be a survivor, but its failure to maintain high standards puts it at risk.

ANALYSIS

Who Is Our Customer?

Silverman insisted that he had weeded out negligent franchisees, but he was also quoted as saying that "the [quality-assurance] inspectors are not cops, and they are supposed to get along with franchisees. . . . The franchisee is our customer."[12]

Is the franchisee truly the Days Inns customer? Or should the traveler be? The interests of the two did not prove to be wholly compatible. The best interests of travelers can be sacrificed by those franchisees most interested in short-term profits achieved by putting as little into the business as possible.

Bastardizing the Inspection Process

Inspectors in any chain organization ensure that all members meet reasonable performance and maintenance standards. For franchise chains, inspec-

---

[11]As reported in Standard & Poor's Industry Surveys (March 11, 1993), p. L42. This data is based on Smith Travel Research's *Lodging Outlook*.

[12]Ibid.

tions are crucial because the franchisees are independent and less bound by corporate policies than are company-owned outlets with their hired managers. Anecdotal evidence suggests that Days Inns abuses of reasonable standards were widespread and that inspectors were more figureheads than enforcers of corporate standards and controls. The company did terminate some franchises, but usually because they had failed to pay their royalties to the corporation.

With inspectors only desultorily checking on outlets, grading loosely on maintenance and housekeeping and apparently showing little concern about safety and security matters, travelers' best interests were unprotected. Corporate myopia seemed to prevail. But travelers eventually have the final say: Occupancy rates dropped below industry averages, and the better franchises became burdened by the sorry quality image engendered by the weak links in the franchise chain.

WHAT CAN BE LEARNED?

The fallacy of "growth at any cost." At first glance, a growth orientation seems to lie in the same domain as motherhood and apple pie, something intrinsically good and worth seeking. But on deeper reflection, and with the benefit of contrary examples such as Days Inns, Campeau, and many savings and loans, the allure of great growth ought to be sobered by the untoward abuses it can foster.

Unrestrained growth suggests expanding beyond an organization's resources, growing with borrowed funds, being saddled with massive interest overhead commitments. It also suggests pursuing short-run growth goals at the expense of longer-term prudence. In Days Inns the growth mentality restrained any control aspects that might impede the growth, such as careful screening of franchise candidates, high standards for those accepted and for their operational performance, and rigorous enforcement of standards. An unrestrained growth commitment often involves taking short cuts with both accepted ethical standards and sound management procedures.

The rapid growth made possible through a franchise system can be its downfall. Because growth in the number of units can occur easily and quickly, it is tempting to rush headlong into opening ever more units to meet the demand of prospective licensees. Emphasis on growth often means that existing operations are ignored. As a consequence, they are undercontrolled, and emerging problems—such as safety and security issues—do not receive adequate attention. Screening of people and locations becomes superficial.

Firms need to maintain tight controls over far-flung operations if they are to be sufficiently informed about emerging problems and opportunities. Tight controls enable them to best organize their resources and protect a desired image and standard of performance. In franchise operations such controls are essential because franchisees are independent entrepreneurs.

Beware of weak links in a chain. In any organization with many outlets, all identifiable as members of the same group, the actions of a few can enhance or tarnish the image of all. Where incompetent, unsafe, and cheapening operations are permitted, then customers' negative perceptions may be transferred to the whole operation. Even though the poorly performing and disgraceful outlets may constitute only a small minority, their negative actions have wider impact. The moral: chain and franchise operations need to quickly deal with those units unable or unwilling to conform to corporate policies and dictates. At stake is the preservation of the integrity of the total enterprise. Truly, the chain can quickly become as vulnerable as its weakest link.

INVITATION

What other learning insights does the Days Inns case provide?

QUESTIONS

1. "Silverman has maneuvered so as to become a very wealthy man. You can't argue with success." Discuss.
2. Days Inns is pursuing a strategy of accepting older, run-down motels that might otherwise have to be abandoned or perhaps sold as nursing homes. Discuss the desirability of this strategy from the following perspectives:
    (a) the Days Inns Corporation
    (b) the new franchisees accepted by Days Inns
    (c) the older franchisees
    (d) society in general
3. How can a motel/hotel beef up security in a time of increasing crime?
4. "If Days Inns is the largest hotel chain, the company must be doing something right." Discuss.
5. What parallels do you see in this case and the Sears Auto Centers' problems? (See Chapter 8.)
6. Critique the hypothesis that a few weak links in the chain can have a serious effect on the entire company.

INVITATION TO ROLE PLAY

1. You have been the owner of a Days Inn franchise for 10 years (since before the 1984 buyout and subsequent change in policy). You are incensed and deeply troubled by the dilution of quality and security standards. What plan of action do you suggest for correcting the worst of the abuses?

2. As the CEO of Days Inns, how would you seek to achieve extensive growth without diminishing quality of service and facilities, as well as security? Be as specific as possible.

INVITATION TO RESEARCH

Update the performance of Days Inns. Is it still growing? Is it profitable? Does this performance suggest any insights to you?

22

Contrast—McDonald's: Maximizing Controls and Sustaining Vigorous Growth

Few business firms anywhere in the world can match the sustained growth of McDonald's. Initially, it grew with one simple product—a hamburger—and although McDonald's today has broadened its product mix somewhat, it still remains uniquely undiversified.

The foundation of the great success of McDonald's as the world's largest restaurant chain has always been the most rigid standards and controls to be found anywhere. Its undeviating insistence on controls by all its outlets, company-owned as well as franchised, posits the greatest example we can find of the desirability of rigorous controls over all aspects of an operation.

RAY KROC

Ray Kroc faced a serious dilemma. He was 57 years old and all his life had dreamed of becoming rich. Ever since he returned from World War I (at 15 he had falsified his age), he had worked hard at becoming rich. He played piano with dance bands, then turned to selling paper cups for a firm called Lily-Tulip. He also moonlighted by working for a Chicago radio station (WGES), playing the piano, arranging the music programs, and accompanying singers. Then he thought that perhaps he could make his fortune in a big Florida land boom in the mid-1920s, so he left Chicago and tried selling land. But things did not work out, and he returned to Chicago a year later almost broke. Lily-Tulip gave him his old job back, and he stayed there for more than 10 years. In 1937 he stumbled onto a new gadget, a simple electric appliance that could mix six milkshakes at the same time, so he quit Lily-Tulip again and made a deal with the inventor. He soon became the world's exclusive agent for the Prince Castle Multi-Mixer and, for the next 20 years, traveled all over the country peddling it. He earned a fair living but was by no means rich.

Thus far wealth had remained an illusion. But finally Kroc stumbled onto the opportunity of a lifetime. He needed $1.5 million to make it work; unfortunately, he had neither money nor credit. His main source of income had dried up when he was forced to sell his mixer business for $100,000 to pay for a divorce. Now his total assets, including his house, were $90,000. Was this grand opportunity going to elude him?

HISTORY

In 1954 Kroc had received an order for eight of the Multi-Mixers from a small hamburger stand in San Bernardino, California. This was so unusual that he decided to go out himself and get a first-hand look at an operation that needed to make 48 milkshakes at the same time.

Maurice and Richard McDonald had come to California from New England in 1928, thinking that the west was the land of opportunity. They opened their first restaurant in Pasadena in 1940 and then in 1948 opened a self-service hamburger stand in San Bernardino. They had had trouble staffing their restaurant after World War II: Unskilled job seekers were primarily drunks and drifters. Dick McDonald recalled thinking, "Let's get rid of it all. Out went dishes, glasses, and silverware. Out went service, the dishwashers, and the long menu. We decided to serve just hamburgers, drinks, and french fries on paper plates. Everything prepared in advance, everything uniform."[1] These operations proved so successful that they had offers by those who wanted to buy them out or work out franchising deals. But they were conservative and had cautiously sold six other franchises in California while passing up other deals. The brothers lived in a small town, were netting $75,000 a year, and were afraid of getting too big.

When Ray Kroc arrived, he was amazed. He saw crowds of people waiting in line under golden arches, and he estimated that the hamburger stand did $250,000 a year. He was even more impressed with the speed of service and the cleanliness. The McDonalds served a standard hamburger for 15¢, and the french fries were always fresh and crispy, kept warm under

---

[1]"What McDonald's Had, the Others Didn't," *Forbes* (January 1973), p. 26.

infrared heat lamps. The customers moved in and out quickly so that only a small facility was needed to generate the substantial sales volume.

Ray Kroc badly wanted in on this business. He hounded the McDonald brothers for two days until they finally relented and allowed him to start selling franchises. The agreement was to charge 1.9 percent of revenues for each franchise, of which Kroc got 1.4 percent and the McDonald brothers, 0.5 percent.

At the time of the deal, Kroc was most interested in expanding the chain in order to sell more Multi-Mixer machines. By 1960 he had sold some 200 franchises, giving him gross franchise income per year of about $700,000. However, he had substantial travel expenses, and he had taken a partner, Harry Sonneborn, a former vice-president of Tastee Freez, who was drawing $100 a week. Kroc's secretary was taking her wages in stock (when she retired, she had an estimated 1 million shares of McDonald's stock).[2]

Sonneborn had convinced Kroc of the merits of a whole new approach. All new franchisees would also be tenants. Accordingly, the company would select the site, build the store, provide the equipment, and then rent the total package to an operator. This franchisee would then pay a rental fee, so McDonald's would have a profit from the lease as well as from the franchising fees. A great plan, but it required money—about $1.5 million. And with Kroc's meager $90,000 in assets, bank credit was unattainable.

ONWARD TO SUCCESS

Of course, we know that Ray Kroc got the money he needed, and this propelled McDonald's to a huge success. In only 22 years his firm reached the billion-dollar milestone. It took corporations such as Xerox and IBM 63 years and 46 years, respectively, to reach this milestone. Kroc could boast in his autobiography that the company was responsible for making more than 1000 millionaires, the franchise holders.[3]

Kroc got the $1.5 million he needed from several insurance companies. As a premium on the loan, they took 20 percent of the company; this they later sold for a $7 million profit. However, had they held on to the stock, it eventually would have been worth $500 million.

A year later Kroc bought out the McDonald brothers, paying them $2.7 million for everything—trademarks, copyrights, formulas, the "Golden Arches," and the name. The brothers took their money and quietly retired

[2]"For Ray Kroc, Life Began at 50. Or Was It 60?" *Forbes* (January 15, 1973), p. 25.
[3]Ray Kroc and Robert Anderson, *Grinding It Out: The Making of McDonald's* (New York: Berkley Publishing, 1977), p. 200.

to their hometown of Bedford, New Hampshire. Sonneborn also left a few years later; as Sonneborn's health began to fail, Kroc offered him $10 million in cash and $100,000 a year for life, and Sonneborn retired to Florida.

Figures 22.1 and 22.2 show the tremendous growth of McDonald's in number of outlets and in sales from 1955 to 1975. An investment of $5,000 in McDonald's in 1967 was worth $100,000 by 1973.[4] Table 22.1 shows the market dominance of McDonald's against its major fast-food competitors. Notice the steady increase in market share over this four-year period of rapid growth.

THE MARKETING STRATEGY

Ray Kroc saw a market opportunity in catering to "budget-conscious families on wheels who wanted quick service, clean surroundings, and high-quality food."[5] This was seen as a desirable alternative to the wide variety of drive-ins with car hops, juke boxes, tipping, waiting, and food of inconsistent and rather questionable quality. Kroc defended his approach because "all of those things create unproductive traffic in a store and encourage loitering that can disrupt customers. This would downgrade the family image we wanted to create for McDonald's. Furthermore, in some areas the

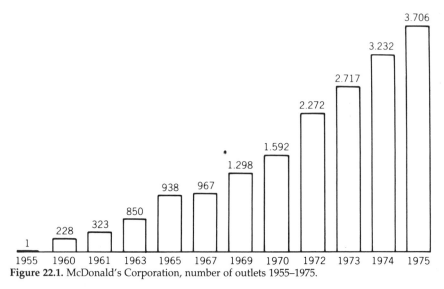

Figure 22.1. McDonald's Corporation, number of outlets 1955–1975.

[4]"What McDonald's Had, the Others Didn't," *Forbes* (January 1973), p. 26.

[5]Carol White and Merle Klingman, "'Hamburger,' McDonald's Takes It Seriously," *Advertising Age* (May 22, 1972), p. 117.

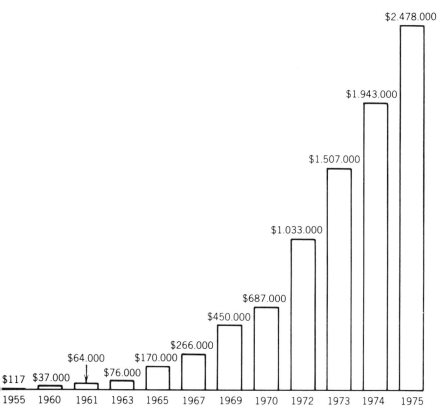

Figure 22.2. McDonald's Corporation, sales growth analysis 1955–1975 (figures in thousands of dollars).

vending machines were controlled by the crime syndicate, and I wanted no part of that."[6] As the executive vice president, Fred L. Turner, said, "We want young families in the tricycle and bicycle neighborhoods—the station wagon set, or one car going on two."[7]

During the company's early years, Ray Kroc used the company air-plane to spot good locations; he would fly over a community looking for schools and church steeples and then follow with site surveys. In those days, McDonald's favored above-average-income and residential areas, preferably near shopping centers. The rule was that new store sites should contain 50,000 residents within a three-mile radius. This changed by the 1970s, when marketing research revealed that three-fourths of McDonald's

[6]Kroc and Anderson, op. cit., p. 84.
[7]"McDonald's Makes a Franchise Sizzle," *Business Week* (June 15, 1968), p. 107.

Table 22.1 Top 25 Fast-Food Restaurants

	1974		1973		1972		1971	
	A^a	B^b	A	B	A	B	A	B
McDonald's	1,940,000	19.8	1,507,000	17.7	1,032,000	15.2	784,000	18.4
Kentucky Fried Chicken	1,150,000	11.7	1,000,000	11.8	840,000	12.4	900,000	15.4
International Dairy Queen	590,000	6.0	530,000	6.0	510,000	7.5	424,000	7.3
Burger King	466,500	4.8	388,600	4.0	270,700	4.0	226,000	3.9
Burger Chef	275,000	2.8	225,000	2.6	200,000	2.9	225,000	3.9
A & W International	265,000	2.7	200,000	3.1	241,000	3.5		
Hardee's	259,000	2.6	200,000	2.4	136,000	2.0	107,000	1.8
Denny's	252,964	2.6	204,016	2.4	163,411	2.4	132,332	2.1
Jack-in-the-Box	244,000	2.6	170,000	2.1	132,000	1.9		
Pizza Hut	242,000	2.5	160,000	2.0	115,000	1.7	77,680	1.8
Bonanza	193,000	1.9	140,700	1.7	92,846	1.4	64,000	1.1
Sambo's	190,000	1.9	138,000	1.7	92,152	1.4	61,582	1.1
Gino's	170,521	1.7	170,521	2.1	128,044	1.9	95,300	1.6
Dunkin' Donuts	169,474	1.7	141,757	1.7	126,693	1.8	99,593	1.8
Ponderosa	155,000	1.6	96,552	1.1	96,552	1.4	64,065	1.1
Church's Fried Chicken	126,000	1.3	101,600	1.3	79,354	1.2	51,200	0.9
Shoney's	120,401	1.2	101,349	1.2				
Arby's International	120,175	1.2	100,000	1.2				
Jerrico	98,870	1.0	61,678	0.7				
Frisch's Big Boy	91,000	0.9	88,000	1.0	79,000	1.2	73,000	1.2
Morrison's	90,800	0.9	66,000	0.8	52,250	0.8		
Friendly Ice Cream	90,000	0.9	71,775	0.8	61,249	0.9	49,379	0.8
Shakey's	87,000	0.9	74,500	0.9	63,650	0.9	73,000	1.2
Mr. Steak	85,000	0.9	81,700	1.0	64,000	0.9	49,800	0.9
Sizzler	85,500	0.9	62,200	0.6	43,443	0.7		

^{a}A represents total sales (in thousands of dollars).
^{b}B represents market share (%).

Sources: Advertising Age (June 3, 1974), p. 52; *Advertising Age* (May 14, 1973), p. 93; and *Advertising Age* (June 30, 1975), p. 49. Permission granted by Becker Paribas Inc., 55 Water St., New York, N.Y., 10041.

customers stopped by in conjunction with some other activity. As a consequence, stores were located by patterns of customer activity and traffic flows.

Kroc offered the public a clean, family atmosphere in which service was quick and cheerful. Cleanliness of outlets, including the toilets, and friendliness of salespeople became major competitive advantages; great pains were taken to maintain these standards. Hamburger University, a special McDonald's training school for managers and owners, placed heavy emphasis on customer service. A 350-page operating manual required adherence to strict standards, not only for the preparation of food but also for the care and maintenance of facilities. For example, the manual called for door windows to be washed twice daily. Similar tight standards concerned service, food, and cooking procedures. There was even an employee dress code, with men required to keep their hair cropped to military length and their shoes highly polished. Women were to wear dark, low shoes, hair nets, and only very light makeup. All employees wore uniforms.

The cooking was completely standardized: A pound of meat was to have less than 19 percent fat; buns were to measure 3½ in. wide, no more than one-quarter ounce of onions was to be used per hamburger, and so on. The holding time for each of the cooked products was set by the corporate headquarters: for example, french fries, 7 minutes; burgers, 10 minutes; coffee, 30 minutes. Products held longer than that had to be thrown out. Company auditors closely scrutinized this part of the operation to ensure that all food served was of the same quality.

Consistency in adhering to the high standards was another notable aspect of the marketing strategy. Store operation was closely supervised by strong regional offices to prevent a detrimental effect on other stores in the system caused by a weakness in one restaurant. For example, field consultants made two three-day inspections of each outlet every year, grading operators on quality, cleanliness, quick service, and friendliness. This grading system could determine whether an existing operator would be granted desirable additional franchises. On rare occasions a franchise could be terminated if prescribed standards were not met.

Franchises were granted store by store. This contrasted with the practice of most other franchisers, who granted area franchises to large investors who promised to put up a given number of outlets within a specified period of time. Although the rate of growth was rapid, there were few problems with substandard conditions at either company-owned or franchised outlets.

McDonald's rigorously analyzed potential sites to ensure the maximum chance of success for each unit; failures due to poor locations were few. The distinctive buildings and the arches, of course, made a McDonald's unit visible and even conspicuous from a distance.

Among all retailers McDonald's was one of the biggest users of mass media advertising, budgeting over $50 million each year. (A familiar jingle was "You Deserve a Break Today.") How successful has this mass advertising been? In a survey of school children in the early 1970s, 96 percent identified Ronald McDonald, ranking him second only to Santa Claus.[8]

THE YEARS AFTER RAY KROC

In 1968 Ray Kroc stepped aside and appointed 35-year-old Fred Turner president of the company. Turner had been Kroc's understudy for several years, having started as a cook and worked his way up.

Despite Turner's allegiance and admiration for Kroc, he began instituting a number of changes in established policies. The major changes involved the appearance of the stores. He replaced the red-and-white-tile exteriors with dull-brown brick, more plate glass windows, and a shingled roof. The garish neon Golden Arches gave way to a more sedate logo. Turner modified the interiors so that people could more comfortably eat on the premises and changed the name "hamburger stands" to "restaurants." He gave certain outlets more flexibility in decor: such as a nautical theme in Boston and a campus theme at UCLA.

As McDonald's gained financial strength, Turner made efforts to increase the number of company-owned, as opposed to franchised, outlets. An aggressive "buy-back" policy encouraged old franchise-holders to sell out to McDonald's, and an increasing number of new outlets were company operated. Company stores proved to be more desirable because of their higher profitability and more centralized control. In 1968 McDonald's owned only 15 percent of the outlets, but by 1974 the company owned 40 percent.

As choice highway locations became increasingly scarce, McDonald's moved into some downtown locations and into shopping malls, zoos, office buildings, hospitals, and even a high school. Central city locations involved some adjustments. Salaries and occupancy costs were higher, and selling hours tended to be much shorter, with little business typically done on weekends. But much higher volume—averaging twice the volume of the suburban stores—offset these drawbacks. Along with the central city expansion came the overseas market. By 1980 McDonald's had located 1050 stores abroad, of which 250 were in Japan and 50 in England; 19 percent of total company sales volume came from this international operations.[9]

[8]"The Burger That Conquered the Country," *Time* (September 17, 1973), pp. 84–92.
[9]McDonald's 1980 Annual Report, p. 16.

McDonald's continued its traditional Saturday morning television ads promoting Ronald. According to a McDonald's official, "It only takes one child to influence a meal out."[10] In addition to directing advertising at children, McDonald's increasingly developed ads aimed at specific segments of the public, such as blue-collar workers, a group that had been hard for McDonald's to draw. Special promotions and giveaways aimed at children have also influenced sales: for example, "Kid's Day," featuring free sundaes; premiums in "play value" packages; and in certain cities even a "Fun Bus" that takes school children on field trips with, of course, a stop at a McDonald's restaurant for lunch.

The traditional product offering of McDonald's has been simplicity itself. In the early days the product line was only hamburgers, french fries, milk shakes, and soft drinks. The first successful menu expansion came with the Filet-o-Fish in 1962, which was invented by an operator in Cincinnati, Ohio, who was located in a large Catholic neighborhood and was faced with weak Friday sales. Before the sandwich was introduced chain-wide (not until 1965) the company developed standards such as how long to cook it, what type of breading to use, how thick to make it, and what kind of tartar sauce to use; it was then test marketed, being offered on Fridays only in a limited number of outlets. Chicken likewise was intensively tested, beginning in 1971, and was not made generally available until 1981. Even the Big Mac was tested for some years before it was made widely available.

The most notable success with product expansion was the breakfast menu. The Egg McMuffin was first tested in 1972, with other breakfast items added shortly after. Breakfast menus were initially tested in Chicago, Pittsburgh, and Washington, DC. They proved so successful there that the breakfast menu became available nationwide in 1976 and by 1977 accounted for 10 percent of the company's sales. A major advantage of these breakfast sales was that they brought additional business during the time when these outlets previously had sat idle. In addition, the breakfast menu lured older customers whom the company had previously had trouble attracting. In 1971, only one year after the nationwide rollout of the breakfast menu, patronage from customers over 35 years of age jumped from 18 percent to 22.5 percent of McDonald's sales.[11] Thoroughly testing selected menu additions has been a hallmark of the product strategy. The company uses its company-owned stores to test market new product candidates before making them more widely available.

[10]Christy Marshall, "McDonald's '79' Plan: Beat Back the Competition," *Advertising Age* (February 2, 1979), p. 88.
[11]"McDonald's Blends New Products with Savvy Merchandising," *Business Week* July 11, 1977), p. 59.

COMPARISON OF MCDONALD'S WITH FAILING FRANCHISE OPERATIONS

Many franchise firms faded in the late 1960s and 1970s because of oversaturation. Competitors had put up more outlets than the market could support, and marginal operations faltered and went under.

Some franchisers failed because of difficulty in obtaining qualified franchisees or licensees. McDonald's believed that a key factor for success was for a licensee initially to work full time in the business. The unsuccessful franchisers failed to attract or insist on licensees who met prescribed qualifications. They tended to be interested primarily in getting the initial franchise fee. Business was viewed as a quick-buck scheme, to be milked dry before the franchisers exit.

Poor site selection plagued some operations. In their eagerness to secure footholds in major markets, some franchisers failed to research locations. Too-fast expansion led to indiscriminate site selection, sometimes influenced by opportunistic realtors. Another factor leading to poor locations was lack of capital to purchase the more desirable sites.

When business and the economy in general are going well, ineffective management controls are not always readily apparent. However, when the economy experiences a downturn and, more important, when competition intensifies, lack of effective controls can be fatal to these businesses.

In order to gain quick public attention and recognition, many fast-food franchisers used the name of either an entertainer or a professional sports figure to lure potential licenses: Minnie Pearl's Chicken, Here's Johnny Restaurant (Johnny Carson), Al Hirt Sandwich Saloon, Broadway Joe's (Joe Namath), Jerry Lucas Beef 'n Shake, and Mickey Mantle's Country Cookin' Restaurant. But although the public would pay to see the entertainer or sports figure perform, they would not necessarily frequent a fast-food outlet simply because of the famous name unless the food and service warranted their patronage, and mostly they did not.

Burger King—Why Not Another McDonald's?

At the same time as McDonald's was positioning itself for rapid growth, a competitor, with initially better prospects than all other competitors, was striking out.

In 1967 General Foods Corporation acquired Burger Chef Systems, a fast-food franchising operation of some 700 units, for $16 million. In less than four years, General Foods amassed a pretax loss of $83 million from the venture, while, during the same period, McDonald's net income rose

285 percent. Some marginal fast-food franchisors collapsed during this period, in which there appeared to be a saturation of hamburger, chicken, and other restaurants, but General Foods was no marginal firm. It was the nation's largest manufacturer of convenience foods, with sales approaching $3 billion. It was an astute and aggressive marketer and the country's third largest national advertiser, spending over $150 million a year. It had an unbroken string of annual sales increases dating back to 1935. With such backing for an already established and growing franchise chain, how could disaster strike, and in just a few years?

General Foods undertook a vigorous expansion program for Burger Chef. By March 1969, not much more than a year after the acquisition, 900 outlets were operating across the country. That same month, Burger Chef moved into Canada with an outlet in Toronto.

By December 1969 Burger Chef had 1022 outlets in the United States and 29 in Canada. One year later it had more than 1200 outlets in the United States and 36 in Canada, representing an increase of over 70 percent in three years. Approximately 84 percent of the outlets were franchised and 16 percent operated by Burger Chef. Advertising expenditures averaged $2.5 million a year.

General Foods lost several of its key executives in its fast-food acquisitions. The founder of Burger Chef left to pursue other interests shortly after the acquisition, and another key executive had a heart attack. Other departures for various reasons resulted in an almost complete management turnover during the first two years. This seemed to pose no severe problems, however, because General Foods supplied the new management for its acquisition from its own ranks.

The faster General Foods tried to expand its fast-food operation, the bigger the problems became. The bad news, when it came, was sudden and shocking. In January 1972 General Foods announced a write-down amounting to $83 million pretax dollars, nearly $1 a share after taxes. General Foods informed its stockholders that it was cutting back its ambitious expansion into fast food. It closed all 70 of its Rix roast beef restaurants, closed 100 of the 1200 Burger Chef units, and announced that it was writing off many more.

Forbes magazine questioned how so big a company could go so wrong in as simple a business as frying hamburgers and slicing roast beef. In an interview with *Forbes's* reporters, President Larkin explained: "We couldn't get enough people to come into our stores. The kids didn't want roast beef and later the adults didn't want it either. Roast beef was just a fad." Regarding the Burger Chef operation, Larkin admitted the problem was simply management: "The key man had a heart attack. We sent one of our own men and he just did not know his way around this kind of operation."[12]

For 19 consecutive years, General Foods had managed to achieve gains in per-share earnings, but the hamburger and roast-beef disaster broke the trend in 1972. The viability of the multibillion dollar company was not in danger, and the company was still profitable despite the fast-food drain. However, Burger Chef's substantial losses hurt the image of the company, especially with its major food chain customers. This image further suffered when General Foods cut back on some customer services in order to absorb the fast-food losses.

Arthur Larkin, the heir apparent for the chairman's position, took an early retirement. As part of the company-wide efficiency drive, General Foods cut salaried personnel by 10 percent and took a hard look at its total operation.

While other aspects of the corporation were also causing problems, the biggest rebuilding job continued to be the Burger Chef chain. The total number of units was pruned to about 1000, and more attention was given to clustering these in major markets to obtain a more efficient sharing of advertising expenditures. More thorough screening and training of franchise owners and managers was instituted. A new building design, new logo, more emphasis on product quality, a more varied menu, and even a new plastic wrapper to keep hamburgers warm longer were belatedly introduced. Yet it seemed likely the fast-food division was years away from making a major contribution to General Food's earnings.

Late in 1981, General Foods sold the Burger Chef subsidiary to Hardee's, a Canadian-owned hamburger fast-food firm with 1396 U.S. outlets. At the time Burger Chef had been pruned to 676 units and, after five years of losses, was finally showing a small profit. The sale to Hardee's resulted in a charge against earnings for General Foods of $12.5 million. The loss was regarded as acceptable to be rid of a burr that had plagued it and which, while showing a profit, was still yielding a lower return on investment than most of its other divisions. Hardee's viewed the acquisition as providing additional sales and earnings growth potential to its already substantial fast-food operation.

The Invincibility of McDonald's

McDonald's remained the king of the hill, with 1989 sales of $5.96 billion and net profits of $707 million. The ingredients of success for

---

[12]"The Bigger They Are . . ." *Forbes* (February 15, 1972), p. 21.

McDonald's were simple, but few competitors were able to effectively emulate them:

- A brief menu, but of consistent quality over thousands of outlets.
- Strictly enforced and rigorous operational standards controlling service, cleanliness, and all other aspects of the operation.
- Friendly employees, despite a high turnover of personnel because of the monotony of automated food handling.
- Heavy mass media advertising directed mostly at families and children.
- Identification of a fertile target market—the family—and direction of the marketing strategy to satisfying it with the product, price, promotional efforts, and site locations (at least in the earlier years, the suburban locations with their high density of families).

The following box discusses strategy countering by competitors and the great difficulty in matching nonprice strengths.

INFORMATION BOX

STRATEGY COUNTERING BY COMPETITORS

Some strategies are easily countered or duplicated by competitors. Price-cutting is the most easily countered. A price cut can often be matched within minutes. Similarly, a different package or a warranty is easily imitated by competitors.

But some strategies are not so easily duplicated. Most of these involve service, a strong and positive company image, or both. A reputation for quality and dependability is not easily countered, at least in the short run. A good company or brand image is hard to match because it usually results from years of good service and satisfied customers. The great controls of McDonald's—the high standards of product quality, service, and cleanliness—would seem to be easily imitated, but they proved not to be, as no other firm could fully match the enforced standards of McDonald's.

Somehow it seems that the strategies and operations that are the most difficult to imitate are not the wildly innovative ones, not the ones that are complex and well researched. Surprisingly—and even difficult to accept—the most difficult to imitate are the very simple ones: simply doing a better job in servicing and satisfying customers and in performing even mundane operations cheerfully and efficiently.

INVITATION TO DISCUSSION
What explanation can you give for competitors' inability to match the standards of McDonald's?

THE BEAT GOES ON

Unlike most firms that eventually find their growth slowing and their competitive dominance eroding, McDonald's has been able to maintain a unique momentum. Table 22.2 shows the compound annual growth rate from 1982 to 1992 for the company on various operational statistics, and it is awesome in its durability. The company plans to increase the pace of new restaurant development by opening 700 to 900 per year for the next several years.

INFORMATION BOX

THE COMPANY LIFE CYCLE

Just as people and products have life cycles—that is, the transition from birth to growth to maturity to decline—business organizations have cycles, as shown here.

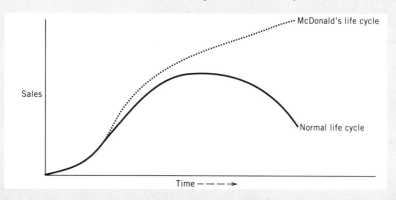

So far, McDonald's seems to have defied the maturity and decline stages and remained perpetually in the growth mode for almost 40 years. While some firms have remained viable for 50 and more years—some even 100 years—few have been able to maintain vigorous growth throughout this period. With most companies, eventually complacency sets in, the innovative mindset erodes, competitors become more aggressive and creative, and the firm loses its ability to adjust quickly in a changing environment. Or perhaps the market becomes saturated, offering little growth opportunity without major diversification.

McDonald's has so far escaped such growth restraints, even as we marvel at how many hamburgers the world can consume. Is there still a belated end in sight for McDonald's?

INVITATION TO DISCUSSION

Do you see any limits to the growth of McDonald's? What, in your opinion, must McDonald's do to sustain its growth over the next decade or two?

Table 22.2 McDonald's Compound Annual Growth Rates, 1981–1991

Systemwide sales	11%
U.S.	8
Outside of the United States	18
Total revenues	10
Operating income	12
United States	8
Outside of the United States	23
Net income	12
Net income per common share	14
Cash provided by operations	13
Total assets	15
Total shareholders' equity	13
Total return to investors on common stock	21

Source: McDonald's 1992 Annual Report.

In 1993 the company had more than 13,000 restaurants in 66 countries, with the end of 1993 seeing debuts in Iceland, Israel, Oman, and Saudi Arabia. According to the 1992 annual report, the company believed that significant growth opportunity also existed in expanding beyond lunch and breakfast business to serve customers at dinner. The information box on p. 344 discusses the life cycle as it pertains to people, products, and organizations. We are left to wonder when McDonald's will finally achieve maturity. How many more hamburgers can the world consume?

WHAT CAN BE LEARNED?

We have to concede that there is nothing exotic about success. It involves simply doing customer-pleasing things better and more consistently than competitors can. Even a unique product is not the essential ingredient for success, although it can certainly help. But a hamburger is a hamburger is a hamburger.

However, franchising presents some significant differences from other types of business operations, offering powerful opportunities as well as lurking dangers. Very rapid growth is possible through franchising—growth that is far more rapid than a firm can achieve on its own, even if it has substantial resources. Because somebody else is putting up most or all of the capital for an outlet, the major impediment to expansion is finding and wooing sufficient investor-licensees and finding sufficient attractive sites for units. Both of these can be done carelessly in the quest for wild expansion or, as with McDonald's, carefully, in controlled expansion.

A further distinction of franchising is that a few poor operations can be detrimental to the other outlets, because all are operating under the same format and logo. Although this is similar to the situation of any chain operation (a few bad stores can hurt the image of the rest of the chain), a franchise system is composed of independent owners who tend to be less controlled than the hired managers of a chain operation.

Illusion of rapid growth. The great growth possible through a franchise system can be its downfall. Because growth in number of units can occur easily and quickly, it is tempting to be a slave to it, to rush headlong into opening ever more units to meet the clamoring demands of prospective licensees. Such emphasis on growth often means that existing operations will be largely ignored. As a consequence they will be undercontrolled, and emerging problems will not receive adequate attention. The screening of people and locations tends to become superficial. Eventually the bubble bursts and the firm is forced to recognize that many outlets are marginal at best and will have to be eliminated. Although the aggressive and ambitious firm seeks growth, it must be prudent and controlled; a slower growth may have to be tolerated in order to achieve adequate assimilation.

Necessity for tight controls. All firms need to maintain tight controls over far-flung outlets to be sufficiently informed of emerging problems and opportunities and to maximize their resources and maintain a desired image and standard of performance. In a franchise operation this is all the more essential, as we have noted before, because we are dealing with independent entrepreneurs rather than hired managers. Controls should mean not only prescribing standards—for example, via the 350-page operating manual of McDonald's—but also monitoring to ensure that the standards are maintained. Regional and/or home office executives should make frequent, unscheduled calls on stores, probably with a checklist in hand, and grade performance according to the prescribed standards. All aspects of the operation should be checked, ranging from the grease content of french fries to the soap supply in restrooms. Where the performance of a particular outlet deviates significantly from that prescribed, remedial action will have to be taken, from warnings to even taking the franchise away in the event of continuing deficiencies.

Other controls are needed for screening and selecting franchisees and for training them. Specifications should also be established for site selection and building standards. Only in this way can uniformity of operation at a desired quality level be achieved and maintained.

Need for a distinctive image. All firms need to develop a distinctive image, one that differs from that of competitors and is unique and idenifiable. This is especially important in a highly competitive environment. Admittedly, uniqueness is not always easy to achieve, especially when many competitors have already come up with the most obvious solutions. But the search should go on. Uniqueness can come from a distinctive design or logo or roof or building style; it can come from a different menu, somewhat different services, or a different promotional approach; it can even be achieved by appealing to a different customer segment.

Imitation should not be disdained. A willingness to imitate may seem a contradiction to the need for a distinctive image, but this is not so. We are talking about adopting proven successful business practices, not imitating a sign or a building style, or even a menu without any changes. McDonald's management and operational procedures were not unknown; indeed, they were highly publicized. It required no genius to recognize the merits in what McDonald's was doing and put these into effect in another operation. But most of the other fast-food operations—such as Burger Chef and even Burger King in its early years—either failed to fully imitate the successful strategy or did so only belatedly, as in the case of Burger King in the late 1970s.

When a firm has developed a proven and successful format, why should other firms hesitate to imitate it? Although imitation may be viewed as uncreative, it represents sound and astute learning. Creativity can be reserved for other aspects of the operation. A firm can still maintain its own distinctive image yet be based on successful management and control practices.

INVITATION

Can you add other learning insights?

QUESTIONS

1. How do you account for the reluctance of competitors to imitate the successful efforts of another firm in their industry? Under what conditions is imitation likely to be embraced?
2. To date McDonald's has shunned diversification into other related and unrelated food retailing operations. Discuss the desirability of such diversification efforts.
3. "Eventually—and this may come sooner than most think—there will no longer be any choice locations anywhere in the world for new hamburger outlets. As a McDonald's stockholder, I am getting worried." Discuss.

4. Can you critique McDonald's operational strategy in recent years?
5. Contrast McDonald's with the earlier case involving Maytag's England operation. What insights can be developed from these two cases?
6. One major challenge facing McDonald's is human resource planning. The traditional McDonald's employee—the suburban teenager—is in short supply. What human resource planning would you recommend for this challenge?
7. "MBA students have been criticized for a 'details be damned' mind set, with overall perspectives cultivated at the expense of attention to details. But McDonald's success illustrates the vital importance of details." Discuss.

INVITATION TO ROLE PLAY

1. As a McDonald's executive, you are strongly in favor of significantly expanding the menu offerings. The firm, however, has traditionally been reluctant to add new items without lengthy testing. Put forth as many arguments as you can for expanding the menu in specific ways. Be prepared to defend your position against that of skeptical executives.
2. Again as a McDonald's executive, what long-term expansion mode do you recommend for your company?

INVITATION TO RESEARCH

Is McDonald's becoming more vulnerable to competitors today? Does it have any emerging problems?

Five

ETHICAL VIOLATIONS

CHAPTER 23

The Dalkon Shield—
Mishandling
the Public Trust

It is February 29, 1984. Three company executives have been summoned to appear in federal district court before Judge Miles Lord in Minneapolis, Minnesota. They are E. Claiborne Robins, Jr., A. H. Robins Company president and CEO; Dr. Carl D. Lunsford, director of research; and William A. Forrest, Jr., the company's general counsel. With them in the courtroom is a horde of lawyers.

To the three executives' acute shock, embarrassment, and anger, they hear Judge Lord publicly chastise them and their company for their conduct regarding the marketing of the Dalkon Shield, an interuterine birth control device.

For some months Judge Lord had been involved with a combined suit against the company by seven women who had been seriously injured by the Shield. The investigation delved into past Dalkon Shield litigation and the legal tactics employed by Robins for over 10 years. The stinging rebuke noted

> And when the time came for these women to make their claims against your company, you attacked their characters. You inquired into their sexual practices and into the identity of their sex partners. You ruined families and reputations and careers in order to intimidate those who would raise their voices against you. You introduced issues that had no relationship to the fact that you had planted in the bodies of these women instruments of death, of mutilation, of disease.... Another of your callous legal tactics is to force women of little

means to withstand the onslaughts of your well-financed team of attorneys. You target your worse tactics at the meek and the poor. . . . You have taken the bottom line as your guiding beacon and the low road as your route.[1]

Judge Lord also ordered a search of the company's files. Court-appointed officials found strong evidence that the company had covered up its knowledge of the Dalkon Shield's dangers. The Robins officials retaliated by bringing a lawsuit against Judge Lord, which they subsequently lost.

Between 1971 and 1975, Robins had sold more than 4 million Dalkon Shield IUDs in 80 countries of the world. In so doing, it had ignored increasing concerns of physicians and others about its effectiveness and safety. In the United States alone, more than 2 million women were fitted with the inadequately tested contraceptive device by doctors who believed the optimistic claims of the company. As a result, thousands of women suffered serious damage caused by the Shield—from pelvic infection to sterility, miscarriage, and even death.

This became one of the biggest business blunders of all time, made so much worse by a firm that at first blinded itself to any danger, then tried to cover it up until finally the dam burst.

How could a respected management, one with the reputation of a multigenerational family firm at stake, have accepted such risks with an untested new product in the crass pursuit of short-term profits? And how could it, in a panic over impending lawsuits, have so deceived itself, as well as the medical profession and the general public, into believing that nothing was wrong, that others—that is, physicians themselves—were to blame?

INTRAUTERINE CONTRACEPTIVES (IUDs) AND THE DALKON SHIELD

Interest in birth control and, in particular, in intrauterine devices (IUDs) as a form of contraception, goes back to ancient times, although most efforts were perilous and unreliable. Medical reports in the 1920s noted many cases of pelvic infection and inflammation with the crude IUD devices available then, and IUDs were generally discredited.

In the early 1960s interest in birth control greatly increased because of two factors. First, fears had begun to emerge of an overpopulated world. These fears seemed justified as a billion people had been added to the world's population between 1930 and 1960. While most of the fears centered on the developing nations of Africa, Asia, and South America, the

---

[1]Miles W. Lord, "A Plea for Corporate Conscience." Speech reprinted in *Harpers* (June 1984), pp. 13–14.

United States was also experiencing a population growth, reaching the psychological milestone of 200 million in the 1960s.

Second, the first oral contraceptive had been approved by the Food and Drug Administration in 1960 and was enthusiastically received by both women and the medical profession. However, worries began to surface about "the pill." Some of these concerned its side effects, such as blood clotting. Of even more concern was the possibility of long-term risks for women using the powerful birth-control hormone during their three decades of childbearing years.

After decades of being discredited, IUDs enjoyed renewed interest following two developments in the 1960s. One was the discovery of a new, malleable, inert plastic from which IUDs could be made, and the second was the development of a new molding process. Two new IUDs were patented in 1966: the Lippes Loop and the Saf-T-Coil.

Meantime, Hugh J. Davis, an associate professor of gynecology at Johns Hopkins, and Irwin Lerner, an inventor, came up with an idea for a new IUD on Christmas Day, 1967. Initial results looked good, and Lerner applied for a patent in 1968. In shape this new IUD resembled a shield, and it was a dime-size, crablike plastic device with a string attached for removal by the physician.

On February 1, 1970, the *American Journal of Obstetrics and Gynecology* published an article by Davis based on his testing at Johns Hopkins Family Planning Clinic of 640 women who had worn the device, named the Dalkon Shield. Davis cited 5 pregnancies, 10 rejections, 9 removals for medical reasons, and 3 removals for personal reasons. He reported a pregnancy rate of 1.1 percent. The article impressed many doctors because of such favorable statistics and because it was tested at the prestigious School of Medicine. As a result, many became interested in obtaining the device for their own patients.

Davis and Lerner decided to market the device themselves, and they formed the Dalkon Company in 1969. They worked to refine the product; by April 1970, they introduced a new, improved device, which made the Shield more flexible and thinner, with barium sulfate added to strengthen the plastic, while retaining its flexibility. However, lacking a sales organization, the owners quickly realized that the Shield would have to be distributed by an established corporation.

Schmid Laboratories turned down the idea, but then Upjohn made an offer. However, at a medical meeting in Bedford, Pennsylvania, another company, A. H. Robins, grew interested. On June 12, 1970, after three days of negotiating, Robins topped the Upjohn offer and bought ownership rights to the Dalkon Shield for $750,000 plus consulting fees and a royalty of 10 percent on all U.S. and Canadian net sales.

THE A. H. ROBINS COMPANY

A. H. Robins Company, headquartered in Richmond, Virginia, was a relatively small company ($135 million in sales at the time), but it had subsidiaries in more than a dozen foreign countries. It was best known for such products as Robitussin cough syrup, Chap Stick lip balm, and Sergeant's Flea and Tick collars. It was no fly-by-night company: For more than a century it had been a solid business citizen.

In 1860 Albert Hanley Robins had opened a small apothecary shop in downtown Richmond. In 1878 he expanded into manufacturing. While A. H. Robins handled walk-in business selling the patent medicines of the day, his son and daughter-in-law had a small pill-rolling operation upstairs.

The mom-and-pop undertaking continued until 1933, when a grandson, Edwin Claiborne Robins, took over management with dreams of expanding. He stopped selling medicines directly to the public and turned instead to selling prescription drugs to physicians and pharmacists. The first such product was a stomach remedy, Donnatel, which still remains a major product. After World War II, the company became a major manufacturer of mass-marketed prescription and nonprescription drugs. In 1963, with net sales of $47 million and profits near $5 million, the firm went public. In the process, E. Claiborne Robins, Sr., turned his family into one of the wealthiest in Virginia. In 1978 E. Claiborne Robins, Jr., became president and CEO.

Since 1965 the company had been interested in the birth control market and particularly in intrauterine devices, although it had never made or sold a medical device or gynecological product before and had no obstetrician or gynecologist on its staff. It had considered buying the rights for the Lippes Loop, but then the Dalkon Shield opportunity surfaced.

The potential for IUDs as a group seemed attractive. But perhaps the biggest plus for IUDs was that they did not require filing a new-drug application (NDA) with the Food and Drug Administration. Since the agency only had jurisdiction over drugs and not over medical devices (which was how IUDs were classified), a manufacturer did not have to file an NDA demonstrating that it had established relative safety with reliable and sufficient clinical and animal testing. Thus the lengthy research and safety testing of the Dalkon Shield could be avoided. (On May 28, 1976, the Medical Device Amendments were enacted to bring medical devices under the supervision of the Food and Drug Administration, but these amendments came five years after the Dalkon Shield was first brought to market.)

Robins quickly made plans to bring the Shield to market, and its assembly was assigned to the Chap Stick division. The company saw an urgent need to get into the market before potential competitors could rush in. In January 1971, just six months after it acquired the rights, the Dalkon Shield was ready for national distribution. The profitability potential was intriguing: The production cost was only about 25 cents, but the Shield was priced at $4.35. Although there were some quality control problems, they were deemed not to be particularly serious.

Promoting the Dalkon Shield

An aggressive marketing strategy was put in place. Several hundred salesmen were trained to contact physicians. The advertising itself was directed at both the medical professionals—physicians as well as agencies and clinics that provided IUDs—and women directly to persuade them to accept the Shield if their physicians should so recommend, and even to request and insist on the device if their physicians were skeptical. Consequently, in addition to advertising in medical journals, *Family Circle, Mademoiselle,* and similar magazines carried Dalkon Shield advertising.

Robins wanted to position the Shield as a superior product. It was promoted in 1970 as a modern superior IUD, with the lowest pregnancy rate (1.1%), lowest expulsion rate (2.3%), and the highest continuation rate (94%). Other promotional literature stated that it was the only IUD anatomically engineered for optimal uterine placement, fit, tolerance, and retention.

In the ads in major medical journals, Dr. Davis (the original researcher and coinventor) was impressively noted as a research physician with citations from the article he had published. Not disclosed was his financial interest in the product and the fact that he was hardly the objective and unbiased researcher deemed essential to sound medical research.

The Shield proved to be a popular product in the contraceptive market. By 1972 an estimated 12 million IUDs were in use worldwide, with 3 million in the United States. The Shield was in the forefront: Approximately 1,146,000 were sold in 1971, with an estimated market share of 40 percent. In one month, April 1972, some 88,000 women were fitted with the Shield.

But physician complaints began to mount. Many of them in the early months focused on the difficulty of inserting the Shield, but later these complaints would assume a more serious nature.

Despite all objections, by August 1973, more than 5 million pieces of promotional literature had been printed. The sales pitch did not change: "No general effects on the body, blood, or brain . . . safe and troublefree . . . the safest and most satisfactory method of contraception . . . truly superior."[2] A new, smaller shield had been brought out, and this was especially directed to women who had never borne children. However, no safety and effectiveness testing was ever done with this new version.

---

[2]Morton Mintz, *At Any Cost: Corporate Greed, Women, and the Dalkon Shield* (New York: Pantheon Books, 1985), p. 75.

Storm Clouds

In June 1973 Henry S. Kahn, a researcher working for the Center for Disease Control, headed a study to assess the safety of IUDs in general. In a survey of physicians in the United States and Puerto Rico, some surprising and troubling things surfaced. There seemed to be a significant correlation between the Dalkon Shield and the incidence of women hospitalized for a complicated pregnancy. He suggested that a more detailed investigation was warranted. At about the same time, Representative Fountain was chairing a subcommittee investigating whether or not medical devices should be subject to the same kinds of controls as regular drugs.

In the months that followed, more serious problems came to light, including some Shield-related deaths. In October 1973 the Robins Company changed its package label of the Shield to include the warning, "Severe sepsis with fatal outcome, most often associated with spontaneous abortion following pregnancy with the Dalkon Shield *in situ*, has been reported. In view of this, serious consideration should be given to removing the device when the diagnosis of pregnancy is made with the Dalkon Shield *in situ*."

Robins convened its own OB-Gyn Advisory Panel in February 1974 to evaluate information on cases of spontaneous septic abortion among women who became pregnant with the Shield in place. The panel finally concluded that there was inadequate information to establish a cause-and-effect relationship.

But problems continued to multiply. The Shield had a multifilament tail, compared with the monofilament tails used in all other IUDs. This tail was shown in several studies to be an excellent harbor for bacteria. In a letter dated May 8, 1974, Robins informed over 125,000 doctors that the Dalkon Shield should be removed immediately if a patient became pregnant and, if this was impossible, to perform a therapeutic abortion. The letter did not advise removal of the Shield from nonpregnant women. The company also stated that it felt the problems shown with the Shield were common to all IUDs. This letter was reported in *The Wall Street Journal*, and Robins quickly issued a press release stating that it had no intention of canceling production of the Shield.

There were more deaths, and by the end of June 1974, the Food and Drug Administration asked (not ordered) Robins to cease marketing the Shield. Bowing to public pressure, the company announced that it would cease marketing the Shield until FDA tests were finalized. However, it still insisted that women who were currently using the Shield were in no danger. Meanwhile, the directors of Planned Parenthood and federally funded Family Planning Programs urged the discontinuance of the Shield.

In October 1974 a preliminary report from the FDA concluded that the Shield was as safe as any other IUD and attributed the problem to the fact that the Shield was the newest IUD on the market and was still undergoing a "shakedown" period. In December 1974 Alexander Schmidt, then commissioner of the FDA, announced that Robins could continue to market the Shield as long as accurate records were kept of all wearers.

The Crisis

Robins was never to market the device again. Where the FDA failed, the judicial system took over. By March 1975, 186 suits had been filed against Robins. Also in March, the first judicial award was made: $10,000 compensatory and $75,000 punitive damages against Robins. In May a $475,000 judgment was awarded to the estate of a woman who had died while using the Shield. In August 1975, Robins formally announced that it would not remarket the Shield, but it still insisted that women who had had it inserted previously were in no danger.

Not until September of 1980, six years after the problems with the Shield had begun to surface, did Robins finally send a letter to 200,000 doctors, urging them to remove the device from all women who were still using it. The company stated that a "new" study showed that other problems, such as an infection called pelvic actinomycosis, were more likely the longer the device was worn. This move followed a $6.8 million judgment in Colorado in June 1980, in which $600,000 was awarded in compensatory damages and $6.2 million in punitive damages. The punitive award was of serious concern to the company since Robins' liability insurance covered only compensatory damages.

By 1980, 4300 suits were pending against Robins. Some attorneys were spending their entire time suing Robins; this became so popular a cause that a newsletter was published covering IUD litigation, and four-day yearly seminars were held so that more experienced lawyers could instruct others on how best to sue Robins.

The 1981 annual report noted that 2300 cases were still pending, while 4200 cases had been settled. Up to now, the company and its insurer (Aetna) had paid out $98 million for Dalkon Shield litigation. Lawsuits continued to multiply and became increasingly expensive for the company to handle. For example, the average settlement in 1976 was $8000; in 1984 the average was in the $400,000 range.

As 1985 approached, Robins' sales had continued to climb, reflecting the strength in its other product lines and its international operations. Profits had risen more grudgingly because of the heavy legal costs until 1984. (See Table 23.1 for the trend in sales and profits and a chronology of major events.)

In 1984, hounded by mounting legal costs and judgments and the running out of liability insurance coverage from Aetna, Robins took an

Table 23.1   Trend in Sales and Profits, 1970–1984; and Chronology of Major Events

	Sales (000,000)	Profits (000,000)	Profits as Percent of Sales	Major Events
1970	$132.6	$15.7	11.8	June 12, 1970, Robins buys the Dalkon Shield
1971	151.4	19.1	12.6	January 1971, Robins begins to market it
				April 1972, peak month for number of women fitted with the shield
1973	189.2	25.4	13.4	October 1973, Robins puts warnings on packages
				June 1974, Robins suspends Shield sales in United States
1975	241.1	26.6	11.0	April 1975, Robins suspends Shield sales in other coun-tries
1977	366.7	26.8	7.2	
1979	386.4	44.7	11.6	June 1980, $6.8 million judgment against Robins
1981	450.9	44.2	9.8	
1983	563.5	58.2	10.3	
1984	631.9	(461.6) loss		February 1984, Judge Miles Lord chastises Robins in Minneapolis court
				October 1984, Robins urges removal of all Shields
				Robins establishes $615 million reserve for claims
				August 21, 1985, Robins files for bankruptcy

extraordinary charge of $615 million as a Reserve for Claims. This resulted in a paper loss of $461.6 million in 1984. In August 1985 Robins filed Chapter 11 bankruptcy. Under Chapter 11 bankruptcy, all litigation against a company is stayed while the company and its creditors attempt to devise a plan to pay the bankrupt company's debts. E. Claiborne Robins, Jr., said the action was necessary to protect the company's economic vitality against those who would destroy it for the benefit of a few. Attorneys for the victims found this action to be fraudulent and in bad faith and an attempt by Robins to escape responsibility for the thousands of injuries the Shield had caused.

Not even Aetna was to escape unscathed. In 1986 a group of former Dalkon Shield users sued Aetna, charging that it had conspired with Robins to keep the alleged health hazards of the IUD from the public. The women claimed that Aetna also participated in intentional destruction of evidence that would have helped the plaintiffs prove the dangers of the device.

A bidding war developed for the troubled Robins Company. Rorer Group, a Pennsylvania pharmaceutical concern, made the first offer. Late in 1987, Sanofi, a French drug maker, made another takeover proposal. A week later, American Home Products Corporation joined the fast-developing bidding war. On January 20, 1988, the bid by American Home Products was accepted. John Stafford, chairman and CEO of American Home Products, was interested in Robins because of the tax advantages and the acquisition of two popular consumer brands: Robitussin and Dimetapp. "Franchises that powerful come along every few decades," he said.[3] And American Home could deduct its funding of Dalkon Shield liabilities from federal taxes.

American Home offered Robins' shareholders $700 million in American Home stock and agreed to pay $2.15 billion in cash to the trust fund of claims. The final modification had the two top executives of Robins each giving $5 million in exchange for protection against being sued personally over the Shield. This plan, Robins' fourth in its 29 months of bankruptcy proceedings, was the first to receive endorsement from both the company's shareholders and the committee representing the Shield claimants.

POSTMORTEM

The conduct of A. H. Robins' management led a well-regarded firm with a 100-year history down the road to bankruptcy; but even worse, its conduct brutalized an innocent public. How could this have happened? After all, these were not deliberately vicious men: They were well intentioned, albeit badly misguided. Perhaps their worst sin was that of trying to ignore and then cover up the increasingly apparent serious health problems with their

---

[3]Michael Waldholz, "American Home Expects Most of its Price for A. H. Robins Will be Tax-Deductible," *The Wall Street Journal* (January 21, 1988), p. 1.

product, doing this to such an extent that a federal judge castigated them and their company for corporate immorality. How could this situation—in which everyone lost but lawyers—have possibly been permitted to get so out of hand?

The situation began innocently enough, and in accordance with sound business strategy. Robins recognized an emerging opportunity: the birth control market. While competitors were already in the oral contraceptive market, the IUD sector of this market was virtually untapped and seemed to offer enormous potential. This sector appeared to be in the early stages of development, with no serious competitors as yet. But the likelihood of strong competitive entry could not be ignored, and Robins thus saw the need to enter this IUD market quickly and secure a major share of it—that is, beat competitors to the punch. We have to recognize that this is textbook business strategy.

In accordance with the desirability of quickly entering the market, Robins made many decisions with little deliberation. One such decision was to assign production of the Dalkon Shield to the Chap Stick division of the company. The two products had no similarities, but this assignment seemed a matter of expediency and a means of offering lower labor costs. And it might be argued that with such a new and unique product, there was not much more compatibility with any other division of the company.

Now we come to the point where Robins deviated from sound business strategy. It was entering a market in which it had no previous experience whatsoever, one in which health dangers ought to have been carefully evaluated. Yet Robins had not a single obstetrician or gynecologist on its staff. The company also neglected to conduct its own testing of the product, relying instead on the limited research that had been done by the Dalkon Shield's inventors. Robins did not question the original research and testing, flawed though it soon proved to be. Rather, it rushed the product to market, thankful that the Food and Drug Administration did not have to be involved. Good judgment would have mandated confirmation of the safety of the product by independent parties, but this would have taken time, time that Robins was fearful of spending.

Recognizing an emerging and spectacular strategic opportunity, Robins pursued it with single-minded determination. Unfortunately, such determination ignored prudent and even ethical considerations. For example, much of the product information and advertising that was used was taken from Davis and Lerner's admittedly biased research, and the financial interest that these two "researchers" had in the Dalkon Shield was ignored, and certainly never publicly mentioned. Physicians were thereby misled into thinking that the research was objective and unbiased.

The impressive research figures cited in the ads soon conflicted with studies done by others. As one example, Robins's ads originally claimed that the Shield had a low pregnancy rate of 1.1 percent; later studies showed pregnancy rates varying from 5 to 10 percent. But Robins continued to use the 1.1 percent rate in its advertising until late 1973, when the claimed pregnancy rate was revised upward.

Other advertising claims attested to the safety and superiority of the Dalkon Shield, stating that "it was generally well tolerated by even the most sensitive women," and that no anesthetic was required. Only after many physicians complained about the difficulty of insertion was the advertising literature changed in November 1971, by removing the statement that no anesthetic was required. But the claim of being safe and superior went unchanged.

Robins continued to ignore reports of major problems—such as massive bleeding, pelvic inflammatory diseases, miscarriages, and even deaths—that kept coming in over the years following the introduction of the Shield.

Admittedly, the term "safety" was relative. Was the Shield as safe or safer than the Pill? After all, the Pill was known not to be completely safe—it could cause serious side effects. Still, the evidence was mounting that there were significant dangers associated with the Shield, dangers beyond reasonable risk. And these Robins opted to ignore for far longer than was prudent and ethical.

The Robins Company maintained that its product was safe—and it proclaimed so publicly. But evidence suggests that the company knew otherwise. Internal memos indicated that the company knew of potential danger less than a month after it acquired rights to the Shield. And more internal company memos were to surface during subsequent litigation: two to three truckloads of incriminating papers.

The basic component of Robins's strategy now became strictly defensive: to cooperate when necessary, but to spend most of its time on lobbying Congress and defending itself against lawsuits. Major concern was thus on legal and not ethical considerations regarding its past actions.

So, what seemed at first to be an unassailable strategy was found seriously wanting. Was the company guilty of subordinating everything to the profit maximization goal, in an end-justifies-the-means perspective? Or did it simply panic, faced with a calamity of extraordinarily severe consequences, and resort to the defense mechanism of denial?

Roger L. Tuttle, a former A. H. Robins attorney, believed the latter:

> I've got to believe that had they known early on what they were dealing with they wouldn't have touched it with a 10-foot pole. It was just that one step led to another, until they had the grenade spinning in the middle of the floor.[4]

---

[4]Mintz, *op. cit.*, pp. 51–52.

Regardless, the dire consequences to the company and to its innocent customer victims represents a classic example of a monumental management mistake that should have been handled better. (See the following Issue Box.

ISSUE BOX

MUST MANAGEMENT ASSUME THE WORST SCENARIO?

The Dalkon Shield turned out to be an unmitigated disaster for the thousands of women who were victims and also for the company. Certainly, no organization would choose to undertake a venture that was likely to produce such results. There should be a commonality of interests on the part of consumers and firms to prevent such happenings. Besides the issue of a company's culpability for not noticing and then covering up the danger, another question should be asked: Does ignorance of possible dire future consequences relieve a firm of much of its blame? The contentious segment of the general public—lawyers as well as politicians eager to mollify their constituents—sees a "no mercy" scenario: The corporation is guilty despite ignorance of any wrongdoing, or any danger, at the time. But is this the most equitable viewpoint?

We live in a complex world, and our products are increasingly more complex technologically; some products, such as drugs, asbestos, and cigarettes, may well have long-term consequences far beyond our ability to predict at this time. Was this the case with the Dalkon Shield?

In today's environment, firms are unable to escape the long-term negative consequences of their products. The litigious environment will not permit this, however ignorant the firm may have been. Ethically, the blame has to be more muted for a firm that could not see any dire consequences. But does the very fact of not knowing really excuse?

Although knowledge of long-term consequences for any product may be limited, this ignorance does not preclude adequate and objective testing to achieve a high level of safety assurance. This Robins did not do. Furthermore, it ignored and even concealed the early suspicions of possible problems. Here was Robins' great ethical and moral misdeed: It placed short-term company profits above very strong doubts of customer health and safety.

INVITATION TO DISCUSSION

Robins' executives argue that if they had had any idea of the serious danger of the shield, they would have jerked it from the market, but that they had had nothing to confirm this until too late. Therefore, they should be exonerated from any serious wrongdoing. Discuss the pros and cons of this defense.

WHAT CAN BE LEARNED?

The Robins Company's actions seemed exemplary, at first:

1. Identify a business opportunity or strategic window.
2. Find or develop a product to tap this strategic window.
3. Beat competition in being the first to capitalize on this opportunity.

But there was one basic difference with other effective strategies: Health and safety was at stake with this particular product. This should have necessitated a more cautious approach to tapping the window of opportunity to ensure that the product had no risks to customers. Yet with Robins, health and safety considerations were ignored in a single-minded pursuit of profits. Everything else was secondary to this profit orientation.

Does our business system necessarily motivate firms toward such a profit-at-any-cost perspective? The answer is no. A firm, as we will see in Chapter 25, can be scrupulously honest and prudent in protecting health and safety considerations of its customers—and in so doing, protecting its reputation or public image—even at the cost of severe current diminishment of profits.

A firm today must zealously guard against product liability suits. Any responsible executive now has to recognize that product liability suits, in today's increasingly litigious environment, can bankrupt a firm. The business arena has become more risky, more fraught with peril for the unwary or the naively unconcerned. Consequently, any firm needs careful and objective testing of any product that can even remotely affect customer health and safety, and this testing must be undertaken even if product introduction is delayed and competitive entry encouraged.

Suspicions and complaints about product safety must be thoroughly investigated. We should learn unequivocally from this case that immediate and thorough investigation of any suspicions or complaints must be undertaken, regardless of the confidence management may have in the product or of the glowing recommendations of persons whose objectivity could be suspect. To procrastinate or ignore complaints poses what should be unacceptable risks.

If the worst happens and lawsuits begin to mount, a salvage strategy is best undertaken, regardless of costs. Robins faced a crossroads in 1974. Scary reports of problems and lawsuits were flooding in. How should the company react? One course of action was to tough it out, trying to combat the bad press, denying culpability, and resorting to the strongest possible legal defense. This Robins opted to do. At stake was its reputation, its economic life, and the welfare of tens of thousands of women.

The other recourse was what we might call a salvage strategy: recognition and full admission of the problem and removal of the Shield from more than 4 million women amid a full-market withdrawal. Expensive, yes, but far less risky for the viability of the company and certainly for the health of the women involved.

Neither strategy is without major costs. The first course of action puts major cost consequences in the future, however, where they may turn out to be vastly greater. The second course of action has an immediate impact on profitability but may save the company and its reputation and return it to profitability in the future.

This is an era of caveat vendidor—*"let the seller beware."* Businesses today have to recognize that this is no longer an age of caveat emptor—"let the buyer beware." Such a philosophy ruled the business environment for many decades, but now the pendulum has swung to *caveat vendidor*—"let the seller beware." Products or business practices that are perceived as not in the best interest of the public are subject to reprisals, be these in customer resentment and public outcry or in lawsuits. Woe to the firm that does not recognize this or underestimates the environmental constraints.

QUESTIONS

1. Can a firm guarantee complete product safety? Discuss.
2. Design a strategy for the Dalkon Shield that would have minimized the problems Robins eventually faced. What might be some concerns with such a strategy?
3. After this disaster, do you think Robins could ever have regained a sufficiently respected image to be a viable business under the same management? Why or why not?
4. "In essence, Robins exploited women's bodies for profit." Discuss.
5. The Dalkon Shield has proven to be a bonanza for lawyers. Do you think the legal profession has been allowed to go too far in seeking multi-million dollar suits and in having newsletters and seminars on how best to sue Robins?
6. Can you defend Robins' conduct regarding the Dalkon Shield—that is, were there any mitigating circumstances?

INVITATION TO ROLE PLAY

You are the public relations director for Robins in late 1972. Some disquieting information has come to you about numerous physician complaints about the Shield. Top management has so far been unconcerned about such reports, especially in view of Food and Drug Administration complacency.

Develop a plan of action for dealing with potential product safety problems that can be persuasively presented to top management.

INVITATION TO RESEARCH

Investigate the performance of American Home Products since it took over Robins in 1988. Was this a wise acquisition?

24

Customer Abuses: Cigarettes, Health Clubs, Small Loans

Cigarettes are among the world's most profitable consumer products. A cigarette "costs a penny to make, sell it for a dollar, it's addictive, and there's fantastic brand loyalty." So said takeover specialist Warren Buffett as he unsuccessfully sought to take over RJR Nabisco, the tobacco conglomerate.[1] Perhaps because of its profitability, the morality of the business has long been suspect.

Abusive practices toward consumers seem to gravitate to certain other industries as well, such as the health club industry and small consumer loans. They typify the range of unethical practices aimed at those who may or may not be naive and unsophisticated, but certainly have less technical knowledge and are consequently at the mercy of unscrupulous sellers.

CIGARETTES: CONTROVERSIAL STRATEGIES IN A SHRINKING MARKET

Faced with a steadily declining market in the United States, the tobacco industry has responded with a proliferation of brands: More than 300 brands were created, boasting of such features as being longer, slimmer, cheaper, flavored, microfiltered, pastel colored, and even striped. One of these new brands was an R. J. Reynolds brand called Uptown.

---

[1]"The Tobacco Trade: The Search for El Dorado," *Economist* (May 16, 1992), p. 21.

The Controversy over Uptown

Uptown was packaged in a showy black-and-gold box and was a menthol blend. R. J. Reynolds designed the product to appeal to a particular market segment, much as the other new brands had been designed for.

Because cigarette consumption had fallen in the United States, tobacco companies were increasingly directing their efforts to specific groups, such as women, Hispanics, and African-Americans. The last group in particular seemed a fruitful target market: 39 percent of black men smoke, whereas 30.5 percent of white men do.[2] Using careful research and design, everything about Uptown—even the name—was tailored to the tastes of black consumers. It was, indeed, the first cigarette aimed specifically at African-American smokers. This was the rub.

A storm of protests quickly ensued. Critics maintained that the marketing of Uptown represented a cold-blooded targeting of blacks, who already suffered a lung cancer rate 58 percent higher than whites. The protests even reached the office of Louis Sullivan, the Secretary of Health and Human Services. Sullivan quickly sided with the critics: "Uptown's message is more disease, more suffering and more death for a group already bearing more than its share of smoking-related illness and mortality."[3] He called for an "all-out effort to resist the attempts of tobacco merchants to earn profits at the expense of the health and well-being of our poor and minority citizens."[4]

Given the virulence of the protests, R. J. Reynolds abandoned its plans to test market the cigarettes in Philadelphia. It decried the negative attention being focused on the brand by a few zealots and angrily compared the acceptability of a retailer designing a line of clothing for blacks with the outcry accompanying the same marketing strategy for a cigarette.

On March 16, 1990, the *Chicago Tribune* announced that R. J. Reynolds Tobacco Company had stated that it was unlikely to pursue the controversial marketing of Uptown. The company defended its marketing efforts, but the critics had won.[5]

A Similar Controversy: Dakota. Another new cigarette brand, also targeted to a specific group, found itself beset with controversy. This was Dakota, aimed at "virile females."[6] Critics of tobacco's relationship with

---

[2]Michael Quinn, "Don't Aim That Pack at Us," *Time* (January 29, 1990), p. 60.
[3]Ibid.
[4]Ben Wildavsky, "Tilting at Billboards," *New Republic* (August 20, 1990), p. 19.
[5]Janet Cawley, "Target Marketing Lights Smoky Fire," *Chicago Tribune* (March 16, 1990), p. 1.
[6]Paul Cotton, "Tobacco Foes Attack Ads that Target Women, Minorities, Teens and the Poor," *Journal of the American Medical Association* (September 26, 1990), p. 1505.

lung cancer and heart disease were quick to attack this as a blatant appeal to women.

Another group was especially upset. In some Native American languages, *dakota* means friend. Yet, to a group that already had high rates of smoking addiction, such a brand name seemed a betrayal.

Controversies over Tobacco Company Sponsorships

As a result of the 1971 ban on the use of TV and radio cigarette commercials, the tobacco companies desperately sought other media in which to place their hundreds of millions of advertising dollars. They were fairly successful in doing so, but by the early 1990s serious questions were being raised about their use of certain media.

For example, there were great criticisms and aggressive actions taken against billboards promoting cigarettes and alcohol in African-American communities. Advertising support of black media by tobacco companies was also coming under fire, yet such support for many years existed in a vacuum, with few other major firms and industries supporting advertising in black media.

Tobacco company support for minority organizations also began to be questioned. The National Association of Black Journalists turned down a $40,000 Philip Morris donation: "We couldn't take money from an organization deliberately targeting minority populations with a substance that clearly causes cancer," said the group's president, Thomas Morgan. "We simply became more aggressive in our fund-raising so we could do without it."[7] But for many small minority publications, this was not an option: They would simply have folded without the advertising dollars furnished by tobacco companies.

Women's organizations also are beholden to support from the tobacco industry, which has liberally provided money to such groups at a time when other sources were virtually nonexistent. As a major example of such support, Virginia Slims brought women's tennis into prominence at a time when no one else would. And this issue raises another major controversy, discussed in the following box.

The Old Joe Camel Controversy

In 1988 R. J. Reynolds Tobacco Company stumbled upon a promotional theme for its slumping Camel brand. Using a sunglass-clad, bulbous-nosed cartoon camel that it called Joe, it instituted a $75 million-a-year advertising

[7]Ibid., p. 1506.

ISSUE BOX

TOBACCO COMPANY SPONSORSHIP OF ATHLETIC EVENTS

Is it right to allow tobacco companies to sponsor certain athletic events? What seems like a simple and uncontroversial question becomes far more complex when we consider the sponsorship of tennis tournaments such as Virginia Slims. There is no longer any doubt that cigarette smoking causes serious damage to the heart and lungs, yet tennis requires top physical fitness and aerobic capacity.

Although the sponsorship of athletic events came about as the industry sought alternative media after being banned from TV and radio, cigarette company sponsorship has particular advantages from the industry's perspective. It creates the false association of cigarette smoking with vitality and good health, and it directly targets women. The company is essentially taking advantage of the inadequate funding of women's sports by making itself a strong presence in this sector.

So we have an unhealthy product—as almost all experts but the tobacco industry stoutly maintain—sponsoring a prestigious athletic event for women, an event that would probably never be able to exist without such funding. Do we refuse to accept this sponsorship? Do we ban all cigarette promotions that appear to have some tie-in with health and fitness? Does the evil outweigh the good?

INVITATION TO DISCUSSION

You are a feminist leader with convictions that women's athletic events should be promoted more strongly. The major source of funding for tennis and golf tournaments has been the tobacco industry, with no alternative sponsors likely in the near future. Discuss your position regarding the acceptability of tobacco company sponsorships. What is your position on this controversy? Present your rationale as persuasively as you can.

---

campaign. The company featured Joe in an array of macho gear and targeted the campaign to appeal to younger male smokers who had been deserting the Camel brand in droves.

The campaign was an outstanding success. In only three years, Camel's share of sales among the 18- to 24-year age group almost doubled, from 4.4 percent to 7.9 percent.

But the appeal of Old Joe went far beyond the target age group. It was too potent. It was found to be highly effective in reaching young people, especially children under 13. Children were enamored with the camel character. Six-year olds in the United States recognized Joe Camel at a rate nearly equal to their recognition of Mickey Mouse.[8]

[8]Judann Dagnoli, "'JAMA' Lights New Fire Under Camel's Ads," *Advertising Age* (December 16, 1991), pp. 3, 32.

According to another study published in the *Journal of the American Medical Association*, teenagers are far better able than adults to identify the Camel logo. Children as young as three could even identify the cartoon character with cigarettes. Of even more concern, Camel's share of the market of underage children who smoke is nearly 33 percent, up from less than a percentage point before the Old Joe campaign. See Table 24.1 for the results of the survey.

THE PROTESTS EXPAND

Uptown

Critics of Uptown initially focused attention on its billboard advertising in African-American neighborhoods. They soon expanded their protests beyond a single cigarette brand to cigarettes in general and to alcohol and began whitewashing offending billboards. Their only recourse, they argued, was to use civil disobedience to attract attention to their cause. Maintaining that they had nothing against billboards in general, protestors demanded more educational themes as well as such wholesome products as orange juice for these billboards in these neighborhoods.

Dr. Harold Freeman, director of surgery at Harlem Hospital, is coauthor of a study that found that men in Harlem have a lower life expectancy than men in Bangladesh, at least partly because of alcohol and tobacco use. Speaking to an audience at Harlem's Abyssinian Baptist Church, Dr. Freeman asked, "Is it ethical, is it moral, to sell cigarettes and alcohol specifically to a community that is dying at a much higher rate than others?"[9] And with this, the church's pastor, Reverend Calvin O. Butts III, led his flock out of the church and throughout the city, painting signs with black paint to denote their Afrocentric perspective.

Table 24.1 Survey Results of Knowledge and Attitudes Regarding Camel's Old Joe Advertisements

	Students	Adults
Have seen Old Joe	97.7%	72.2%
Know the product	97.5	67.0
Think ads look cool	58.0	39.9
Like Joe as friend	35.0	14.4
Smokers who identify Camel as favorite brand	33.0	8.7

Source: Data from the *Journal of the American Medical Assn.*, as presented in Walecia Konrad, "I'd Toddle a Mile for a Camel," *Business Week* (December 23, 1991), 34. The results are based on a survey of 1055 students, ages 12 to 19 years, and 345 adults, aged 21 to 87 years.

[9]Ibid.

The agitation against billboards was by no means limited to Harlem. In Dallas, for example, County Commissioner John Wiley Price led a group that whitewashed 25 billboards, resulting in arrests and misdemeanor charges. And Chicago priest Michael Pfleger was also arrested for allegedly painting billboards and throwing paint at a billboard company employee.

Antismoking and antibillboard activists were having a field day. California launched a $28.6 million antismoking campaign using money from cigarette taxes. Similarly, the Office of Substance Abuse Policy began a nationwide 7000-billboard campaign targeting drug and alcohol abuse.

Business began heeding the mounting pressure. In June 1990 the Outdoor Advertising Association of America, representing 80 percent of billboard companies, announced a new policy encouraging its members to keep billboard ads for products that are illegal for minors at least 500 feet from schools as well as from places of worship and hospitals. The association also recommended voluntary limits on the number of billboards that advertise cigarettes and alcohol in any given area, such as minority neighborhoods. Gannet Outdoor, the largest billboard company in North America, began putting decals on billboards near schools and churches indicating that no alcohol or tobacco ads were to be posted there.

Assessment of the Controversy of Targeting Minorities. Was R. J. Reynolds Company an ogre, as some critics depicted it? Or were the critics self-seeking extremists more interested in publicity and crying wolf when the wolf was really rather toothless?

Without question, inner-city African-Americans have shown higher rates of tobacco and alcohol use than their suburban contemporaries; they also have higher incidences of the accompanying health problems. And despite a few weak company disclaimers, there can be little doubt that tobacco firms thought they had developed a new and effective market targeting strategy. The dispute hinges on this question:

> Are certain minority groups—such as African-Americans and women—particularly susceptible to marketing blandishments so that they need to be protected from potentially unsafe products?

Although the proponents of controls argue that certain groups, such as young blacks, need such protection, others see that protection as paternalism. Even some black leaders decry the billboard whitewashing and the contentious preachings of certain ministers. To Adolph Hauntz, president of the Dallas Merchants and Concessionaires Association, whitewashing signs "treats blacks as if we are a stupid bunch of people that are overly influenced by billboards." And former NAACP Executive Director Benjamin

Hooks makes the same point, condemning billboard whitewashing for "saying that white people have enough sense to read the signs and disregard them and black people don't."[10] Certainly tempting people is hardly the same as oppressing them. After all, no one has to buy cigarettes and alcohol.

Butts, Sullivan, and others countered that comments such as those of Hooks simply reflected the tobacco and alcohol industries' success in muting criticisms of their minority targeting policies by their large donations to such groups as the NAACP, the United Negro College Fund, and the National Urban League.

Regardless of the pro and con arguments concerning the susceptibility of inner-city youth to advertisements for unhealthy products, there is more validity to the contentions of susceptibility when we consider the vulnerability of children to the attractive and sophisticated models found in most of these commercials.

Finally, if local, state, or federal legislation is enacted to ban certain products from being promoted on billboards, as was done with radio and TV advertising two decades ago, where should the line be drawn? Should promotions in minority neighborhoods be banned for products that are economically extravagant, such as expensive athletic shoes? Or should promotions be banned for high-cholesterol foods that might cause high blood pressure? Or for high-powered "muscle" cars?

Joe Camel

Not surprisingly, a storm of criticism ensued after the American Medical Association's disclosure of the study that found that Joe Camel appealed far more to children than to adults. Health advocates demanded that the Federal Trade Commission ban the ads. Surgeon General Antonia Novella took the unprecedented step of asking RJR to cancel its campaign voluntarily. Even *Advertising Age* published an editorial entitled "Old Joe Must Go."[11] The basis for the concern, of course, was that the popular ads might encourage underage children to start smoking.

RJR refused to yield. It denied that the ads are effective with children: "Just because children can identify our logo doesn't mean they will use the product."[12] Defensively, Reynolds moved to counter the bad press. It distributed pamphlets and bumper stickers and put up billboards discouraging kids from smoking, and it stoutly maintained its right to freedom of speech.

---

[10]Wildavsky, op. cit., p. 20.
[11]"Old Joe Must Go," *Advertising Age* (January 13, 1992).
[12]Ibid.

Assessment of the Old Joe Controversy. Some advertising people believed RJR's stubbornness was badly misguided: "RJR . . . is taking a huge chance. By placing Old Joe as a freedom-of-speech issue instead of an unintentional marketing overshoot, the conglomerate risks goading Congress into bans and restrictions on all tobacco advertising. Lawmakers might, for instance, look more favorably on legislation just introduced . . . which would shift responsibility for tobacco products to the Food and Drug Administration [which] could regulate the tobacco industry into oblivion."[13]

Old Joe was a marketing success beyond all management expectation. But in a time of increasingly critical attention by society, should any firm in a sensitive industry hold itself aloof from a groundswell of denunciations? Are some bumper stickers and billboards with messages to discourage kids from smoking likely to be more than token and impotent efforts, given the popularity of a cartoon character that commands virtually as much recognition and affection as Mickey Mouse?

Then this thought may be raised (while we hesitate to denigrate any firm): Could it be that targeting the young is seen as a long-range strategy for gaining future smokers? Perish the thought! See the following box for identification of more cigarette issues.

ISSUE BOX

CIGARETTES AND SMOKING

The controversies concerning cigarettes go beyond those detailed in this chapter.

- Should smoking be restricted in the workplace? In restaurants? In airplanes?
- What about some firms not allowing employees to smoke even when they are not at work?
- Should the tobacco industry pay for employee suits concerning their "right to smoke"?
- Should nonsmokers be protected against passive smoke?
- In general, are the rights of smokers being violated?

INVITATION TO DISCUSSION
Discuss, and even debate, these questions and any other smoking issues you come up with.

---

[13]Craig Stoltz, "RJR Appears Intent on Sticking with Old Joe to the Bitter End," *Adweek Eastern Edition* (March 23, 1992), p. 18.

TARGETING FOREIGN MARKETS

With increasing restraints on cigarette advertising in the United States and the steadily diminishing per capita consumption of cigarettes, it is not surprising that the industry began focusing greater attention on foreign markets. Unfortunately for cigarette makers, criticisms and restraints did not long remain subdued in these markets, either.

At least as early as 1984, the Royal College of Physicians in the United Kingdom harshly denounced tobacco usage, stating that smoking killed 100,000 people a year in the United Kingdom and resulted in 50 million lost working days a year.[14] But the Royal College particularly condemned the lack of availability of low-tar cigarettes, "which are practically unknown in the Third World. The incidence of lung cancer among men in the Natal Bantustan in South Africa has increased 600 percent in the last 11 years. Developed countries bear a heavy responsibility for the worldwide epidemic of smoking."[15]

By 1990 *The New York Times* was reporting strong criticisms by women's groups and health organizations in India over attempts to promote Ms, a new cigarette brand aimed at upwardly mobile Indian women. Billboards and print ads for the products showed strong, happy Indian women in Western-style clothes and affluent settings. Opposition groups condemned the "evil message that cigarette smoking is part of a healthy and logical way of feminine life."[16]

Despite intense lobbying by the tobacco industry, two European Community directives on tobacco advertising were proposed by the European Commission in 1989. The first, barring television advertisements, was readily accepted by EC governments and went into effect in October 1991. The second directive would ban other advertising and was backed by the European Parliament. This measure awaiting passage would ban tobacco advertising in "any form of communication, printed, written, oral, by radio and television broadcast and cinema." Even logos on cigarette lighters and matches would be forbidden. The tobacco industry, which claimed there was no link between tobacco publicity and the 430,000 deaths a year in Europe from smoking-related diseases, not surprisingly was frantic at this possible outcome.[17] But John Major, Prime Minister of Great Britain, opposed the measure, and a minority of countries were likely to block it

---

[14]"Developing Countries: Governments Should Take Action Against Cigarettes before Too Many People Acquire the Potentially Lethal Habit," *New Scientist* (December 1, 1983), p. 42.

[15]*Ibid.*

[16]"Women in Delhi Angered by Smoking Pitch," *The New York Times* (National Edition), (March 18, 1990), p. 11.

[17]"EP Backs Ban on Tobacco Advertising," *Europe 2000* (March 1992), p. R41.

temporarily. (However, bans on print ads for tobacco are already in force in such EC countries as France, Italy, and Portugal.)

With Western Europe's mounting inhospitality to the industry, U.S. tobacco firms today are eagerly pushing into Asia, Africa, Eastern Europe, and the former Soviet Union. These markets are big—$90 billion a year—and the local cigarette makers appear highly vulnerable to the slick and aggressive efforts of U.S. firms. For example, Marlboro's cowboy is even more widely known in most of Asia than it is in the United States. As a result, Philip Morris can get its message across simply by playing the brand's theme song or flashing a single image of the cowboy.[18]

For years, Western companies were kept out of these lucrative markets by governments eager to preserve state tobacco monopolies or anticapitalist ideologies, but these barriers have crumbled, especially in Eastern Europe. Tobacco companies have been invited into enormous new markets such as the former Soviet Union, where "cigarette famines" have long existed. Now Philip Morris is shipping billions of cigarettes to Russia.

Countries in the expanding sales area have few marketing or health labeling controls. In Hungary, for example, Marlboro cigarettes are even handed out to young fans at pop music concerts.[19]

In Asia, foreign tobacco firms had to crack protectionist tariffs and import bans before entering these markets. The United States was successful in using Section 301 of its 1974 Trade Act to threaten retaliatory tariffs on the exports of such countries as Japan, South Korea, Taiwan, and Thailand if their markets were not opened to U.S. tobacco firms. Tobacco-state representatives in Congress have been strong influences in such pressures, and they were successful in opening up these markets. By 1992 cigarette advertising on television in Japan—not allowed in the United States—had soared from fortieth to second place in air time since 1987 and even appears during children's shows. Smoking has greatly increased among women, who were largely ignored before the Western firms arrived but are now prime targets. Tobacco companies found good market potential among women in such Asian areas as Hong Kong, where fewer than 5 percent of women smoke. Philip Morris is tapping this market with its Virginia Slims, a feminine brand famous for its slogan "You've come a long way, baby."[20]

Assessment of the Overseas Push by U.S. Tobacco Firms. A firm seems entitled to make all the profit it can make. If certain markets are drying up

---

[18]Mike Levin, "U.S. Tobacco Firms Push Eagerly into Asian Market," *Marketing News* (January 21, 1991), p. 2.

[19]"The Tobacco Trade: The Search for El Dorado," *Economist* (May 16, 1992), p. 23.

[20]Ibid., p. 24.

or are being severely constrained, should not a firm have the right to seek other markets aggressively? This is what the tobacco companies are doing.

The issue is clouded because cigarette smoking is generally conceded to be hazardous to health, though the health risks are not immediate. As long as many people are willing to take the risk, how can the tobacco makers and growers and advertisers and retailers be so negatively judged?

When sophisticated and aggressive promotional efforts are directed at the developing countries where consumers are more easily swayed and far more vulnerable to promotional blandishments, does our perception of what is ethical and what is undesirable conduct change? Should it?

HEALTH CLUB ABUSES

Over the last few decades, more and more Americans have turned to the pursuit of physical fitness, which is promoted as a means to a more attractive and satisfactory lifestyle and also as an assurance of healthy longevity. Many people have joined health clubs for the equipment and expertise to pursue such healthy lifestyles and for the social encouragement that they need to persevere in these efforts. Alas, some health clubs have failed their dedicated fitness seekers. Some have evinced outright fraud in their solicitation of memberships; most have shown the extremes of high-pressure selling; others have been built on flimsy financial structures and have closed, taking the money of members who have paid advance fees or leaving them no alternative memberships.

Health Club Closings

Some health clubs have fraudulently solicited memberships with the intention to fold their tents and slink away when sufficient funds are gained, leaving their erstwhile patrons with little recourse while the promoters count their gains. But it is a thin line between such scams and the enterprise that is poorly funded, poorly planned, and cannot survive and thus presents its patrons with the same consequences, even though the intent may not have been quite so evil.

Business Atlanta pointed out such problems in the Atlanta area where health clubs folded and left their members stranded. For example, the two largest facilities in the area, Richard Simmons Anatomy Asylum and Mademoiselle Spa Figure and Fitness, together generated 1500 complaints to the state Office of Consumer Affairs. Four smaller clubs also went under for a total of 57 clubs that closed, out of 122 listed in the yellow pages.

People complaining about useless health club contracts say their spas showed no hint of impending disaster. For example, Nancy George got little use out of her $500 Richard Simmons membership before that center folded. She said to reporters, "I was cheated out of a lot of money, and it just closed down on me with no warning. I was worried, too, because one of the other clubs had been in trouble, so I asked the managers who ran my club about it. They assured me it would not close."[21] But close it did, with no warning.

Barry Reid, administrator of the governor's Office of Consumer Affairs, noted that a major problem was that spas asked for large amounts of money in advance. While they operated under the guise of legitimacy, some clubs were set up from the beginning as a scam.[22]

In many instances of failed and/or closed health clubs, the members still owed money on their contracts. It would seem an easy solution for members simply to refuse to make any further payments. Alas, this solution was not that simple. Invariably, the health clubs had sold the contracts to a third party, a loan company, now supposedly an innocent holder in due course that was entitled to full recompense. Customers were threatened with the loss of their credit ratings if they did not continue paying for the defunct membership. (The information box discusses the traditional rights of the holder in due course and the consequences for the consumer.)

Defenders of the larger health club chains pointed out that they were operating completely within the law. Existing corporate rules permit a chain to set up many stores, each as an individual entity, so that the potential failure of one does not drag down the others. Therefore, the other units of a chain are insulated from the incompetencies and inefficiencies of some outlets.

High-Pressure Selling

High-pressure sales efforts have prevailed with many health clubs despite the fact that most potential customers are neither poor nor unsophisticated but are young professionals and executives who should be more resistant and turned off by high pressure.

The larger organizations appear to have been more successful in this type of selling. Because of greater resources than smaller health spas, they are able to use the media more effectively to bring potential clients to their premises. They can afford more impressive equipment, and they can hire people who are experienced in hard sell and whose own compensation and even jobs depend on how many contracts they can write.

Potential customers, even though they may be well educated and with good jobs, seem particularly vulnerable to appeals to health, beauty, and

---

[21]Maxine Rock, "Health Club Hijinks," *Business Atlanta* (October 1988), p. 104.
[22]Ibid.

INFORMATION BOX

THE HOLDER IN DUE COURSE CONTROVERSY

Traditional legal doctrine prescribes that when a seller sells a note or credit contract to a third party such as a bank or loan company, this new owner is the innocent holder in due course; the purchaser must pay the full amount of the obligation to this third party *regardless* of his or her satisfaction with the purchase, whether it is even usable or, in the case of health club memberships, even in business. Thus the rights of the third party are fully protected, whereas the purchaser's rights are no longer protected once the credit obligation has been sold to a third party.

You can see the inequity this system can impose on the innocent purchaser. Not to pay the full amount of the contract can bring legal action and destroy a credit rating. No wonder the purchasers of memberships in health clubs that went under feared to stop their payments. The injustice for the consumer of holder in due course obligations has come under public scrutiny, and some states have moved to modify the full ramifications of this law of long standing.

For example, in 1984 laws regulating health clubs in Georgia were enacted requiring reimbursement of members on defunct spa contracts through posting by the club of a bond or a letter of credit with the state. The law also stated that consumers have the right to refuse payment to a finance company holding the contract under certain circumstances, even under the holder in due course rule. Consumers must notify the finance company in writing of their intention to cease monthly payments and explain why they are doing so, but many persons are unclear about the law and fear consequent actions by finance companies for nonpayment.

INVITATION TO DISCUSSION
Either to enforce the holder in due course rule or to rescind it poses inequities. The innocent third party is protected with the rule; the innocent consumer is better protected if it is rescinded. As a state legislator considering the issue of rescinding, how will you try to resolve the issue? How will you balance off the competing claims? Which position do you expect to carry the most weight, and why?

---

social attractiveness. Such emotional appeals, when coupled with the right atmosphere of attractive customers and employees, can be powerfully persuasive. Strenuous efforts to induce the potential customer, often called a "target," to make a commitment on the spot often succeed.

With employees themselves under pressure to make the sale—in some cases under surveillance through monitoring devices and one-way mirrors—the unscrupulous health spa has reasonable assurance that only the most sales-resistant potential customers will be "allowed" to escape.

State Efforts to Curb Abusive Practices

A number of states have attempted to regulate health clubs more closely. For example, Pennsylvania Attorney General LeRoy S. Zimmerman testified before the state legislature in support of a bill for a health club act that was drafted by the state House Consumer Affairs Committee.

The attorney general displayed boxes filled with consumer complaints. He told the committee that in only five months his office had received more than 2500 complaints regarding health clubs.

In particular, the proposed legislation would require health clubs to post bonds or letters of credit to ensure that money would be available to reimburse clients if the facility closed. The bill would also remedy another frequent source of complaints, the decision by a health club with two or more locations to close one of these locations. Usually, such clubs refuse to give refunds to members who used the closed location, reasoning that those members can use one of the remaining locations. "This sounds reasonable, and may be acceptable to members when the other location is just down the street," Zimmerman noted. "But it is neither reasonable nor acceptable when, as happened recently, a club closed [one facility], and told members to use a related facility . . . more than 50 miles away."[23]

Other provisions needed to protect consumers would allow for cancellation of membership and a refund if the member dies, is disabled, or moves out of the area. And an important protection against high pressure to finalize the sale on the spot is a three-day waiting period after signing the contract, during which it can be canceled without penalty.

SMALL-LOAN COMPANY ABUSES

Most people needing personal loans are not financially sophisticated. California Attorney General John Van de Kamp noted that most of the victims of an alleged scam were poor people who were easy prey. "These are people who are often desperate," he said. "They're borrowing money for food for their children."[24]

The vulnerability of many such customers is increased by their youth (they lack experience) or advanced age (they may become easily confused and hesitant to ask for explanations or clarifications). Furthermore, many of these customers are in precarious financial situations and have few alternatives to doing business with a small loan company.

---

[23]"Pennsylvania Attorney General Speaks in Favor of H.B. 819, the `Health Club Act,'" *PR Newswire* (May 21, 1987), p. 8.

[24]Charles McCoy, "ITT Unit Settles Fraud Charges in California," *The Wall Street Journal* (September 22, 1989), p. A3.

Here, then, is a situation that can motivate loan companies to take less than scrupulously honest actions. While abuses are by no means limited to the following example, this particular large company epitomizes the type of questionable practices that can occur in this industry.

ITT Consumer Financial Corporation

ITT Consumer Financial Corporation is a unit of ITT (formerly called IT&T), a multinational firm diversified into such areas as communications, information and financial services, manufacturing, and hotels. ITT Consumer specializes in small consumer loans, and its practices have come to the critical attention of attorneys general in a number of states. The complaints have centered mostly on high-pressure selling techniques, inadequate or nonexistent disclosure that certain add-ons were optional and cost more, and uselessness of some of these add-ons. Added to these specific allegations against ITT were the more pervasive charges against most small loan firms in general: exorbitant interest rates and aggressive and abusive collection techniques.

The attorneys general were particularly concerned with "packing," a lucrative practice in which the lender adds payments for "optional" insurance and other products to the amount of the loan without the customer's requesting them, sometimes without the customer's knowledge either that they have been added or that they could have been refused. For example, take the case of Katherine Snow.

Needing money for Christmas, she sought out Wisconsin's biggest consumer-loan company, a division of ITT. It agreed to lend her $126.72. But Snow was also induced to borrow $14.74 for credit life insurance, $73.44 for property insurance, and $202 for term life insurance. Not satisfied with this, the lender also pressured her to become a member of the ITT Consumer Thrift Club, entitling her to discounts on consumer products. All of these add-ons were financed at interest rates above 22 percent.[25]

Although the company maintained in defense that its policies were to emphasize to customers that all these additional purchases were voluntary, internal company memoranda suggested otherwise—that branch managers were ordered to sell certain amounts of add-ons in connection with loans, or face disciplinary action.

The profitability in selling insurance with consumer loans has not gone unnoticed by other lenders. Banks, auto dealers, and other consumer-loan companies have also moved to tap this fertile field. But ITT's profi-

---

[25]Walt Bogdanish, "Irate Borrowers Accuse ITT's Loan Companies of Deceptive Practices," *The Wall Street Journal* (February 26, 1985), p. 1.

ciency was unsurpassed, with the result that a number of states either took or threatened legal action against ITT. An out-of-court settlement was reached with the Wisconsin attorney general whereby ITT agreed to return as much as $12 million to Wisconsin policyholders. A similar settlement was reached with the Iowa attorney general, and class action suits alleging insurance packing were pending against ITT in Wisconsin, Alabama, and Arizona. Minnesota and Colorado were also investigating the company's lending practices.

But the biggest case and decision occurred in California. In one of the largest settlements ever in a consumer fraud case, ITT Consumer Financial Corporation agreed to pay restitution, fines, and other penalties that could eventually total $100 million. The California Attorney General's Office had alleged that ITT defrauded thousands of California consumers by promising them preapproved credit, inducing them to take out loans that sometimes carried rates as high as 35 percent, and then illegally charging them for insurance, club memberships, and other services that the customers did not request and frequently had no idea they were paying for and receiving.[26]

In addition to complaints about packing, other complaints, such as the following, focused on bait and switch (as discussed in the information box on p. 382), exorbitant interest, and harassment.[27]

> Interest rates quoted over phone were 18.5 percent, raised to 28.5 percent when papers were signed.

> My loan was for $1200. When they finished in the end I was to pay back $3500.

> They harassed me at home and on my job and I was only a day late.

ASSESSMENT OF HEALTH CLUB AND SMALL-LOAN ABUSES

The examples described are hardly symptomatic of the entire business community's interactions with consumers. These are the exceptions to forthright conduct. But we have to recognize from these examples that consumers are vulnerable to abuse in at least two arenas:

1. When advance payments are required for services to be rendered later.
2. When consumers are in financial straits and are desperate for relief through loans.

---

[26]Charles McCoy, "ITT Unit Settles Fraud Charges in California," *The Wall Street Journal* (September 22, 1989), p. A3.
[27]A sample of an unpublished survey of small loan customers in Cleveland, Ohio, 1990.

INFORMATION BOX

BAIT AND SWITCH—WHEN IS IT ETHICAL?

In bait and switch, the customer is enticed into a store because of very low prices, only to find that such goods are "no longer available," and is then led to look at more expensive items. This practice can be deceptive and abusive. The abuse is more prevalent in minority neighborhood stores: An appliance or a set of furniture may be advertised at an unreasonably low price to entice customers into the store. But when they attempt to purchase the "sale" item they find it, in the parlance of retailing, "nailed to the floor." In other words, it is not available; the only piece at that price may be broken, shopworn, have missing parts, or carry a "sold" tag. The customer is then traded up to a more expensive and more profitable product.

But this is the extreme. It is commonplace for reputable retailers to advertise their most attractively priced items and then attempt to sell a customer something else. Some retailers even offer items below cost (so-called loss leaders) to generate customer traffic, expecting that regular-price items will be bought as well. Some weekly grocery ads use this technique. The difference between such bait-and-switch advertising and the deceptive kind is that the sale item is available; customers can buy it if they so desire (and some, indeed, may buy nothing else but loss leaders).

INVITATION TO DISCUSSION

Bait and switch, where the product or the price advertised is not available or the interest rate stated over the phone is incorrect, is illegal as well as unethical. Yet it is still practiced. What accounts for the pervasiveness of the practice, despite its illegality?

(We might propose another area offering great potential for consumer abuse: repair services, be these with automobiles, appliances, home repairs, or other items. Here most consumers are helpless before the expertise of the repair person in assessing the validity of the charges and parts replacements. We discussed the problem with auto repairs in Chapter 8.)

These situations create serious temptations for sellers to take advantage of naive and hapless consumers. When no repeat business is likely, at least in the short run, and when customer loyalty is not a major consideration, temptations will arise to overcharge even to the point of fraud.

It is evident today that large firms are the focus of regulatory attention and attorney general purview. These are the visible players in their respective industries. As we saw with the ITT small-loan investigations and the previously described allegations against Sears' auto servicing (Chapter 8), the social and legal environment today makes any large firm particularly vulnerable to public scrutiny, especially if its practices are not scrupulously honest. A small firm may be far more guilty of abuses but generally will escape most public condemnation.

WHAT CAN BE LEARNED?

Public perception of unethical conduct is growing, and large firms are particularly vulnerable. Formerly, deceptive practices or unsafe products were the most commonly condemned examples of misconduct. But as we have seen in this chapter, perceptions of misconduct have expanded. The ethical arena for a firm is no longer finite and predictable. It is a lurking quicksand for the unwary or the unconcerned. Consequently, the need for vigilance is greater, especially in large firms.

Effective strategies may need to be reconsidered today. Strategies accepted in the past may no longer be appropriate and may even be vulnerable to public protests, boycotts, negative publicity, and governmental pressure and regulation. How is a firm to cope with this changed environment?

The answer seems to lie in increased sensitivity, especially concerning relations with minorities, whether of race, sex, or other categories. A new brand or a new strategy should be carefully assessed for its acceptability and freedom from potential criticism before widespread introduction. Even then, surprises may come. Stoutly maintaining a strategy in the face of mounting opposition may not be the best course of action: Sometimes criticism may necessitate scrapping a successful product, brand, or advertising campaign to prevent bad publicity and protect future sales.

Beware transferring unacceptable actions to another environment. Cigarette firms, finding the domestic market hostile to aggressive promotions, turned their efforts to more hospitable sectors and countries. Not many years ago, such efforts would have been effective and would have activated little critical attention or publicity. Today, however, criticism tends to become contagious, even though oceans may separate the activists. A firm may no longer be insulated from adverse publicity and possible punitive regulations when it attempts to move aggressively into minority sectors and foreign markets.

Issue: Does a vocal minority represent acceptable behavior in aggressively promoting its own self-interest? In a pluralistic society, minorities are encouraged to present their positions. The issue becomes one of degree: What level of critical behavior is acceptable? Is whitewashing or destroying billboards acceptable behavior? Is firebombing the stores of opportunistic shopowners of different ethnic origins acceptable? Where do we draw the line?

Unfortunately, there is no common ground for society's approval; inconsistencies abound. For example, most people view burning stores to be unacceptable, but many find whitewashing offending billboards to be acceptable. Where should the line be drawn, and who is to be the judge: A preacher? A government agency? The police department? The courts?

Issue: Is it ethically right for a firm to vigorously promote a product seen by most as unsafe and even deadly? This issue points directly at the tobacco industry. Generally considered by health experts as dangerous and, in the long term, life threatening, tobacco smoking is still protected by powerful governmental interests.

The industry stubbornly refuses to admit the health charges, citing its own research to the contrary. The industry is huge, with many stakeholders: tobacco growers, processors, retailers, tax collectors. And many of these stakeholders have influential proponents in the halls of government. Not the least of the proponents are the users themselves, even though their numbers are declining. Smokers discount the health dangers as being far in the future and affecting only a minority of users.

The morality? It is easy for stakeholders to rationalize that any bad consequences are uncertain at best, that the good outweighs any bad possibilities. But somehow, some of us are left with the sneaky feeling that maybe, just maybe, the profit motive is deemed stronger than any possible dire consequences to customers.

Heavy selling incentives invite abusive practices in such consumer service areas as health clubs, small-loan firms, and repair businesses. Selling incentives such as lucrative commissions, bonuses, and sales targets encourage aggressive selling. These almost invariably lead to high-pressure tactics, but they also may stimulate false promises, fraudulent claims, and the attitude that "the customer is prey." The poor, the elderly, and the young and unsophisticated are particularly vulnerable. As we saw with the health clubs, however, even the well educated and affluent can be vulnerable. Particularly in the repair area, incentives promote padded and phony diagnoses to bilk the consumer.

INVITATION

Can you think of other learning insights related to these ethical issues?

QUESTIONS

1. Most of the patrons of health clubs are educated and have fairly good incomes and jobs. How do you account for their susceptibility to high pressure, fraud, and other abuses?

2. Amid the rather large number of small-loan firms, shouldn't a consumer be able to shop around for the best deal and thus escape the worst of the abuses mentioned in the chapter?
3. How do you feel about activist ministers leading their followers to whitewash offensive billboards? Is tearing down such billboards acceptable? Please discuss this issue as objectively as possible.
4. Do you consider the proof adequate that cigarettes pose a substantial health threat and should be banned or tightly constrained? If you accept this position, should tobacco growers be allowed to continue growing such "unsafe" harvests?
5. Playing devil's advocate (one who argues an opposing point for the sake of argument), what arguments can you put forth that cigarette manufacturers should be permitted complete freedom in targeting developing countries?
6. What is the ethical difference between promoting and selling cigarettes, and promoting fatty, cholesterol-laden foods?
7. Are the rights of non-smokers being too highly emphasized? Do smokers have any rights?

INVITATION TO ROLE PLAY

1. You are the public relations spokesperson for a major cigarette maker. How do you defend your company's aggressive marketing practices in developing countries?
2. You are a young African-American woman who uses Uptown cigarettes and likes them. At a church outing, your minister denounces Uptowns and the company that makes them. Describe how you might respond to such a tirade against your favorite brand.
3. You are the chief executive of a chain of small-loan outlets. After hearing the bad publicity about the alleged practices of ITT's Consumer Loan Division, you want to be certain that your managers and employees are not guilty of similar practices. What policies might you establish to minimize abuses in your business?

INVITATION TO RESEARCH

1. Has the hubbub over minority targeting by cigarette companies subsided?
2. What is the most current situation regarding overseas incursions by U.S. tobacco companies?
3. Have the abuses in the small-loan industry been fairly well corrected? How about home and auto repairs?

25

Contrast—Johnson & Johnson's Tylenol: Regaining Public Trust—and Yet . . . ?

It is a surprising anomaly that a firm (or a person) can exhibit exemplary behavior, yet later fall to a lower common denominator of conduct. In its handling of a catastrophe of major proportions, the criminal and deadly contamination of its highly profitable Tylenol capsules, Johnson & Johnson exhibited what has become a model for corporate responsibility to its customers, regardless of costs. Yet in a later day, the company has come under fire for price gouging with one of its cancer drugs.

PRELUDE

It was September 30, 1982. On the fifth floor of the Johnson & Johnson (J & J) headquarters in New Brunswick, New Jersey, Chairman James E. Burke was having a quiet meeting with President David R. Clair. The two top executives of the company liked to hold such informal meetings every two months to talk over important but nonpressing matters that they usually did not get around to dealing with in the normal course of events. That day both men had reason to feel good, for J & J's sales and earnings were up sharply and the trend of business could hardly have been more promising. They even had time to dwell on some nonbusiness matters that sunny September morning.

Their complacency and self-satisfaction did not last long. Arthur Quill, a member of the executive committee, burst into the meeting. Consternation and anguish flooded the room as he brought word of cyanide deaths in

Chicago that were connected to J & J's most important and profitable product, Extra-Strength Tylenol capsules.

THE PRODUCT

The success of Tylenol in the late 1970s and early 1980s had been sensational. It had been introduced in 1955 by McNeil Laboratories as an alternative drug to aspirin, one that avoided aspirin's side effects. In 1959 Johnson & Johnson had acquired McNeil Laboratories, and the company ran it as an independent subsidiary.

By 1974 Tylenol sales had grown to $50 million at retail, primarily achieved through heavy advertising to physicians. A national consumer advertising campaign, instituted in 1976, proved very effective. By 1979 Tylenol had become the largest selling health and beauty aid in drug and food mass merchandising, breaking the 18-year domination of Procter & Gamble's Crest toothpaste. By 1982 Tylenol had captured 35.3 percent of the over-the-counter analgesic market. This was more than the market shares of Bayer, Bufferin, and Anacin combined. Table 25.1 shows the competitive positions of Tylenol and its principal competitors in this analgesic market. Total sales of all Tylenol products went from $115 million in 1976 to $350 million in 1982, a whopping 204 percent increase in a highly competitive market. As such, Tylenol accounted for 7 percent of all J & J sales. More important, it contributed 17 percent of all profits.

Then catastrophe struck.

THE COMPANY

Johnson & Johnson manufactures and markets a broad range of health care products in many countries of the world. Table 25.2 shows the various categories of products and their percent of total corporate sales. In 1981 J & J was number 68 on the *Fortune* 500 list of the largest industrial companies in the United States, and it had sales of $5.4 billion. It was organized into four

Table 25.1 Market Shares of Major Brands—Over-the-Counter Analgesic Market, 1981

Brand	Percent of Market
Tylenol	35.3
Anacin	13
Bayer	11
Excedrin	10.1
Bufferin	9

Source: "A Death Blow for Tylenol?" Business Week (October 18, 1982) p. 151.

Table 25.2   Contribution to Total Johnson & Johnson Sales of Product
Categories, 1983

Product Classification	Sales (Millions)	Percent of Total Company Sales
Surgical and First-Aid Supplies	$1,268	21%
Pharmaceuticals	1,200	20
Sanitary Napkins and Tampons	933	16
Baby Products	555	9
Diagnostic Equipment	518	9
Tylenol and Variants	460	8
Other (includes hospital supplies, dental products, contraceptives	1,039	17
Total	$5,973	100%

Source: "After Its Recovery, New Headaches for Tylenol," Business Week (May 14, 1984) p.137.

industry categories: professional, pharmaceutical, industrial, and consumer. The professional division included products such as ligatures, sutures, surgical dressings, and other surgery-related items. The pharmaceutical division included prescription drugs, and the industrial area included textile products, industrial tapes, and fine chemicals.

The largest division was the consumer division, consisting of toiletries and hygienic products such as baby care items, first aid products, and nonprescription drugs. These products were marketed primarily to the general public and distributed through wholesalers and directly to independent and chain retail outlets.

Tylenol was one of the major brands included in the consumer division. An acetaminophen-based, or nonaspirin, analgesic, it was the most profitable product for Johnson & Johnson in the early 1980s.

Through the years, J & J had assiduously worked to cultivate an image of responsibility and trust. Its products were associated with gentleness and safety—for all customers, from babies to the elderly. The corporate sense of responsibility fully covered the products and actions of any firms that it acquired, such as McNeil Laboratories.

THE CRISIS

The catastrophe started on a Wednesday morning in late September 1982. Adam Janus had a minor chest pain, so he purchased a bottle of Extra-Strength Tylenol capsules. He took one capsule and was dead by midafternoon. Later that same day, Stanley Janus and his wife also took capsules from the same bottle—both were dead by Friday afternoon. By the weekend four more Chicago-area residents had died under similar circumstances. The cause of death was cyanide, a deadly poison that can kill within 15 minutes by disrupting the blood's ability to carry oxygen through the body, thereby affecting the heart, lungs, and brain. The cyanide had been used to contaminate Extra-Strength Tylenol capsules. Dr. Thomas Kim, chief of the critical care unit of Northwest Community Hospital in Arlington Heights, Illinois, noted, "The victims never had a chance. Death was certain within minutes."[1]

Medical examiners retrieved bottles from the victims' homes and found another 10 capsules laced with cyanide. In each case the red half of the capsule was discolored and slightly swollen, and its usual dry white powder had been replaced with a gray substance that had an almond odor. One of the capsules had 65 mg of cyanide—a lethal dose is considered to be 50 mg.

The McNeil executives learned of the poisonings from reporters calling for comment about the tragedy—calls came from all the media, and then from pharmacies, doctors, hospitals, poison control centers, and hundreds of panicky consumers. McNeil quickly gathered information on the victims, causes of deaths, lot numbers on the poisoned Tylenol bottles, outlets where they had been purchased, dates when they had been manufactured, and the route they had taken through the distribution system.

After the deaths were linked to Tylenol, one of the biggest consumer alerts ever took place. Johnson & Johnson recalled batches and advised consumers not to take any Extra-Strength Tylenol capsules until the mystery had been solved. Drugstores and supermarkets across the country pulled Tylenol products from their shelves; it soon became virtually impossible to obtain Tylenol anywhere.

Those tracking down the mysterious contamination quickly determined that the poisoning did not occur in manufacturing, either intentionally or accidentally. The poisoned capsules had come from lots manufactured at both McNeil plants. Therefore, the tampering had to have happened in Chicago, since poisoning at both plants at the same time would have been almost impossible. The FDA suspected that someone unconnected with the manufacturer had bought the Tylenol over the counter, inserted cyanide in some capsules, then returned the bottles to the stores. Otherwise, the contamination would have been widespread, and not only in the Chicago area.

At this point, Johnson & Johnson was virtually cleared of any wrongdoing, but the company was stuck with having one of its major products publicly associated with poison and death, no matter how innocent it was. Perhaps the task of coping with the devastating impact of the tragedy would have been easier for Johnson & Johnson if the perpetrator were conclusively identified and caught. This was not to be, despite a special task force of 100 FBI agents and Illinois investigators who chased down more than 2000 leads and filed 57 volumes of reports.[2]

---

[1]Susan Tifft, "Poison Madness in the Midwest,"*Time* (October 11, 1982), p. 18.
[2]"Tylenol Comes Back as Case Grows Cold," *Newsweek* (April 25, 1983), p. 16.

COMPANY REACTION

Johnson & Johnson decided to elevate the management of the crisis to the corporate level and a game plan developed that company executives hoped would ensure eventual recovery. The game plan consisted of three phases: Phase I was to figure out what had actually happened; Phase II was to assess and contain the damage; and Phase III was to try to get Tylenol back into the market.

The company that had always tried to keep a low profile now turned to the media to provide it with the most accurate and current information, as well as to help it prevent a panic. Twenty-five public relations specialists were recruited from Johnson & Johnson's other divisions to help McNeil's regular staff of 15. Advertising was suspended at first. All Tylenol capsules were recalled—31 million bottles with a retail value of more than $100 million. Through advertisements promising to exchange tablets for capsules, through 500,000 telegrams to doctors, hospitals, and distributors, and through statements to the media, J & J hoped to demystify the situation.

With proof that the tampering had not occurred in the manufacturing process, the company moved into Phase II. Financially it experienced immediate losses amounting to over $100 million, the bulk coming from the expense of buying unused Tylenol bottles from retailers and consumers and shipping them to disposal points. The cost of sending the telegrams was estimated at $500,000, and the costs associated with expected product liability suits were expected to run in the millions.

Of more concern to the management was the impact of the poisoning on the brand itself. Many predicted that Tylenol as a brand could no longer survive. Some suggested that Johnson & Johnson reintroduce the product under a new name to give it a fresh start and thus rid itself of the devastated brand image.

Surveys conducted by Johnson & Johnson about a month after the poisonings seemed to buttress the death of Tylenol as a brand name. In one survey 94 percent of the consumers were aware that Tylenol was involved with the poisonings. Although 87 percent of these respondents realized that the maker of Tylenol was not to blame for the deaths, 61 percent said they were not likely to buy Tylenol in the future. Even worse, 50 percent of the consumers said they would not use the Tylenol tablets either. The only promising result from the research was that 49 percent of the *frequent* users answered that they would eventually use Tylenol.[3]

The company found itself in a real dilemma. It wanted so much to keep the Tylenol name; after all, the acceptance had been developed by years of advertising. Now, was it all to be destroyed in a few days of adversity? On

---

[3]Thomas Moore, "The Fight to Save Tylenol," *Fortune,* (November 29, 1982), p. 48.

the one hand, if J & J brought Tylenol back too soon, before the hysteria had subsided, the product could die on the shelves. On the other hand, if the company waited too long to bring the product back, competitors might well gain an unassailable market share lead. The marketing research results were not entirely acceptable to Johnson & Johnson executives. One manager expressed the company's doubts: "The problem with consumer research is that it reflects attitudes and not behavior. The best way to know what consumers are really going to do is put the product back on the shelves and let them vote with their hands."[4] But what was the right timing?

Johnson & Johnson decided to rebuild the brand by focusing on the frequent users and then to expand to include other consumers. It hoped that a core of loyal users would want the product in both its tablet and capsule forms. In order to regain regular user confidence, J & J ran television commercials informing the public that the company would do everything it could to regain their trust. The commercials featured Dr. Thomas Gates, medical director of McNeil, urging consumers to continue to trust Tylenol: "Tylenol has had the trust of the medical profession and 100 million Americans for over 20 years. We value that trust too much to let any individual tamper with it. We want you to continue to trust Tylenol."[5]

Johnson & Johnson also tried to encourage Tylenol capsule users to switch to tablets, which are more difficult to sabotage. In an advertising campaign it offered to exchange tablets for capsules at no charge. In addition, it placed 76 million coupons in Sunday newspaper ads good for $2.50 toward the purchase of Tylenol.

Finally, it designed a tamper-resistant package to prevent the kind of tragedy that occurred in Chicago. Extra-strength capsules were now sold only in new triple-sealed packages. The flaps of the box were glued shut and were visibly torn apart when opened. The bottle's cap and neck were covered with a tight plastic seal printed with the company name, and the mouth of the bottle was covered with an inner foil seal. Both the box and the bottle were labeled, "Do Not Use If Safety Seals Are Broken." This triple-seal package cost an additional 2.4 cents per bottle, but Johnson & Johnson hoped it would instill consumer confidence in the safety of the product and spur sales. In addition, the company offered retailers higher-than-normal discounts—up to 25 percent on orders.

Consumers who said they had thrown away their Tylenol after the scare were given a toll-free number to call, and they received $2.50 in coupons too—in effect a free bottle, since bottles of 24 capsules or 30 tablets sold for about $2.50.

[4]Ibid., p.49
[5]Judith B. Gardner, "When a Brand Names Gets Hit by Bad News,"*U. S. News & World Report* (November 8, 1982), p. 71.

Over 2000 salespeople from all Johnson & Johnson domestic subsidiaries were mobilized to persuade doctors and pharmacists to again begin recommending Tylenol tablets to patients and customers. This was similar to the strategy initially used when the product was introduced some 25 years before.

The Outcome

Immediately after the crisis, J & J's market share plunged from 35.3 percent of the pain reliever market to below 7 percent. Competitors were quick to take advantage of the situation. Upjohn Company and American Home Products Corporation were seeking Food and Drug Administration permission to sell an over-the-counter version of ibuprofen, a popular prescription pain reliever. Upjohn also granted marketing rights for its brand, Nuprin, to Bristol-Myers Co., maker of Bufferin, Excedrin, and Datril. Upjohn's prescription brand, Motrin—a stronger formulation than Nuprin—was generating some $200 million in 1982, making Motrin the company's biggest-selling drug. And lurking in the wings was mighty Procter & Gamble Company (P&G), the world's heaviest advertiser. P&G was launching national ads for Norwich aspirin and was test-marketing a coated capsule containing aspirin granules.

Yet, there were some encouraging signs for J & J. When *Psychology Today* polled its readers regarding whether Tylenol would survive as a brand name, 92 percent thought Tylenol would survive the incident. This figure corresponded closely with the results of another survey conducted by Leo Shapiro, an independent market researcher, just two weeks after the deaths occurred, in which 91 percent said they would probably buy the product again.

Psychology Today tried to get at the roots of such loyalty and roused comments such as these:

> A 23-year old woman wrote that she would continue to use Tylenol because she felt that it was "tried and true."

> A 61-year old woman said that the company had been "honest and sincere."

> And a young man thought Tylenol was an easy name to say.[6]

Such survey results presaged an amazing comeback: J & J's conscientious actions paid off. By May 1983 Tylenol had regained almost all the market share lost the previous September; its market share reached 35 percent, which it held until 1986, when another calamity struck.

New industry safety standards had been developed by the over-the-counter drug industry in concert with the Food and Drug Administration for

---

[6]Carin Rubenstein, "The Tylenol Tradition,"*Psychology Today* (April 1983), p. 16.

tamper-resistant packaging. Marketers under law had to select a package "having an indicator or barrier to entry, which if breached or missing, can reasonably be expected to provide visible evidence to the consumer that the package has been tampered with or opened."[7] Despite toughened package standards, in February 1986, a Westchester, New York, woman died from cyanide-laced Extra-Strength Tylenol capsules. The tragedy of 3½ years before was being replayed. J & J immediately removed all Tylenol capsules from the market and offered refunds for capsules consumers had already bought.

Now the company made a major decision. It decided no longer to manufacture any over-the-counter capsules because it could not guarantee their safety from criminal contamination. Henceforth, the company would market only tablets and so-called caplets, which were coated and elongated tablets that are easy to swallow. This decision was expected to cost $150 million. The president explained: "People think of this company as extraordinarily trustworthy and responsible, and we don't want to do anything to damage that."[8]

By July 1986 Tylenol had regained most of the market share lost in February, and it now stood at 32 percent.

INGREDIENTS OF SUCCESS AND THE CONTRAST WITH A. H. ROBINS

Johnson & Johnson was truly a business success in its handling of the Tylenol problem. It overcame the worst kind of adversity, that in which human life was lost in association with one of its products. In only a few months it recouped most of its lost market share and regained its public image of corporate responsibility and trust. Admittedly, the injury to customers was by no means as great as that perpetrated by Robins and its Dalkon Shield; still, the public limelight was more intense, and the trauma of the deaths greater because of the way they occurred. What accounted for the success of J & J in overcoming the adversity?

We can identify five significant factors:

1. Keeping communication channels open.
2. Taking quick corrective action.
3. Keeping faith in the product.
4. Protecting the public image at all costs.
5. Aggressively bringing back the brand.

[7]"Package Guides Studied," *Advertising Age* (October 18, 1982), p. 82.
[8]Richard W. Stevenson, "Johnson & Johnson's Recovery," *The New York Times* (July 5, 1986), pp. 33–34.

Effective communication has seldom been better illustrated. It is vital to gain rapport with the media, to enlist their support and even their sympathy. And this is not easily done, for the press is inclined to sensationalize, criticize, and take sides against the big corporation. Johnson & Johnson gained the needed rapport through corporate openness and cooperation. In the early days of the disaster it sought good two-way communication, with the media furnishing information from the field while J & J gave full and honest disclosure of its internal investigation and corrective actions. For good rapport company officials need to be freely available and open to the press. Unfortunately, this usually goes against executives' natural bent so that a spirit of antipathy often is fostered—not so with J & J during its time of greatest trial.

When product safety is in jeopardy, quick corrective action must be taken, *regardless* of the cost. This usually means immediate recall of the affected product, and such action can run into many millions of dollars. Even if the fault lies with only an isolated batch of products, a firm may have to consider recalling them all, since the problem and danger can quickly become transferable to all items of that brand. Robin's grudging and delayed recall of the shield simply exacerbated the problem and led to costs many times greater than would have occurred if the recall had taken place years before, when the problems were first brought to light.

Johnson & Johnson kept faith with its products and brand name, despite the counsel of experts who thought that the Tylenol name should be abandoned and that public trust could never be regained. Of course the company was not at fault: There was no culpability, no carelessness. The cause was right. With Robins the situation was vastly different: The company was culpable, with research carelessness heaped on callous disregard for real and potential health problems associated with the product. Admittedly, in keeping faith with a product there is a thin line between a positive commitment and recalcitrant stubbornness to face up to any problem and accept any blame. Without J & J's faith in Tylenol, the company would have had no chance of resurrecting the product and its market share.

Johnson & Johnson strove to protect its public image of being a socially responsible and caring firm. (The following Information Box discusses *social responsibility* and presents the J & J credo regarding this.) If there was to be any chance for a fairly quick recovery from adversity, this public image had to be guarded, no matter how beset it was. While the plight of Tylenol was well known, the corrective actions were prompt and thorough, and many people were thus assured that safety was restored. We should note here that for the public image to be regained under adverse circumstances, the corrective actions must be well publicized. Public relations efforts and good communication with the media are essential for this. Of course, it helps when the fault of the catastrophe is clearly not the firm's.

INFORMATION BOX

SOCIAL RESPONSIBILITY AND THE JOHNSON & JOHNSON CREDO REGARDING IT

We can define social responsibility as the sense of responsibility a firm has for the needs of society, over and above its commitment to maximizing profits and stockholders interests. The following credo of J & J illustrates the wide circle of corporate social responsibility that more and more firms are beginning to accept.

JOHNSON & JOHNSON'S CREDO[9]

We believe our first responsibility is to the doctors, nurses, and patients, to mothers and all others who use our products and services. In meeting their needs everything we do must be of high quality. We must constantly strive to reduce our costs in order to maintain reasonable prices. Customers' orders must be serviced promptly and accurately. Our suppliers and distributors must have an opportunity to make a fair profit.

We are responsible to our employees, the men and women who work with us throughout the world. Everyone must be considered as an individual. We must respect their dignity and recognize their merit. They must have a sense of security in their jobs. Compensation must be fair and adequate, and working conditions clean, orderly, and safe. Employees must feel free to make suggestions and complaints. There must be equal opportunity for employment, development, and advancement for those qualified. We must provide competent management, and their actions must be just and ethical.

We are responsible to the communities in which we live and work and to the world community as well. We must be good citizens—support good works and charities and bear our fair share of taxes. We must encourage civic improvements and better health and education. We must maintain in good order the property we are privileged to use, protecting the environment and natural resources.

Our final responsibility is to our stockholders. Business must make a sound profit. We must experiment with new ideas. Research must be carried on, innovative programs developed and mistakes paid for. New equipment must be purchased, new facilities provided, and new products launched. Reserves must be created to provide for adverse times. When we operate according to these principles, the stockholders should realize a fair return.

Johnson & Johnson did a superb job of aggressively bringing back the Tylenol brand. In so doing, all efforts had to be coordinated: Efforts to safeguard the public image had to be reasonably successful; the cause of the disaster needed to be conclusively established; the likelihood of the event happening again had to be made virtually impossible. Then aggressive promotional efforts could fuel the recovery.

[9]From a company recruiting brochure.

Johnson & Johnson's efforts to come back necessarily focused on correcting the problem. Initially it designed a tamper-resistant container to prevent the kind of tragedy that had occurred in Chicago. Extra-strength capsules were now to be sold only in new triple-sealed packages. When another death occurred in 1986, the company dropped capsules entirely and offered Tylenol only in tablet form.

With the safety features in place, J & J then used heavy promotion. This included consumer advertising, with the theme of safety assurance and company social responsibility. J & J offered to exchange capsules for tablets at no charge. It offered millions of newspaper coupons good for $2.50 toward the purchase of Tylenol. Retailers were also given incentives to back Tylenol through discounts, advertising allowances, and full refunds for recalled capsules with all handling costs paid. These efforts, directed to consumers and retailers alike, bolstered dealer confidence in the resurgence of the brand.

INFORMATION BOX

RECENT DRUG PRICING ABUSES BY J & J?

In May 1992 publicity surfaced that Johnson & Johnson was guilty of "unconscionable" pricing of levamisole, the drug used to treat colon cancer. The charge came from a distinguished physician and cancer expert, Charles G. Moertel of the Mayo Comprehensive Cancer Center, at the annual meeting of the American Society of Clinical Oncology. Under Johnson & Johnson's brand name, Ergamisol, levamisole cost patients $1250 to $1500 for a year's supply.

The controversy arose not so much from the absolute price of a life-saving drug, but from its price relative to a 30-year-old veterinary version of the drug, which farmers used to treat their sheep for parasites. This version cost only $14. The dispute first came to light when an Illinois farmer being treated for cancer noticed that her pills contained the same active ingredients she used to deworm her sheep.

Under sponsorship of the National Cancer Institute, Dr. Moertel and others found that levamisole, combined with a staple chemotherapy drug, 5-fluorouracil, was spectacularly effective in patients with advanced colon cancer, reducing recurrence by 40 percent and cutting deaths by 33 percent. "It's an unequivocal success," he said. "We now have a therapy with a national impact" against the second-largest cause of cancer deaths, after lung cancer. "We were specifically promised that it would be marketed at a reasonable price."[10]

Johnson & Johnson defended its pricing of the consumer version of the drug thus: "The price of the product reflects costly research over decades to determine possible uses in humans for other diseases."[11] J & J also pointed out that sales were less than $15 million a year, a relatively modest amount for a pharmaceutical

---

[10]Marilyn Chase, "Doctor Assails J & J Price Tag on Cancer Drug," *The Wall Street Journal* (May 20, 1992), pp. B1, B8.

[11]Ibid., p. B1.

product. At the same time, the company claimed to have rerun parts of 1400 studies involving 40,000 patients in seeking new applications of the drug in humans.

Dr. Moertel dismissed Johnson & Johnson's justification for the high prices as necessary to meet the higher research and regulatory costs in preparing the drug for human consumption. He maintained that the National Cancer Institute, funded by American taxpayers, sponsored the studies. "The company just supplied the pills, which cost pennies." Moertel raised the question whether a new use for an old drug—a windfall—should justify a price surge: "Just because aspirin was found to improve your risk of heart attack, should you charge more?"[12]

The bad publicity now confronting J & J was not confined to the print media. TV news programs, such as "20/20", soon featured this controversy along with criticisms of drug pricing of the entire pharmaceutical industry. Compounding the problem, the spokespersons for J & J and the other pharmaceutical companies hardly upheld their positions with conviction.

WHAT CAN BE LEARNED?

Any company's nightmare is having its product linked to death or injury. Such a calamity invariably results in fear and loss of public confidence in the product and the firm. At worst, such a disaster can kill a company, as happened with some canned-food firms whose products were contaminated with the deadly botulism toxin. And we cannot forget the grudging demise of Chevrolet's rear-engine Corvair, whose lack of safety was the object of Ralph Nader's best-selling book *Unsafe at Any Speed*. We saw the delayed but serious consequences to Robins with the Dalkon Shield. At best a firm may lose years of time and money it has invested in a brand, with the brand unable to regain its former robustness. In the throes of the catastrophe, J & J executives grappled with the major decision of abandoning the brand at the height of its popularity or keeping it. The decision could have gone either way. Now with hindsight, we know that the decision not to abandon was unmistakably correct; but at the time how could anyone know?

In event of a catastrophe, heroic efforts may still save the brand, although the costs may be staggering. Even though J & J successfully brought back Tylenol, the cost was in the hundreds of millions of dollars. The company's size, with over $5 billion in sales from a diversified product line, enabled it to handle the costs without jeopardy. A smaller firm would not have been able to weather it, especially without a broad product line.

Whenever product safety is an issue, the danger of lawsuits must be reckoned with. In the Dalkon Shield case (Chapter 23), litigation brought A. H. Robins into bankruptcy and eventual takeover. Legal action finally was effective in curbing its abuses and procrastination in the absence of strong government regulation. This recourse upheld the rights of the general

[12]Ibid., p. B8.

public, even though lawyers were perhaps the biggest beneficiaries. With J & J the danger of litigation was muted, although hundreds of millions of dollars in lawsuits were filed. But in the absence of corporate neglect, the swift constructive reaction, and the fact that the company could hardly have guarded against the actions of a madman, it escaped the worst scenario regarding litigation. Still, suits accused J & J of failing to package Tylenol in a tamper-proof container, and the legal expenses of defending itself were high. The threat of litigation must be a major consideration for any firm. Even if the organization is relatively blameless, legal costs can run into the millions, and no one can predict the decisions of juries.

Other firms may also be vulnerable to actions taken against their competitor. While other firms in the industry stand to gain an advantage in a competitor's crisis, they and firms in related industries need to be particularly vigilant because of the tendency toward "copycat crimes." By November, a month after the deaths, the Food and Drug Administration had received more than 270 reports of chemicals, pills, poisons, needles, pins, and razor blades in everything from food to drinks to medications. Fortunately, no deaths resulted from these incidents. But FDA Commissioner Hayes worried: "My greatest fear is that because of the notoriety of the case and the financial damage to the company, someone else will take out his or her grudges on a product and do something similar."[13] Actually, the Tylenol case was not the first time products had been deliberately contaminated. Eyedrops, nasal sprays, milk of magnesia, foods, and cosmetics have all been targets of tampering. An Oregon man was even sentenced to 20 years in prison for attempting to extort diamonds from grocery chains by putting cyanide in food products on their shelves.

It is possible to bounce back from extreme adversity. Certainly, one of the major things we can learn from this case is that it is possible to bounce back from extreme adversity. Before the Tylenol episode, this was not realized by most experts: The general opinion was that severe negative publicity resulted in such an image destruction that recovery could take years. The most optimistic predictions were that Tylenol might recover to about a 20 to 21 percent market share in a year; the pessimistic predictions were that the brand would never recover and should be abandoned.[14] Actually, in eight months, Tylenol had regained almost all of its market share, to a satisfactory 35 percent. For such a recovery, a firm has to manifest unselfish concern, quick corrective action, and unsparing spending, and it must have a base of a good public image before the catastrophe.

---

[13]"Lessons That Emerge from Tylenol Disaster," *U. S. News & World Report* (October 18, 1982), p. 68.

[14]"J & J Will Pay Dearly to Cure Tylenol," *Business Week* (November 29, 1982), p. 37.

Behavior may lapse: Good deeds and favorable publicity in the past do not protect from future criticism. Accusations in 1992 against J & J of "unconscionable" drug pricing quickly became widely publicized. On the surface, J & J appeared highly vulnerable to such criticism: $14 for sheep versus $1250 to $1500 for humans whose lives are threatened. Where is the compassion and best interest of consumers that J & J had evinced some years before?

Perhaps there was ample justification for the company's position that the press and public opinion did not understand. The enhanced public image from the Tylenol troubles were quickly forgotten and replaced by public notions of profiteering and price-gouging. Given public criticism because of a dubious strategy, a firm should marshall its defenses more persuasively than J & J did, or else bow to the pressure and recant the strategy.

INVITATION

Can you think of other learning insights?

QUESTIONS

1. Did J & J move too far in recalling all Extra-Strength Tylenol capsules? Would not a sufficient action have been to recall only those in the Chicago area, thus saving millions of dollars? Discuss.
2. How helpful do you think the marketing research results were in the decision to keep the Tylenol name?
3. "We must assume that someone had a terrible grudge against J & J to have perpetrated such a crime." Discuss.
4. What justification do you think Johnson & Johnson could offer for its levamisole pricing that would be generally acceptable to the press and public opinion?
5. How do you reconcile the seemingly great concern of J & J for its customers during the Tylenol scare, and its seemingly callousness over levamisole pricing? On balance, what is your assessment of the company regarding (*a*) its public image, (*b*) its concern for customers, (*c*) its ethical commitment?
6. "The Tylenol episode represents great crisis management. Ethics was hardly a factor." Do you agree that this case does not really belong in the ethical section of this book?

INVITATION TO ROLE PLAY

1. Assume this scenario: It has been established that the fault of the contamination was accidental introduction of cyanide at a company

plant. How will you, as CEO of J & J, direct your recovery strategy? Give your rationale.

2. Assume the role of the person responsible for the pricing of levamisole for treatment of colon cancer. What do you advise the executive committee regarding any pricing changes after the negative publicity in May 1992?

INVITATION TO RESEARCH

1. Has Tylenol been able to maintain its competitive position since the contamination crises? How successful has Johnson & Johnson been in recent years?
2. What, if anything, has J & J done regarding its pricing of levamisole (Ergamisol) since May 1992?

CHAPTER 26

Conclusions—What Can Be Learned?

In considering mistakes, two things are worth noting: (1) even the most successful organizations make mistakes but survive as long as they can maintain a good "batting average," and (2) making mistakes can be an effective teaching tool, thereby enabling a firm to avoid similar errors.

We can make a number of generalizations from companies' mistakes and successes. Of course we need to recognize that management is a discipline that does not lend itself to laws or axioms. Examples of exceptions to every principle or generalization can be found. However, the business executive does well to heed the following insights. For the most part, they are based on specific corporate experiences and are transferable to other situations and other times.

INSIGHTS REGARDING OVERALL ENTERPRISE PERSPECTIVES

Importance of Public Image

The impact, for good or bad, of the public image was a common thread through a number of cases. For example, the Edsel, Gilbert, the Yugo, Robins, and Johnson & Johnson.

The Edsel and the Yugo were haunted by early product defects and could never overcome the poor quality image. With Gilbert we saw how quickly a superior image, a quality image, one built up from decades of carefully designed toys, could be cut down. In Gilbert's case, two or three

401

years of an image-destructive strategy ruined the company. Robins and its Dalkon Shield catastrophe showed the fallacy of trying to ignore health-related product problems by denials and legal maneuverings.

The Genentech case exemplified the price opportunism that has cast the entire pharmaceutical industry as callous and profiteering at the expense of a helpless public and which has made it a ready target for regulation and public criticism at the highest levels of government. Continental Air with Frank Lorenzo at the helm exhibited a similar disdain, this time for its employees, and found its public image a lodestone. And United Way was brought to its knees by revelations about the excesses of its long-time chief executive, William Aramony. Donations dwindled and local chapters withheld funds from the national organization as the public image of the largest charitable organization was sullied.

Some image problems stem from a hazy or indistinct image. Burger Chef's lack of a distinctive image placed it at a major disadvantage vis-à-vis McDonald's and other successful fast-food operations.

But we saw some successes in protecting and enhancing an image. Johnson & Johnson's ability to regain its image of trust and product safety after tragic deaths were related to its product is a great success story. Honda performed a surprising success in totally reversing the image of people who rode motorcycles. And Saturn, Wal-Mart, and Southwest Air were able to nurture positive public images that enhanced their growth.

The importance of a firm's public image is undeniable, yet some firms continue to disregard this and either act in ways detrimental to image or else ignore the constraints and opportunities that a reputation affords.

Power of the Media

We have seen or suspected the power of the media in a number of cases. Coca-Cola, the Edsel, the Yugo, Robins, United Way, and Johnson & Johnson are obvious examples. This power is often used in a critical sense—to hurt a firm's public image. The media can fan a problem or exacerbate an embarrassing or imprudent action. In particular, this media focus can trigger the herd instinct, in which increasing numbers of people join in with protests and public criticism. But it is possible to use the media in a positive role, as Johnson & Johnson demonstrated.

We can make five key generalizations regarding image:

1. It is important to maintain a stable, clear-cut image and undeviating objectives.
2. It is very difficult and time-consuming to upgrade an image.
3. An episode of poor quality control has a lasting stigma.

4. A good image can be quickly lost if a firm relaxes in an environment of aggressive competition.
5. Well-known firms, and particularly not-for-profit firms depending on voluntary contributions, are especially vulnerable to critical public scrutiny and must be prudent in maintaining their reputation.

PLANNING INSIGHTS

What Should Our Business Be?

An organization's business, its mission and purpose, should be thought through, spelled out clearly, and well communicated by executives involved in policy making. Otherwise, the organization lacks unified and coordinated goals and objectives, which makes running it like trying to navigate unknown terrain without a map.

Good judgment suggests choosing safe rather than courageous goals. Campeau's acquisition efforts and the expansion efforts of Frank Lorenzo in the airline industry epitomized the excesses of the merger mania of the 1980s. In the total perspective, the high-risk orientations of hundreds of savings and loans represented perhaps the worst abuses of business judgment this country has ever seen.

Determining what a firm's business is or ought to be is a starting point for specifying goals. Several elements help with this determination.

The *history of the organization* should be considered, since it affects employees, suppliers, and customers alike. Some S & L's completely disavowed their tradition in the quest for wild speculations of all kinds. The firm's *resources* and *distinctive abilities and strengths* must play a major role in determining its goals. It is not enough to wish for a certain status or position if the firm's resources and competence do not warrant it. To take an extreme example, a railroad company can hardly expect to transform itself into an airline, even though both may be in the transportation business.

Finally, *environmental and competitive opportunities* ought to be considered. The inroads of foreign carmakers in the United States stemmed from environmental opportunities for energy-efficient vehicles and the lack of formidable U. S. competition in this area.

Need for Cautious Growth Orientation

The opposite of a growth commitment is a status quo philosophy, one that is not interested in expansion or the problems and work involved. With Gilbert, contentment with status quo was extreme, until a drastically worsening sales and profit picture and a takeover by new management set the company on its path of ill-conceived expansion efforts. Harley Davidson also was content, despite being pushed around by foreign competitors, until eventually a new management reawakened it several decades later.

In general, how tenable is a low-growth or no-growth philosophy? Although at first glance it seems workable, such a philosophy can sow the seeds of its own destruction. More than three decades ago the following lesson was pointed out:

> Vitality is required even for survival; but vitality is difficult to maintain without growth, at least in the American business climate. The vitality of a firm depends on the vigor and ambition of its members. The prospect of growth is one of the principal means by which a firm can attract able and vigorous recruits.[1]

Consequently, if a firm is obviously not growth-minded, its ability to attract able people diminishes. Customers see a growing firm as reliable, eager to please, and constantly improving. Suppliers and creditors tend to give preferential treatment to a growth-oriented firm because they hope to retain it as a customer and client when it reaches large size.

But an emphasis on growth can be carried too far. Somehow the growth must be kept within the abilities of the firm to handle it. Several examples, such as Wal-Mart and Southwest Air, showed how firms can grow rapidly without losing control; other cases—such as some savings and loans, and Campeau's buyout, the epitome of unsound leveraged buyouts—revealed that imprudent growth can lead to corporate destruction. And then we have the bungled growth efforts of Maytag's Hoover Division in the United Kingdom. Good financial judgment must not be sacrificed to the siren call of growth.

McDonald's is the premier example of rapid growth achieved through franchised units rather than company-owned outlets. However, other franchised fast-food operations expanded just as fast and either went out of business or had to cut back drastically and rid themselves of marginal operations. What was the secret of McDonald's handling of rapid growth? The essentials can be narrowed down to very tight controls, careful screening of prospective franchisees and locations, and continual monitoring of existing units even during the excitement of opening new ones.

We can make seven generalizations about the most desirable growth perspectives:

1. Growth targets should not exceed the abilities of the organization to assimilate, control, and provide sufficient managerial and fi-

---

[1]Wroe Alderson, *Marketing Behavior and Executive Action* (Homewood, IL: Irwin, 1957), p. 59.

nancial resources. Growth at any cost—especially at the expense of profits and financial stability—must be shunned. In particular, tight controls over inventories and expenses should be established, and performance should be monitored promptly and completely.

2. The most prudent approach to growth is to keep the organization and operation as simple and uniform as possible, to be flexible in case sales do not meet expectations, and to keep the break-even point as low as possible, especially for new and untried ventures.

3. Concentrating maximum efforts on the expansion opportunity is like an army exploiting a breakthrough. The concentration strategy usually wins out over more timid competitors who diffuse efforts and resources. But such concentration is not without risk.

4. Rapidly expanding markets pose dangers from both too conservative and overly optimistic sales forecasts. The latter may overextend resources and jeopardize viability should demand contract; the former opens the door to more aggressive competitors. There is no definite answer to this dilemma, but the firm should be aware of the risks and the rewards of both extremes.

5. A strategy emphasizing rapid growth should not neglect other aspects of the operation. For example, older stores should not be ignored in the quest to open new outlets. Basic merchandising principles, such as inventory control and new merchandise planning, should not be violated. Otherwise, the sales coming from expansion are built on a shaky foundation, growth is not assimilated, and an illusion is created of strength and success.

6. Decentralized management is more compatible with rapid growth than a centralized organization since it puts less strain on home office executives. However, delegation of decision making to field executives must be accompanied by well-defined standards and controls and executed by high-caliber field personnel.

7. In the quest for rapid growth, the integrity of the product and the reputation of the firm must not be sacrificed. This should be a major consideration when customers' health and safety may be jeopardized. Today the risk of providing poor-quality or unsafe products and services may affect the very viability of the firm.

Strategic Windows of Opportunity

Two of the great successes we examined resulted from a company's finding and exploiting strategic windows of opportunity. Wal-Mart became the nation's largest retailer by giving small-town consumers a variety of goods at the lowest prices, despite the conventional thinking that small towns offered no opportunities. Wal-Mart further exploited its strategic window by developing efficiencies unmatched by other retailers and providing the ultimate in friendly service. Southwest Air found its opportunity by being so cost effective that it could offer cut-rate yet highly dependable short-haul service that no other airline could match.

We can make several generalizations regarding opportunities and the finding of strategic windows:

1. Opportunities often exist when a traditional way of doing business has prevailed in the industry for a long time.
2. Opportunities often exist when there are gaps in serving customers' needs by existing firms.
3. Innovations are not limited to products but can involve services as well as elements such as the method of distribution.
4. For industries with rapidly changing technologies—often new industries—heavy research and development expenditures are usually required if a firm is to avoid falling behind its competitors. But heavy R & D expenditures do not guarantee being in the vanguard, as shown by the tribulations of IBM despite its huge expenditures.

Power of Judicious Imitation

Some firms are reluctant to copy successful practices of their competitors; they want to be leaders, not followers. But successful practices or innovations may need to be copied in order for a company to survive. Sometimes the imitator outdoes the innovator. Success can lie in doing the ordinary better than competitors.

GM's Saturn achieved its initial success by imitating many of the successful practices of its Japanese competitors. Iacocca did the same with Chrysler. On the other hand, any competitors of McDonald's ignored its successful format, even though its high standards and rigid controls were obvious to all. Admittedly, it is not easy to develop high standards and controls and to insist that they be followed. We can make this generalization:

> It makes sense for a company to identify the characteristics of successful competitors (and even similar but noncompeting firms) that contributed to their success, and then to adopt these characteristics if they are compatible with the resources of the imitator. Let someone else do the experimenting and risk taking: The imitator faces some risk in waiting too long, but it usually is far less than the risk that the innovator is taking.

ORGANIZATIONAL INSIGHTS

Importance of Organizational Compatibility

Organizational structure is often taken for granted. Its role in the success or failure of the enterprise or a particular venture or division tends to be downgraded in favor of the supposedly more important strategic planning. But sometimes organizational problems dominate the mistake.

Although Edsel's mistakes were varied, a crucial one was its establishment of a separate organization to sell and service Edsels. This greatly increased the breakeven point, managerial workloads, and search for adequate dealers. By contrast, the Mustang was created with organizational simplicity, using the existing organization and available resources.

We saw in the Campeau case the worst of the abuses of the raider modus operandi, with the acquisitions being stripped, employees terminated in ruthless downsizing, and the previously successful organizations placed in hock for billions of dollars of debt.

Frank Lorenzo, in his confrontational and union-busting policies with Continental and Eastern Airline employees, succeeded in making these carriers low-cost, but he destroyed organizational spirit and commitment and brought his acquisitions to bankruptcy.

Lean and Mean

A new organizational climate is sweeping our country's major corporations. In one sense it is good, but it can be destructive. Wal-Mart and Southwest Airlines have been in the forefront of the lean-and-mean movement. They developed flat organizations with few management layers, thus keeping overhead low, improving communication, and involving employees in greater self-management. Iacocca in the early 1980s was also able to make Chrysler the lowest cost domestic automaker. However, illustrative of how difficult it is to keep costs under control, rising overhead forced him to institute another cost-cutting crusade in the late 1980s.

In contrast, we saw the organizational bloat of such behemoths as IBM, Sears, and General Motors, with their many management levels, entrenched bureaucracies, and massive overhead. A virtual cause-and-effect relationship exists between the proportion of total overhead committed to administration/staff and the ability to cope with change and innovate. It is like trying to maneuver a huge ship: Bureaucratic weight slows the response time.

The problem with the lemming-like pursuit of the lean-and-mean structure is knowing how far to downsize without cutting into bone and muscle, which then becomes counterproductive. And as thousands of managers and staff specialists and college graduates can attest, the loss of jobs and the destruction of career paths has been traumatic both for the economy and for society.

Resistance to Change

People as well as organizations are naturally reluctant to embrace change. Change is disruptive; it destroys accepted ways of doing things and muddles familiar authority and responsibility patterns. It makes people uneasy because their routines are disrupted and their interpersonal relationships with subordinates, coworkers, and superiors are modified. Previously important positions may be downgraded or even eliminated, and people who view themselves as highly competent in a particular job may be forced to assume unfamiliar duties amid the fear that they cannot master the new assignments. When the change involves wholesale terminations in a major downsizing, as Campeau foisted on his Allied and Federated buyouts, the resistance and fear of change can become so great that personnel efficiency is seriously jeopardized.

Normal resistance to change can be combated by good communication with participants about forthcoming change. Without such communication, rumors and fears assume monumental proportions. Acceptance of change is facilitated if employees are involved as fully as possible in planning the changes, if their participation is solicited and welcomed, and if assurance can be given that positions will not be impaired, only changed. Gradual rather than abrupt changes also make a transition smoother.

In the final analysis, however, making needed changes and embracing different opportunities should not be delayed or canceled because of possible negative repercussions on the organization. If change is desirable, as it usually is with long-established bureaucratic organizations, it should be initiated. Individuals and organizations can adapt to change—it just takes some time.

LEADERSHIP AND STRATEGY EXECUTION

The Need for Prudent Crisis Management

Crises are unexpected happenings that pose threats, ranging from moderate to catastrophic, to the organization's well-being. With the Gilbert Company, frenetic efforts to correct a suddenly realized crisis vastly exacerbated the problem. With Robins, a denial of the extent of the crisis until far too late resulted in the downfall of the company. Johnson & Johnson, however, handled a crisis of the worst possible kind with prompt and judicious actions. And United Way of America reacted reasonably well to the crisis following the public scrutiny of Aramony and associates, although fully regaining public trust may take much longer.

Most crises can be minimized if a company takes precautions, is alert to changing conditions, has contingency plans, and practices risk avoidance. For example, it is prudent to prohibit key executives from traveling on the same air flight; it is prudent to insure key executives so that their incapacity will not endanger the organization; and it is prudent to set up contingency plans for a strike, an equipment failure or plant shutdown, unexpected economic conditions, or a serious lawsuit. Some risks can be covered by insurance; others need good planning in a calm atmosphere. The mettle of any organization may be severely tested by an unexpected crisis. Such crises need not cause the demise of the company, however, if alternatives are weighed and actions taken only after due deliberation.

Crises may necessitate some changes in the organization and the way of doing business. Firms should avoid making hasty or disruptive changes or, the other extreme, making too few changes too late. The middle ground is usually best. Advanced planning can help a company minimize trauma and enact effective solutions.

A Long-Term Management Orientation

The desperate situation in the early 1980s that faced Chrysler, and to a lesser extent the rest of the U.S. auto industry and other major industries, brought to light a disturbing realization. The prevalent management thinking, with its emphasis on short-term profit objectives, was vulnerable to aggressive foreign competitors that were willing to sacrifice for the short term in order to build for the future. As we saw with Chrysler, the diminishing relative productivity of large parts of U.S. industry could be attributed to numerous factors, some of which management had little or no direct control over, such as government regulations and tax policies. Still, substantial blame must lie with a management unwilling to commit enough resources to research and development, to invest in the newest technologies for plant and equipment, or to work more closely and encourage teamwork with labor. Management can also be faulted for complacency about quality control and customer dissatisfaction. A columnist in an editorial in a major newspaper commented about the U.S. automakers' plight as follows:

> Perhaps the public's apathy toward the current plight of the American auto companies . . . suggests . . . that the industry today is paying for yesterday's arrogance and dishonesty in dealing with its customers. Did your new car in 1965 turn out to be a lemon? Tough luck, but you were on your own. And did your 1971 automobile turn from shiny beauty into a rusty monstrosity inside

of two or three years, only to have the manufacturer and his dealer shrug off the tragedy?[2]

Perhaps we can learn from these past sins of omission. Not only should long-term strategy objectives involve investment goals and labor incentives aimed at increasing productivity, but customer satisfaction must also be given priority attention, not just lip service. Saturn has been a shining example of such customer satisfaction.

In several other cases, we saw the contrast in management thinking of short-term profit objectives versus long-term objectives. Robins, with its Dalkon Shield dilemma, focused its attention and strategy on safeguarding short-term profits. Eventually it lost everything because of the contemptible reluctance to pull an unsafe product off the market. With a strange management mind-set, Genentech executives refused to budge on short-term profit maximization for the new heart drug, TPA, even though the high price hurt long-term potential. Johnson & Johnson, however, was willing to sacrifice short-term profits to protect long-run sales.

INSIGHTS REGARDING CONTROLS

Success Does Not Guarantee Continued Success

That success does not guarantee continued success or freedom from adversity is a sobering realization that must come from examining these cases. Many of the mistakes we described occurred in notably successful organizations. Some of these organizations, such as IBM, had exhibited enviable growth records and dominated their industries, yet they succumbed to grievous mistakes, some while at the very pinnacle of their success. How could this possibly have happened to firms with such experience, momentum, and resources, both financial and managerial?

We are forced to conclude that, far from ensuring continued success and mastery, success may actually promote vulnerability. The three C's— complacency, conservatism, and conceit—often blanket the leading firms, such as Harley Davidson, IBM, Sears, and even United Way. We suggest that a constructive attitude of never underestimating a competitor can be fostered in several ways:

- Bringing "fresh blood" into the organization for new ideas and different perspectives
- Establishing a strong and continuing commitment to customer service and satisfaction

[2]George E. Condon, "No Tears Are Wept at Auto-Makers' Plight," *Cleveland Plain Dealer,* (May 18, 1982), p. 3-B.

- Conducting periodic corporate self-analyses designed to detect weaknesses as well as opportunities in their early stages
- Continually monitoring the environment and being alert to any changes

The environment is dynamic, sometimes with subtle and hardly recognizable changes, at other times with violent and unmistakable changes. To operate in this environment, an established firm must constantly be on guard to protect its position. Let us examine several internal tools for doing so.

Management by Exception

With diverse and far-flung operations, it becomes difficult to closely control all aspects. Successful managers therefore focus their attention on performances that deviate significantly from the expected at *strategic control points*. Subordinates can handle ordinary operations and less significant deviations. With this approach to control, the manager is not overburdened by details.

Management by exception failed, however, with Maytag and its overseas Hoover division. The flaw lay in failing to monitor faulty promotional plans: By the time results were coming in, it was too late.

Systematic Evaluations and Controls

Organizations need feedback to determine how well something is being done, whether improvement is possible, where it should occur, how much is needed, and how quickly it must be accomplished. Without feedback or performance evaluation, a worsening situation can go unrecognized until it is too late for corrective action. That was the situation with Gilbert. For some reason, sales declines and loss of competitive position did not arouse any particular concern; certainly, no serious attempt was made to find the causes and take corrective action.

As firms become larger, the need for better controls or feedback increases because top management can no longer personally monitor all aspects of the operation. Here management by exception becomes a must. Diversifications and mergers, which often result in loosely controlled decentralized operations, also call for systematic feedback on performance.

Financial and expense controls are vital. After all, if costs and inventories get severely out of line—and worse, if it is not recognized until too late—then the very viability of the firm can be jeopardized.

Performance standards are another means of control critical to large and widespread operations. Unless operating standards are imposed and enforced, the results are likely to be lack of uniformity of performance, unevenness of quality and service, and a lack of coordination and continuity among the different units. Instead of running a tight ship, managers will have a very loose and undisciplined one. We examined two firms that represented opposites in performance standards. Days Inns, under its new management, let standards slip for its franchised motels to the extent that security and even customer safety were endangered. As we noted, a few weak links in a chain can jeopardize customer patronage of other units. McDonald's is the opposite extreme: an enduring insistence on the tightest standards in its industry, or perhaps any industry.

Environmental Monitoring

A firm must be alert to changes in the business environment: changes in customer preferences and needs, in competition, in the economy, and even in international events such as nationalism in Canada, OPEC machinations, changes in Eastern Europe, and advances in Japanese productivity and quality control. Edsel failed because it did not recognize the trend away from big, high-horsepower cars toward smaller, more economical ones. Gilbert did not recognize changes in the toy industry. IBM, Sears, and Harley Davidson failed to detect and act upon significant changes in their industries.

How can a firm remain alert to subtle and insidious or more obvious changes? A firm must have *sensors* constantly monitoring the environment. The sensor may be a marketing or economic research department, but in many instances such a formal organizational entity is not really necessary to provide primary monitoring. Executive alertness is essential. Most changes do not occur suddenly and without warning. Feedback from customers, sales representatives, and suppliers, news of the latest relevant material and projections in business journals; and even simple observations of what is happening in stores, advertising, prices, and new technologies can provide sufficient information about the environment and how it is changing. But it is surprising and disturbing how many executives overlook or disregard important changing environmental factors that presage impact on their present and future business.

The following are generalizations regarding vulnerability to competition:

1. Initial strategic advantage tends to be rather quickly countered by competitors.
2. Countering by competitors is more likely to occur when innovation is involved than when the advantage concerns more common-place effective management and marketing techniques.
3. An easy-entry industry is particularly vulnerable to new and aggressive competition, especially in an expanding market. In such

new industries, severe price competition usually will weed out marginal firms.

4. Long-dominant firms tend to be vulnerable to upstart competitors because of the older firms' complacency, resistance to change, and myopia concerning a changing environment. Careful monitoring of performance at strategic control points and comparison of similar operating units and their trends in various performance categories can detect weakening positions; alert management can take corrective action before competitors intrude.

5. In expanding markets it is a delusion to judge performance by increases in sales rather than by market share: An increase in sales may hide a deteriorating competitive situation.

INSIGHTS REGARDING SPECIFIC STRATEGY ELEMENTS

Strengths and Limitations of Advertising

We can gain several insights regarding the power and effectiveness of advertising, but we are left with some unanswered questions and some contradictions. On one hand, Ford executives made major advertising and promotional expenditures for the Edsel, but the car flopped. On the other hand, Ford's equal level of commitment to the Mustang contributed to an outstanding success. And then we have Coca-Cola with its steadily declining market share despite the fact that it spent $100 million more on advertising than Pepsi did. Does advertising have much relationship with success?

There are also striking examples of the effectiveness of advertising. Honda successfully used it to change a negative image with modest expenditures of a few million dollars a year. The Pepsi Generation and the Pepsi Challenge promotions are models of the most effective use of advertising.

We can draw these conclusions:

> There is no ensured correlation between expenditures for advertising and sales success. However, given that the other elements of the strategy are relatively attractive, advertising can be an effective tool in generating demand and bringing about the attitude change.

Advertising induced consumers to go to dealers showrooms to look at the Edsel. It performed its primary objective of gaining attention and interest for the product so that consumers would examine it more closely. With the Mustang they liked what they saw; with the Edsel they did not—it is as simple as that.

Planning and budgeting advertising presents some problems. Certain advertisements and campaigns are more effective than others. Other campaigns with higher budgets somehow fall short of expectations. Therein lies the great challenge of advertising. One never knows for sure how much should be spent to get the job done, to reach the planned objectives of perhaps increasing sales by a certain percentage, or gaining market share. Despite the inability to measure directly the effectiveness of advertising, aggressively promoting competitors usually need to be countered, as Harley Davidson belatedly found out.

Limitations of Marketing Research

Marketing research is usually touted as the key to better decision making and the mark of sophisticated professional management. It is commonly thought that the more money spent for marketing research, the less chance for a bad decision. But heavy use of marketing research does not always help the situation, as we saw with the Edsel and Coca-Cola.

Marketing research does not guarantee a correct decision. At best, marketing research increases the "batting average" of correct decisions—maybe only by a little, sometimes by quite a bit. To be effective, research must be current and unbiased. The several million dollars Ford spent on Edsel marketing research came to naught. Most of the research on consumer preferences and attitudes had been done several years before the Edsel came on the market, and the decision to use the name Edsel was made despite its negative connotation to many people. From the Edsel example we can further conclude that planning and long lead time do not ensure success, especially when based on faulty premises.

And the several million dollars in taste-test research for Coca-Cola can hardly reassure us about the validity of marketing research. Admittedly, results of taste tests are difficult to rely on, simply because of the subjective nature of taste preferences. But the Coca-Cola research did not even uncover the latent and powerful loyalty toward tradition, and it gave a completely false "go" signal for the new flavor.

We do not want to imply that marketing research has little value. Some of the flawed studies would have been invaluable with better design and planning. As an example of the possibilities, Lee Iacocca used marketing research to identify the most promising markets for the Mustang, to guide the design of the car, and to determine its price.

Surprisingly, we see that many successful new ventures used little formal research. Southwest Air and Wal-Mart initially relied on entrepreneurial hunch rather than sophisticated research. Ray Kroc of McDonald's recognized a good thing when he saw it, although McDonald's later relied heavily on research, especially for its site selections. It is doubtful if Honda's invasion of the U. S. motorcycle market was bolstered by formal research.

Why have we not seen more extensive use of marketing research in new ventures? Consider the following major reasons:

1. Most of the founding entrepreneurs did not have marketing backgrounds and therefore were not familiar and confident with such research.
2. Available tools and techniques are not always appropriate to handle some problems and opportunities. There may be too many variables, and some that are intangible and incapable of precise measurement. Much research consists of collecting past and present data that, although helpful in predicting a stable future, are of little help in charting revolutionary new ventures. But the higher risks for such ventures are often offset by the potential for great rewards.

ETHICAL CONSIDERATIONS

We have contrasted the Dalkon Shield and the Tylenol cases but have devoted less attention to other examples of consumer abuses: Health clubs, cigarettes, and small loans. Each of these areas of consumer abuse is different but critics would say that all are reprehensible. Health clubs directed high-pressure sales tactics to the educated and affluent, small-loan firms to the poor and desperate. And the cigarette makers came under fire for directing promotional efforts of their allegedly unsafe products to minority neighborhoods, to children, and to certain foreign markets. Where do we draw the line in our targeting of prospective customers?

We do not have space in this book to delve very deeply into social and ethical issues.[3] However, several insights are worth noting:

1. A firm can no longer disavow itself from the possibility of ethical appraisal. Activist groups will publicize alleged misdeeds long before governmental regulators will. Legal actions may follow.
2. Public protests may take a colorful path, with marches, picketing, billboard whitewashing, and the like, and may enlist public and media support for their criticisms.

Should a firm attempt to resist or to defend itself? No! The bad press, the confrontation, and the effect on public image are hardly worth such a confrontation. The better course of action is to back down as quietly as possible, controversial though such an action may be to a management convinced of the reasonableness of its position.

---

[3]See R. F. Hartley, *Business Ethics* (New York: Wiley, 1993) if you have more interest in this topic.

GENERAL INSIGHTS

Impact of One Person

In many of the cases one person had a powerful impact on the organization. Sam Walton and Wal-Mart is perhaps the most outstanding example, but we also have Ray Kroc of McDonald's, who converted a small hamburger stand into the world's largest restaurant operation. The accomplishments of Lee Iacocca are well known, both with the Mustang and with the resurrection of Chrysler. And we should not forget Herb Kelleher of Southwest Airlines, tormentor of the mighty airlines.

One person can also have a negative impact on an organization. How can we forget Robert Campeau, the destructive raider of our most prestigious department stores? And Frank Lorenzo, who destroyed Eastern Airlines and almost ruined Continental? The same goes for William Aramony of United Way. A lesser-known name is that of Henry Silverman, the shrewd manipulator of Days Inns. The impact of one person, for good or ill, is one of the recurring marvels of history, whether business history or world history.

Prevalence of Opportunities for Entrepreneurship Today

Despite the maturing of our economy and the growing size and power of many firms in many industries, there still is abundant opportunity for entrepreneurship today. Such opportunity exists not only for the change maker or innovator, but even for the person who only seeks to do things a little better than existing, and complacent, competition.

Thousands of entrepreneurial successes are unheralded, although dozens are widely publicized. In this book we have examined two of the latter: Wal-Mart and Southwest Airlines. Many other analysts would point out Bill Gates of Microsoft. Opportunities are there for the dedicated. Venture capital to support promising new businesses is increasing to more than $1 billion a year. We are in the midst of the greatest boom in new stock issues and new company formations since the late 1960s.

Of course, not all of us have what it takes to be an entrepreneur. It takes more than the "great idea." Nolan Bushnell, who founded Atari in 1972 with $500, says: "A lot of people have ideas, but there are few who decide to do something about them now. Not tomorrow. Not next week. But today."[4] Dreamers do not make entrepreneurs; "doers" do. The great venture capitalists look at the person, not the idea. Typically they distribute their seed money to resourceful people who are courageous enough to give

[4]John Merwin, "Have You Got What It Takes?" *Forbes*, (August 3, 1981), p. 60.

up security for the unknown consequences of their embryonic venture, who have great self confidence, and who demonstrate a tremendous will to win.

The Role of Greed

We can define greed as an extreme desire to amass wealth; it might even be seen as rapaciousness or plundering. Are there any examples of greed in these cases? Certainly some of the S&L excesses smack of greed. Campeau's acquisitive drive suggests greed outweighing good judgment. Many of the corporate raiders in the leveraged buyout frenzy of the 1980s were bent on plundering their targets.

Does ambition and a strong growth commitment constitute greed? Was Ray Kroc greedy for much greater size and growth for McDonald's? Was Sam Walton a greedy man, in the most negative sense? And was Lee Iacocca, while he reveled in the acclaim, really greedy in any negative sense?

Some people say that greed comes into play when the great quest for growth is entirely self-seeking and hurts somebody—perhaps customers, investors or creditors, or employees—and therefore exceeds reasonable expectations of ethical and socially responsible behavior. Then extreme ambition becomes negative, whereas ambition should be a positive spur for our society.

Socialist Shortcomings

The Yugo case showed the particular vulnerabilities of Eastern European firms: vulnerabilities in technological backwardness, in worker motivation, and in managerial competence. Their deficiencies result in poor and inconsistent quality and in products that are below par in technology, attractiveness, and competitive stature. Because of these shortcomings, such firms usually are forced to compete by offering the lowest prices in the industry, and this creates the continuing public image problems of low quality.

U.S. firms can learn from the Yugo example that it is not always desirable to be the lowest-price firm. They can learn the importance of quality control and assurance and worker motivation. The Yugo represents the worst of manufacturer mistakes, which all firms should avoid.

CONCLUSION

We learn from mistakes and from successes, although every management problem seems cast in a unique setting. One author has likened business strategy to military strategy:

Strategies which are flexible rather than static embrace optimum use and offer the greatest number of alternative objectives. A good commander knows that he cannot control his environment to suit a prescribed strategy. Natural phenomena pose their own restraints to strategic planning, whether physical, geographic, regional, or psychological and sociological.[5]

He later adds:

Planning leadership recognizes the unpleasant fact that, despite every effort, the war may be lost. Therefore, the aim is to retain the maximum number of facilities and the basic organization. Indicators of a deteriorating and unsalvageable total situation are, therefore, mandatory. . . . No possible combination of strategies and tactics, no mobilization of resources . . . can supply a magic formula which guarantees victory; it is possible only to increase the probability of victory.[6]

Thus, we can pull two concepts from military strategy to help guide business strategy: the desirability of flexibility in an unknown or changing environment and the idea that a basic core should be maintained in crisis. The first suggests that the firm should be prepared for adjustments in strategy as conditions warrant. The second suggests that there is a basic core of a firm's business that should be unchanging; it should be the final bastion to fall back on for regrouping if necessary. Harley Davidson stolidly maintained its core position, even though it let expansion opportunities slither away. Sears and IBM have solid cores that they should be able to maintain and from which they can mount new attacks. Gilbert abandoned its core and its life.

In regard to the basic core of a firm, every viable firm has some distinctive function or "ecological niche" in the business environment:

Every business firm occupies a position which is in some respects unique. Its location, the product it sells, its operating methods, or the customers it serves tend to set it off in some degree from every other firm. Each firm competes by making the most of its individuality and its special character.[7]

Woe to the firm that loses its ecological niche.

---

[5]Myron S. Heidingsfield, *Changing Patterns in Marketing*, (Boston: Allyn & Bacon, 1968), p. 11.

[6]*Ibid.*

[7]Alderson, *op. cit.*, p. 101.

QUESTIONS

1. Design a program aimed at mistake avoidance. Be as specific, as creative, and as complete as possible.
2. How would you build controls into an organization to ensure that similar mistakes do not happen in the future?
3. Would you advise a firm to be an imitator or an innovator? Why?
4. A number of cases involved ethical issues, among them Genentech, Continental, United Way, S&L's. Identify the ethical issues of these and any other cases you think appropriate.
5. Can you reconcile the desirability of management by exception with the basic importance of details, as characterized by McDonald's, Southwest Air, and Wal-Mart?
6. "There is no such thing as a sustainable competitive advantage." Discuss.

INVITATION TO ROLE PLAY

Your firm has had a history of reacting rather than anticipating changes in its industry. As the staff assistant to the CEO, you have been assigned the responsibility of developing adequate sensors of the marketplace. How will you go about developing such sensors?